The Collected Works of
James M. Buchanan

VOLUME 1

*The Logical Foundations of
Constitutional Liberty*

*James M. Buchanan receiving the Alfred Nobel Memorial
Prize in Economic Sciences from Carl XVI Gustaf,
king of Sweden, 1986*

The Collected Works of

James M. Buchanan

VOLUME 1

The Logical Foundations of Constitutional Liberty

LIBERTY FUND

Indianapolis

Frontispiece photograph from Pressens Bild, Stockholm, Sweden

01 15 16 17 18 19 20 C 8 7 6 5 4 3 2
    16 17 18 19 20 P 11 10 9 8 7 6

Library of Congress Cataloging-in-Publication Data
Buchanan, James M.
The logical foundations of constitutional liberty.
p.   cm. — (The collected works of James M. Buchanan ; v. 1)
Includes bibliographical references and index.
ISBN 978-0-86597-213-1(alk. paper). – ISBN 978-0-86597-214-8(pbk. : alk. paper)
1. Economic policy.   2. Liberty.   3. Economics.   4. Buchanan,
James M.   I. Title.   II. Series: Buchanan, James M.   Works.   1999 ; v. 1.
HD82.B763   1999
338.9—dc21   98-45534

LIBERTY FUND, INC.
8335 Allison Pointe Trail, Suite 300
Indianapolis, IN 46250-1684

Contents

4. The Economist and Economic Order

5. Ethics and Economics

6. The Reason of Rules

Appendixes

Foreword

The Logical Foundations of Constitutional Liberty is the first volume in a series comprising the Collected Works of James M. Buchanan.[1] The series consists of twenty volumes involving all of the major monographs and scholarly papers that Buchanan wrote from 1949, the date of the first published paper, to the point at which the final decisions on the collected works project were effectively taken in early 1998—an exact fifty-year span. The arrangement of the volumes is as follows:

Vol. 1   *The Logical Foundations of Constitutional Liberty*

Vol. 2   *Public Principles of Public Debt: A Defense and Restatement*

Vol. 3   *The Calculus of Consent: Logical Foundations of Constitutional Democracy* (with Gordon Tullock)

Vol. 4   *Public Finance in Democratic Process: Fiscal Institutions and Individual Choice*

Vol. 5   *The Demand and Supply of Public Goods*

Vol. 6   *Cost and Choice: An Inquiry in Economic Theory*

Vol. 7   *The Limits of Liberty: Between Anarchy and Leviathan*

Vol. 8   *Democracy in Deficit: The Political Legacy of Lord Keynes* (with Richard E. Wagner)

Vol. 9   *The Power to Tax: Analytical Foundations of a Fiscal Constitution* (with Geoffrey Brennan)

---

1. Hereafter referred to as the Collected Works or the series.

Vol. 10   *The Reason of Rules: Constitutional Political Economy*
(with Geoffrey Brennan)

Vol. 11   *Politics by Principle, Not Interest: Toward Nondiscriminatory Democracy* (with Roger D. Congleton)

Vol. 12   *Economic Inquiry and Its Logic*

Vol. 13   *Politics as Public Choice*

Vol. 14   *Debt and Taxes*

Vol. 15   *Externalities and Public Expenditure Theory*

Vol. 16   *Choice, Contract, and Constitutions*

Vol. 17   *Moral Science and Moral Order*

Vol. 18   *Federalism, Liberty, and the Law*

Vol. 19   *Ideas, Persons, and Events*

A final volume is planned, containing an index to the series and a full curriculum vitae. Volumes 2 through 11 were originally published as monographs and are here republished in their entirety, including all the original prefaces, introductions, forewords, and any appendices or afterwords. Volumes 1 and 12 through 19 are collections of papers and essays by Buchanan, arranged according to theme. The editing of the monographs, and of the papers collected in volumes 1 and 12 through 19, has been restricted to ensuring homogeneity of style and reference conventions in each paper and correction of typographical errors, conspicuous grammatical errors, and errors of fact. Editors' forewords written for the series have been added to each volume. *The Calculus of Consent*, written with Gordon Tullock, is produced here with an index prepared by Buchanan expressly for the Collected Works version, and *Cost and Choice* will have a subject index (also prepared by Buchanan) to accompany the author index that appeared in the original. No other changes in the written texts have been made.[2]

2. James M. Buchanan and Gordon Tullock, *The Calculus of Consent: Logical Foundations of Constitutional Democracy* (Ann Arbor: University of Michigan Press, 1962), volume 3 in the series; James M. Buchanan, *Cost and Choice: An Inquiry in Economic Theory* (Chicago: Markham Publishing Co., 1969), volume 6 in the series.

Several of Buchanan's books and a small proportion of the articles have been omitted from the "*collected* works." In particular, textbooks, volumes of papers by other authors edited by Buchanan, and previously published collections of Buchanan's own papers (whether collected by Buchanan or by others) have all been left out. Most of the Buchanan papers are republished here, but they have been rearranged to fit within the thematic structure that has been designed for this series. Articles have been omitted only where the degree of overlap with other papers actually included was such that publication of both versions seemed unnecessary or where Buchanan's contribution took the form of a comment on another scholar's work and was such that the Buchanan commentary would not stand intelligibly on its own. In other words, although the series does not quite literally represent Buchanan's "*complete* works," the intellectual coverage is, we believe, complete in all essential respects. There have been no papers independently written for this series: all have been published previously in either professional journals or edited volumes.

The omission of two monographs requires specific discussion. One is Buchanan's set of autobiographical essays, *Better than Plowing*. Several of these essays were excluded on the basis of a judgment that the scope of the series should encompass Buchanan's academic and professional work rather than the entire range of his writings. The second exclusion is the book *Academia in Anarchy*, written with Nicos Devletoglou. The grounds for exclusion in this case lie in the judgment that the book is really an extended occasional essay written in response to the crisis in universities in the late sixties: as such, we considered it too long to include as an essay and too time-specific to be published as a separate book.[3]

3. James M. Buchanan, *Better than Plowing: And Other Personal Essays* (Chicago: University of Chicago Press, 1992); however, the essay "Better than Plowing" has been included in this first volume, and three other chapters from the book, "Italian Retrospective," "Born-again Economist," and "Virginia Political Economy—Some Personal Reflections," have been reprinted in *Ideas, Persons, and Events*, volume 19 in the series; "Better than Plowing," 1–18, originally published in *Banca Nazionale del Lavoro Quarterly Review* 159 (December 1986): 359–75; "Italian Retrospective," 82–92; "Born-again Economist," 68–81, originally published in *Lives of the Laureates: Ten Nobel Economists*, ed. William Breit (Cambridge: MIT Press, 1990), 163–80; "Virginia Political Economy—Some Personal Reflections," 93–107; James M. Buchanan and Nicos E. Devletoglou, *Academia in Anarchy: An Economic Diagnosis* (New York: Basic Books, 1970).

As editors for the series, we have not wanted to construe our tasks expansively. Buchanan is a contemporary scholar, so there has been none of the detailed exegetical work that might be required in preparing a "scholarly edition" of some seventeenth- or eighteenth-century text. Our presumption has been that Buchanan can speak for himself—and certainly, better than we could speak for him. Specifically, we have not wanted to obscure Buchanan's voice with our own particular interpretations. There are, therefore, no extended essays attempting to explain this or that aspect of Buchanan's thought, or to locate Buchanan in relation to particular intellectual traditions, or to specify how Buchanan's position on major issues relates to that of other notable scholars. All of these interpretative tasks are worthy ones, but they seem to us to be better pursued in other contexts. Our aim in this series is, basically, to provide in an accessible form the raw material for such further analysis. To the extent that we offer any remarks of an interpretative kind, the object is merely to point up links with other themes in Buchanan's work or to indicate connections to specific pieces in other volumes. In only one or two cases, where it has seemed especially desirable, have we gone further to discuss the significance of the relevant monograph or group of papers in Buchanan's thought or to place Buchanan's work in the context of other literature. This we have attempted to do briefly and with no suggestion of exhaustiveness.

This first volume, however, is a special case. The object in this volume has been to provide a selection from Buchanan's academic papers and published essays that would introduce the whole series and offer a representative picture of Buchanan's work. For this reason, rather more in the way of explanation and justification of the selection made may be required.

The volume begins with the only piece in the Collected Works that is not by Buchanan himself. This is the press statement released by the Royal Swedish Academy of Sciences in October 1986 that James M. Buchanan was to be awarded the Alfred Nobel Memorial Prize in Economic Sciences.[4] Because this statement is an attempt to describe Buchanan's contribution in terms that sought to justify what is undoubtedly the highest professional award an economist can receive, and because in our judgment the authors did a par-

---

4. Press release (Stockholm: Royal Swedish Academy of Sciences, 1986). With the exception of one minor deletion, it is reprinted here in its entirety.

ticularly fine job in providing such justification, the press release struck us as an apt way to introduce the Collected Works.

The press release is followed immediately by an introductory section beginning with an autobiographical paper, "Better than Plowing," originally published shortly before the Nobel announcement. We have thought it better to allow Buchanan himself to speak on his life than to offer biographical material ourselves (often the lot of collected works editors), not least because in this article Buchanan provides a personal history that connects very much to his intellectual development over the course of his life and that gives a systematic account of the Buchanan contribution from the contributor's own viewpoint. At the close of the current volume, appendix A sets out in summary form Buchanan's honors, awards, education, and professional affiliations.

The second introductory essay is the piece "What Should Economists Do?" which also forms an element in, and the title of, an earlier book—a collection of essays published by Liberty Fund on the occasion of Buchanan's sixtieth birthday. That earlier collection is rendered somewhat obsolete by the current series because all of the essays in *What Should Economists Do?* are caught up in one or another of the volumes in this series, though they appear in a different array according to the dictates of the thematic structure.[5]

The remaining twenty-nine essays in this volume are divided into five parts. The first of these includes essays dealing directly with public choice theory. After all, it is the public choice ingredient—the insistence, that is, on the inclusion of a plausible and appropriately theorized political element in all policy analysis—that is the most characteristic aspect of the Buchanan contribution. The title of this section and of the initial paper, "Politics without Romance," captures the essence of the public choice approach.[6] In this sense, public choice theory is defined as much by what it is *against* as by what it is *for*. More specifically, public choice stands in vivid contrast both to the

---

5. James M. Buchanan, "What Should Economists Do?" *Southern Economic Journal* 30 (January 1964): 213–22; *What Should Economists Do?* (Indianapolis: Liberty Fund, 1979).

6. James M. Buchanan, "Politics without Romance: A Sketch of Positive Public Choice Theory and Its Normative Implications," Inaugural Lecture, Institute for Advanced Studies, Vienna, Austria, *IHS-Journal, Zeitschrift des Instituts für Höhere Studien, Wien* 3 (1979): B1–B11.

naively optimistic "benevolent despot" model of politics that implicitly inhabits most conventional economic analysis of public policy and to the tradition in political theory that views politics as the search for the "true," the
"good," the "beautiful" in total isolation from the *feasible*. Public choice is an
attempt, quite literally, to conduct political analysis in a way that is shorn of
romantic illusion.

Absence of romantic illusion does not mean an absence of normative
commitment—and certainly does not in Buchanan's case. What it does mean
is that normative analysis must be mediated by a proper sense of the feasible—with "feasibility" understood both in terms of plausible assumptions
about human motivations and behavior and in terms of the ways in which
different institutional forms structure human interactions to produce social
outcomes. Public choice theory borrows more broadly from economics both
a sense of the constrained nature of human activity and an essentially individualistic approach to understanding social phenomena.

In making our selections of Buchanan's public choice writings—and indeed throughout this first volume—earlier more "classic" statements have
been deliberately favored over later restatements. Consequently, there are
here two papers from the 1950s—Buchanan's appraisal of Arrow's impossibility theorem in "Social Choice, Democracy, and Free Markets" and "Individual Choice in Voting and the Market," which is his early treatment of the
contrast between individual choice in voting and choice in the market.[7] We
also have chosen the classic piece "Politics, Policy, and the Pigovian Margins," written in what was for Buchanan a "classic" year. This was the year,
for example, of the publication of *The Calculus of Consent* and the famous
paper "Externality," as well as "The Relevance of Pareto Optimality," included in part 4 of this introductory volume. We close part 2 with "Rent
Seeking and Profit Seeking." Buchanan's contribution to the "rent-seeking"

---

7. James M. Buchanan, "Social Choice, Democracy, and Free Markets," *Journal of Political Economy* 62 (April 1954): 114–23; "Individual Choice in Voting and the Market,"
Journal of Political Economy 62 (August 1954): 334–43. This latter paper connects with
those in part 3 of volume 13 in the series, *Politics as Public Choice*, as well as with more
recent developments in the so-called expressive theory of voting, for example in Geoffrey
Brennan and Loren Lomasky's 1993 book *Democracy and Decision: The Pure Theory of
Electoral Preference* (Cambridge and New York: Cambridge University Press, 1993).

literature has been extremely significant and has not always had the attention it deserves.[8]

The second substantive section (part 3) deals with Buchanan's contributions to public finance. As Buchanan puts it in the preface to *The Power to Tax*, he sees himself primarily as "a public-finance economist . . . despite . . . various excursions into ethics, law, politics, and philosophy." Certainly, public finance economics represents a substantial part of Buchanan's work, as the two volumes of papers in the Collected Works assigned to this area indicate.[9] With such an array to choose from, the selection here is only the barest tip of the iceberg. However, the distinctiveness of Buchanan's approach is reflected clearly enough. For one thing, in the Buchanan scheme, public finance is to be viewed through the lens of "democratic process" and not merely as some isolated policy phenomenon, hence the title to part 3. The reference to Buchanan's book *Public Finance in Democratic Process* is intentional, though the degree of overlap between the essays included here and the essays in that volume is minimal. We begin with "The Pure Theory of Government Finance," an amazingly prescient paper from 1949. This is one of Buchanan's earliest papers; yet it lays out in broad form much of the work in public economics that Buchanan was to pursue over the course of the ensuing half century. It is worth noting that the "suggested approach" that Buchanan outlines predates by six or seven years the rise of public goods theory in public finance orthodoxy and, by almost a decade Musgrave's in-

---

8. James M. Buchanan, "Politics, Policy, and the Pigovian Margins," *Economica* 29 (February 1962): 17–28; James M. Buchanan and W. C. Stubblebine, "Externality," *Economica* 29 (November 1962): 371–84, see *Externalities and Public Expenditure Theory*, volume 15 in the series; James M. Buchanan, "The Relevance of Pareto Optimality," *Journal of Conflict Resolution* 6 (December 1962): 341–54; "Rent Seeking and Profit Seeking," in *Toward a Theory of the Rent-Seeking Society*, eds. James M. Buchanan, Robert D. Tollison, and Gordon Tullock (College Station: Texas A&M University Press, 1980), 3–15. Other Buchanan papers on rent seeking appear in part 5 of volume 13 in the series, *Politics as Public Choice*, and deal with Buchanan's public choice contribution in greater detail. Of course, the five papers presented in part 2 should be read in association with all those in volume 13: our aim here is to give a flavor of the fuller feast, not to substitute for it.

9. Geoffrey Brennan and James M. Buchanan, *The Power to Tax: Analytical Foundations of a Fiscal Constitution* (New York: Cambridge University Press, 1980), volume 9 in the series; see volumes 14 and 15 in the series, *Debt and Taxes* and *Externalities and Public Expenditure Theory*, respectively.

fluential attempt at synthesizing public finance in his *The Theory of Public Finance*. The second paper, "Taxation in Fiscal Exchange," shows Buchanan's attempt to meld tax theory with his general contractarianism. The third and fourth papers, "Public Debt, Cost Theory, and the Fiscal Illusion" and "Keynesian Follies," respectively, reflect his lifelong interest in debt financing and its political consequences.[10] The fifth paper, "Socialism Is Dead but Leviathan Lives On," represents a blend of concerns about unconstrained governmental expenditure powers combined with the postsocialist euphoria of 1989–90.[11]

Buchanan is a relatively self-conscious theorist, and much of his writing has a methodological flavor. Here in part 4, we present, in turn, two important papers on the interpretation of welfare economics, "Positive Economics, Welfare Economics, and Political Economy" and "The Relevance of Pareto Optimality"; two papers that deal with the nature of political and social order, "Politics and Science: Reflections on Knight's Critique of Polanyi" and "Order Defined in the Process of Its Emergence"; one paper, "Natural and Artifactual Man," on the operation of basic human nature; and one paper, "Rights, Efficiency, and Exchange: The Irrelevance of Transactions Cost," which deals with transaction costs in economic analysis.[12] This set of papers

10. James M. Buchanan, *Public Finance in Democratic Process: Fiscal Institutions and Individual Choice* (Chapel Hill: University of North Carolina Press, 1966), volume 4 in the series; "The Pure Theory of Government Finance: A Suggested Approach," *Journal of Political Economy* 57 (December 1949): 496–505; Richard A. Musgrave, *The Theory of Public Finance* (New York: McGraw-Hill, 1959); James M. Buchanan, "Taxation in Fiscal Exchange," *Journal of Public Economics* 6 (1976): 17–29; "Public Debt, Cost Theory, and the Fiscal Illusion," in *Public Debt and Future Generations*, ed. J. M. Ferguson (Chapel Hill: University of North Carolina Press, 1964), 150–63; "Keynesian Follies," in *The Legacy of Keynes*, Nobel Conference XXII, ed. David A. Reese (San Francisco: Harper & Row, 1987), 130–45; see also *Public Principles of Public Debt: A Defense and Restatement* (Homewood, Ill.: Richard D. Irwin, 1958), volume 2 in the series, and *Externalities and Public Expenditure Theory* (part 2 specifically), volume 15 in the series.

11. James M. Buchanan, *Socialism Is Dead but Leviathan Lives On*, the John Bonython Lecture, CIS Occasional Paper, 30 (Sydney: Centre for Independent Studies, 1990), 1–9; see also Geoffrey Brennan and James M. Buchanan, *The Power to Tax: Analytical Foundations of a Fiscal Constitution* (New York: Cambridge University Press, 1980), volume 9 in the series, and *Externalities and Public Expenditure Theory* (part 1 specifically), volume 15 in the series.

12. James M. Buchanan, "Positive Economics, Welfare Economics, and Political Econ-

reflects the breadth of Buchanan's interests: there is no single message or topic here, but, rather, a picture of the approach that Buchanan takes to the analysis of economic order.

One important feature of Buchanan's approach—perhaps the most foundational feature—is the normative framework he adopts, and this framework and ethical considerations more generally are the core of part 5. Buchanan's framework is individualist and contractarian. Because it is contractarian, Buchanan takes seriously the values that individuals actually have and how their behavior is influenced by those values in various settings. For example, in "Ethical Rules, Expected Values, and Large Numbers," he examines how the behavior of consequentialist moral agents engaged in collective action is likely to respond to larger numbers. The analysis here develops independently and more concisely the same argument presented almost simultaneously by Mancur Olson in his justly famous *The Logic of Collective Action.* Also included in part 5 is Buchanan's paper "The Samaritan's Dilemma." In terms of its actual reception, this must surely rank as one of Buchanan's most controversial papers. Certainly the paper seems to have had the capacity to reduce Buchanan's opponents to apoplexy. In this paper, Buchanan examines the difficulty for an altruist in dealing with the consequences of his altruism for the recipient's work incentives. One interesting aspect of his treatment here is that, before the issue became fashionable, Buchanan was aware of the problem of commitment power in what was subsequently to be known as "subgame perfectness." Another notable feature is the connection with Buchanan's commitment to the value of the work ethic— a commitment that stands beside and overlays his more abstract contractarian values. Much of Buchanan's attention during the 1990s has been taken up with an attempt to ground this concern with the work ethic within a broader normative frame. This latter strand of Buchanan's thinking is represented in this section in "The Supply of Labour and the Extent of the Mar-

omy," *Journal of Law and Economics* 2 (October 1959): 124–38; "Politics and Science: Reflections on Knight's Critique of Polanyi," *Ethics* 77 (July 1967): 303–10; "Order Defined in the Process of Its Emergence," *Literature of Liberty* 5 (Winter 1982): 5; "Natural and Artifactual Man," in *What Should Economists Do?* 93–112; "Rights, Efficiency and Exchange: The Irrelevance of Transactions Cost," in *Ansprüche, Eigentum und Verfügungsrechte* (Berlin: Duncker and Humblot, 1984), 9–24.

ket." In "Markets, States, and the Extent of Morals," Buchanan examines the connection between moral conduct and institutional form; and, in the final essay in part 5, "The Ethics of Constitutional Order," he looks at the ethics that undergird and support the abstract rules of society.[13]

One aspect of part 5 is worth special mention. Public choice economists are often accused of projecting a picture of human motivation in which only narrow economic self-interest counts. Perhaps in certain contexts, models that make this motivational assumption can be useful. But, it should be clear that Buchanan has a richer picture of human motivation in mind: in that picture, there may be few saints (or "angels," to use Madison's famous term), but ethical presentiments still play some role in individual conduct—a role that can be influenced by the institutional setting in which that conduct is shaped.

No purportedly representative selection of Buchanan's work would be complete without a good dose of "constitutionalism." Whether the concern with rules is an independent feature of Buchanan's work or springs out of a need to make his contractarianism operational (as is suggested for example in "The Relevance of Pareto Optimality" in part 4) can here remain an open issue. What is utterly clear is that "the reason of constitutional rules" has been a lifetime preoccupation for Buchanan and has become an increasingly predominant theme as his work has progressed. In a broad sense, much of Buchanan's work has been, and remains, "constitutional political economy." So it has seemed natural to include in this introductory volume a section focused on the reason of rules and to begin the section with a defining paper, "The Domain of Constitutional Economics," published in the inaugural issue of the journal *Constitutional Political Economy.* Of course, explicit con-

---

13. James M. Buchanan, "Ethical Rules, Expected Values, and Large Numbers," *Ethics* 76 (October 1965): 1–13; Mancur Olson, *The Logic of Collective Action* (Cambridge: Harvard University Press, 1965); James M. Buchanan, "The Samaritan's Dilemma," in *Altruism, Morality and Economic Theory,* ed. E. S. Phelps (New York: Russell Sage Foundation, James 1975), 71–85; "The Supply of Labour and the Extent of the Market," in *Adam Smith's Legacy: His Place in the Development of Modern Economics,* ed. Michael Fry (London: Routledge, 1992), 104–16, see also the papers included in part 7 of volume 12 in the series, *Economic Inquiry and Its Logic;* "Markets, States, and the Extent of Morals," *American Economic Review* 68 (May 1978): 364–68; "The Ethics of Constitutional Order," in *Essays on the Political Economy* (Honolulu: University of Hawai'i Press, 1989), 25–31.

stitutional concern was evident in Buchanan's work long before 1990, as the "predictability" paper (yet another 1962 publication) makes clear. Indeed, the *Calculus of Consent* represents the *locus classicus* of the constitutional approach. Yet Buchanan, almost forty years after the *Calculus,* has not exhausted the topic. More to the point, perhaps it has not exhausted him, as "Generality as a Constitutional Constraint" and the related book with Roger Congleton testify.[14]

A prior "logic of rules" must be derived even before specific analyses of constitutional alternatives are attempted. In "Before Public Choice," a paper that foreshadows much of the extended treatment in *The Limits of Liberty,* Buchanan moves the starting gate back, so to speak, and, in doing so, relates constitutional analysis directly to anarchy.[15]

As longtime associates of Buchanan and as participants in many earnest exchanges with him of the sort that are meat and drink to academics, we felt obliged to include here "The Relatively Absolute Absolutes."[16] It is a feature of these exchanges that, just when you think you have Buchanan in a totally impossible position, he is inclined to make appeal to "the relatively absolute absolutes" as a kind of trump card. Perhaps every academic needs some such concept to be the final repository of all that is ultimately mysterious or unexplored—rather like Adam Smith's "benign deity." Or perhaps there is more in the concept of the "relatively absolute absolutes" than at least some of the editorial team are capable of seeing at this point. After all, this would not be the first time that we have failed to perceive the full depth and subtlety of Buchanan's reasoning: it is indeed in the confidence that there is yet much to

14. James M. Buchanan, "The Domain of Constitutional Economics," *Constitutional Political Economy* 1, no. 1 (1990): 1–18; "Predictability: The Criterion of Monetary Constitutions," in *In Search of a Monetary Constitution,* ed. Leland B. Yeager (Cambridge: Harvard University Press, 1962), 155–83; "Generality as a Constitutional Constraint," in *Trap of Democracy* (Tokyo: Editorial Board of Public Choice Studies); James M. Buchanan and Roger D. Congleton, *Politics by Principle, Not Interest: Toward Nondiscriminatory Democracy* (Cambridge and New York: Cambridge University Press, 1998), volume 11 in the series.

15. James M. Buchanan, "Before Public Choice," *Explorations in the Theory of Anarchy,* ed. Gordon Tullock (Blacksburg, Va.: Center for Study of Public Choice, 1972), 27–37; *The Limits of Liberty: Between Anarchy and Leviathan* (Chicago: University of Chicago Press, 1975), volume 7 in the series.

16. James M. Buchanan, "The Relatively Absolute Absolutes," in *Essays on the Political Economy* (Honolulu: University of Hawai'i Press, 1989), 32–46.

be learned from Buchanan's writings that this Collected Works project is presented.

The last paper in this initial volume is Buchanan's 1986 Alfred Nobel Memorial Prize Lecture, "The Constitution of Economic Policy," a synthesis of the Buchanan contribution by Buchanan himself.[17] We conceive this lecture and the commencing press statement as "bookends" to bracket the elements that compose, as we see it, the essential Buchanan.

Questions might, of course, be raised about the principles of selection we have adopted in forming this initial volume—and more perhaps about what is omitted than about what is included. As already indicated, we have shown a preference in selection for earlier "classic" statements over later reconsiderations. There has also been a preference for single-authored pieces over collaborative ones. Buchanan has been a gregarious intellect and a generous one: many of the important papers and about half the books have been jointly authored, and, though all these works bear the unmistakable Buchanan mind-print, they also reflect in some measure the styles and minds of the collaborators. In this first volume, we have wanted to depict the *unblended* Buchanan voice. All of the papers in volume 1 are therefore solo efforts. Some commentators may be surprised not to see in a collection that purports to offer a picture of the essential Buchanan several of the most famous papers—say, "Externality," a paper written with Craig Stubblebine, or "An Economic Theory of Clubs."[18] The reason for these omissions lies in a desire to avoid, in this initial volume, the more technical papers and, more particularly, to locate these classics within the context of other papers that show the same style and thematic concern. We are confident that those readers who would want to consult those papers for scholarly purposes would also want access to associated, similarly technical papers on closely related themes. For such readers, the later volumes (and possibly the entire series) will be essential.

Finally, a word about titles. As anyone who has worked with Buchanan will bear witness, he is one who believes titles to be important. Some care has

17. James M. Buchanan, "The Constitution of Economic Policy," in *Les Prix Nobel* (Stockholm: Almquist and Wicksell International, 1986), 334–43.

18. James M. Buchanan, "An Economic Theory of Clubs," *Economica* 32 (February 1965): 1–14; see volume 15 in the series, *Externalities and Public Expenditure Theory*.

therefore been taken with the title for this particular volume. We have wanted to be descriptive. And we have sought a certain euphony. On the one hand, in the spirit of Buchanan's distinction between the "logic" and the "science" of choice, the work is represented as primarily "logical" in that sense.[19] On the other hand, there should be no misapprehension that Buchanan's work is mere logic-chopping for its own sake: *this* logic is foundational. Further, the title should recognize the distinctive constitutionalist orientation that characterizes the Buchanan approach. We have, in addition, wanted to include some reference to liberty—both because liberty is a central element in Buchanan's normative structure and because liberty is the core concern of the organization under whose aegis the Buchanan Collected Works are being produced. Whether the chosen title is a reasonable compromise among these various considerations is an issue we shall have to leave to the judgment of (we hope, sympathetic) readers. We are ourselves tolerably satisfied. Indeed, we should take this opportunity to record our pleasure and satisfaction with this entire project. We have been both honored and delighted to have acted as editors. Apart from anything else, the editorial role has provided us the opportunity to acquaint ourselves in greater depth with the remarkable work of a truly remarkable scholar. We feel privileged to have participated in an exercise that will extend that opportunity more broadly.

We should in particular place on record here our debt to Liberty Fund for initiating this project and for pursuing it with their customary dedication and skill. In particular, Alan Russell, chairman of the board; George B. Martin, president; Emilio J. Pacheco, vice president; David A. Bovenizer, director of publications; and Madelaine R. Cooke, managing editor, deserve our thanks for their enthusiasm and support. In the final analysis, it is entirely appropriate that the Buchanan Collected Works are appearing under Liberty Fund aegis. Not only is there a long-standing Buchanan association with Liberty Fund (for many years Buchanan held the record for the most Liberty Fund conferences ever attended), but there is also the centrality of liberty as an organizing normative principle in Buchanan's writings. Liberty Fund was established to "explore the idea of a society of free and responsible individuals." Buchanan's work has been devoted to precisely that exploration.

No Buchanan project would be complete without the mention of Mrs.

---

19. See volume 17, part 1, in the series, *Moral Science and Moral Order.*

Betty H. Tillman, who has served as Jim Buchanan's secretary and executive assistant for more than thirty years. In this project, Betty provided much needed guidance and assistance and, as ever, an encompassing moral support for all things Buchanan and all things Public Choice. We should also acknowledge the contribution of Jo Ann Burgess at the Center for Study of Public Choice, who has been an indispensable piece of the whole operation: as project editorial officer she has been the coordinating, shaping, and, occasionally, whip-cracking hand. She has never lost her cool, despite provocation. We should be remiss if we did not acknowledge the invaluable assistance of Allison Blizzard.

Finally, behind the scenes and from an appropriately remote distance, Jim Buchanan himself has also been an important source of information and advice, when the editorial trio felt that some expert input might be useful. We have, obstinately, retained the final determination on all matters of inclusion and location—a situation that has always been respected. But it has helped immeasurably to have the "master's voice" available for consultation when we wanted it.

Geoffrey Brennan
Australian National University

Hartmut Kliemt
University of Duisburg

Robert D. Tollison
University of Mississippi

1998

The Logical Foundations of
Constitutional Liberty

The Royal Swedish Academy of Sciences Press Release

For further information please contact
The Royal Swedish Academy of Sciences
Information Department
Box 50005, S-104 05 Stockholm, Sweden, tel. 08/15 04 30
Telex 17073 royacad s

The Royal Swedish Academy of Sciences has decided to award the 1986 Alfred Nobel Memorial Prize in Economic Sciences to *Professor James McGill Buchanan*, George Mason University, Virginia, USA, for his development of the contractual and constitutional bases for the theory of economic and political decision-making.

THIS YEAR'S ECONOMICS PRIZE AWARDED FOR A SYNTHESIS OF THE THEORIES OF POLITICAL AND ECONOMIC DECISION-MAKING (PUBLIC CHOICE)

Summary

This year's Alfred Nobel Memorial Prize in Economic Sciences is awarded to *James M. Buchanan* for his contributions to the theory of political decision-making and public economics. Traditional economic theory explains in great

KUNGL.
VETENSKAPSAKADEMIEN
THE ROYAL SWEDISH
ACADEMY OF SCIENCES   16 October 1986

detail how consumers and entrepreneurs make decisions regarding purchase of goods, choice of work, production, investments, etc. In a series of studies, Buchanan has developed a corresponding theory of decision-making in the public sector. This comprehensive theoretical formulation which goes under the name the New Political Economy or "Public choice," and lies on the boundary between economics and political science and has some of its origins in the work of the Swedish economist Knut Wicksell. Buchanan's contribution is that he has transferred the concept of gain derived from mutual exchange between individuals to the realm of political decision-making. The political process thus becomes a means of cooperation aimed at achieving reciprocal advantages. But the result of this process depends on "rules of the game," i.e., the constitution in a broad sense. This in turn emphasizes the vital importance of the formulation of constitutional rules and the possibility of constitutional reforms. According to Buchanan, it is often futile to advise politicians or influence the outcome of specific issues. In a given system of rules, the outcome is to a large extent determined by established political constellations. A relevant example is that those who would like to correct individual tariffs should concentrate instead on the fundamental rules of international trade, such as GATT regulations.

For nearly forty years, James M. Buchanan has devoted himself to development of the contractual and constitutional bases for the theory of economic and political decision-making. In so doing, he has become the leading researcher in the field which has come to be known as "public choice theory."

For a long time, traditional economics lacked an independent theory of political decision-making. Modern welfare theory often relied on the premise that public authorities could apply relatively mechanical methods to correct different types of so-called market failures. Stabilization policy theory— regardless of whether it was Keynesian or monetarist—appeared to assume that political authorities endeavored to achieve certain macroeconomic or socioeconomic goals regarding employment, inflation or growth rates. Buchanan and others in the public choice school have not accepted this simplified view of political life. Instead, they have sought explanations for political behavior that resemble those used to analyze behavior on markets.

Individuals who behave selfishly on markets can hardly behave wholly altruistically in political life. This results in analyses which indicate that political parties or authorities that to at least some extent act out of self-interest will try to obtain as many votes as possible in order to reach positions of power or receive large budget allocations. This type of analyses has become universal in recent years, and is perhaps the most widely known aspect of public choice theory.

Principles of Unanimity

Buchanan has extended the parallels between economic and political decision-making even further. Market behavior is based primarily on voluntary agreements and the exchange of goods and services which give rise to mutual advantages for the agents in market transactions. A prerequisite of the market system, however, is the establishment of a legal system that protects ownership rights and the realization of contractual agreements. The political system may also be regarded as a system based on voluntary agreements.

Beginning with Knut Wicksell's early analysis of the relation between public expenditures and taxes, Buchanan has formulated a theory of the public sector and political decision-making based on the principle of unanimity. As a result, decisions concerning the dimensioning and financing of collective efforts may be regarded as the outcome of voluntary agreements among citizens. Every citizen would thus in theory receive a welfare gain if the value, to him, of collective measures exceeds what he must forego in the form of taxes.

In this perspective the political process becomes primarily a way of co-operating to achieve mutual advantages—and not a means for redistributing resources among individuals. Owing to the high costs of arriving at decisions, however, the unanimity principle is difficult to apply in practice. The costs of making decisions based on a high degree of mutual agreement have to be weighed against the costs an individual faces when a majority decision goes against him. It thus becomes imperative to distinguish between fundamental decisions concerning the rules which govern future decisions on all kinds of issues and the decisions themselves.

Once constitutional rules are adopted, the outcome on concrete issues is often given by the internal dynamics of the political system. Thus the design of constitutional rules and the possibility of constitutional reforms take on great importance. Attempts to advise politicians or affect the outcome of specific issues are often futile: for any given rule system, the outcome is determined largely by prevailing political constellations.

The Importance of Fixed Rules

Buchanan's foremost achievement is that he has consistently and tenaciously emphasized the significance of fundamental rules and applied the concept of the political system as an exchange process for the achievement of mutual advantages. He has used his method with great success in the analysis of many specific problems and issues. Long before large budget deficits arose, for example, he showed how debt financing dissolves the relation between expenditures and taxes in the decision-making process.

Developments over the last few decades have confirmed Buchanan's realistic view of the scope of economic policy and the importance of continuously reconsidering fundamental rules of the game, while retaining stable rules. Economists now working in the area of stabilization policy are much more interested in fixed rules than they were a few decades ago when "fine tuning" was in fashion. Earmarked taxes and qualified majority as methods of achieving better correspondence between public expenditures and taxes are now considerably more topical questions than they were twenty years ago when attempts were made to restrict the political administrative decision-making process as little as possible.

Important Publications

Buchanan's best-known work is probably *Calculus of Consent* (1962; written in collaboration with his colleague Gordon Tullock). Different applications are given in e.g. *Public Finance in Democratic Process* (1966) and *The Demand and Supply of Public Goods* (1968).

Buchanan's visionary approach is presented in *The Limits of Liberty* (1975) and *Freedom in Constitutional Contract: Perspectives of a Political Economist* (1977). In more recent works, Buchanan has continued his analysis of the tax state and systems of rules in *The Power to Tax* (1980; with G. Brennan) and *The Reason of Rules* (1985; with G. Brennan).

In addition to these monographs, Buchanan has published numerous articles in scientific journals; collections have appeared in *What Should Economists Do?* (1979) and *Liberty, Market and State* (1986).

James McGill Buchanan was born in Tennessee, USA, on October 3, 1919. After academic studies at Middle Tennessee State College and the University of Tennessee, his research work at Chicago University resulted in a doctorate in 1948. Between 1957 and 1967, he served as professor at the University of Virginia in Charlottesville, where he directed the Thomas Jefferson Center for Studies in Political Economy and Social Philosophy. After a short interlude at the University of California in Los Angeles, he became professor at the Virginia Polytechnic Institute in Blacksburg in 1969, where he with Gordon Tullock founded and led the Center for Study of Public Choice. In 1982 the Center was moved to George Mason University, Fairfax, Virginia, near Washington, D.C., where Buchanan now works.

PART ONE

Introduction

Better than Plowing

Family Origins

My title's description of an academic career is taken directly from Frank H. Knight, from whom I take so much. Nonetheless, my origins in the rural agricultural poverty of the upper south (Tennessee) in the United States, along with the sometimes pretentious efforts of the middle-class poor to impose social distinctions, are surely explanatory elements in any narrative account of my own history.

My family was poor, but, in the county, it was important. My grandfather, John P. Buchanan, was the county's only Governor of the State of Tennessee. He was a one-term phenomenon, having been elected as the nominee of the Farmers' Alliance Party, one of the several successful Populist electoral triumphs in 1891. By 1893, the Democratic Party had put its house in order, and the Populists had seen their best days. But Buchanan's governorship established the family in the community. The local public school which I attended for ten years was named "Buchanan School."

My father was the youngest of a large family, to whose lot fell the operation of the family farm after his siblings had departed. I grew up in a huge house on a hill, in varying states of disrepair, on a farm that had no owner. It was owned by "the Buchanan estate," which was not divided until the farm was sold in 1944, and long after I had entered military service. My father had no incentive for effective maintenance. He was a jack of all trades, a farmer, a sometime carpenter, veterinarian, insulator, and equipment operator. He

From *Banca Nazionale del Lavoro Quarterly Review* 159 (December 1986): 359–75. Reprinted by permission of the publisher. Contribution to a series of recollections and reflections on professional experiences of distinguished economists. This series opened with the September 1979 issue of this *Review*.

was locally political, a community Justice of the Peace during all of my childhood. A handsome man, he had been a fine athlete (two years varsity football
at the University of Oklahoma); and with a fine sense of humor, he was a
favorite with the ladies. He was possessed by intense personal courage; he
made no pretense to intellectual interests.

My mother was the best and the brightest of a family of deputy sheriffs
and Presbyterian preachers which had roughly the same class standing as my
father's. As was general in rural Tennessee in the early years of this century,
both families were pure Scots-Irish. My mother, Lila Scott, finished high
school, took teacher training, and taught for a decade before meeting my father. Hers was the most curious mind I have known; she devoured anything
she could find to read, and she was not discriminating, with interests ranging
at least from Latin grammar through calculus through Zane Grey westerns.
She, too, assumed easily a leadership role in the local community, organizing
the parents' association for the school, rising rapidly to county and regional
offices. But, for this narrative, she was my teacher, and beyond the teacher
that is in all mothers. She advanced me two grades by home instruction, and
helped me in assignments through college years.

Early Education

From my early years, I was assigned the role as family successor to my grandfather. I was to be the lawyer-politician, and Vanderbilt University (pre-law,
then law) was understood as the final rung on my educational ladder. There
were early family misgivings about my personality; I did not exhibit the behavior of the exaggerated extrovert required for any budding politician. But
law remained my career focus, and I was trained in public speaking. Economic reality destroyed this dream; Vanderbilt moved beyond the possible as
the Great Depression moved in. College was what I could afford, Middle
Tennessee State Teachers' College in Murfreesboro, which allowed me to live
at home and to earn enough for fees and books by milking dairy cows morn-
ing and night for four years.

My college education was non-systematic and stochastic. There was waste
in the requirements in formal education, and poor instruction in biology,
history, psychology, economics, and other subjects. But there was much of
value in my exposure to Shakespeare, modern poetry, mathematics, and

physics. When I finished, I had accumulated majors in three areas—mathematics, English literature, and social science, including economics. These college years were important as confidence builders; by the end of my second year my academic standing was the best in the college; the country boy more than held his own against the boys and girls from the towns.

Upon graduation in 1940, I faced three options—school teaching at $65 per month; employment in a Nashville bank at $75 per month; and a $50 per month fellowship in economics at the University of Tennessee. My career as an economist was settled by the dominance of the third opportunity, not by any desire to save the world. The 1940–41 graduate year in Knoxville, Tennessee, helped me meet the world beyond. I learned no economics during that year, but that I did learn about women and whiskey, which, after all, are important parts of an education. There were few good economists on the faculty, but I was exposed to a genuine scholar, a man whose work habits were important in shaping my own. Charles P. White became my example of the research economist, who took his position seriously and conveyed to me the notion that there is, after all, a moral element in academic employment. It was White also who, despite his own self-acknowledged limits in these respects, strongly advised me to stick with economic theory as the basis for all applications.

Plans were open beyond the one year until I secured a fellowship in statistics at Columbia University for the 1941–42 academic year. But before I could take up this appointment, I was drafted into military service, and found myself in the United States Navy by August 1941.

I had an easy war. After officer training in New York, and a special stint at the Naval War College, I was assigned to the operations staff of Admiral C. W. Nimitz, Commander-in-Chief, Pacific Fleet. Aside from a six-week experience-gathering tour at sea during one of the island invasions, I worked throughout the war at Pearl Harbor and at Guam at fleet headquarters control deep in the bowels of the earth. I enjoyed the military, the colleagues, the work, and the setting; and I was good at the job. For the first and only time in my life, I worked closely with men who were important in shaping the lives and destinies of many others. I saw these military leaders as ordinary mortals, trying to do their job within the constraints they faced, and burdened with their own prejudices like everyone else. This experience has helped me throughout my academic career; I have been able to relegate to the third order of smalls the sometime petty quarrels that seem to motivate professors everywhere, both in their roles as instructors and as research scholars.

In one sense my only career choice involved the decision to leave the navy and to return to civilian life. This decision was not easy; I knew the important persons, who urged me to stay; I had enjoyed the four years. But I made the correct choice, and was discharged in late 1945. With the GI government subsidy for further schooling available, and with a new wife for partial support, I considered alternative graduate schools. Columbia University no longer beckoned because New York City had not made me want to return. I knew nothing about the competence or the ideological makeup of the University of Chicago economics faculty. But a teacher from my undergraduate days at Middle Tennessee, with a Chicago Ph.D. in political science, conveyed to me the intellectual excitement of the place. Off to Chicago I went in late 1945, along with the many others who were just returning from military service.

Chicago, Frank Knight, and Knut Wicksell

Had I known about the ideological character of the Chicago faculty I might have chosen to go elsewhere. I was not overtly political or ideological in my salad days; emerging from the family populist tradition, I grew up in a solidly Democratic setting, with Roosevelt emerging as the popular leader in the 1930's. I was basically populist and pacifist. But officer-training school in New York radicalized me. Along with many others, I was subjected to overt discrimination based on favoritism for products of the eastern-establishment universities. This sobering experience made me forever sympathetic to those who suffer discriminatory treatment, and it forestalled any desire to be a part of any eastern-establishment institution.

When I reached the University of Chicago, I was what I now best describe as a libertarian socialist. I had always been anti-state, anti-government, anti-establishment. But this included the establishment that controlled the United States economy. I had grown up on a reading diet from my grandfather's attic piled high with the radical pamphlets of the 1890's. The robber barons were very real to me.

At Chicago, I found myself no different from my graduate-student colleagues, almost all of whom were socialist of one or another stripe. But within six weeks after enrollment in Frank Knight's course in price theory, I had been converted into a zealous advocate of the market order. Frank Knight was not an ideologue, and he made no attempt to convert anybody. But I was, somehow, ready for the understanding of economic process that his teaching offered. I was converted by the power of ideas, by an understanding of the model of the market. This experience shaped my attitude toward the use and purpose of economic instruction; if I could be converted so could others.

Frank Knight was *the* intellectual influence during my years at the University of Chicago, and his influence increased over subsequent years, enhanced by the development of a close personal relationship. Knight became my role model, without which I wonder what turns I might have taken. The qualities of mind that Knight exhibited were, and remain, those that I seek to emulate: the willingness to question anything, and anybody, on any subject anytime; the categorical refusal to accept anything as sacred; the genuine openness to all ideas; and, finally, the basic conviction that most ideas peddled about are nonsense or worse when examined critically.

A second Chicago event profoundly affected my career. Having finished my work, including the German-language examination, I had the leisure of a scholar without assignments in the Harper Library stacks during three months of the summer of 1948. By sheer chance, I pulled Knut Wicksell's 1896 dissertation on taxation from the shelves, a book that was untranslated and unknown.[1] The effect on me was dramatic. Wicksell laid out before me a set of ideas that seemed to correspond precisely with those that I had already in my head, ideas that I could not have expressed and would not have dared to express in the public-finance mind-set of the time. Wicksell told us that if economists really want to apply the test of efficiency to the public sector, only the rule of unanimity for collective choice offers the procedural guarantee. If we seek reform in economic policy, we should change the rules under which political agents or representatives act. Economists should, once and for all, cease and desist proffering advice to non-existent benevolent des-

---

1. Knut Wicksell, *Finanztheoretische Untersuchungen* (Jena: Gustav Fischer, 1896).

pots. Wicksell's were heady words, and from that day, I was determined to translate Wicksell's contribution into English.[2]

Visitors to my office know that photographs of only two economists grace the walls, Frank Knight and Knut Wicksell. I consider them co-equals, Knight in his influence on my attitudes toward the world of ideas generally, and Wicksell in his influence on the specific ideas that have come to be associated with my work in public choice and constitutional economics. Both of these influences were embedded in my psyche when I left Chicago in mid-1948.

I entered the highly competitive world of American academia with no conscious sense of intellectual direction. In one of my first articles, based in part on the Wicksell exposure and, in part, by reading a translation of de Viti de Marco,[3] I called for a tie-in between the theory of the state and norms for taxation. The point seemed so simple, indeed obvious, yet so locked in was the utilitarian mind-set of orthodox public finance that the article was widely cited as seminal. In 1951, Kenneth Arrow published his widely-heralded book on the general impossibility theorem.[4] For three years, I was bemused by the failure of reviewers and critics to make the obvious point that the whole Arrow construction was inappropriate for a democratic society. Why should the social ordering satisfy consistency norms if individual values and preferences generated inconsistencies? I published a review article in 1954 that few economists understood then, or understand now. Almost as a footnote, I published a second short article comparing individual choice in voting and in the market. Again, the points made seemed simple, but surprisingly no one had made such a basic comparison. In those two papers, there were elements of much that was later to be developed in my contributions to public choice.

The two 1954 papers were published in the *Journal of Political Economy*, under the editorship of Earl J. Hamilton, who deserves special mention in this narrative. I had not taken his courses at the University of Chicago, and

2. My translation of the centrally important part of the book was published as "A New Principle of Just Taxation," in *Classics in the Theory of Public Finance*, ed. E. P. Musgrave and A. T. Peacock (London: Macmillan, 1958), 72–118.

3. Antonio de Viti de Marco, *First Principles of Public Finance*, trans. E. P. Marget (London: Jonathan Cape, 1936).

4. Kenneth Arrow, *Social Choice and Individual Values* (New York: Wiley, 1951).

only in my last few months there did I get to know him personally. But we did establish a friendship, and from him I got the advice that one major key to academic success was to "keep the ass to the chair," a rule that I have followed and that I have passed along to several generations of students. But Hamilton's influence was not primarily in this piece of advice. Through his editorship of the journal, he encouraged rather than discouraged me as potential author; he was a tough editor, but his comments-reactions were never wholly negative, and it was only after several submissions that the two 1954 pieces were hammered into acceptable shape. Negation at that stage of my career might have been fatal.

The Italian Year

Hamilton was also influential in encouraging me to keep up with the languages, and I commenced to learn to read Italian. I wanted to go to Italy for a year's reading in the classical works in public finance theory. I got a Fulbright grant for the 1955–56 academic year, which I spent in Perugia and Rome. This Italian year was critical in the development of my ideas on the importance of the relationship between the political structure and the positive and normative theory of economic policy. The Italians had escaped the delusions of state omniscience and benevolence that had clouded the minds of English- and German-language social philosophers and scientists. The Italians had long since cut through the absurdities of Benthamite utilitarianism and Hegelian idealism. Real rather than idealized politics, with real persons as actors—these were the building blocks in the Italian constructions, whether those of the cooperative-democratic state or the ruling class–monopoly state. Exposure to this Italian conceptualization of the state was necessary to enable me to break out of the idealistic-utilitarian mind-set that still imposes its intellectual straitjacket on many of my peers in social science. The Italian year was also important in the more general sense of offering insights into the distinctly non-American historical-cultural environment.

Public Debt and Opportunity Cost

The Italian research year was indirectly responsible for one strand of my work that may seem to represent a side alley, namely, my work in the theory of public debt, which was less successful in convincing my economist peers than other work in public choice and public finance. At the very end of the Italian year, I suddenly "saw the light." I realized that the whole conventional wisdom on public debt was simply wrong, and that the time had come for a restoration of the classical theory, which was correct in all its essentials. I was as excited by this personal discovery as I had been by the discovery of the Wicksell book almost a decade earlier. Immediately on my return to America in 1956, I commenced my first singly-authored book, *Public Principles of Public Debt*.[5]

In my overall assessment, the work on public debt was not a digression. This work was simply another extension or application of what can be discerned as a central theme in my efforts from the very first papers written. I have been consistently reductionist in that I have insisted that analysis be factored down to the level of choices faced by individual actors. The orthodox theory of public debt that I challenged embodied a failure to treat relevant choice alternatives. My reasoning, once again, was simple. National economies, as such, cannot enjoy gains or suffer losses. The fact that making guns "uses up" resources in years of war tells us nothing at all about *who* must pay for those guns, and *when*. The whole macroaggregation exercise that had captured the attention of post-Keynesian economists was called into question.

My work on public debt stirred up considerable controversy in the early 1960's, and I realized that the ambiguity stemmed, in part, from an absence of clarity in my initial challenge. Confusion centered around the conception of opportunity cost, and I laid my plans to write a short book, which I consider my best work in economic theory, narrowly defined. This book, *Cost and Choice*, again emphasizes my central theme, the reduction of analysis to individual choice settings which, in this extension, implies the necessity of defining cost in utility rather than commodity dimensions.[6]

---

5. *Public Principles of Public Debt* (Homewood, Ill.: Richard D. Irwin, 1958).

6. *Cost and Choice* (Chicago: Markham, 1969; reprint, University of Chicago Press, 1976).

Gordon Tullock, *The Calculus of Consent,* and Public Choice

I first encountered Gordon Tullock in 1958, when he came to the University of Virginia as a postdoctoral research fellow. I was impressed by his imagination and originality, and by his ability to recognize easily the elements of my own criticism of public debt orthodoxy. Tullock insisted not only that analysis be reduced to individual choice but, also, that individuals be modelled always as maximizers of self-interest, a step that I had sometimes been unwilling to take, despite my exposure to the Italians. Tullock wrote his seminal paper on the working of simple majority rule, and we decided to collaborate on a book that would examine the individual's choice among alternative political rules. We more or less explicitly considered our exercise to be an implicit defense of the Madisonian structure embodied in the United States Constitution.

The Calculus of Consent was the first work in what we now call "constitutional economics," and it achieved the status of a "classic" in public choice theory.[7] In retrospect, it is interesting, to me, that there was no sense of "discovery" at any point in that book's construction, no moment of excitement akin to those accompanying either the discovery of the Wicksell book or the insight into public debt theory. Tullock and I considered ourselves to be applying relatively simple economic analysis to the choice among alternative political decision rules, with more or less predictable results. We realized that no one had attempted to do precisely what we were doing, but the exercise was essentially one of "writing out the obvious" rather than opening up wholly new areas for inquiry.

We were wrong. Public choice, as a subdiscipline in its own right, emerged in the early 1960's, in part from the reception of our book, in part from our own organizational-entrepreneurial efforts which later emerged in the Public Choice Society, in part from others' works. Once the whole complex web of political-decision rules and procedures was opened up for economic analysis, the range of application seemed open-ended. Public choice in the 1960's was both exciting and easy; it is not surprising that graduate students

---

7. James Buchanan and Gordon Tullock, *The Calculus of Consent* (Ann Arbor: University of Michigan Press, 1962).

in our program at Virginia were highly successful and that budding economists and political scientists quickly latched onto the new subdiscipline.[8]

My own work does not exhibit a dramatic switching to public choice economics from standard public finance. As I have noted above, from my earliest papers I had emphasized the importance of political structure, a conviction that was strengthened by my exposure to the Italians. Immediately after
my excursion into the theory of public debt and before collaboration with
Tullock on *The Calculus of Consent*, I wrote a long survey essay on the Italian
tradition in public finance and published this essay, along with other pieces
in *Fiscal Theory and Political Economy*. Considered as a package, my work
over the decade, 1956–66, involved filling in gaps in the taxonomy of public
goods theory along with various attempts to factor down familiar propositions in theoretical welfare economics into individualized choice settings.
The paper "Externality," written jointly with W. C. Stubblebine, was an amalgamation of strands of argument from Wicksell, Coase, and Pigou. The paper "An Economic Theory of Clubs" was a filling-in of an obvious gap in the
theory of public goods.[9]

During the early 1960's, my work specifically shifted toward an attempt to
tie two quasi-independent strands of inquiry together, those of orthodox
public finance and the theory of political-decision structure. The result was
a relatively neglected book, *Public Finance in Democratic Process*, which contained implications for normative theory that remain unrecognized by modern research scholars.[10]

The research program embodied in elementary public choice theory developed almost naturally in a sequence of applications to the theory of economic policy. The whole of the Keynesian and post-Keynesian theory of
macroeconomic management (including monetarism) depends critically on

8. For two volumes devoted largely to applications, see James M. Buchanan and Robert Tollison, eds., *Theory of Public Choice: Political Applications of Economics* (Ann Arbor:
University of Michigan Press, 1972); James M. Buchanan and Robert Tollison, eds., *Theory
of Public Choice, II* (Ann Arbor: University of Michigan Press, 1984).

9. *Fiscal Theory and Political Economy* (Chapel Hill: University of North Carolina
Press, 1960); James M. Buchanan and W. C. Stubblebine, "Externality," *Economica* 29
(November 1962): 371–84; "An Economic Theory of Clubs," *Economica* 32 (February
1965): 1–14.

10. *Public Finance in Democratic Process* (Chapel Hill: University of North Carolina
Press, 1967).

the presumption that political agents respond to considerations of "public interest" rather than to the incentives imposed upon them by constituents. Once these agents are modelled as ordinary persons, the whole policy structure crumbles. This basic public-choice critique of the Keynesian theory of policy was presented in *Democracy in Deficit*, written jointly with Richard E. Wagner.[11] I have often used the central argument of this book as the clearest example of the applicability of elementary public choice theory, the implications of which have been corroborated in the accumulating evidence provided by the regime of quasi-permanent budget deficits.

Between Anarchy and Leviathan

Through the middle 1960's, my analysis and interpretation of the workings of democratic politics were grounded in a relatively secure belief that, despite the many political failures that public choice theory allows us to identify, ultimately the governing authorities, as constrained by constitutional structure respond to and implement the values and preferences of individual citizens. This belief in the final efficacy of democratic process surely affected my analysis, even if unconsciously, and allowed me to defend the essential "logic" of political institutions in being against the sometime naive proposals made by social reformers.

This foundational belief was changed by the events of the late 1960's. I lost my "faith" in the effectiveness of government as I observed the explosive take-off in spending rates and new programs, engineered by self-interested political agents and seemingly divorced from the interests of citizens. At the same time, I observed what seemed to me to be a failure of the institutional structure, at all levels, to respond effectively to mounting behavioral disorder. The United States government seemed to take on aspects of an agent-driven Leviathan simultaneously with the emergence of anarchy in civil society.

What was happening, and how could my explanatory model be applied to the modified reality of the late 1960's and early 1970's? I sensed the necessity of plunging much deeper into basic political philosophy than heretofore, and

---

11. James M. Buchanan and Richard E. Wagner, *Democracy in Deficit* (New York: Academic Press, 1977).

I found it useful to examine more closely the predicted operating properties of both anarchy and Leviathan. I was fortunate in that I located colleagues who assisted and greatly complemented my efforts in each case. Winston C. Bush formalized the anarchy of the Hobbesian jungle in terms of modern economic theory. Bush's independent and foundational analysis provided me with the starting point for the book that remains the most coherent single statement of my research program, *The Limits of Liberty*.[12]

Although chapters in that book raised the threat of the Leviathan state, I had not worked out the formal analysis. Again I was lucky to be able to work with Geoffrey Brennan in pushing along this frontier of inquiry. We commenced the exciting project that emerged as *The Power to Tax*.[13] That book explored the implications of the hypothesis that government maximizes revenues from any taxing authority constitutionally granted to it. Such analysis seems required for any informed constitutional calculus involving a grant of taxing power to government. As reviewers noted, the result of our analysis here was to stand much of the conventional wisdom in normative tax theory on its head.

Constitutionalism and the Social Contract

As I noted earlier, *The Calculus of Consent* was the first explicit contribution in the research program that we now call "constitutional economics" or "constitutional political economy." Gordon Tullock and I were analyzing the individual's choice among alternative rules for reaching political decisions, rules to which he, along with others, would be subject in subsequent periods of operation. Such a choice setting is necessarily different in kind from that normally treated by economists, which is the choice among end objects within well-defined constraints. In a very real sense, the choice among rules becomes a choice among constraints, and, hence, involves a higher-state calculus of decision than that which most economists examine.

We were initially influenced to analyze the choice among political rules by at least two factors that I can now identify. First, we were dissatisfied by the

---

12. *The Limits of Liberty* (Chicago: University of Chicago Press, 1975).

13. Geoffrey Brennan and James M. Buchanan, *The Power to Tax* (Cambridge: Cambridge University Press, 1980).

apparent near-universal and unquestioned acceptance of majority rule as the ideal for collective decision processes. Secondly, we were influenced by our then colleague, Rutledge Vining, himself an early student of Frank Knight, who hammered home to all who would listen that economic-policy choices are not made among allocations or distributions, but are, necessarily, among rules or institutions that generate patterns of allocations and distributions. Vining's emphasis was on the stochastic nature of these patterns of outcomes and on the necessity for an appreciation for and understanding of the elementary theory of probability.

How does a person choose among the rules to which he will be subject? Vining took from Knight, and passed along to me, a fully sympathetic listener, the analogy with the choice of rules in ordinary games, from poker to basketball. The chooser, at the rule-choosing or constitutional stage of deliberation, cannot identify how any particular rule will precisely affect his own position in subsequent rounds of play. Who can know how the cards will fall? The choice among rules is, therefore, necessarily made under what we should now call a "veil of uncertainty." *The Calculus of Consent* was our straightforward extension of this nascent research program to the game of politics.

In constitutional choice there is no well-defined maximand analogous to that which describes garden-variety economic choice. The individual may still be modelled as a utility maximizer, but there is no readily available means of arraying alternatives. The formal properties of choice under uncertainty, properties that have been exhaustively explored during the middle decades of this century, did not concern us. But we did sense the positive value of the uncertainty setting in opening up the potential for agreement on rules. If an individual cannot know how specific rules will affect his own position, he will be led to choose among rules in accordance with some criterion of generality rather than particularity. And if all persons reason similarly, the prospects for some Wicksellian-like agreement on rules are much more favorable than prospects for agreement on political choices to be made within a defined rules structure. In my own interpretation, in *The Calculus of Consent*, Tullock and I were shifting the Wicksellian unanimity norm for efficiency in collective choice from the in-period level, where its limits are severe, to the constitutional level where no comparable limits are present.

This construction in *The Calculus of Consent* was essentially worked out independently of the comparable construction of John Rawls. But discovery of his early paper on "Justice as Fairness" during the course of writing our book served to give us confidence that we were on a reasonable track. As early as the late 1950's, Rawls had spelled out his justice-as-fairness criterion and had introduced early versions of his veil of ignorance, which was to become universally familiar after the publication of his acclaimed treatise, *A Theory of Justice*.[14] The coincidence both in the timing of our initial work and in the basic similarity in analytical constructions has made me share an affinity with Rawls that has seemed mysterious to critics of both of us.

The subject matter of economics has always seemed to me to be the institution of exchange, embodying agreement between or among choosing parties. The Wicksellian extension of the exchange paradigm to the many-person collective has its most direct application in the theory of public finance, but when applied to the choices among political rules the analysis moves into areas of inquiry that are foreign to economists. At this research juncture, the disciplinary base merges into political philosophy, and the exchange paradigm becomes a natural component of a general contractarian theory of political interaction. Almost by definition, the economist who shifts his attention to political process while retaining his methodological individualism must be contractarian.

As noted earlier, my emphasis has been on factoring down complex interactions into individual choice components and, where possible, to explain and interpret such interactions in terms of cooperation rather than conflict models. Interpersonal, intergroup, and interparty conflict can scarcely be left out of consideration when we examine ordinary politics within defined constitutional structures. The contractarian or exchange program must shift, almost by necessity, to the stage of choices among rules. The contractarian becomes a constitutionalist, and I have often classified my own position with both these terms.

I have continued to be surprised at the reluctance of my colleagues in the social sciences, and especially in economics, to share the contractarian-constitutionalist research program and to understand the relevance of looking at politics and governance in terms of the two-stage decision process. A substantial share of my work over the decade, 1975–85, involved varying attempts to persuade my peers to adopt the constitutional attitude. In two vol-

---

14. John Rawls, *A Theory of Justice* (Cambridge: Harvard University Press, 1971).

umes of collected essays, *Freedom in Constitutional Contract* and *Liberty, Market and State*, as well as in a book jointly with Geoffrey Brennan, *The Reason of Rules*, I sought to defend the contractarian-constitutionalist methodology in many applications.[15]

Academic Exit and Virginia Political Economy

Both in response to the demands of the series of autobiographical essays in which this paper appears and to my own preferences, I have, aside from the first two background sections, concentrated on the intellectual record, on the development of the ideas that have characterized my work, and on the persons and events that seem to have affected these ideas. I have deliberately left out of account the details of my personal, private experiences over the course of a long career. My essay would, however, be seriously incomplete if I should neglect totally the influences of the academic-intellectual environments within which I have been able to pursue my work, including the stimulation I have secured from colleagues, staff, and students whose names are not entered in these accounts.

I cannot, of course, test what "might have been" had I chosen academic settings other than those I did select. I feel no acute sense of highly-valued opportunities missed, nor do I classify any choices made as having been grossly mistaken. I have exercised the academic exit option that the competitive structure of the United States academy offers. In so doing, I have reduced the ability of those who might have sought to modify the direction of my research and teaching efforts, while, at the same time, I have secured the benefits from the unintended consequences that shifts in location always guarantee.

This much said, I would be remiss if I did not include some form of tribute to the three academic settings within Virginia that have provided me with professional breathing space for almost all of my career. Mr. Jefferson's "academical village," the University of Virginia, where I spent twelve years, 1956—

---

15. *Freedom in Constitutional Contract* (College Station: Texas A&M University Press, 1978); *Liberty, Market and State* (New York: New York University Press, 1986); Geoffrey Brennan and James M. Buchanan, *The Reason of Rules* (Cambridge: Cambridge University Press, 1985).

68, allowed Warren Nutter and me full rein in establishing the Thomas Jefferson Center for Studies in Political Economy. This Center, as an institution, encouraged me, and others, to counter the increasing technical specialization of economics and, for me, to keep the subject matter interesting when the discipline, in more orthodox hands, threatened to become boring in the extreme. Virginia Polytechnic Institute, or VPI, where I spent fourteen years, 1969–83, allowed Charles Goetz, Gordon Tullock, and me to organize the Center for Study of Public Choice, a Center that became, for a period in the 1970's and early 1980's, an international haven for research scholars who sought some exposure to the blossoming new subdiscipline of public choice. Finally, George Mason University, to which the whole Center shifted in 1983, insured a continuity in my research emphasis and tradition, even beyond that of my active career.

Retrospective

Other contributors to this series have discussed the influences on their developments as "economists." I am not at all sure that I qualify for inclusion in terms of this professional or disciplinary classification. I am not, and have never been, an "economist" in any narrowly-defined meaning. My interests in understanding how the economic interaction process works has always been instrumental to the more inclusive purpose of understanding how we can learn to live one with another without engaging in Hobbesian war and without subjecting ourselves to the dictates of the state. The "wealth of nations," as such, has never commanded my attention save as a valued by-product of an effectively free society. The ways and means through which the social order might be made more "efficient" in the standard meaning—these orthodox guidelines have carried relatively little weight for me.

Neither have I considered myself a "pure scientist" and my work as "pure science." I have not been engaged in some exciting quest for discovery of a reality that exists independently of our own making. I have sensed acutely the exhilaration in ideas that is shared by all scientists in the broader meaning, but the ideas that capture my attention are those that, directly or indirectly, explain how freely choosing individuals can secure jointly desired goals. The simple exchange of apples and oranges between two traders—this institutional model is the starting point for all that I have done. Contrast this with the choice between apples and oranges in the utility-maximizing calculus of Robinson Crusoe. The second model is the starting point for most of what most economists do.

If this difference between my foundational model and that of other economists is recognized, my work takes on an internal coherence and consistency that may not be apparent absent such recognition. The coherence was not, of course, a deliberately-chosen element of a research program. I have written largely in response to ideas that beckoned, ideas that offered some intellectual challenge and that had not, to my knowledge, been developed by others. I have rarely been teased by either the currency of policy topics or the fads of academic fashion, and when I have been so tempted my work has suffered. The coherence that the work does possess stems from the simple fact that I have worked from a single methodological perspective during the four decades that span my career to date, along with the fact that I have accepted the normative implications of this perspective. The methodological perspective and the normative stance are shared by few of my peers in modern social science. This location of my position outside the mainstream has the inestimable value of providing me with the continuing challenge to seek still other ideas and applications that may, ultimately, shift the frontier of effective agreement outward.

What Should Economists Do?

But it is not the popular movement, but the travelling of the minds of men who sit in the seat of Adam Smith that is really serious and worthy of all attention.

—Lord Acton, *Letters of Lord Acton to Mary Gladstone,*
edited by Herbert Paul (London: George Allen, 1904), 212.

I propose to examine the "travelling of the minds of men who sit in the seat of Adam Smith," those who try to remain within the "strict domain of science," and to ask the following questions: What are economists doing? What "should" they be doing? In these efforts to heed the counsel of Lord Acton, I proceed squarely against the advice of a modern economist whose opinions I regard with respect, George Stigler. He tells us that it is folly to become concerned with methodology before the age of sixty-five. As a value statement, Stigler's admonition can hardly be discussed. But, as a hypothesis, it can be refuted, at least by analogy with an ordinary road map. I remain notorious for my failure to look quickly enough at highway-route maps, hoping always that some intuitive directional instinct will keep me along the planned pattern of my journey. I learned many years ago that "optimal" behavior involves stopping soon after one gets "lost," after uncertainty beyond a certain limit is reached, and consulting a properly drawn map. The analogy with scientific methodology seems to be a close one. Unless we can, for some reason, accept the ever-changing activities of economists as being always a part of the necessary evolution of the discipline through time, as being "on the highway," it is essential that we look occasionally at the map or model for scien-

From *Southern Economic Journal* 30 (January 1964): 213–22. Reprinted by permission of the publisher.

tific progress that each of us surely carries around, consciously or unconsciously, in his head.

By proposing to examine critically what economists do you will note that I am also rejecting the familiar proposition advanced by Jacob Viner that "economics is what economists do," a proposition that Frank Knight converted into full circle when he added "and economists are those who do economics." This functional definition of our discipline begs the very question that I want to raise, if not to answer, here. Economists should, I think, face up to their basic responsibility; they should at least try to know their subject matter.

Let me call your attention to a much-neglected principle enunciated by Adam Smith. In Chapter II of *The Wealth of Nations* he states that the principle which gives rise to the division of labor, from which so many advantages are derived,

> is not originally the effects of any human wisdom, which foresees and intends that general opulence to which it gives occasion. It is the necessary, though very slow and gradual, consequence of a certain propensity in human nature which has in view no such extensive utility; the propensity to truck, barter, and exchange one thing for another.

Somewhat surprisingly, it seems to me, the relevance and the significance of this "propensity to truck, barter, and exchange" has been overlooked in most of the exegetical treatments of Smith's work. But surely here is his answer to what economics or political economy is all about.

Economists "should" concentrate their attention on a particular form of human activity, and upon the various institutional arrangements that arise as a result of this form of activity. Man's behavior in the market relationship, reflecting the propensity to truck and to barter, and the manifold variations in structure that this relationship can take; these are the proper subjects for the economist's study. In saying this, I am, of course, making a value statement that you may or may not support. Consider this paper, if you will, as an "essay in persuasion."

The elementary and basic approach that I suggest places "the theory of markets" and not the "theory of resource allocation" at center stage. My plea is really for the adoption of a sophisticated "catallactics," an approach to our discipline that has been advanced earlier, much earlier, by Archbishop

Whately and the Dublin School, by H. D. Macleod, by the American Arthur Latham Perry, by Alfred Ammon and still others.[1] It is not my purpose here, and it is not within my competence, to review the reasons for the failures of these men to convince their colleagues and their descendants. I note only that the view that they advanced, and one which has never been wholly absent from the main stream of thinking,[2] is perhaps more in need of stress now than it was during the times in which they worked.

In a brief treatment it is helpful to make bold charges against ideas or positions taken by leading figures. In this respect I propose to take on Lord Robbins as an adversary and to state, categorically, that his all-too-persuasive delineation of our subject field has served to retard, rather than to advance, scientific progress. You are, of course, all familiar with the Robbins statement of the definition of the economic problem, the one that has found its way into almost all of our textbooks. The economic problem involves the allocation of scarce means among alternative or competing ends. The problem is one of *allocation*, made necessary by the fact of *scarcity*, the necessity to *choose*. Only since *The Nature and Significance of Economic Science*[3] have economists so exclusively devoted their energies to the problems raised by scarcity, broadly considered, and to the necessity for the making of allocative decisions.

In Robbins' vision, our subject field is a problem or set of problems, not a characteristic form of human activity. We were better off, methodologically speaking, in the less-definitive Marshallian world when economists did, in fact, study man in his ordinary business of making a living. In his attempt to remain wholly neutral as to ends, Robbins left economics "open-ended," so to speak. Search him as you will, and you will not find an explicit statement as to *whose* ends are alternatives. His neutrality extends to the point of remaining wholly silent on the identity of the choosing agent, and few economists seem to have bothered with the difficult issue of identifying properly

---

1. For a review of this approach in terms of the doctrinal history, see Israel Kirzner, *The Economic Point of View* (New York: D. Van Nostrand, 1960), chap. 4. This book provides a good summary of the various approaches to the "economic point of view."

2. For a recent paper in which the exchange basis for economic analysis is plainly accepted, see Kenneth E. Boulding, "Towards a Pure Theory of Threat Systems," *American Economic Review*, May 1963, 421–34, especially 424–26.

3. Robbins (London: Macmillan, 1932).

the entity for whom the defined economic problem exists. It is thus by quite natural or normal extension that the economic problem moves from that one which is confronted by the individual person to that facing the larger family group, the business firm, the trade union, the trade association, the church, the local community, the regional or state government, the national government, and, finally, the world.[4]

To illustrate the confusion that this lack of identification introduces, let me mention my most respected of all professors, Frank Knight, who has taught us all to think in terms of the five functions of "an economic system," presumably, "any economic system." In the Knightian introduction to our subject we talk about the "social organization" that performs these five familiar "social" functions. For whom? This is the question to which I return. Presumably, the answer is for the whole of the relevant collective group, for society. To be somewhat more explicit, let me cite Milton Friedman who says, if I remember his classroom introduction correctly, "economics is the study of how a particular society solves its economic problem."

Knight and Friedman are good examples for my purposes, since both of these men, despite their own differences on many particulars of economic policy, are men with whom, broadly and generally, I agree on principles of political-philosophical order. In their introductions to economics, both of these men seem to identify "society" as the entity that confronts the economic problem about which we, as professional economists, should be concerned, the entity, presumably, whose ends are to count in the appropriate calculus of margins. If they should be explicitly questioned, I am sure that both Knight and Friedman, and Robbins as well, would say that "society," as such, must always be conceived in terms of its individual members. Hence, when reference is made to a particular society solving its economic problem, this is really only shorthand for saying "a particular group of individuals who have organized themselves socially solving their economic problem."

---

4. In his presidential address to the American Economic Association delivered in 1949, Howard S. Ellis criticized the arbitrariness with which ends may be selected under the Robbins definition. Ellis' whole approach has much in common with that taken in this paper. In my view, however, Ellis, through his overemphasis on the "choice" aspects of economics, failed to make his critique of Robbins as effective as it might have been. See Howard S. Ellis, "The Economic Way of Thinking," *American Economic Review,* March 1950, 1–12.

The important point is, however, that we do, in ordinary and everyday usage, require a supplementary or an additional step in our basic definitional process before we break down the societal language into its meaningful individual components. This amounts to locking the barn door without being sure that we have ever had or will have a horse inside. Somewhat more technically, this procedure assumes that there is meaningful content in economics for "social welfare"; it prejudges the central issue that has been debated in theoretical welfare economics, and comes down squarely with the utilitarians. This seems to be a clear case where the basic conceptual apparatus has not yet been brought into line with modern developments. But this conceptual apparatus is extremely important, especially when most practitioners are too busy to bother with methodology. The definition of our subject makes it all too easy to slip across the bridge between personal or individual units of decision and "social" aggregates. In principle, this bridge is most difficult to cross, as most economists fully recognize when put to it. And, in one sense, my whole plea here is summarized by saying to economists, "get back or stay on the side of the bridge where you belong."

The utilitarians tried to cross the bridge by summing utilities. Robbins quite properly told them to cease and desist. But in remaining what I have called "open-ended," in emphasizing the universality of the allocation problem without at the same time defining the identity of the choosing agent, Robbins' contribution to method has tended to promote a proliferation of the very confusion that he had hoped to prevent. Economists, paying heed to Robbins, now know when they cross the bridge; they explicitly state their own value judgments in the form of "social welfare functions." Once having done this, they feel free to maximize to their own hearts' content. And they do so within the bounds of methodological propriety, à la Robbins. They have, of course, abandoned his neutrality-of-ends position, but they have been straightforward about this. And, by the very fact of this neutrality, their explicitly stated personal version of "social" value is as acceptable as any other. They continue to work on an *economic* problem, as such, and this problem appears superficially to be the one that is generally referred to in the definitional introduction to our subject. These "social" economists are wholly concerned with the allocation of scarce resources among competing ends or uses.

I submit that theirs is not legitimate activity for practitioners in economics, as I want to define the discipline. In hastening to explain my heresy, I should emphasize that my argument is not centered on whether or not economists explicitly introduce value judgments into their work. This important issue is a wholly different one from that which I am trying to advance here. I want economists to quit concerning themselves with allocation problems, *per se*, with *the problem*, as it has been traditionally defined. The vocabulary of science is important here, and as T. D. Weldon once suggested, the very word "problem" in and of itself implies the presence of "solution." Once the format has been established in allocation terms, some solution is more or less automatically suggested. Our whole study becomes one of applied maximization of a relatively simple computational sort. Once the ends to be maximized are provided by the social welfare function, everything becomes computational, as my colleague, Rutledge Vining, has properly noted. If there is really nothing more to economics than this, we had as well turn it all over to the applied mathematicians. This does, in fact, seem to be the direction in which we are moving, professionally, and developments of note, or notoriety, during the past two decades consist largely in improvements in what are essentially computing techniques, in the mathematics of social engineering. What I am saying is that we should keep these contributions in perspective; I am urging that they be recognized for what they are, contributions to applied mathematics, to managerial science if you will, but not to our chosen subject field which we, for better or for worse, call "economics."

Let me illustrate with reference to the familiar distinction, or presumed distinction, between an economic and a technological problem. What is the sophomore, who has completed his "principles," expected to reply to the question: What is the difference between an economic and a technological problem? He might respond something like the following: "An economic problem arises when mutually conflicting ends are present, when choices must be made among them. A technological problem, by comparison, is characterized by the fact that there is only one end to be maximized. There is a single best or optimal solution." We conclude that the sophomore has read the standard textbooks. We then proceed to ask that he give us practical examples. He might then say: "The consumer finds that she has only $10 to spend in the supermarket; she confronts an economic problem in choosing among the many competing products that are available for meeting diverse ends and objectives. By contrast, the construction engineer has $1,000,000 allotted to build a dam to certain specifications. There is only one best way to do this; locating this way constitutes the technological problem." Most of us would, I suspect, be inclined to give this student good grades for such answers until another, erratic and eccentric, student on the back row says: "But there is really no difference."

I need not continue the illustration in detail. In the context of my earlier remarks, it seems clear that the second student has the proper answer, and that the orthodox textbook reply is wrong. Surely any difference between what we normally call the economic problem and what we call the technological problem is one of degree only, of the degree to which the function to be maximized is specified in advance of the choices to be made.

In one sense, the theory of choice presents a paradox. If the utility function of the choosing agent is fully defined in advance, choice becomes purely mechanical. No "decision," as such, is required; there is no weighing of alternatives. On the other hand, if the utility function is not wholly defined, choice becomes real, and decisions become unpredictable mental events. If I know what I want, a computer can make all of my choices for me. If I do not know what I want, no possible computer can derive my utility function since it does not really exist. But the distinction to be drawn here is surely that about the knowledge of the utility function. The difference is analogous to driving on a clear and on a foggy highway. It is not that between economics and technology. Neither the consumer in the supermarket nor the construction engineer faces an economic problem; both face essentially technological problems.

The theory of choice must be removed from its position of eminence in the economist's thought processes. The theory of choice, of resource allocation, call it what you will, assumes no special role for the economist, as opposed to any other scientist who examines human behavior. Lest you get overly concerned, however, let me hasten to say that most, if not all, of what now passes muster in the theory of choice will remain even in my ideal manual of instructions. I should emphasize that what I am suggesting is not so much a change in the basic content of what we study, but rather a change in the way we approach our material. I want economists to modify their thought processes, to look at the same phenomena through "another window," to use Nietzsche's appropriate metaphor. I want them to concentrate on "exchange" rather than on "choice."

The very word "economics," in and of itself, is partially responsible for some of the intellectual confusion. The "economizing" process leads us to think directly in terms of the theory of choice. I think it was Irving Babbit who said that revolutions begin in dictionaries. Should I have my say, I should propose that we cease, forthwith, to talk about "economics" or "political economy," although the latter is the much superior term. Were it possible to wipe the slate clean, I should recommend that we take up a wholly different term such as "catallactics," or "symbiotics." The second of these would, on balance, be preferred. Symbiotics is defined as the study of the association between dissimilar organisms, and the connotation of the term is that the association is mutually beneficial to all parties. This conveys, more or less precisely, the idea that should be central to our discipline. It draws attention to a unique sort of relationship, that which involves the cooperative association of individuals, one with another, even when individual interests are different. It concentrates on Adam Smith's "invisible hand," which so few non-economists properly understand. As suggested above, important elements of the theory of choice remain in symbiotics. On the other hand, certain choice situations that are confronted by human beings remain wholly outside the symbiotic frame of reference. Robinson Crusoe, on his island before Friday arrives, makes decisions; his is the economic problem in the sense traditionally defined. This choice situation is not, however, an appropriate starting point for our discipline, even at the broadest conceptual level, as Whately correctly noted more than a century ago.[5] Crusoe's problem is, as I have said, essentially a computational one, and all that he need do to solve it is to program the built-in computer that he has in his mind. The uniquely symbiotic aspects of behavior, of human choice, arise only when Friday steps on the island, and Crusoe is forced into *association* with another human being. The fact of association requires that a wholly different, and wholly new, sort of behavior take place, that of "exchange," "trade," or "agreement." Crusoe may, of course, fail to recognize this new fact. He may treat Friday simply as a means to his own ends, as a part of "nature," so to speak. If he does so, a "fight" ensues, and to the victor go the spoils. Symbiotics does not include

5. Richard Whately, *Introductory Lectures on Political Economy* (London: B. Fellowes, 1831), 7; the same point is made by Perry. See Arthur Latham Perry, *Elements of Political Economy* (New York: Charles Scribner & Company, 1868), 27.

the strategic choices that are present in such situations of pure conflict. On the other extreme, it does not include the choices that are involved in purely "integrative" systems, where the separate individual participants desire identical results.[6]

Crusoe, if he chooses to avoid pure conflict, and if he realizes that Friday's interests are likely to be different from his own, will recognize that mutual gains can be secured through cooperative endeavor, that is, through exchange or trade. This mutuality of advantage that may be secured by different organisms as a result of cooperative arrangements, be these simple or complex, is the one important truth in our discipline. There is no comparable principle, and the important place that has been traditionally assigned to the maximization norm that is called the "economic principle" reflects misguided emphasis.

Almost at the other extreme from the Crusoe models, the refinements in the theoretical model of perfectly competitive general equilibrium have been equally, if not more, productive of intellectual muddle. By imposing the condition that no participant in the economic process can independently influence the outcome of this process, all "social" content is squeezed out of individual behavior in market organization. The individual responds to a set of externally-determined, exogenous variables, and his choice problem again becomes purely mechanical. The basic flaw in this model of perfect competition is not its lack of correspondence with observed reality; no model of predictive value exhibits this. Its flaw lies in its conversion of individual choice behavior from a social-institutional context to a physical-computational one. Given the "rules of the market," the perfectly competitive model yields a unique "optimum" or "equilibrium," a single point on the Paretian welfare surface. But surely this is nonsensical social science, and the institutionalist critics have been broadly on target in some of their attacks. Frank Knight has consistently stressed that, in perfect competition, there is no competition. He is, of course, correct, but, and for the same reason, there is no "trade," as such.

A market is not competitive by assumption or by construction. A market *becomes* competitive, and competitive rules *come to be* established as institu-

---

6. Boulding distinguishes threat systems, exchange systems, and integrative systems of social order. Boulding, "Towards a Pure Theory of Threat Systems."

tions emerge to place limits on individual behavior patterns. It is this *becoming* process, brought about by the continuous pressure of human behavior in exchange, that is the central part of our discipline, if we have one, not the dry-rot of postulated perfection. A solution to a general-equilibrium set of equations is not predetermined by exogenously-determined rules. A general solution, if there is one, *emerges* as a result of a whole network of evolving exchanges, bargains, trades, side payments, agreements, contracts which, finally at some point, ceases to renew itself. At each stage in this evolution towards solution, there are *gains* to be made, there are exchanges possible, and this being true, the direction of movement is modified.

It is for these reasons that the model of perfect competition is of such limited explanatory value except when changes in variables exogenous to the system are introduced. There is no place in the structure of the model for internal change, change that is brought about by the men who continue to be haunted by the Smithean propensity. But surely the dynamic element in the economic system is precisely this continual evolution of the exchange process, as Schumpeter recognized in his treatment of entrepreneurial function.

How should the economist conceive the market organization? This is a central question, and the relevance of the difference in approach that I am emphasizing is directly shown by the two sharply conflicting answers. If the classical and currently renewed emphasis on the "wealth of nations" remains paramount, and if the logic of choice or allocation constitutes the "problem" element, the economist will look on market order as a *means* of accomplishing the basic economic functions that must be carried out in any society. The "market" becomes an engineered construction, a "mechanism," an "analogue calculating machine,"[7] a "computational device,"[8] one that processes information, accepts inputs, and transforms these into outputs which it then distributes. In this conception, the "market," as a mechanism, is appropriately compared with "government," as an alternative mechanism for accomplishing similar tasks. The second answer to the question is wholly different,

7. Paul A. Samuelson, "The Pure Theory of Public Expenditure," *Review of Economics and Statistics,* November 1954, 388.

8. Takashi Negishi, "The Stability of a Competitive Economy: A Survey Article," *Econometrica,* October 1962, 639.

although subtly so, and it is this second conception that I am trying to stress in this paper. The "market" or market organization is not a *means* toward the accomplishment of anything. It is, instead, the institutional embodiment of the voluntary exchange processes that are entered into by individuals in their several capacities. This is all that there is to it. Individuals are observed to cooperate with one another, to reach agreements, to trade. The network of relationships that emerges or evolves out of this trading process, the institutional framework, is called "the market." It is a setting, an arena, in which we, as economists, as theorists (as "onlookers"), observe men attempting to accomplish their own purposes, whatever these may be. And it is about these attempts that our basic theory is exclusively concerned if we would only recognize it as such. The boundaries are set by the limits of such cooperative endeavor; unilateral action is not part of the behavior pattern within our purview. In this conception, there is no explicit meaning of the term "efficiency" as applied to aggregative or composite results. It is contradictory to talk of the market as achieving "national goals," efficiently or inefficiently.

This does not imply that efficiency considerations are wholly eliminated in the conception that I am proposing. In fact, the opposite is true. The motivation for individuals to engage in trade, the source of the propensity, is surely that of "efficiency," defined in the personal sense of moving from less-preferred to more-preferred positions, and doing so under mutually acceptable terms. An "inefficient" institution, one that produces largely "inefficient" results, cannot, by the nature of man, survive until and unless coercion is introduced to prevent the emergence of alternative arrangements.

Let me illustrate this point and, at the same time, indicate the extension of the approach I am suggesting by referring to a familiar and simple example. Suppose that the local swamp requires draining to eliminate or reduce mosquito breeding. Let us postulate that no single citizen in the community has sufficient incentive to finance the full costs of this essentially indivisible operation. Defined in the orthodox, narrow way, the "market" fails; bilateral behavior of buyers and sellers does not remove the nuisance. "Inefficiency" presumably results. This is, however, surely an overly restricted conception of market behavior. If the market institutions, defined so narrowly, will not work, they will not meet individual objectives. Individual citizens will be led, because of the same propensity, to search voluntarily for more-inclusive trading or exchange arrangements. A more-complex institution may emerge to drain the swamp. The task of the economist includes the study of all such cooperative trading arrangements which become merely extensions of markets as more restrictively defined.

I have not got out of all the difficulties yet, however. You may ask: Will it really be to the interest of any single citizen to contribute to the voluntary program of mosquito control? How is the "free rider" problem to be handled? This spectre of the "free rider," found in many shapes and forms in the literature of modern public finance theory, must be carefully examined. In the first place, there has been some confusion between total and marginal effects here. If a pretty woman strolls through the hotel lobby many tired convention delegates may get some external benefits, but, presumably, she finds it to her own advantage to stroll, and few delegates would pay her to stroll more than she already does. Nevertheless, to return to the swamp, there may be cases where the expected benefits from draining are not sufficiently high to warrant the emergence of some voluntary cooperative arrangement. And, in addition, the known or predicted presence of free riders may inhibit the cooperation of individuals who would otherwise contribute. In such situations, voluntary cooperation may never produce an "efficient" outcome, for the individual members of the group. Hence, the "market," even in its most extended sense, may be said to "fail." What recourse is left to the individual in this case? It is surely that of transferring, again voluntarily, at least at some ultimate constitutional level, activities of the swamp-clearing sort to the community as a collective unit, with decisions delegated to specifically designated rules for making choices, and these decisions coercively enforced once they are made. Therefore, in the most general sense (perhaps too general for most of you to accept), the approach to economics that I am advancing extends to cover the emergence of a political constitution. At the conceptual level, this can be brought under the framework of a voluntaristic exchange process. The contract theory of the state, and most of the writing in that tradition, represents the sort of approach to human activity that I think modern economics should be taking.[9]

---

9. In our recent book, *The Calculus of Consent* (Ann Arbor: University of Michigan Press, 1962), Gordon Tullock and I develop the theory of the political constitution in the manner sketched out here.

I propose to extend the system of human relationships brought within the economist's scope widely enough to include collective as well as private organization. This being so, you may ask, How are "politics" and "economics" to be distinguished? This is a proper question, and it helps me to illustrate the central point of the paper in yet another way. The distinction to be drawn between economics and politics, as disciplines, lies in the nature of the social relationships among individuals that is examined in each. Insofar as individuals exchange, trade, as freely-contracting units, the predominant characteristic of their behavior is "economic." And this, of course, extends our range far beyond the ordinary price-money nexus. Insofar as individuals meet one another in a relationship of superior-inferior, leader to follower, principal to agent, the predominant characteristic in their behavior is "political,"[10] stemming, of course, from our everyday usage of the word "politician." Economics is the study of the whole system of exchange relationships. Politics is the study of the whole system of coercive or potentially coercive relationships. In almost any particular social institution, there are elements of both types of behavior, and it is appropriate that both the economist and the political scientist study such institutions. What I should stress is the potentiality of exchange in those socio-political institutions that we normally consider to embody primarily coercive or quasi-coercive elements. To the extent that man has available to him alternatives of action, he meets his associates as, in some sense, an "equal," in other words, in a trading relationship. Only in those situations where pure rent is the sole element in return is the economic relationship wholly replaced by the political.

As I have noted, almost all of the institutions and relationships that economists currently study will remain subject to examination in the disciplinary frame that I propose to draw around "economics." The same basic data are central to the allocation approach and the exchange approach. But the interpretation of these data, and even the very questions that we ask of them, will depend critically on the reference system within which we operate. What will the shift in reference system produce? The most important single result will be the making of a sharp and categorical distinction between the discipline to which our theory of markets applies and that which we may call "so-

---

10. This distinction has been developed at some length by Gordon Tullock. See his *Politics in Bureaucracy: A General Theory of Administrative Hierarchies* (to be published).

cial engineering," for want of any better term. Note that I am not here saying that social engineering is not legitimate endeavor. I am suggesting only that the implications concerning the uses of individuals as means to non-individual ends be explicitly recognized. My criticism of the orthodox approach to economics is based, at least in part, on its failure to allow such implications to be appropriately made. If the economic problem is viewed as the general means-ends problem, the social engineer is a working economist in the full sense of the term. Thus it is that we now observe him developing more and more complicated schemata designed to maximize more and more complex functions, under more and more specifically-defined constraints. We applaud all of this as "scientific" advance, and consider the aids that we may provide to the practicing social engineer in these respects as our "social" purpose. There is, I submit, something wholly confused about all of this. I, too, applaud and admire the ingenuity of the applied mathematicians who have helped, and are helping, choosers to solve more-complex computational problems. But I shall continue to insist that our "purpose," if you will, is no more that of providing the social engineer with these tools than it is of providing the monopolist with tools to make more profits, or Wicksteed's housewife with instructions how better to divide out the mashed potatoes among her children. The proper role of the economist is not providing the means of making "better" choices, and to imply this, as the resource allocation–choice approach does, tends to confuse most of us at the very outset of our training.

I want to note especially here that I am not, through rejecting the allocation approach, decrying the desirability, indeed the necessity, for mathematical competence. In fact, advances in our understanding of symbiotic relationships may well require considerably more-sophisticated mathematical tools than those required in what I have called social engineering. For example, we need to learn much more about the theory of n-person cooperative games. It seems but natural that the mathematics finally required to systematize a set of relationships involving voluntary behavior on the part of many persons will be more complicated than that required to solve even the most complex computational problem where the ends are ordered in a single function.

Although this will, of course, be challenged, the position that I advance is neutral with respect to ideological or normative content. I am simply proposing, in various ways, that economists concentrate attention on the institutions, the relationships, among individuals as they participate in voluntarily organized activity, in trade or exchange, broadly considered. People may, as in my swamp-clearing example, decide to do things collectively. Or they may not. The analysis, as such, is neutral in respect to the proper private sector–public sector mix. I am stating that economists should be "market economists," but only because I think they should concentrate on market or exchange institutions, again recalling that these are to be conceived in the widest possible sense. This need not bias or prejudice them for or against any particular form of social order. Learning more about how markets work means learning more about how markets work. They may work better or worse, in terms of whatever criteria that might be imposed, than uninformed opinion leads one to expect.

To an extent, of course, we must all follow along the road that is functionally determined by the behavior of our disciplinary colleagues. The growth and development of a discipline is somewhat like language, and despite the fact that we may think that the current direction of change is misleading and productive of intellectual confusions, we must try to continue communicating one with another. It would be naive in the extreme for me to think that I could, through individual persuasion such as this, or in concert with a few others who might agree broadly with me on such matters, change the drift of a whole social science. Economics, as a well-defined subject of scholarship, seems to be disintegrating, and for the reasons I have outlined, and realistic appraisal suggests that this inexorable process will not be stopped. Nevertheless, it is useful, or so it seems to me, to stop occasionally and look at the road map.

I may conclude by recalling a little adage that Frank Ward, of the University of Tennessee, had clipped on his office door when I first met him in 1940, when I was a very green beginning graduate student. The adage said: "The study of economics won't keep you out of the breadline; but at least you'll know why you're there." I can paraphrase this to apply to methodology: "Concentration on methodology won't solve any of the problems for you, but at least you should know what the problems are."

PART TWO

Politics without Romance

Politics without Romance
A Sketch of Positive Public Choice Theory
and Its Normative Implications

Abstract: "Public choice theory," or "the economic theory of politics," has emerged only in the decades after World War II. In summary, this theory models the *realities* rather than the romance of
political institutions. It commences with the utility-maximizing
behavior of individuals who participate in their various public-
choosing capacities, as voters, as legislators, as bureaucrats. It analyzes the effects of varying institutional constraints on generating alternative political outcomes.

Normatively, public choice forces the analyst to compare relevant institutional alternatives. In one sense, public choice is a
"theory of governmental failure" comparable to the "theory of
market failure" that emerged from theoretical welfare economics.

1. Introduction

In this lecture, I propose to summarize the emergence and the content of the
"theory of public choice," or, alternatively, the economic theory of politics,
or "the new political economy."[1] This area of research has become important
only in the decades after World War II. Indeed in Europe and Japan, the the-

From Inaugural Lecture, Institute for Advanced Studies, Vienna, Austria, *IHS-Journal,
Zeitschrift des Instituts für Höhere Studien, Wien* 3 (1979): B1–B11. Reprinted by permission
of the publisher.

1. For an earlier, and differently organized, discussion, see James M. Buchanan, "From
Private Preferences to Public Philosophy: The Development of Public Choice," in *The
Economics of Politics* (London, 1978), 1–18; for a more technical survey, see D. Mueller,
"Public Choice: A Survey," *Journal of Economic Literature* 14, no. 2 (1976): 395–433.

ory has come to command the attention of scholars only within the 1970's; developments in America stem from the 1950's and 1960's. As I hope that my remarks here will suggest, the theory of public choice is not without antecedents, and especially in the European thought of the 18th and 19th centuries. Ecclesiastes tells us that there is nothing new under the sun, and in a genuine sense, such a claim is surely correct, and especially in the so-called "social sciences." (I am reminded of this every week when I see my mathematically-inclined younger colleagues in economics rediscovering almost every wheel that older economists have ever talked about.) In terms of its impact on the realm of prevailing ideas, however, "public choice" is *new*, and this subdiscipline that falls halfway between economics and political science has turned around the thinking of many persons. If I am allowed to use Thomas Kuhn's overly-used word here, we can, I think, say that a new *paradigm* has been substituted for an old one. Or, to go somewhat further back, and to use Nietzsche's metaphor, we now look at some aspects of our world, and specifically our world of politics, through a different window.

My primary title for this lecture, "Politics without Romance," was chosen for its descriptive accuracy. Public choice theory has been the avenue through which a romantic and illusory set of notions about the workings of governments and the behavior of persons who govern has been replaced by a set of notions that embody more skepticism about what governments can do and what governors will do, notions that are surely more consistent with the political reality that we may all observe about us. I have often said that public choice offers a "theory of governmental failure" that is fully comparable to the "theory of market failure" that emerged from the theoretical welfare economics of the 1930's and 1940's. In that earlier effort, the system of private markets was shown to "fail" in certain respects when tested against the idealized criteria for efficiency in resource allocation and distribution. In the later effort, in public choice, government or political organization is shown to "fail" in certain respects when tested for the satisfaction of idealized criteria for efficiency and equity. What has happened is that today we find few informed scholars who would try to test markets against idealized models. The private sector–public sector decision that each community must make is now more likely to be discussed in more-meaningful terms, with organizational arrangements analyzed by comparisons between realistically modelled alternatives.

It seems to be nothing more than simple and obvious wisdom to compare social institutions as they might be expected actually to operate rather than to compare romantic models of how such institutions might be hoped to operate. But such simple and obvious wisdom was lost to the informed consciousness of Western man for more than a century. Nor is such wisdom today by any means universally accepted. The socialist mystique to the effect that the state, that politics, somehow works its way toward some transcendent "public good" is with us yet, in many guises, as we must surely acknowledge. And, even among those who reject such mystique, there are many who unceasingly search for the ideal that will resolve the dilemma of politics.

Especially at this early point in my lecture, however, I do not want to appear to place too much emphasis on the normative implications of public choice theory. These implications can stand on their own, and they can be allowed to emerge as they will or will not from the positive analysis. The *theory* of public choice, as such, is or can be a wholly positive theory, wholly scientific and *wertfrei* in the standard meanings of these terms. The implications for the comparative evaluation of institutions, noted above, have to do with methods of making such comparisons, not with specific results. I do not want to commit the naturalistic fallacy, and I make no claim that public choice theory, any more than economic theory, can tell a community of persons what they "should" choose to do.

2. Definition

Let me now be somewhat more concrete and try to define "public choice theory" more directly. Such a definition can perhaps best be clarified by reference to economic theory, if only because the latter is more familiar. What is economic theory? It is a body of analysis that offers an understanding, an explanation, of the complex exchange process that we call "an economy." It is a body of analysis that allows us to relate the behavior of individual participants in market activity, as buyers, sellers, investors, producers, entrepreneurs, to the results that are attained for the whole community, results that are not within the purposes or the knowledge of the separate participants themselves. (I should note here that Austria has a very proud and important heritage in the development of economic theory as I have here defined it, and I may say in passing that one of the most exciting and most encouraging developments within economics in the United States today is the observed resurgence of interest in "Austrian economics," and notably as among young research scholars.)

Public choice theory essentially takes the tools and methods of approach that have been developed to quite sophisticated analytical levels in economic theory and applies these tools and methods to the political or governmental sector, to politics, to the public economy. As with economic theory, the analysis attempts to relate the behavior of individual actors in the governmental sector, that is, the behavior of persons in their various capacities as voters, as candidates for office, as elected representatives, as leaders or members of political parties, as bureaucrats (all of these are "public choice" roles) to the composite of outcomes that we observe or might observe. Public choice theory attempts to offer an understanding, an explanation, of the complex institutional interactions that go on within the political sector. I emphasize the word "complex" here, since the appropriate contrast to be made is with the approach that models government as some sort of monolith, with a being of its own, somehow separate and apart from the individuals who actually participate in the process.

3. Methodological Individualism

As my definition suggests, public choice theory is methodologically individualistic, in the same sense that economic theory is. The basic units are choosing, acting, behaving persons rather than organic units such as parties, provinces, or nations. Indeed, yet another label for the subject matter here is "An Individualistic Theory of Politics."

There is no formal connection between the methodological individualism that describes formal public choice theory and the motivations that are attributed to persons as they behave in their various public-choice capacities or roles listed above. It would be possible to construct a fully consistent and methodologically individualistic theory of politics on the romantic assumption that all persons in their political roles seek only to further their own conceptions of some "common good," and with utter and total disregard for their own more narrowly defined self-interest. Such a theory would not escape problems of reconciling differing persons' differing conceptions of just what defines "common good." But testable propositions might emerge from such a theory, and empirical work might be commenced to test these propositions.

But most of the scholars who have been instrumental in developing public choice theory have themselves been trained initially as economists. There has been, therefore, a tendency for these scholars to bring with them models of man that have been found useful within economic theory, models that have been used to develop empirically testable and empirically corroborated hypotheses. These models embody the presumption that persons seek to maximize their own utilities, and that their own narrowly-defined economic well-being is an important component of these utilities. At this point, however, I do not want to enter into either a defense of or an attack on the usefulness of *Homo economicus*, either in economics or in any theory of politics. I would say only, as I have many times before, that the burden of proof should rest with those who suggest that wholly different models of man apply in the political and the economic realms of behavior. Logical consistency suggests that, at least initially, we examine the implications of using the *same* models in different settings.

As I have already noted, we commence with individuals as utility maximizers. And, for present purposes, we do not need to specify just what arguments are contained in a person's utility function. We can, at this stage, allow for saints as well as sinners. In one sense, we can simply define a person in terms of his set of preferences, his utility function. This function defines or describes a set of possible trade-offs among alternatives for potential choice, whether the latter be those between apples and oranges at the fruit stand or between peace and war for the nation.

Once we begin analysis in terms of preference or utility functions, we are led almost immediately to inquire about possible differences among persons. Since there seems to be no self-evident reason why separate persons should exhibit the same preferences, it seems best to commence with the presumption that preferences may differ. Within economic theory, such differences present no problem. Indeed, quite the opposite. If one person places a relatively higher value on apples as compared with oranges than another person, an exchange opportunity is presented. Both persons can gain utility by trade. Indeed this trading to mutual advantage is what economic theory is all about, no matter how esoteric its modern practitioners may make it seem to be in its detail.

4. Political Exchange

By any comparison with politics, economic theory is *simple*. The process of "political exchange" is necessarily more complex than that of economic exchange through orderly markets, and for two quite separate reasons. In the first place, basic "political exchange," the conceptual contract under which the constitutional order is itself established, must precede any meaningful economic interaction. Orderly trade in private goods and services can take place only within a defined legal structure that establishes individuals' rights of ownership and control of resources, that enforces private contracts, and that places limits on the exercise of governmental powers. In the second place, even within a well-defined and functioning legal order, "political exchange" necessarily involves *all* members of the relevant community rather than the two trading partners that characterize economic exchange.[2]

The two levels of "political exchange" provide a somewhat natural classification for two related but separate areas of inquiry, both of which fall within the corpus of public choice. The first area of inquiry may be called an "economic theory of constitutions."[3] This theory has historical antecedents in the theory of social contract, and it also has modern philosophical generalization in the work of Rawls.[4] The second area of inquiry involves the "theory of political institutions" as these might be predicted to work within a constitutional-legal structure. The subject matter incorporates theories of voting and voting rules, theories of electoral and party competition, and theories of bureaucracy.[5]

---

2. For a development of the distinction between political exchange at the constitutional and the postconstitutional levels, see James M. Buchanan, *The Limits of Liberty* (Chicago, 1975).

3. The development of such a theory was the primary purpose of the book that I wrote jointly with Tullock. See James M. Buchanan and Gordon Tullock, *The Calculus of Consent* (Ann Arbor, 1962).

4. John Rawls, *A Theory of Justice* (Cambridge, 1971).

5. In modern public choice theory, the theory of voting rules commences with Duncan Black, *Theory of Committees and Elections* (Cambridge, 1958). The theory of electoral, or party, competition stems largely from the work of Anthony Downs, *An Economic Theory of Democracy* (New York, 1957). The theory of bureaucracy in its modern sense was first developed in Gordon Tullock, *The Politics of Bureaucracy* (Washington, 1965).

5. The Economic Theory of Constitutions

As I have stated, this aspect of modern public choice theory is closely related to an important strand of ideas in traditional political theory or political philosophy, namely, the theory of the social contract or compact. The whole discussion here is directly relevant to the classic set of issues involving the *legitimacy* of political order. What gives legitimacy to governments, or to governors? What rights can some men possess to rule over other men?

At some basic philosophical level, the individualist must reject the notion that any such "rights of governance" exist. In this sense, I have often called myself a philosophical anarchist. Nonetheless, we are obligated to look squarely at the alternative social order that anarchy would represent, and without the romantic blinders that putative anarchists have always worn, then and now. And we look to Thomas Hobbes, whose 17th-century vision becomes very appealing to those of us who live in the late 20th century. Hobbes described the life of persons in a society without government, without laws, as "solitary, poor, nasty, brutish, and short." In this Hobbesian perspective, any person in such a jungle would value security to life and property so highly that any contract with a sovereign government would seem highly beneficial. The person would agree to abide by the laws laid down by the sovereign, even if he recognizes that there were essentially no limits that could be placed on the sovereign's use of these laws for its own exploitative purposes.

Montesquieu, John Locke, and the American Founding Fathers were more optimistic than Hobbes in their conception of constitutional contract as potentially binding on the activities of government. And I think that a reading of history will, to an extent at least, bear out their conception. Governments have been limited by constitutions, and part of the Western heritage to this day reflects the 18th-century wisdom that imposed some limits on governmental powers. But the 19th- and 20th-century fallacy in political thought was embodied in the presumption that electoral requirements were in themselves sufficient to hold government's Leviathan-like proclivities in check, the presumption that, so long as there were constitutional guarantees for free and periodic elections, the range and extent of governmental action would be controlled. Only in the middle of this century have we come to recognize that such electoral constraints do not keep governments within the implied "contract" through which they might have been established, the "contract" which alone can give governments any claim to legitimacy in the eyes of citizens.

The theory of constitutions that makes up a central part of public choice represents, in part, a return to the 18th-, as opposed to the 19th- or 20th-, century perspective. The theory raises questions about how governments may be constrained, and about how governments should be constrained. What should governments be allowed to do? What is the appropriate sphere of political action? How large a share of national product should be available for political disposition? What sort of political decision-structures should be adopted at the constitutional stage? Under what conditions and to what extent should individuals be franchised?

These questions, and many others like them, clearly depend for answers on some positive, predictive analysis of how different political institutions will operate if, in fact, they are constitutionally authorized. An informed, and meaningful, theory of constitutions cannot be constructed until and unless there exists some theory of the operation of alternative political rules.

6. Postconstitutional Politics

In a postconstitutional setting, with a defined legal order, there will remain opportunities for mutually advantageous "political exchanges." That is to say, after the conceptualized constitutional "contract" has established what has been variously called the "protective," "minimal" or "night-watchman" state, there are still likely to be efficiency-enhancing complex trades among all persons in the community. The "productive state" may emerge to provide "public goods," goods that are nonexcludable as among separate beneficiaries and that may be more cheaply produced jointly than separately.

How should the complex political exchanges be organized so as to insure that all beneficiaries secure net gains in the process? Voluntaristic trade akin to the pairwise matching of buyers and sellers that characterizes private-goods market exchange may not be possible. A role for governmental action is suggested, but how are government decisions to be made and by whom? By what rules? And how might various rules be predicted to work?

The theory here, as it has developed, has involved two distinct types of question. First, it has attempted to look at how differing individual preferences over joint outcomes are reconciled, or might be reconciled. That is, how do groups of persons reach collective decisions under differing procedural rules? This type of theory has not been concerned with government, as such. In effect, it is a theory of *demand* for government goods and services without an accompanying theory of *supply.* The second, and more recent, development has addressed the quite different set of questions relating to the behavior of persons who are themselves charged with powers of governance, with supplying the goods and services that might be demanded by the citizenry. It will be useful to summarize the strands of postconstitutional political analysis separately.

THEORY OF VOTING RULES

We may commence with the work of Black who asked the simple question: How do committees reach decisions under simple majority voting rules? Building on only bits and pieces of precursory work by Condorcet, Lewis Carroll, and a few others, Black was led to analyze the properties of majority voting, and he discovered the problem of the majority cycle, the problem that has occupied perhaps an undue amount of attention in public choice theory. There may exist situations where no single one of the possible alternatives for choice can command majority support over all other alternatives, despite the consistency of the preference sets of all members of the choosing group. In such a cyclical majority setting, there is no stable group decision attainable by majority rule; the group cannot make up its collective mind; it cannot decide.

Simultaneously with Black, and for a different purpose, Arrow was examining the desirable properties of a "social welfare function," and he was attempting to determine whether such a function could ever be constructed from a set of individual orderings.[6] He reached the conclusion that no such function satisfying minimally acceptable properties could be found, and for basically the same reasons that Black developed more closely in connection with majority voting rules [Arrow]. Arrow's work is not narrowly within what we might call the "public choice tradition," since he was, and is, con-

---

6. Kenneth Arrow, *Social Choice and Individual Values* (New York, 1951).

cerned not with how institutions work but the logical structure of collective or social choice. Nonetheless, it was Arrow's work that exerted a major influence on the thinking of social scientists; his work was taken to have demonstrated that government cannot work, if work here is defined in terms of the standard economist's criteria for consistency in choice. Collectivities in which individual preferences differ cannot, à la Black, make up their collective or group mind. And, à la Arrow, such groups cannot be assigned an ordering that will array all possible outcomes that is itself both consistent and reflective of individual orderings. Since the 1950's, since Arrow and Black, social choice theorists have explored in exhaustive logical and mathematical detail possible ways and means of escaping from the implications of the Arrow impossibility theorem, but they have had little or no success. "Social choice theory" has itself become a major growth industry, with an equilibrium not yet in sight.

Let me return to the work of Black, who, when confronted with the prospect of majority rule cycles, discovered that under certain configurations of preferences, such cycles would not arise. If the alternatives for collective choice can be arrayed in such a fashion that individual orderings over these alternatives are single-peaked, for all voters in the group, there will be a unique majority outcome, one that will defeat any other outcome in a series of pairwise majority votes. This outcome or option will be that one which best satisfies or which is most preferred by the voter who is *median* among all voters, with respect to preferences over the options. The conditions required for single-peakedness are plausibly applicable in situations where the alternatives for collective choice are reducible to quantitative variations along a single dimension, for example, proposed amounts of public spending on a given public service. Consider a school board or committee of three members, one of whom prefers high spending on education, one of whom prefers medium spending, and the third of whom prefers low spending. So long as the high spender prefers medium to low spending, and so long as the low spender prefers medium to high spending, majority voting as within the three-member committee will produce a stable medium-spending outcome.

This tendency of majority voting rules to produce determinate outcomes that correspond to the preferences of the median voter under certain conditions has led to many studies, both analytical and empirical, notably in public-finance applications of public choice, and particularly with reference to the budgetary decisions made in local governments. Median-voter models break down, however, even with simple budgetary allocation problems, when more than one dimension is introduced. If voters, or members of committee, consider simultaneously several issues or dimensions, such as, say, spending on education and spending on police, the cyclical majority problem returns. And, related to this return, the multiplicity of dimensions allows for vote trading and "log-rolling," the analysis of which has been important in public choice theory from its inception.

As I have already noted, the theory of voting and voting rules sketched here in summary is not a theory of government or of politics at all. It is, instead, a theory or set of theories about how groups of persons reach some decision or choice on what might be *demanded*, by the group, from some supplying agent or agency. Implicitly, the analysis proceeds on the presumption that the goods or services demanded are supplied passively and that the motivations of suppliers may be neglected. It is as if all collective decisions are somehow analogous to the decision made by a group meeting in a closed room about the setting for the thermostat, the presumption being that, once a joint decision is made, the heating or cooling system will respond automatically and passively to the demands placed on it.

REPRESENTATION AND ELECTORAL COMPETITION

Once we so much as move beyond the simple committee or town-meeting setting, however, something other than the passive response of suppliers must be reckoned with in any theory of politics that can pretend to model reality. Even if we take only the single step from town-meeting democracy to representative democracy, we must introduce the possible divergence between the interests of the representative or agent who is elected or appointed to act for the group and the interests of the group members themselves.

It is at this point that electoral competition, as an institution, plays a role that has some similarities with that played by market competition in the economy. In the latter, the principle of consumer sovereignty prevails if sellers are sufficiently competitive. At the idealized limit, no single seller can exercise any power over buyers. But to what extent does a system of electoral competition generate comparable results? To what extent is voter sovereignty analogous to consumer sovereignty? There are major differences that should be recognized, despite the underlying similarities. Persons or parties who seek to represent the interests of voters compete for approval or favor much in the manner as the sellers of products in imperfectly competitive markets for private goods and services. But politics differs categorically from markets in that, in political competition, there are mutually exclusive sets of losers and winners. Only one candidate or party wins; all others lose. Only one party is the governing party. One way of stating the basic difference here is to say that, in economic exchange, decisions are made at the margin, in terms of more or less, whereas in politics, decisions are made among mutually exclusive alternatives, in terms of all-or-none prospects. The voter may be disappointed when his candidate or party or policy proposal loses in a sense that is not experienced in market exchange.

At best electoral competition places limits on the exercise of discretionary power on the part of those who are successful in securing office. Re-election prospects tend to keep the self-interests of politicians within reasonable range of those of the median voter, but there is nothing to channel outcomes toward the needs of the non-median voting groups.

Theory of bureaucracy

Even if we ignore the possible divergencies between the interests of legislative representatives, as elected agents of the voters, and those interests of the voters themselves, we remain without an effective model of government because we have not accounted for the behavior of those persons who actually *supply* the goods and services that are provided via governmental auspices. Voters elect members of legislatures or parliaments. Members of legislatures, through coalitions or through parties, make selections as among various policy alternatives or options. But the implementation of policy, the actual process of government, remains with persons who hold positions in the bureaucracy. How do these persons behave? How are the conflicts between their own interests and those of the voters reconciled?

Recent developments in public choice theory have demonstrated the limits of legislative control over the discretionary powers of the bureaucracy. Modern government is complex and many-sided, so much so that it would be impossible for legislatures to make more than a tiny fraction of all genuine policy decisions. Discretionary power must be granted to bureaucrats over wide ranges of decision. Further, the bureaucracy can manipulate the agenda for legislative action for the purpose of securing outcomes favorable to its own interests. The bureaucracy can play off one set of constituents against others, insuring that budgets rise much beyond plausible efficiency limits.

Increasingly, public choice scholars have started to model governments in monopoly rather than competitive terms. Electoral competition has come more and more to be viewed as competition among prospective monopolists, all of whom are bidding for an exclusive franchise, with profit-maximizing assumed to characterize the behavior of the successful bidder. Governments are viewed as exploiters of the citizenry, rather than the means through which the citizenry secures for itself goods and services that can best be provided jointly or collectively. Both the modern analysis and the observed empirical record suggests that governments have, indeed, got out of hand.

7. Can Leviathan Be Limited?

The rapidly accumulating developments in the theory of public choice, ranging from sophisticated analyses of schemes for amalgamating individual preferences into consistent collective outcomes, through the many models that demonstrate with convincing logic how political rules and institutions fail to work as their idealizations might promise, and finally to the array of empirical studies that corroborate the basic economic model of politics— these have all been influential in modifying the way that modern man views government and political process. The romance is gone, perhaps never to be regained. The socialist paradise is lost. Politicians and bureaucrats are seen as ordinary persons much like the rest of us, and "politics" is viewed as a set of arrangements, a game if you will, in which many players with quite disparate objectives interact so as to generate a set of outcomes that may not be either internally consistent or efficient by any standards.

I do not want to claim, or to be taken to claim, too much for the contribution of public choice theory in turning attitudes around here, in being responsible for the paradigm shift. For social scientists, for scholars and intellectuals, the availability of an alternative model of political process probably has been of some considerable importance. But for members of the general public, the simple observation of failure on the part of governments to deliver on their promises, these failures have been much more important in modifying attitudes than any set of ideas or any ideology.

I noted earlier that the fallacy of the 19th- and 20th-century political thought lay in an implicit faith that electoral constraints would alone be sufficient to hold the Leviathan-like proclivities of government in check. The experience in Western nations since World War II has exposed this fallacy for what it is. And we are now seeking to reimpose constitutional limits on government over and beyond those exercised through democratic electoral constraints. At least we are trying to do so in the United States. Beyond minimal efforts, I am not sure that there is a comparable movement at work in Europe. It seems to me highly doubtful that this objective can be successfully accomplished. Having come to command shares in national income or product that were undreamt of, even in the most roseate of the early democratic socialist predictions, modern governmental bureaucracies will not relinquish their relative positions in society without struggle.

Nonetheless, the effort is being made and will be made. In America, 1978 was the year of Proposition 13, when the voters of California turned back, by a two-to-one margin, the growth of government spending and taxing. This event sent political shock waves throughout the Western world. The United States is now (1979) inundated with various proposals, at all levels of government, designed to limit the expansion of governmental powers. "Bridling the passions of the sovereign"—this 18th-century slogan has resurfaced to command political respectability.

I have indicated that developments in public choice theory may have been in some small way influential in generating this shift in attitudes toward bureaucracies, politicians, and government. But the question remains as to what contribution public choice theory might make in the face of the developing distrust of traditional political institutions. It is here that the economic theory of constitutions, discussed earlier as a part of public choice analysis, becomes relatively the most important area of emphasis. Western societies face a task of *reconstruction*; basic political institutions must be re-examined and rebuilt so as to keep governments as well as citizens within limits of tolerance. But we are approaching a period when critical diagnosis is not enough. Criticism alone can generate chaos, whether this be in the form of gradual breakdown or in the form of violent disruption. The reconstructive reform in our institutions can be accomplished without revolution of either the left or right, but this path toward the future requires that the public come to understand the limits of change as well as the value. Zealotry in the cause of anti-politics, anti-government, anti-institutions movements can result in a drift toward anarchistic terror, the jungle against which Hobbes warned us all. We must indeed keep the "miracle" of social order clearly in our mind as we seek ways and means of reforming arrangements that seem to have got out of hand. I think that public choice theory offers an analytical setting that allows us to discuss genuine reconstruction in our constitutions that may be made without major social costs.

Politics, Policy,
and the Pigovian Margins

Since Sidgwick and Marshall, and notably since Pigou's *The Economics of Welfare*, economists have accepted the presence or absence of external effects in production and consumption as a primary criterion of market efficiency. When private decisions exert effects that are external to the decision-maker, "ideal" output is not obtained through the competitive organisation of economic activity even if the remaining conditions necessary for efficiency are satisfied. The market "fails" to the extent that there exist divergencies between marginal private products and marginal social products and/or between marginal private costs and marginal social costs. This basic Pigovian theorem has been theoretically refined and elaborated in numerous works, but its conceptual validity has rarely been challenged.[1] The purpose of this paper is to bring into question a fundamental implication of this aspect of theoretical welfare economics, namely, the implication that externalities are either reduced or eliminated by the shift of an activity from market to political organisation. I shall try to show that this implication will stand up to critical scrutiny only under certain highly restricted assumptions about hu-

From *Economica* 29 (February 1962): 17–28. Reprinted by permission of the publisher.

Although independently developed, this note draws upon and extends certain ideas that have been developed in a larger work undertaken in collaboration with Gordon Tullock. See *The Calculus of Consent* (forthcoming). I should acknowledge Tullock's indirect as well as his direct influence on the general ideas presented in this paper.

1. The current work of my colleague, Ronald Coase, should be mentioned as a notable exception. Coase's criticism of the Pigovian analysis concerns the implications of externality for resource allocation. For a preliminary statement of Coase's position, see his "The Federal Communications Commission," *Journal of Law and Economics* 2 (1959), especially 26–27. A more complete statement appears in "The Problem of Social Cost," *Journal of Law and Economics* 3 (1960).

man behaviour in modern political systems. When these restrictive assumptions are modified, the concept of divergence between marginal "social" product (cost) and marginal private product (cost) loses most of its usefulness.[2]

"Imperfection" and "failure" are descriptive nouns that tell something about the operation of the organism, the activity, or the organisation that is under discussion. These words, and others like them, are meaningful only if the alternative states of "perfection" and "success" are either specifically described or are assumed to be tacitly recognised by participants in the discussion. In the analysis of market organisation, the "perfectly-working" order has been quite carefully defined. The necessary conditions for Paretian optimality are now a part of the professional economist's stock-in-trade, and these conditions are known to be satisfied only when all of the relevant costs and benefits resulting from an action are incorporated into the calculus of the decision-maker that selects the action. By contrast with this state of perfection, almost all ordinary or real-world markets are "imperfect," in greater or lesser degree. Most private decisions exert external effects. So far, so good. If this were the end of it, however, there would be little point in all of the effort. Economists must imply or suggest that the imperfectly-working organisation is, in fact, "perfectible": that is, they must do so if they are to justify their own professional existence. The analysis of an existing social order must, almost by the nature of science itself, imply that some "improvement" in results can be produced by changes that can be imposed on the variables subject to social control.

Such improvements in the organisation of economic activity have, almost

2. It should be noted that I shall not be concerned with the conceptual ability of welfare economists to make specific policy prescriptions, a problem that has been central to much of the modern discussion. It is now widely acknowledged that welfare economics, as such, can provide few guides to positive policy-making in a specific sense. But the analysis continues to be employed for the purposes of demonstrating the existence of market failure. If, as J. de V. Graaff suggests, "*laissez-faire* welfare theory" was "largely concerned with demonstrating the optimal properties of free competition and the unfettered price system," it is surely equally accurate to suggest that modern welfare theory has been largely concerned with demonstrating that these conclusions are invalid: that is, that competitive markets do not satisfy the necessary conditions for optimality. Graaff's own work is, perhaps, the most elegant example. See his *Theoretical Welfare Economics*, 1957, 170.

without exception, involved the placing of restrictions on the private behaviour of individuals through the implementation of some *political* action. The various proposals that have been advanced by economists are sufficiently familiar to make a listing at this point unnecessary. They run the gamut from the relatively straightforward tax-subsidy schemes of Marshall to the more sophisticated and highly intricate proposals for multi-part pricing, counter-speculation, collective simulation of ideal market processes, and many other intriguing methods designed to promote and to insure the attainment of economic efficiency. Indeed, economists tend to be so enmeshed with efficiency notions that it seems extremely difficult for them to resist the ever-present temptation to propose yet more complex gimmicks and gadgets for producing greater "efficiency." In almost every case, and often quite unconsciously, the suggested improvement is assumed to be within the realm of the genuinely attainable. And, if some sceptic dare raise a question on this point, the economist is likely to respond to the effect that his task is not that of the politician, that he does not appropriately concern himself with the political feasibility or workability of his proposals. But if political obstacles to realisation are not, in fact, discussed, the implication is clear that the proposals which are advanced are attainable as a result of some conceivable politically-imposed modifications in the institutional framework within which decisions are made. It seems fully appropriate to charge welfare economists, generally, with an implicit acceptance of this implication of their analyses. If this were not the case, it is difficult to see why, for example, William J. Baumol should have attempted to construct a theory of the state, of collective action, on the basis of the externality argument,[3] why K. W. Kapp should have entitled his work, *The Social Costs of Private Enterprise*,[4] and why Francis Bator should have called his recent summary analysis, "The Anatomy of Market Failure."[5]

I shall not be concerned here with the analysis of market imperfection or failure, as such. The primary criticism of theoretical welfare economics (and economists) that is advanced in this note is that its failure to include analyses

3. William J. Baumol, *Welfare Economics and the Theory of the State*, 1952.

4. K.W. Kapp, *The Social Costs of Private Enterprise*, 1950.

5. Francis Bator, "The Anatomy of Market Failure," *Quarterly Journal of Economics* 72 (1958): 351–79.

of similar imperfections in realistic and attainable alternative solutions causes the analysis itself to take on implications for institutional change that are, at best, highly misleading. To argue that an existing order is "imperfect" in comparison with an alternative order of affairs that turns out, upon careful inspection, to be unattainable may not be different from arguing that the existing order is "perfect."[6] The existence of demonstrated imperfection in terms of an unattainable state of affairs should imply nothing at all about the possibility of actual improvement to an existing state. To take this step, considerably more is required than the preliminary analysis of "ideal output." This is not to suggest, of course, that the preliminary analysis is not essential and important.

In what follows I shall try to show that, with consistent assumptions about human behaviour in both market and political institutions, any attempt to replace or to modify an existing market situation, admitted to be characterised by serious externalities, will produce solutions that embody externalities which are different, but precisely analogous, to those previously existing. Indeed, the Pigovian analysis lends itself readily to the analysis of political imperfection.

I

In order to analyse political processes in a manner that is even remotely similar to the methods of economic theory, great simplification and abstraction are required. To the political scientist, accustomed as he is to working with more "realistic" models of human behaviour, the simplified models with which the economist must analyse political institutions can only seem to be grossly inadequate caricatures of the operation of complex organisational structures. This rather sharp methodological gap between the two social sciences incorporated in "political economy" provides an important reason why the political scientist has not filled, and could hardly be expected to fill, the analytical void left open by the incompleteness of welfare economics.

I shall assume the existence of a community composed of separate indi-

---

6. Professor Frank Knight's statement that "to call a situation hopeless is equivalent to calling it ideal" may be reversed. To call a situation ideal is merely another means of calling it hopeless: that is, not perfectible.

viduals in which all collective decisions are reached by a voting rule of simple majority with universal suffrage. More complex, and realistic, models introducing representation, political parties, leadership, etc., could be employed but without significantly altering the conclusions reached. Almost any political order described by the term, "democratic," in the modern Western usage of this term may, for present purposes, be simplified into this extreme model of "pure" democracy. Characteristics of the political structure may modify the majority equivalent in the simple model. That is to say, a model of two-thirds or three-fourths majority may be more appropriate to the analysis of some political structures under certain conditions than the simple majority model. However, this quantitative variation in the voting rule equivalent does not affect the conclusions of this paper. Each particular rule, save that of unanimity, leads to conclusions that are identical to those reached in the simple majority model. The magnitude of the distortions produced is, of course, affected by the voting rule. The analysis here is concerned solely with indicating the direction of these effects, not with their magnitude. A distinction among the various "majority equivalents" is not, therefore, necessary.

In the first model, the orthodox assumptions of positive economics will be retained in so far as these concern individual motivation and action. Private individuals are assumed to be sufficiently informed and rational to conduct the required calculus and to reach decisions on the basis of a comparison of private costs and benefits at the relevant margins. No considerations of the "public" or the "social" interest are assumed to enter into this individual calculus within the relationship in question except in so far as this should coincide with individual interest. In determining his voting behaviour on each issue confronted by the group, the individual is assumed, quite simply, to act in that manner which he considers to advance his own interest. The model embodies, therefore, a rather straightforward extension of the behavioural assumptions of orthodox economic theory, as a predictive, explanatory theory, to political choice-making.

If no institutional restrictions are placed on this majority-rule model of the collective choice process, the characteristics of the "solution" should be intuitively clear. The minimum-size effective or dominating coalition of individuals, as determined by the voting rule, will be able to secure net gains at the expense of the other members of the political group. These gains, secured through the political process, will tend to be shared symmetrically (equally) among all members of the dominant coalition. In the simple majority-rule model, this involves, in the limit, fifty plus per cent. of the total membership in the dominating coalition and fifty minus per cent. of the total membership in the losing or minority coalition. That such a solution will, in fact, tend to emerge under the conditions of the model seems hardly subject to question. It is helpful, however, to note that such a solution, and only such, satisfies fully the von Neumann–Morgenstern requirements for solutions to *n*-person games which, of course, all political "games" must be.[7]

It is useful to apply the familiar Pigovian calculus to this model of political behaviour. To the individual member of the effective majority, the political process provides a means through which he may secure private gain at the expense of other citizens. In determining the margins to which political activity shall be extended, the individual member of the dominant coalition will include in his calculus a share of the net benefits from public activity that will be larger than the offsetting individualised share or proportion of the net costs of the activity. In the calculus of the individuals effectively making the final collective decision, marginal private benefits will tend to exceed marginal social benefits and/or marginal private costs will tend to fall short of marginal social costs. The distortions produced are, therefore, precisely analogous, in opposing directions, to those present in the market solution characterised by the familiar Pigovian divergencies. In essence, the value of a political vote in this model lies in its potential power to impose external costs on other members of the group. Externalities must be present in any solution reached by the voting process under all less-than-unanimity rules. If the possible "perfectibility" of market organisation is to be determined under these conditions, it is clearly necessary to compare two separate imperfections, in each of which significant divergencies of the Pigovian sort may exist at the individualised margins of decision-making. Since there will be nothing in the collective choice process that will tend to produce the "ideal" solution, as determined by the welfare economist, the presence or absence of a Pigovian marginal divergency in the market solution, even of sufficient serious-

7. J. von Neumann and O. Morgenstern, *Theory of Games and Economic Behavior*, third ed., 1953, 264.

ness to warrant concern, provides in itself no implication for the desirability of institutional change.[8]

II

This conclusion holds so long as consistency in individual behaviour patterns over market and voting processes is retained, independently of the specific motivation that may be assumed to direct this behaviour. The oversimplified model of Part I may be criticised on the grounds that individuals do not act in the way postulated: that is, they do not follow their own interests when they participate in the formation of social decisions for the community. Several responses might be advanced to such criticism, but it is not the purpose of this note to defend the validity, methodologically or otherwise, of the self-interest assumption about behaviour. The relevant response to the charge of unrealism at this point is surely the frank admission that, of course, individuals do not always act as the model of Part I postulates. A model is a construction that isolates one element of behaviour and, upon this, the analyst may erect conceptually refutable hypotheses. The model of majority rule in the simple pure democracy is not different in this respect from the competitive model of economic theory. Both models isolate that part of human behaviour that does reflect the rational pursuit of private gain by individuals in particular institutional relationships and both models fail to the extent that individuals do not, in fact, behave in this fashion in the relationships under consideration.[9]

8. I am not suggesting that deliberate exploitation of minority by majority need be the only purpose of collective activity, even in this polar model. The point is rather that, independently of the motivation for collective activity, majority-rule institutions of decision-making create opportunities within which Pigovian-like externalities may arise. There will, of course, arise situations in which the self-interest of the individual dictates the collectivisation of an activity in order that the application of general rules to *all* members of the group can be effected. It is precisely in such cases that, conceptually, unanimity may replace majority rule as the decision device, and the propositions of modern welfare economics become fully appropriate. But so long as majority rule prevails, the "political externalities" are present, whether these be purposeful or ancillary to collective action designed to accomplish other ends.

9. Care must be taken to distinguish between the self-interest assumption, as the basis for a "logic of choice" and the self-interest assumption as the basis of a predictive, ex-

Any number of models of individual behaviour can be constructed. The only real limitation lies, ultimately, in the testing of the predictions made. It will not be necessary, however, to develop any large number of additional and complex models to illustrate the central point of this note. One additional extremely simple model will suffice for this purpose. In this second model, I shall drop the assumption that individuals, in both their market and in their political behaviour, act in pursuit of their own narrowly defined self-interest. Instead, I now postulate that individuals act in the other extreme: I assume that each individual, in all aspects of his behaviour, tries to identify himself with the community of which he is a member and to act in accordance with his own view of the overall "public" or "social" interest. Each member of the group tries to act in the genuine interest of the whole group as this is determined for him through the application of some appropriately-chosen Kantian-like rule of action.

The results are again almost intuitively clear. Since each member of the group acts on the basis of identifying his own interest with that of the larger group, no deliberate exploitation of minority by majority can take place through the political process regardless of the voting rule that is applied. Differences that may arise, and which must be resolved by voting, stem solely from differences in individual conceptions of what the group interest on particular issues is. The Pigovian-type marginal divergencies between private and social costs or benefits disappear from the individual calculus in this model of behaviour. It is in application to market, rather than to political, behaviour that this model seems somewhat unorthodox. Under the assumptions of the model, the individual in his market behaviour will also try to

---

planatory theory of human action. In the first sense, all action of individuals must be based on self-interest, and it becomes meaningless to discuss alternative models of behaviour. The pure logic of individual choice is not without value, but it should be emphasised that the argument of this paper employs the second version of the self-interest assumption. If conceptually refutable hypotheses are to be developed, the behaviour of choice-making individuals must be externally observable in terms of measurable criteria of choice. In the market relationship, this degree of operational validity is often introduced by stating that the minimal requirement is that individuals, when confronted with choice, choose "more" rather than "less." But "more" or "less" take on full operational meaning only when they become measurable in something other than subjective utility of the choosers. The "measuring rod of money" must be allowed to enter before the generalised logic of choice can produce even so much as the first law of demand.

identify himself with the group as a whole and to act in accordance with what he considers to be the "public" interest. If his chimney pours out smoke that soils his neighbours' laundry, he will assess these costs as if they were his own in reaching a decision concerning the possible introduction of a smoke-abatement device. The familiar analysis of welfare economics simply does not apply. Each individual decision-maker does, in fact, attempt to balance off "social" benefits against "social" costs at the margin. While, as in the collective sector, differences may arise among members of the group concerning the proper definition of social benefits and social costs, these differences cannot be interpreted in the standard way. The Pigovian divergence between marginal private product and marginal social product disappears in both the market and the political organisation of activity in this universal benevolence model. The policy conclusions are, however, identical with those reached from the use of the extreme self-interest model. If chimneys smoke, or if the majority is observed to impose discriminatory taxes on the minority, these facts carry with them no implications for institutional changes. In this case, they must represent the decision-makers' estimates of genuine community interest. Neither "real" nor "apparent" externalities can, in themselves, provide grounds for suggesting organisational changes.

III

From the analysis of these two extreme and contrasting models of human behaviour, the inference is clear that so long as individuals are assumed to be similarly motivated under market and under political institutions there can be no direct implications drawn about the organisational structure of an activity on the basis of a Pigovian-like analysis of observed externalities. The orthodox implication of Pigovian welfare economics follows only on the assumption that individuals respond to *different* motives when they participate in market and in political activity. The only behavioural model appropriate to the Pigovian analysis is that which has been called "the bifurcated man." Man must be assumed to shift his psychological and moral gears when he moves from the realm of organised market activity to that of organised political activity and *vice-versa*. Only if there can be demonstrated to be something in the nature of market organisation, as such, that brings out the selfish motives in man, and something in the political organisation, as such, which, in turn, suppresses these motives and brings out the more "noble" ones, can there be assumed to exist any "bridge" between the orthodox externality analysis and practical policy, even apart from problems of specific policy prescription.

The characteristics of the organisational structure within which choices must be made may affect the nature of the value system upon which individual action is based. It seems probable that the individual in his voting behaviour, will tend to choose among alternatives on the basis of a somewhat broader and more inclusive value scale than that which will direct his behaviour in the making of market choices. One reason for this is that, in political behaviour, the individual is made fully conscious of the fact that he is choosing *for* the whole group, that his individual action will exert external effects on other members of the group, that he is acting "socially." In his market behaviour, on the other hand, the external effects of individual choice are sensed only indirectly by the chooser.[10] But this recognition that the individual value scale may be, to some extent, modified by the institutional structure within which choice is exercised is quite different from accepting the idea that the motivation for individual action is wholly transformed as between two separate structures. While it may be acknowledged as "realistic" to assume that the model of individual choice based on self-interest motivation, the "economic" model, is somewhat more applicable to an analysis of markets than of voting processes, this is far removed from accepting the applicability of the universal benevolence model for the latter. At most, the influence of the different organisational structures, as such, on motivation would seem to be conceptually represented by a reasonably narrow distance on some motivational spectrum. If, at the elementary stages of analysis, a choice must be made between that conception of behaviour that assumes this possible institutionally-generated difference to be absent or negligible (models that I have called consistent) and the conception that assumes wholly different behavioural patterns solely due to the institutional structure, the first alternative seems obviously to be preferred. Yet, as I have shown, it is the second, and clearly extreme, conception of human behaviour that is implicit in much of the discussion of Pigovian welfare economics.

10. For a further discussion on these points see my "Individual Choice in Voting and the Market," *Journal of Political Economy* 62 (1954): 334–43.

This assumption of behavioural dichotomy, as opposed to behavioural consistency, is most openly expressed in the early literature on socialism, especially that of the Christian and Fabian varieties. The criticism of the market order of affairs was often made by referring to the pursuit of private gain, and the case for socialism was based on the replacement of this pursuit of private gain by that of public good. Although this rather naive conception has perhaps lost some of its appeal since World War II, it continues to be implied in much of the popular discussion. While this is not in itself surprising, it does seem notable that the analytical structure based on this conception of human behaviour should have remained largely unchallenged in the scientific literature.[11]

IV

Up to this point the discussion has been concerned with the most general case in which no limitations are placed on the activities that may be organised through the political process. Can the implications of the Pigovian welfare analytics be rescued by restricting the movement of the political-institutional variables? If collective action can take place only within prescribed limits, which can be assumed to be fixed by constitutional rules, a model may be constructed in which the policy implications of the Pigovian-type of analysis do not run into immediate conflict with reasonable assumptions concerning human motivation. To accomplish this result, however, the range of possible political action must be restricted to such an extent as to make the analysis practically worthless.

Let it be assumed that constitutional rules dictate that all human activity shall be organised privately and voluntarily except that which involves the provision of genuinely collective goods and services. These are defined as those goods and services which, when a unit is made available to one individual member of the group, an equal amount, one unit, is also made avail-

---

11. The behavioural inconsistency here has been, of course, indirectly recognised by many writers. However, the only explicit reference to the private-cost–social-cost analysis, to my knowledge, is contained in the paper by William H. Meckling and Armen A. Alchian, "Incentives in the United States," *American Economic Review* 50 (1960): 55–61, and, even here, the reference is only a passing one.

able to each other member of the group. These goods and services are completely indivisible. Let it be further assumed that the constitution states that the provision of such goods and services, if politically organised, shall be financed by taxes that are levied on the "marginal benefit principle." That is to say, each individual shall be required to contribute a "tax-price" that is exactly proportional to his own marginal rate of substitution between the collective good and money (all other goods). This marginal tax will be different for different individuals in the group because, although the good is genuinely collective, the relative marginal utility of it will vary from individual to individual.

If the provision of such a good or service should be organised privately rather than collectively, and if individuals are assumed to be motivated by self-interest considerations, the market solution will be characterised by the presence of significant externalities. The individual, acting privately, will take into account only that share of total marginal benefit or product that he expects to enjoy. By comparison, he will take into account the full amount of the marginal costs which, by hypothesis, he must bear individually. In other words, he cannot exclude other members of the group from the enjoyment of the benefits provided by the good: but there is no way that he may include these other members of the group in the payment of the costs. This market organisation produces, therefore, the familiar result; the private calculus of individuals embodies the Pigovian divergence at the margins of decision. Compared to a Pareto-optimal situation, relatively too few resources will be devoted to the provision of the common good or service.

Under this situation, a shift in organisation from the private or market sector to the collective sector will, under the conditions specified, tend to eliminate the Pigovian divergence, even if the self-interest motivation of individual action is retained. If the individual, in making a political or voting choice concerning the possible marginal extension of the provision of the collective good or service, is required to include in his calculus a share of the total marginal cost of the extension that is proportional to his individualised share of the total marginal benefits provided by the extension, a "solution" will tend to be produced by political choice that will meet all of the necessary conditions for Pareto optimality. If the total marginal costs of extending the activity fall short of the total marginal benefits, individuals will not be in equilibrium and they will, accordingly, vote to extend the activity. At the "solution," all of the necessary conditions are satisfied, and total incremental benefits equal total marginal costs. No externalities exist.[12]

The reason for this result is not difficult to understand. By imposing the restriction that the individual voter must pay for the marginal unit of the collective good or service in proportion to the marginal benefit enjoyed, it is insured that the individual's private calculus becomes a miniature reflection of the aggregate or "social" calculus that would be made by an omniscient, benevolent despot acting in the interests of all persons in the community. The individual voter cannot, because of the restrictions on the model, impose external costs on others in the group through the political process. In his private voting decision he will recognise that additional units of the collective good will yield benefits to others than himself. But he will, under the self-interest assumption, not be influenced by these spillover benefits at all. There are, however, also spillover marginal costs that the provision of the additional units of the collective good will impose on his fellows, and the neglected external benefits will tend to offset these neglected external costs.

This highly restricted model has several interesting features. First of all, note that the sharp difference in result as between the market and the political solution emerges only if the self-interest assumption about human motivation is consistently adopted and applied. If, by contrast, the universal benevolence assumption is introduced, the market organisation and the political organisation will tend to produce similar results, as in the earlier analyses. Secondly, if the self-interest assumption is adopted, the political result in the restricted model here will tend to be identical under *any* voting rule. Any rule will, under the constitutional restrictions imposed, tend to produce a solution that satisfies all of the necessary conditions for Pareto optimality. The single individual acting as a dictator, the simple majority, and the rule of unanimity: each of these will tend to produce the same results. These separate rules for making political decisions only become important because they reflect differences in the ability of some members of the group to impose

---

12. This solution is that which has been rigorously defined by Paul A. Samuelson. See his "The Pure Theory of Public Expenditure," *Review of Economics and Statistics* 36 (1954): 386–89; "Diagrammatic Exposition of a Theory of Public Expenditure," *Review of Economics and Statistics* 37 (1955): 350–56.

costs on other members, an ability that is specifically eliminated by the constitutional restrictions postulated.

It is not, of course, surprising to find that the Pigovian analysis has relevant policy implications only for the provision of genuinely collective (perfectly indivisible) goods and services. Indeed, the statement that externalities exist in any private market solution is one means of stating that genuinely collective elements characterise the activity under consideration. This restricted model indicates clearly, however, that the good must be wholly collective if the implications of the Pigovian analysis are to apply. If an activity is only quasi-collective, that is to say, if it contains elements that are privately divisible as well as collective elements, the political solution must also involve externalities. The restricted model analysed here is perhaps even more useful in pointing up the extremely limited tax scheme that is required for the analysis to apply at all. Even for those goods and services that are wholly collective in nature, the provision of them through the political process will produce Pigovian-like externalities at the margin unless taxes are collected on the basis of marginal benefits. In the real world, very few, if any, goods and services are wholly collective. And even if these few could be isolated, they would not be financed by taxes levied on this principle of incremental benefits enjoyed. Such a principle is not only politically unimaginable in modern democracy: it is also conceptually impossible. Its application would require that the taxing authorities be able to determine, in advance, all individual preference functions. It must be concluded, therefore, that the restricted institutional model in which the implications of the standard externality analysis might apply is nothing but a conceptual toy. In the real world, political results must embody externalities to the extent that individuals follow self-interest in their capacities as collective decision-makers: individuals are able, by political means, to impose costs on other individuals.

V

In Part III it was demonstrated that the generalised implications of the Pigovian analysis could be supported only on the adoption of a highly questionable conception of human motivation. In Part IV it was demonstrated that these implications would be drawn from a consistent motivational model only if this model should be so highly restricted as to make the analysis of little practical value. It is much easier, however, to explain the reasons for economists neglecting to examine these aspects of their analysis than it is to justify their neglect. As Knut Wicksell suggested many years ago, most economists are content with assuming the presence of a benevolent despot. In so far as their analysis points toward policy at all, as it must, the improvements in efficiency advanced are assumed to be attainable within the realm of the politically possible. The almost universal neglect of the imperfections that might arise from the political attempts at applying the economists' efficiency criteria represents a serious deficiency in the work of welfare economists and economists generally. To shy away from considerations of the politically feasible has been deemed an admirable trait, but to refuse to examine the politically possible is incomplete scholarship.

Individual Choice in Voting
and the Market

This paper will compare individual choice in the political voting process and in the market process, with both considered as ideal types. A substantial portion of the analysis will be intuitively familiar to all social scientists, since it serves as a basis for a large part of political theory, on the one hand, and economic theory, on the other. Perhaps as a result of disciplinary specialization, however, the similarities and the differences between these two methods of individual decision-making in liberal society are often overlooked. The state of things is illustrated in the prosaic "one-dollar–one-vote" analogy, which is, at best, only partially appropriate and which tends to conceal extremely important differences.

It is necessary to emphasize the limitations of this analysis. No attempt will be made to compare market choice and voting choice in terms of the relative efficiency in achieving specified social goals or, in other words, as means of *social* decision-making. Many comparisons of this sort have been made. In the great debate over the possibility of rational socialist calculation, the discussion has been concerned primarily with the workability of political decision-making processes when confronted with the social criterion of economic efficiency. The issue has been framed, appropriately, in terms of the relative efficiency of centralized and decentralized decision-making. Collective choice implies centralized choice, whatever the process of choosing;

From *Journal of Political Economy* 62 (August 1954): 334–43. Copyright 1954 by The University of Chicago. All rights reserved. Reprinted by permission of the University of Chicago Press, publisher.

I am indebted to Marshall Colberg, Jerome Milliman, and Vincent Thursby for helpful comments and suggestions.

hence the market has been compared with the whole subset of political choice processes ranging from pure democracy to authoritarian dictatorship.

This paper will compare the *individual* choices involved in the price system and in a single form of centralized decision-making—pure democracy. The individual act of participation in the choice process will be the point of reference. The comparison does not, of course, imply that these two processes will be presented as genuine alternatives to the individual, even in their somewhat less pure forms. A more complete understanding of individual behavior in each process should, however, provide some basis for deciding between the two, if and when they do exist as alternatives.

The following distinctions between individual choice in voting and the market will be discussed: (1) the degree of certainty, (2) the degree of social participation, (3) the degree of responsibility, (4) the nature of the alternatives presented, (5) the degree of coercion, and, finally, (6) the power relations among individuals. Quite obviously, these distinctions are somewhat arbitrarily isolated from one another, and, in a broad sense, each implies others. After these are discussed, some attention will be given to their influence on the selection of voting or the market as a decision-making process for the social group.

I

It will be assumed that the individual chooser possesses the same degree of knowledge concerning the results of alternative decisions in the polling place that he does in the market place.[1] It is essential that this assumption be made at this stage, in order that the first important distinction, that of the degree of certainty, between individual choice in voting and individual choice in the market may be made clear.

In market choice the individual is the acting or choosing entity, as well as

---

1. This is a simplifying assumption; there is reason for believing that the individual possesses a greater knowledge of alternatives in the market. This is due, first, to the greater continuity of market choice and, second, to the difference in the degree of knowledge required to compare alternatives in each case. The latter difference has been stressed by Professor Hayek (see F. A. Hayek, "Individualism: True and False," *Individualism and Economic Order* [Chicago: University of Chicago Press, 1948]; see also Robert A. Dahl and Charles E. Lindblom, *Politics, Economics, and Welfare* [New York: Harper & Bros., 1953], 63).

the entity for which choices are made. In voting, the individual is an acting or choosing entity, but the collectivity is the entity for which decisions are made. The individual in the market can predict with absolute certainty the direct or immediate result of his action. The act of choosing and the consequences of choosing stand in a one-to-one correspondence.[2] On the other hand, the voter, even if he is fully omniscient in his foresight of the consequences of each possible collective decision, can never predict with certainty which of the alternatives presented will be chosen. He can never predict the behavior of other voters in the polling place. Reciprocal behavior prediction of this sort becomes a logical impossibility if individual choice is accepted as meaningful.[3] This inherent uncertainty confronting the voter can perhaps be classified as genuine uncertainty in the Knightian sense; it is not subject to the application of the probability calculus.

This uncertainty must influence to some degree the behavior of the individual in choosing among the possible social alternatives offered to him. Whereas the chooser in the market,[4] assumed to know what he wants, will always take the attainable combination of goods and services standing highest on his preference scale, the voter will not necessarily, or perhaps even probably, choose the alternative most desirable to him. The actual behavior of the voter must be examined within the framework of a theory of choice under uncertainty. As is well known, there is no fully acceptable theory of behavior here, and there are some students of the problem who deny the possibility of rational behavior in uncertain conditions.[5]

II

The second fundamental difference in the two-choice processes is found in the sense or degree of participation in social decision-making. In the market the individual is confronted with a range of commodities and services,

2. Cf. Kenneth J. Arrow, "Alternative Approaches to the Theory of Choice in Risk-taking Situations," *Econometrica* 19 (1951): 405.

3. Cf. Frank H. Knight, "Economic Theory and Nationalism," in his *The Ethics of Competition* (London: Allen & Unwin, 1935), 340.

4. The device of considering productive services as negatively desired and hence carrying negative prices enables both the buying and the selling activity of the individual to be encompassed in "market choice."

5. See Arrow, "Alternative Approaches," for an excellent summary of the various theories of choice under uncertainty.

each of which is offered at a given price. Individually, the buyer or seller considers both the range of alternatives and the set of prices to be beyond his power to alter.[6] He is able, therefore, to assume himself apart from, or external to, the social organization which does influence the alternatives made available. He is unconscious of the secondary repercussions of his act of choice which serve to alter the allocation of economic resources.[7] The individual tends to act *as if* all the social variables are determined outside his own behavior, which, in this subjective sense, is nonparticipating and therefore nonsocial.[8] The influence of the individual's actual behavior on the ultimate social decision made has no impact upon such behavior.[9]

The individual in the polling place, by contrast, recognizes that his vote is influential in determining the final collective choice; he is fully conscious of his participation in social decision-making. The individual act of choosing is, therefore, social, even in a purely subjective sense.

The sense of participation in social choice may exert important effects on the behavior of the individual. It seems probable that the representative individual will act in accordance with a different preference scale when he realizes that he is choosing for the group rather than merely for himself. There are two reasons for this. First, his identification will tend to be broadened,[10]

6. Cf. Ludwig von Mises, *Human Action: A Treatise on Economics* (New Haven: Yale University Press, 1949), 312.

7. The fact that individual behavior in the market sets off reactions which are not recognized or intended by the actor, but which do control society's utilization of resources, is stressed in a somewhat different context by Dahl and Lindblom (*Politics, Economics, and Welfare*, 99–102). They are concerned with the "spontaneous field control" exerted over the individual in this manner. "Control" in this sense, however, is no different from that imposed by the natural environment or any other set of forces external to the individual (see Sec. V).

8. For a definition of social action see Max Weber, *The Theory of Social and Economic Organization*, trans. A. M. Henderson and Talcott Parsons (New York: Oxford University Press, 1947), 88.

9. It has been advanced as a merit of the price system that it does place the individual in a position of adapting his behavior to the anonymous forces of the market without at the same time feeling that he can participate in changing these forces. On this point see Hayek, "Individualism," 24.

Market behavior can, of course, become "social" if the individual is made to realize the secondary repercussions of his action. Exceptional cases of such realization may be present even in the perfectly competitive economy, e.g., "buyers' strikes."

10. Dahl and Lindblom, *Politics, Economics, and Welfare*, 422.

and his "values" will be more likely to influence his ordering of alternatives, whereas in market choice his "tastes" may determine his decision.[11] As an example, the individual may cast a ballot-box vote for the enforcement of prohibition at the same time that he visits his bootlegger, without feeling that he is acting inconsistently. Even if the individual's welfare horizon is not modified in a shift from market to voting choice, or vice versa, there is a second, and perhaps equally important, reason for a rearrangement of his preference scale and hence for some difference in behavior. The individual's ranking of alternatives in market choice assumes no action on the part of other individuals in specific correspondence to his own. In voting, the choice is determined from a ranking of alternative situations in each of which the position of the individual is collectively determined for him and for *all* other individuals in the group.[12] As an example of this difference, businessmen in a perfectly competitive industry marketing a product with an inelastic demand may vote to approve governmentally imposed production limitations, while, if left to operate independently, they would have no incentive to restrict production. A further example may be used to illustrate the case in which both these effects on individual choice may be operative. A man who in the unregulated market economy would construct a billboard advertising his product might vote for the abolition of billboards because he considers such action preferable in terms of group welfare and/or because his own interests will be better served by such collectively imposed action.

III

The difference in the individual's sense of social participation has its obverse, however, which may be introduced as a third distinction between the voting and market processes. Since voting implies collective choice, the responsibility for making any particular social or collective decision is necessarily divided. This seems clearly to affect the individual's interest in the choosing

---

11. Cf. Kenneth J. Arrow, *Social Choice and Individual Values* (New York: John Wiley & Sons, 1951), 82.

12. Cf. William J. Baumol, *Welfare Economics and the Theory of the State* (Cambridge: Harvard University Press, 1952), 15; Trygve Haavelmo, "The Notion of Involuntary Economic Decisions," *Econometrica* 18 (1950): 3, 8.

process. Since a decision is to be made in any case, the single individual need not act at all; he may abstain from voting while other individuals act.

The responsibility for market decisions is uniquely concentrated on the chooser; there can be no abstention. There is a tangible benefit as well as a cost involved in each market chooser's decision, while there is neither an immediately realizable and certain benefit nor an imputable cost normally involved in the voter's choice.[13] This difference tends to guarantee that a more precise and objective consideration of alternative costs takes place in the minds of individuals choosing in the market. This does not suggest, however, that the greater precision in the consideration of alternatives by individuals in the market implies that the costs and benefits taken into account are necessarily the proper ones from the social point of view.[14]

It seems quite possible that in many instances the apparent placing of "the public interest" above mere individual or group interest in political decisions represents nothing more than a failure of the voters to consider fully the real costs of the activity to be undertaken. It is extremely difficult to determine whether the affirmative vote of a nonbeneficiary individual for a public welfare project implies that he is either acting socially in accordance with a "nobler" ordering of alternatives or is estimating his own self-interest in accordance with a "collective-action" preference scale, or whether it suggests that he has failed to weigh adequately the opportunity costs of the project.

The difference in responsibility provides a basis for Professor Mises' argument that an individual is "less corruptible" in the market.[15] This might plausibly be advanced without necessarily contradicting the claim that ballot-box choice, if uncorrupted, is made in accordance with a more inclusive and modified value scale. A somewhat related point has been made by Professor Spengler when he says that there is, in voting as compared with the market, "the tendency of the individual (especially when he is a part of a large and

13. On this point see Alfred C. Neal, "The 'Planning Approach' in Public Economy," *Quarterly Journal of Economics* 54 (1940): 251.

14. In cases where spill-over effects are significant, the costs taken into account by the individual in the market will clearly exclude some important elements of social costs (positive or negative) which should be considered in the making of a social decision (see Dahl and Lindblom, *Politics, Economics, and Welfare*, 419).

15. Ludwig von Mises, *Socialism* (new ed.; New Haven: Yale University Press, 1951), 21.

disciplined organization) more easily to lose . . . political than economic autonomy."[16]

IV

A fourth distinction, and perhaps one of the most important, between individual choice in voting and the market lies in the nature of the alternatives offered to the individual in each case. Choice implies that alternatives are mutually conflicting; otherwise, all would be chosen, which is equivalent to saying that none would be chosen. It is in the precise way in which the alternatives mutually conflict that the voting process must be sharply distinguished from the market mechanism.

Alternatives of market choice normally conflict only in the sense that the law of diminishing returns is operative. This is true at the level both of the individual chooser and of the social group. If an individual desires *more* of a particular commodity or service, the market normally requires only that he take *less* of another commodity or service. If all individuals, through their market choices, indicate that *more* resources should be devoted to the production of a particular commodity, this requires only that *less* resources be devoted to the production of other commodities.

Alternatives of voting choice are more normally mutually exclusive, that is, the selection of one precludes the selection of another. This, too, is true at the level both of the individual chooser and of the whole system. The individual voter normally faces mutually exclusive choices because of the indivisibility of his vote. Group choices tend to be mutually exclusive by the very nature of the alternatives, which are regularly of the "all-or-none" variety.

For the individual, market choice amounts to the allocation of an unspecialized and highly divisible resource (income-yielding capacity) among a range of alternatives. On the other hand, few voting schemes include means which enable an individual to break his total voting strength down into fractional parts. The attribute of scarcity has never been applied to voting strength; an additional vote is granted to each individual when each new collective decision is made. In order for market choice to be made similar to

16. J. J. Spengler, "Generalists versus Specialists in Social Science: An Economist's View," *American Political Science Review* 44 (1950): 378.

voting in this respect, each individual would be required to devote his whole capacity in each market period to one commodity or service. If only the buying side is taken into account, this means that the consumer's whole expenditure should be on one commodity. It seems clear that this feature of the choice process can itself affect the nature of the alternatives presented. If the individual were required to spend the whole of his income on one commodity, market alternatives would tend to become mutually exclusive and to become severely limited in number and variety. Most of the normally available goods and services would disappear from the market places.

The major share of the difference in the nature of the alternatives presented in the two choice processes must, however, be attributed to fundamental differences in the objects of choice themselves. In a very real sense many voting choices can never be made in the market because they are inherently more difficult, involving, as they do, considerations which cannot be taken into account effectively by the individual choosing only for himself. The choice to be made is normally among two or more alternatives, only one of which may be chosen, with its very selection precluding the selection of the others. Even if the results of the voting were to be based upon the proportionate number of votes cast for each alternative, combinations or composite solutions of the market type would not be possible in most cases. Inherent in the market solution, by contrast, is choice among an almost infinite number of *combinations* of goods and services, in each of which some of almost every conceivable good and service will be included.[17] As a result of this difference, individual choice in the market can be more articulate than in the voting booth.

V

There follows directly from the difference in the nature of alternatives an extremely important fifth distinction between the voting process and the market process as faced by the individual choice-maker. If production indivisibilities may be disregarded (they would not be present in the ideally

---

17. The market is thus the only system of proportional representation which will likely work at all (cf. Clarence Philbrook, "Capitalism and the Rule of Love," *Southern Economic Journal* 19 [1953]: 466).

competitive world), each dollar vote in the market becomes positively effective[18] to the individual, not only in providing him with a unit of the chosen commodity or service, but also in generating changes in the economic environment. In either of these senses a dollar vote is never overruled; the individual is never placed in the position of being a member of a dissenting minority.[19] When a commodity or service is exchanged in the market, the individual chooses from among *existing* alternatives; at the secondary stage, of which he is unconscious, his behavior tends to direct economic resources in a specific manner.

In voting, the individual does not choose among *existing* but rather among *potential* alternatives, and, as mentioned earlier, he is never secure in his belief that his vote will count positively. He may lose his vote and be placed in the position of having cast his vote in opposition to the alternative finally chosen by the social group. He may be compelled to accept a result contrary to his expressed preference. A similar sort of coercion is never present in market choice. It has been argued that pressure toward social conformity "compels those outvoted to make an expenditure against their will."[20] While it is no doubt true that both the individual's earning and expenditure patterns are conditioned to a large degree by the average patterns of his social group, the distinction between this indirectly coercive effect involved in the social urge to conform and the direct and unavoidable coercion involved in collective decision seems an extremely important one.

If the assumption of production divisibility is relaxed, some modifications of this conclusion must be made. Given the presence of indivisibility, the individual's dollar vote may be overruled at the secondary stage of the market choice process. On the buying side, if the consumer's dollar vote is not accompanied by enough other votes to maintain the production of the particular good or service, it may be "lost," and, at this stage, the buyer may be in

18. A decision to sell productive services may be considered as a vote for generalized purchasing power (i.e., dollars), and thus may be considered positively effective if the sale is consummated.

19. For an excellent summary discussion of this point see Mises, *Human Action: A Treatise on Economics*, 271.

20. Dahl and Lindblom, *Politics, Economics, and Welfare*, 424. A similar position is taken by Professor Howard Bowen (see his *Toward Social Economy* [New York: Rinehart & Co., 1948], 44).

a position apparently equivalent to that of the ballot-box supporter of the losing side of an issue. On the selling side, if there are not enough final demand dollar votes to warrant production of those commodities or services embodying the individual's productive contribution, then the attempt to convert productive services into generalized purchasing power on former terms may be thwarted. But in each case, at the initial or primary stage of the market process, the individual's expressed choice is never overruled. The buyer would never have possessed the opportunity to choose, had not the commodity or service been existent in the market; and the seller of productive services would have never been able to develop particular skills, had not a derived demand for those skills been present. And since the one-to-one correspondence between the act of choice and its result is the only condition directly influencing the individual's behavior, there can never be present the sense of directly losing one's market vote. There may, of course, arise a sense of regret when the consumer returns to the market place and finds a desired commodity no longer available and when the individual no longer is able to market productive services previously adapted to particular uses. The consumer may also regret that certain desired goods have never been placed in the market in the first place, and the individual seller may be concerned that there has never existed a ready market for his peculiar talents. This sort of regret does not, however, apply uniquely to market choice. It applies equally to political voting, and it does not, therefore, constitute the market's equivalent of the "lost" ballot-box vote. It is true that there may be commodities and services not offered for sale which the individual would be willing to purchase, but there may also be many potential alternatives never presented for a vote which an individual might desire to support.

VI

Each of the five preceding distinctions in the individual participation in voting and market choice is present even when the relative power positions of individuals are made equivalent in the two processes, that is, when there is absolute equality in the distribution of income-earning capacity among market choosers. All these distinctions tend, therefore, to be neglected in the simple "one-dollar–one-vote" analogy, which concentrates attention only upon the difference in the relative power of individuals. Market choice is normally conducted under conditions of inequality among individuals, while voting tends, at least ideally, to be conducted under conditions of equality.

The essential point to be emphasized in this connection is that the inequalities present in market choice are inequalities in individual power and not in individual freedom, if care is taken to define freedom and power in such a way as to maximize the usefulness of these two concepts in discussion. As Knight has suggested, it seems desirable for this reason to define freedom somewhat narrowly as the absence of coercion and unfreedom as the state of being prevented from utilizing the normally available capacities for action.[21]

VII

There remains the task of evaluating the foregoing differences in the position of the individual chooser in voting and in the market, with a view toward determining the relative appropriateness of the two choice processes for the social group when they are, in fact, possible alternatives. If rationality in individual behavior is considered a desirable feature of a choice process,[22] there would appear to be several reasons for claiming that market choice should be preferred. The greater degree of certainty seems clearly to produce more rational behavior; the uniquely centered responsibility tends to work in the same direction. Even if voting and the market are genuinely alternative means of making choices in a particular situation (thereby eliminating the inherent difficulties in voting choice when this is the only alternative), the difference in the divisibility of voting tends to make market choices finer and more articulate. The fact that market choice tends to embody greater rationality in *individual behavior* than does voting choice does not suggest that market choice tends to produce greater *social* rationality.[23]

21. See Frank H. Knight, "The Meaning of Freedom," in *The Philosophy of American Democracy,* ed. Charles M. Perry (Chicago: University of Chicago Press, 1943), 64; "Conflict of Values: Freedom and Justice," in *Goals of Economic Life,* ed. Dudley Ward (New York: Harper & Bros., 1953), 207, 226. For supporting views see Michael Polanyi, *The Logic of Liberty* (Chicago: University of Chicago Press, 1951), 159; E. F. Carritt, *Morals and Politics* (London: Oxford University Press, 1953), 195 f.

22. Rationality in individual behavior is defined in the normal manner, that is, the individual is able to rank alternatives, and such ranking is transitive.

23. It is on this basis that Dahl and Lindblom appear to reject the argument that mar-

The market should also be preferred as a choice process when individual freedom is considered in isolation. The absence of negative results of individual choices and, therefore, of the direct coercion which requires that the individual accept unchosen alternatives makes for a greater degree of freedom in market choice.

On the other hand, voting should perhaps be preferred to the market when individual motivation in choice is the attribute examined. Voting choice does provide individuals with a greater sense of participation in social decision-making, and, in this way, it may bring forth the "best" in man and tend to make individuals take somewhat more account of the "public interest." This attribute of the voting process has probably been somewhat neglected by liberal students and somewhat overemphasized in importance by socialists. It should be noted, however, that, even if this proves to be an important difference, voting will produce consistent or "rational" *social* choice only if men are able to agree on the ultimate social goals.[24] If men are not able to agree on what is genuine morality, the adoption of a choice process in which they act more morally cannot be justified on this ground.[25]

It is in the power structure among individuals antecedent to choice that the market may, and most often does, prove unacceptable. Political voting is characterized by an alternative power structure which may be deemed preferable to that of the market. And the selection of the one-for-one power relation among individuals appears to carry with it the selection of voting over market choice. If, however, the market power structure can be effectively modified independently of the choice process, this apparent advantage of political voting need not be present.

It should be noted that the fundamental decision to modify the power structure, as well as the extent of such modification, clearly must be made by the ballot box. And in this type of decision especially it is essential that indi-

---

ket choice is more rational (*Politics, Economics, and Welfare,* chap. 15). They do so because they are concerned with rationality in the social sense, defined as that action which maximizes the achievement of certain postulated social goals. If rationality is defined purely in terms of individual behavior, their argument appears to support that of this paper, although they seem explicitly to deny this at one point (ibid., 422).

24. Cf. Arrow, *Social Choice and Individual Values.*

25. If they cannot agree, the possible irrationality of collective choice may be a desirable rather than an undesirable feature, since rationality could be imposed only at the cost of minority coercion (see my "Social Choice, Democracy, and Free Markets," *Journal of Political Economy* 62 [1954]: 114–23).

viduals act in accordance with a value-ordering which is somewhat different from that motivating individual market choice. After a redistributive decision for the group is made, it must be further decided whether a particular choice shall be made by the market or by political voting. This decision on process must also be made by means of the ballot box. In this decision the market should be rejected only if individual market choices are considered by voters to produce a social state less desirable than that which is produced by individual voting choices.

The selection of the choice process, if the redistributive decision can be made separately, will depend to a large degree upon the relative positions of the various social goals in the value scales of individuals comprising the voting group. If consistency in individual behavior and individual freedom are highly regarded relative to other values, the market will tend to be favored. If, on the other hand, the somewhat vague, even though meaningful, concept of "social welfare" is the overriding consideration, voting choice may be preferred. But even here, if the individual's expressed interest is judged to be the best index of social welfare, the market may still be acceptable as a choice process (this was essentially the position of the utilitarians).

The selection of the choice process will also depend on whether or not the voters consider their own self-interest to be better served individualistically or collectively. If the "collective-action" preference scale allows the required majority of individuals to attain a more esteemed position than does the "individual-action" preference scale, voting choice will be selected regardless of the ranking of social goals. In this case it might be irrational for an individual to choose the market process, even though his behavior in the market, once this process was selected by the group, would be more rational than his behavior in the voting booth. The electorate should select the ballot box over the market place in those areas where individually determined market acts tend to produce results which are in conflict either with those which a large group of voters estimate to be their own or the "social welfare" and where the conflict is significant enough to warrant the sacrifice both of the individual freedom and the individual rationality involved.

In so far as market choice must be made under imperfectly competitive conditions[26] and voting choice under conditions of less than "pure" democ-

---

26. Imperfections include, of course, the presence of such monetary and structural factors as may lead to unemployment.

racy, the analysis of individual behavior in each process must be appropriately modified and the conclusions reached earlier changed accordingly. No attempt will be made here to extend the analysis in this direction.

VIII

A major source of confusion in the discussion of economic policy stems from the failure to distinguish carefully between the selection of the power structure among individual choosers and the selection of the choice mechanism. This arises from the more fundamental failure to define freedom in such a way that market freedom and market power may be differentiated conceptually.[27] In many real world situations the market power structure cannot be effectively modified independently, that is, a redistributive decision cannot be made in isolation. It is nevertheless essential for analytical clarity that this ideational distinction be made.

The separation of the power structure and the decision-making process is less inclusive and less complex than the similar and more commonly encountered distinction between the "income" and the "resource" aspects of economic policy. The problem of selecting the desirable structure of power relations among individuals in the market is, of course, equivalent to the income problem broadly considered. The "resource" side of the "income-resource" dichotomy introduces an evaluation of policy in terms of the social criteria of economic efficiency, and these aspects of the market mechanism tend to be emphasized. The "choice" side of the "power-choice" dichotomy which has been developed here tends to concentrate attention upon individual behavior in making choices, and it tends to emphasize the greater range of freedom allowed the individual, as well as the greater degree of individual rationality in market choice.

27. This constitutes one of the major weaknesses in Dahl and Lindblom's otherwise excellent comparison of voting and the market (*Politics, Economics, and Welfare,* 414–27).

Social Choice, Democracy, and Free Markets

Professor Kenneth Arrow's provocative essay, *Social Choice and Individual Values*,[1] has stimulated a great deal of comment and discussion during the two years since its publication. Reviewers and discussants have been primarily concerned with those formal aspects of Arrow's analysis which relate to modern welfare economics. This concentration, which is explained by both the stated purpose of the work and the tools with which it is developed, has resulted in the neglect of the broader philosophical implications of the essay.[2] In this paper I propose to examine the arguments of Arrow and his critics within a more inclusive frame of reference. This approach reveals a weakness in the formal analysis itself and demonstrates that some of the more significant implications drawn from the analysis are inappropriate.

I shall first review briefly Arrow's argument, in order to isolate the source of much of the confusion which has been generated by it. Following this, I shall raise some questions concerning the philosophical basis of the concept of social rationality. In the next section I shall attempt to show that the neg-

From *Journal of Political Economy* 62 (April 1954): 114–23. Copyright 1954 by The University of Chicago. All rights reserved. Reprinted by permission of the University of Chicago Press, publisher.

I am indebted to Marshall Colberg and Jerome Milliman, of Florida State University, and to Proctor Thomson, of the University of Chicago, for helpful comments and suggestions.

1. New York: John Wiley & Sons, 1951.

2. Little's stimulating review article and, to a somewhat lesser extent, Rothenberg's subsequent critique provide partial exceptions to this general statement (see I. M. D. Little, "Social Choice and Individual Values," *Journal of Political Economy* 60 [1952]: 422–32; and Jerome Rothenberg, "Conditions for a Social Welfare Function," *Journal of Political Economy* 61 [1953]: 389–405).

ative results of Arrow's analysis as applied to voting represent established and desirable features of the decision-making process embodied in constitutional democracy. From this it follows that if the conditions required by Arrow were satisfied, certain modifications in the underlying institutional structure would become imperative. Finally, I shall develop the argument that the voting process is fundamentally different from the market when the two are considered as decision-making processes rather than as bases for deriving social welfare functions. Here it will be demonstrated that the market does produce consistent choices and that the market does not belong in the category of collective choice at all.

I. Arrow's Conditions
for the Social Welfare Function

Arrow first defines his problem as that of constructing an ordering relation for society as a whole which will also reflect rational choice-making. This construction requires the establishment of a weak ordering relation among alternative social states. He then defines the social welfare function as a "*process or rule which, for each set of individual orderings . . . states* a corresponding social ordering" (italics mine).[3] The language is extremely important here, and the use of the word "process" seems singularly unfortunate. This usage has apparently been the source of the confusion, which is present in both the original essay and most of the criticism, between the definition of the social welfare function and the actual *processes* of choice: voting and the market. As will be shown in this paper, the decision-making *process* may produce consistent choice, even though the *rule* which *states* the social ordering from the individual values may not exist.

Having defined the social welfare function, Arrow proceeds to set up the conditions which are necessary to insure that it will be based on individual values. These conditions have received the bulk of attention in the discussion of Arrow's work and are so generally familiar that they may be merely listed here. They include the requirements that (1) the function shall not be imposed; (2) it shall not be dictated by any one individual; (3) if one individual prefers one social alternative to another and everyone else is indifferent between the two, the preferred alternative shall not stand lower in the social

3. Arrow, *Social Choice*, 23.

ordering; and (4) irrelevant social alternatives shall not affect the ranking of relevant alternatives.[4]

Having set up these necessary conditions, Arrow develops his General Possibility Theorem (p. 59) which states that, if there are at least three alternatives, every social welfare function satisfying the rationality conditions along with requirements 3 and 4 above must violate the condition either of nonimposition or of nondictatorship. The theorem is proved to be applicable to the method of majority decision *as a welfare function* and to the market *as a welfare function*. It is inapplicable only when there exists unanimous agreement among all individuals concerning alternative social states, when the required majority of individuals possess identical orderings of social alternatives, or when individual orderings are characterized as "single-peaked." Since each of these possibilities appears somewhat remote, the weight of Arrow's argument is to the effect that the individual values which are implicit in the normal decision-making mechanisms of society do not provide methods of deriving social welfare functions that are neither imposed nor dictatorial. So far, so good. But Arrow extends the argument to say that these ordinary decision-making mechanisms do not allow rational social choice.[5] Now this is a horse of quite a different color, with which the Arrow argument should not legitimately concern itself at all. Arrow is not at all clear as to which of these two animals he is chasing. The title of his essay implies that he is concerned with decision-making processes, and he begins his work by reference to the democratic means of decision-making—voting and the market. He states his General Possibility Theorem in terms of "moving from individual tastes to social *preferences*" (italics mine).[6] Yet he slips almost imperceptibly into the terminology of social-ordering relations or social welfare functions when he sets up his required conditions. He fails to see that his *conditions, properly interpreted, apply only to the derivation of the function and do not apply directly to the choice processes.*[7] As will be shown in Section III,

---

4. For the most concise listing of these conditions see William Baumol's review in *Econometrica* 20 (1952): 110.

5. Arrow, *Social Choice*, 59.

6. Ibid.

7. Little objects to Arrow's failure to draw a distinction between the social welfare function and the decision-making process on quite different grounds from those advanced here. His objections are primarily centered on Arrow's labeling the ordering as a "social welfare function" rather than merely as the resultant of the decision-making pro-

this distinction is not important in application to voting, and this appears to be the root of some of the difficulty. As will be shown in Section IV, when the market is considered, this distinction is fundamental. It will be proved that the existence of an Arrow social welfare function is not a necessary condition for consistent decision-making.

Unfortunately, but understandably, the Arrow argument has been widely interpreted in the erroneous sense of proving that the decision-making processes are irrational or inconsistent.[8] To the critics and reviewers of his analysis, almost without exception, Arrow appears to have subjected voting and the market to the test for rationality and to have found both these processes wanting.

II. The Concept of Social Rationality

It is difficult to know exactly what is meant by "rational social choice" in the Arrow analysis. Social rationality appears to imply that the choice-making processes produce results which are indicated to be "rational" by the ordering relation, that is, the social welfare function. But why should this sort of social rationality be expected? Certainly not because it is required for the derivation of the function in the first place. The mere introduction of the idea of social rationality suggests the fundamental philosophical issues involved. Rationality or irrationality as an attribute of the social group implies the imputation to that group of an organic existence apart from that of its individual components. If the social group is so considered, questions may be raised relative to the wisdom or unwisdom of this organic being. But does not the very attempt to examine such rationality in terms of individual values introduce logical inconsistency at the outset? Can the rationality of the social organism be evaluated in accordance with any value-ordering other than its own?

---

cess (Little, "Social Choice," 427–30). He thus fails, along with Arrow, to make the necessary distinction between an ordering of social states possessing certain properties and a decision-making process which is consistent, that is, rational.

Rothenberg, on the other hand, explicitly defines the results of the choice process as the social welfare function ("Conditions," 400). He fails, however, to trace through the effects of this definition on the Arrow analysis.

8. See, e.g., J. C. Weldon, "On the Problem of Social Welfare Functions," *Canadian Journal of Economics and Political Science* 18 (1952): 452–64.

The whole problem seems best considered as one of the "either-or" variety. We may adopt the philosophical bases of individualism in which the individual is the only entity possessing ends or values. In this case no question of social or collective rationality may be raised. A social-value scale as such simply does not exist. Alternatively, we may adopt some variant of the organic philosophical assumptions in which the collectivity is an independent entity possessing its own value-ordering. It is legitimate to test the rationality or irrationality of this entity only against this value-ordering.[9]

The usefulness of either of these opposing philosophical foundations may depend upon the type of problems to be faced.[10] But the two should always be sharply distinguished, and it should be made clear that any social-value scale may be discussed only within an organic framework. Once this approach is taken, the question as to whether or not the social-value scale may be based on individual values may properly be raised,[11] and the individual orderings of all possible social states may be the appropriate starting point in the construction of a social ordering that is to be based on individual values. But the appropriateness of such individual orderings for this purpose does not depend on the fact that these are sufficient to allow the ordinary decision-making processes to function.

Voting and the market, as decision-making mechanisms, have evolved from, and are based upon an acceptance of, the philosophy of individualism which presumes no social entity. These processes are related only indirectly to the individual values entering into any welfare function. This was true even in the pre-Robbins state of welfare economics. The measurability and

9. By his statement that "every value judgment must be someone's judgment of values" ("Social Choice," 427), Little appears fully to accept what I have called the "individualistic assumptions" and, in doing so, to deny the possible existence of an organic social unit. In his critique Rothenberg seems to adhere to the organic conception, when he states that "social valuation as opposed to solely individual valuation is an existential reality" ("Conditions," 397).

10. The point involved here is closely related to a central problem in the pure theory of government finance. The whole body of doctrine in this field has suffered from the failure of theorists to separate the two approaches (see my "The Pure Theory of Government Finance: A Suggested Approach," *Journal of Political Economy* 57 [1949]: 496–505).

11. Whether or not the degree of dependence on individual values is or is not a good criterion of appropriateness for a social ordering depends, in turn, on one's own value scale. We may or may not agree with Rothenberg when he says that consensus is required for a good social welfare function ("Conditions," 398).

comparability of utility did provide a means by which individual psycholog-ical attributes could be amalgamated into a conceptual social magnitude. The social welfare function of the utilitarians was based, in this way, on com-ponents imputable to individuals. But the welfare edifice so constructed was not necessarily coincident with that resulting from the ordinary choice-making processes. It was made to appear so because the utilitarians were also individualists[12] and, in one sense, philosophically inconsistent.

Arrow's work, correctly interpreted, consists in rigorously proving that the individual orderings of alternatives which are sufficient to allow the decision-making processes to function produce no such measuring stick as was provided by the measurability of utility. The overthrow of such measur-ability destroyed the conceptual social welfare function; there are no longer any units of account.[13] Arrow's analysis appears to consist, however, in prov-ing that the decision-making processes themselves define no social welfare function, that is, do not produce rational social choice. And here the impli-cation is strong that this is true only when an ordinal concept of utility is substituted for a cardinal concept. Actually, the decision-making processes do not produce rational social choice, even in the utilitarian framework, un-til and unless certain restrictive assumptions are made.

If social rationality is defined as producing results indicated as rational by the welfare function, that is, maximizing total utility in the utilitarian frame-work, a market decision is socially rational only if individuals are rational and individual utilities are independent. A voting decision is socially rational only if individual voting power is somehow made proportional to individual utility. Cardinal utility allowed the economist to construct a social welfare function from the individual utilities; it did nothing to insure that market or

---

12. Cf. Lionel Robbins, *The Theory of Economic Policy in English Classical Political Econ-omy* (London: Macmillan & Co., Ltd., 1952), 182.

13. Several of the attempts to modify Arrow's conditions in such a way as to define an acceptable social welfare function involve, in one form or another, a revival of the inter-personal comparability of utility (see Murray Kemp and A. Asimakopulos, "A Note on Social Welfare Functions and Cardinal Utility," *Canadian Journal of Economics and Politi-cal Science* 18 [1952]: 195–200; Leo Goodman and Harry Markowitz, "Social Welfare Func-tions Based on Individual Rankings," *American Journal of Sociology* 58 [1952]: 257–62; Clifford Hildreth, "Alternative Conditions for Social Orderings," *Econometrica* 21 [1953]: 81–95).

voting choices were socially rational. Here the distinction between a rational-choice process and an acceptable social welfare function becomes evident.

The proper approach to social welfare functions appears to begin with the frank admission that such functions are social, not individual, and therefore are of a fundamentally different philosophical dimension from individual values or from individualistically oriented decision-making processes. It seems meaningless to attempt to test such choice processes for social rationality. But if the idea of acceptable social welfare functions and of social or collective rationality is completely divorced from the decision-making processes of the group, what is there left of the Arrow analysis? It is still possible to test these processes for consistency;[14] but consistency or rationality in this sense must not be defined in terms of results obtainable from a social ordering. Consistency must be defined in terms of satisfying "the condition of rationality, as we ordinarily understand it."[15] This implies only that choices can be made (are connected) and that the choices are transitive. The implications of the Arrow argument appear to be that such consistency of choice, could it be achieved, would be a highly desirable feature of decision-making. I shall attempt in the following section to show that possible inconsistency of collective choice as applied to voting is a necessary and highly useful characteristic of political democracy.

III. Majority Decision and Collective Choice

The reaching of decisions by majority vote provides the simplest example of voting. In the historical and philosophical context, majority decision evolved as a means through which a social group makes collective choices among alternatives when consensus among the individuals comprising the group cannot be attained. Correctly speaking, majority decision must be viewed primarily as a device for breaking a stalemate and for allowing some collective action to be taken. A decision reached through the approval of a majority with minority dissent has never been, and should never be, correctly interpreted as anything other than a provisional or experimental choice of the

14. Cf. Little, "Social Choice," 432.
15. Arrow, *Social Choice*, 3.

whole social group. As a tentative choice, the majority-determined policy is held to be preferred to inaction,[16] but it is not to be considered as irrevocable. The fact that such decisions may be formally inconsistent provides one of the most important safeguards against abuse through this form of the voting process.[17] If consistency were a required property of decision, majority rule would not prove acceptable, even as a means of reaching provisional choices at the margins of the social decision surface.

One of the most important limitations placed upon the exercise of majority rule lies in the temporary or accidental nature of the majorities. One social alternative may be chosen during a legislative session, but a new and temporary majority may reverse the decision during the same or the next session. A majority may reject C in favor of B, and then select A over B, but still select C over A when put to yet another test. The obvious result of this so-called "paradox" of voting is that the social group cannot make a firm and definite choice among the alternatives offered.[18] Thus the voting process does not necessarily produce consistency of choice, and, within the Arrow framework, the individual rankings required for voting cannot be translated by the economist into a satisfactory social welfare function. The implication is that both these results are undesirable; the transitivity property is not present.

16. For a discussion of the basis for majority decision see Robert A. Dahl and Charles E. Lindblom, *Politics, Economics, and Welfare* (New York: Harper & Bros., 1953), 43 f.

17. Throughout this section the term "inconsistency" will be used in the formal sense without specific reference to the question of time dimension. This is admissible if it is assumed that all individuals have sufficient knowledge of alternatives to enable each to rank all alternatives and if it is assumed further that neither these individual orderings nor the available alternatives change over time. These assumptions, which are central to the Arrow analysis, allow the time dimension of the voting paradox to be neglected. When knowledge of alternatives is not perfect, however, and when the individual orderings do change over time (cf. below) or the alternatives presented vary, the concept of inconsistency itself becomes extremely vague. The argument of this section is applicable, however, whether or not the conditions required for the formal analysis are satisfied.

18. Dahl and Lindblom accept fully this interpretation of the paradox when discussing it in specific reference to Arrow's work. They also dismiss the logical difficulty involved in the paradox as "minor" and "not an empirical observation of a common difficulty." In this latter respect, they apparently fail to see that the potential intransitivity property of ordinary majority voting provides a means of removing one of the greatest of all difficulties in the structure of majority rule (*Politics, Economics, and Welfare*, 422 f.).

But, certainly, majority rule is acceptable in a free society precisely because it allows a sort of jockeying back and forth among alternatives, upon none of which relative unanimity can be obtained. Majority rule encourages such shifting, and it provides the opportunity for any social decision to be altered or reversed at any time by a new and temporary majority grouping. In this way, majority decision-making itself becomes a means through which the whole group ultimately attains consensus, that is, makes a genuine social choice. It serves to insure that competing alternatives may be experimentally and provisionally adopted, tested, and replaced by new compromise alternatives approved by a majority group of ever-changing composition. This is democratic choice process, whatever may be the consequences for welfare economics and social welfare functions.

The paradox is removed, and majority rule produces consistent choices, in the formal sense, if the individual components of a majority possess identical orderings of all social alternatives. If, for example, Joe and Jack both prefer A to B to C, and Tom prefers C to B to A, Joe and Jack can always outvote Tom and adopt A. The selection of A would represent definite and irreversible choice as long as the individual orderings remain unchanged. This is one of the situations in which Arrow's General Possibility Theorem would not hold; a social welfare function may be derived, and the implication appears to be that such a situation would prove a more desirable one than that in which inconsistency is present. In one of the most revealing statements in his essay Arrow says: "Suppose it is assumed in advance that a majority of individuals will have the same ordering of social alternatives. . . . Then the method of majority decision will pick out the agreed-on ordering and make it the social ordering. Again all the . . . conditions will be satisfied. These results reinforce the suggestion . . . that like attitudes toward social alternatives are needed for the formation of social judgments."[19] The above statement also shows that Arrow is primarily interested in individual values as the units of account to be used in deriving social welfare functions. It is the collective rationality with which he is concerned; his approach includes no consideration of individual values as ends as well as means.

If one examines the choices made in this case of identical majority order-

---

19. *Social Choice,* 74.

ings, it becomes evident that collective rationality or consistency is secured here only at a cost of imposing a literal "tyranny of the majority." Minorities under such conditions could no longer accept majority decisions without revolt. If there should exist policy areas in which specific majority groupings possess identical orderings of social alternatives, it would become necessary to impose additional restraints upon the exercise of majority decision. This was one of the considerations which led Wicksell to advocate the adoption of the principle of unanimity in the approval of tax bills. He reasoned that in the imposition of taxes the given majority in power would tend to be too cohesive and would, therefore, be able permanently to impose its will on the minority.[20]

The form in which Arrow states his condition of nondictatorship is closely related to the point discussed above. This condition, as applied to group decision, states that no one individual must dictate the choice without regard to the values of other individuals.[21] From the individual minority member's point of view, however, the acceptance of irrevocable majority decision is not different from the acceptance of irrevocable authoritarian decision. In either case the choice is dictated to the individual in question, since his values are overruled in the decision-making. If one thinks in terms of individual values as ends, "dictated to" seems a more meaningful concept than "dictated by."

The reason that majority rule proves tolerably acceptable and individual authoritarian dictatorship does not lies not in the many versus the one. It is because ordinary majority decision is subject to reversal and change, while individual decision cannot readily be made so. With identical majority orderings, the majority would, of course, always choose the same leaders, and this advantage of majority rule would be lost. It is not evident that we should summarily reject the rule of one individual if we could be assured that every so often a new dictator would be chosen by lot and that everyone's name would be in the lottery.

The attempt to examine the consistency of majority voting requires the assumption that individual values do not themselves change during the decision-making process. The vulnerability of this assumption in the gen-

---

20. Knut Wicksell, *Finanztheoretische Untersuchungen* (Jena: Gustav Fischer, 1896), 122.
21. Arrow, *Social Choice*, 30.

eral case has been shown by Schoeffler.[22] Individual values are, of course, constantly changing; so a postdecision ordering may be different from a predecision ordering. The assumption of constancy may, however, be useful in certain instances. For example, the assumption of given tastes in the decision-making represented by the market is essential for the development of a body of economic theory. But the extension of this assumption to apply to individual values in the voting process disregards one of the most important functions of voting itself.[23] The definition of democracy as "government by discussion" implies that individual values can and do change in the process of decision-making. Men must be free to choose, and they must maintain an open mind if the democratic mechanism is to work at all. If individual values in the Arrow sense of orderings of all social alternatives are unchanging, discussion becomes meaningless. And the discussion must be considered as encompassing more than the activity prior to the initial vote. The whole period of activity during which temporary majority decisions are reached and reversed, new compromises appear and are approved or overthrown, must be considered as one of genuine discussion.

In a very real sense collective choice cannot be considered as being reached by voting until relatively unanimous agreement is achieved. In so far as the attainment of such consensus is impossible, it is preferable that the actual choice processes display possible inconsistency to guaranteed consistency. The molding and solidifying of individual values into fixed ordering relations sufficient to make ordinary majority voting fit the Arrow conditions for consistency would mean the replacement of accepted democratic process by something clearly less desirable. The danger that such solidification will take place becomes more imminent as functional economic groups, subjecting members to considerable internal discipline, seek to institutionalize individual values.

The unanimity requirement need not imply that consistent choice can never be reached by voting. Relatively complete consensus is present in the social group on many major issues, and the securing of such consensus need

22. Sidney Schoeffler, "Note on Modern Welfare Economics," *American Economic Review* 42 (1952): 880–87.

23. The difference in the validity of the constancy assumption in these two situations is stressed by L. J. Richenburg in his review of Duncan Black and R. A. Nevins, *Committee Decisions with Complementary Valuation*, in *Economic Journal* 63 (1952): 131.

not involve the concept of a Rousseau-like general will. As Arrow points out,[24] the unanimity required may be reached at several levels. There may exist relatively general support of the framework within which change shall be allowed to take place, that is, the constitution. This in itself insures that a genuine attempt will be made to attain consensus on controversial issues and, more importantly, to insure that the changes which are made are introduced in an orderly and nonrevolutionary manner. This relative consensus on procedure, however, will exist only so long as majorities on particular issues do not solidify; in other words, as long as ordinary decision-making may be formally inconsistent.

IV. Collective Choice and Free Markets

In his discussion Arrow fails to make any distinction between voting and the market mechanism as decision-making processes, and he specifically defines both as "special cases of the more general category of collective social choice."[25] He is led to this conclusion because he is unable to define a satisfactory social welfare function from the individual orderings required for either process. In the consideration of voting, it is a relatively simple step to discard the social rationality or social welfare function implications and to utilize the Arrow conditions in testing the consistency of the choice process. When this is done, it is found that ordinary majority rule does not necessarily produce consistent choices. Thus the voting process serves neither as a basis for deriving a social welfare function in the Arrow sense nor as a means of producing consistent choices if tested by the Arrow conditions. When the market is considered, however, a different result arises when the process is tested for consistency of choice from that which is forthcoming when one seeks to derive a social welfare function. A necessary condition for deriving a social welfare function is that all possible social states be ordered *outside* or *external to* the decision-making process itself. What is necessary, in effect, is that the one erecting such a function be able to translate the individual values (which are presumably revealed to him) into social building blocks. If these values consist only of individual orderings of social states (which is all that is

24. Arrow, *Social Choice*, 90 f.
25. Ibid., 5.

required for either political voting or market choice), this step cannot be taken. This step in the construction of a social welfare function is the focal point in the Arrow analysis. This is clearly revealed in the statement: "The relation of known preference or indifference is clearly transitive, but it is not connected since, for example, *it does not tell us* how the individual compares two social alternatives, one of which yields him more of one commodity than the second, while the second yields him more of a second commodity than the first" (italics mine).[26]

By the very nature of free markets, however, the only entity required to compare two social alternatives when a choice is actually made is the individual. And, since individual orderings are assumed to be connected and transitive,[27] the market mechanism does provide a means of *making consistent choices* as long as individual values remain unchanged. If, given this constancy in individual tastes (values), the economic environment is allowed to change, consistency requires only that the same social state result always from similar environmental changes. Of course, there is no way of telling what a market-determined result will be (even if we know the individual orderings) except to wait and see what the market produces. The market exists as a means by which the social group is able to move from one social state to another as a result of a change in environment without the necessity of making a collective choice. The consistency of the market arises from what Professor Polanyi has called the system of "spontaneous order" embodied in the free enterprise economy. The order "originates in the independent actions of individuals."[28] And, since the order or consistency does originate in the choice process itself, it is meaningless to attempt to construct the ordering. We should not expect to be told in advance what the market will choose. It will choose what it will choose.

The market does not establish the optimum social state in the sense that individuals, if called upon to vote politically (act collectively) for or against the market-determined state in opposition to a series of alternatives, would consistently choose it. This may or may not be an important conclusion, de-

26. Ibid., 61.

27. Ibid., 34.

28. Michael Polanyi, *The Logic of Liberty* (Chicago: University of Chicago Press, 1951), 160.

pending on the value-judgment made concerning the appropriateness of majority approval as the criterion of optimum collective choice. But the essential point here is that the market does not call upon individuals to make a decision collectively at all. This being the case, market choice is just as consistent as, and no more consistent than, the individual choice of which it is composed.

V. Summary

It is necessary to distinguish between the problem of deriving a social welfare function from the individual orderings required for the operation of the decision-making processes of our society and the problem of testing these processes themselves for consistency. I have shown that the failure to make this distinction clear is the source of much of the confusion surrounding the Arrow analysis. A second distinction must be made between social or collective rationality in terms of producing results indicated by a social ordering and the consistency of choice produced by the mechanisms of decision-making. If rationality is taken to mean only that the choice-making is consistent, the Arrow analysis shows that voting may be inconsistent. But I have argued that possible inconsistency is a necessary characteristic of orderly majority rule. The market, on the other hand, has been shown to produce consistent choice, in spite of the fact that a "satisfactory social welfare function" cannot be derived from the individual rankings implicit in the market mechanism.

The consistency of market choice is achieved without the overruling of minority values, as would be the case if ordinary political voting were made consistent. Therefore, in a very real sense, market decisions are comparable to political decisions only when unanimity is present. The question as to what extent this lends support to the utilization of the market as the decision-making process when it is a genuine alternative to voting opens up still broader areas of inquiry which cannot be developed here.[29]

29. So far as I know, the differences between the market and political voting as choice processes have never been clearly and precisely analyzed. I hope to explore some of these differences in a forthcoming paper.

Rent Seeking and Profit Seeking

Rent seeking, as a specific term, emerged in applied economic theory only in the 1970's. The behavior that it describes, however, has been with us always, and there is surely no prospect that it will fade away. Behaviorally, rent seeking has become more important because institutional changes have opened up opportunities that did not exist in the nineteenth and early twentieth centuries.

What is *rent seeking*? The words seem clear enough at first reading, but economists will sense the ambiguities. Rent seeking does not refer to the behavior of landlords who collect rents on real property. This everyday usage of the word *rent* had best be put in the closet. We move somewhat closer to understanding when we introduce the definition of *rent* found in standard textbooks of economic theory. Rent is that part of the payment to an owner of resources over and above that which those resources could command in any alternative use. Rent is receipt in excess of opportunity cost. In one sense, it is an allocatively unnecessary payment not required to attract the resources to the particular employment. This textbook definition contains ambiguities, some of which will be discussed briefly in this introductory chapter. Nonetheless, the basic definition offers a starting point for any attempt to clarify the meaning of *rent seeking* as a general concept.

So long as owners of resources prefer more to less, they are likely to be engaged in rent seeking, which is simply another word for profit seeking. Traditional economic models of social interaction are based on the presumption that persons seek to maximize present values of expected income streams, and a central demonstration of economic theory involves the rela-

From *Toward a Theory of the Rent-Seeking Society,* ed. James M. Buchanan, Robert D. Tollison, and Gordon Tullock (College Station: Texas A&M University Press, 1980), 3–15. Reprinted by permission.

tionships between such individual profit seeking and desired social results. Since Adam Smith, we have known that the profit-seeking activity of the butcher and baker ensures results beneficial to all members of the community. Only through such activity do markets work in getting resources allocated efficiently among competing uses, in getting production and distribution organized, and in establishing prices as standards of comparative value. In an idealized model of market order, profit seeking as an activity produces consequences neither predicted nor understood by any single participant, but "good" when evaluated as a characteristic of the order itself. In such respect, therefore, profit seeking in an ordered market structure generates external economy; in Pigovian terminology, the social marginal product of profit seeking exceeds private marginal product.

In the preceding paragraph, I have deliberately shifted the terms from *rent seeking* to *profit seeking* as the discussion proceeded. My purpose was to call to mind the familiar proposition that the behavior of persons in trying to maximize returns on their own capacities or opportunities can be socially beneficial in an ordered market structure, behavior that we may here describe to be "profit seeking." The self-same behavior under a different set of institutions, however, may not produce socially beneficial consequences. The unintended results of individual efforts at maximizing returns on opportunities may be "bad" rather than "good." The term *rent seeking* is designed to describe behavior in institutional settings where individual efforts to maximize value generate social waste rather than social surplus. Again I should emphasize that at the level of the individual decision makers, the behavior, as such, is not different from that of profit seeking in market interactions. The unintended consequences of individual value maximization shift from those that may be classified as "good" to those that seem clearly to be "bad," not because individuals become different moral beings and modify their actions accordingly, but because institutional structure changes. The setting within which individual choices are made is transformed. As institutions have moved away from ordered markets toward the near chaos of direct political allocation, rent seeking has emerged as a significant social phenomenon.

Economic Rent

It is useful to return to the definition of *rent* or *economic rent* found in the textbooks. If the owner of a resource unit is paid more than the alternative earning power of that unit, more than opportunity cost, there seems to be no allocative necessity for such excess. The resource unit would have been directed toward the observed employment for any payment above cost, even an infinitesimally small sum. "Economic rent," viewed in this perspective, seems to be a genuine "social surplus," and, indeed, it is this apparent characteristic of rent that has spawned monumental confusion among those who do not fully understand the market process.

In an ordered market structure, the potential attractiveness of economic rents offers the motivation to resource owners and to entrepreneurs who combine resources into production. And it is the action of entrepreneurs that must drive the system. By seeking always to find new opportunities to earn economic rent and to exploit more fully existing opportunities, profit-seeking entrepreneurs generate a dynamic process of continuous resource *re*allocation that ensures economic growth and development, again as an unintended consequence. The role of economic rent in a market structure cannot be properly understood apart from this dynamic.

In the process described, two relevant features of rent require special mention. First, in market systems, all economic rent tends to be eroded or dissipated as adjustments take place through time. Above-cost payments to any entrepreneurs or resource owners must attract other profit-rent seekers to enter identical or closely related employments. As such entry proceeds, rents earned initially are driven down and, in the limit, disappear altogether. In the conceptualized equilibrium of market adjustment, economic rents are eliminated, and all resource owners, including those who have entrepreneurial capacities, earn rates of return established competitively in the whole market system. Second, in the dynamic adjustment process, which, of course, never attains the conceptualized equilibria of the models, economic rents may be negative as well as positive. Resource owners and entrepreneurs who err in their predictions or who overadjust to apparent opportunities that do not materialize may earn less than opportunity costs. This existence of negative rents or losses adds symmetry to the adjustment process and, of course, accelerates resource reallocation.

For completeness, the time dimension of economic rents should be discussed briefly. Economic rent to the owner of a resource that is explicitly locked in to a single use because of its physical characteristics (a particular machine, building, or human talent) may be positive in some short-run sense, but the resource may have little or no prospect of earning an alternative return comparable to that earned in the particular usage. Hence, the owner will have no incentive to reallocate. At the same time, however, the particular investment may be earning negative economic rent in some long-run or planning sense. The earnings may be less than comparable investments could earn in alternative uses. In such a setting, despite positive "quasi-rents," to use a Marshallian term, the negative economic rent applicable to initial allocation will ensure that no additional resources shift toward the particular usage. Reallocation away from the usage will take place via disinvestment as physical facilities wear out and are depreciated.

The Dissipation of Rents in Markets

We are concerned with the net attractiveness of opportunities for new investment. It will be useful to examine in elementary detail the process through which economic rents arise and are dissipated through time in ordered market structures.

Consider a situation where some person, a potential entrepreneur, discovers a use for a resource or a combination of resources that had not been previously discovered.[1] No one else in the economy is aware of this potential opportunity. The entrepreneur organizes production and commences sale of the new commodity or service. By definition, he is a pure monopolist during the initial period. He may be able to secure a return over and above what he might earn in any alternative employment. He receives "economic rent" on his entrepreneurial capacity. And, indeed, it is the prospect of such rent that motivates the activity in the first place. It is important to emphasize, however, that the rent reflects the *creation* of added value in the economy rather than the diversion of value that already exists. The entrepreneurial activity of *rent creation* is functionally quite different from that of *rent seeking*. The fact that the innovating entrepreneur is observed to be receiving rent sends out signals to other noninnovating but potentially imitating producers of the new commodity or service. Unless overt barriers to entry exist, other producers will enter the market and sell the new commodity or a close substitute for it. Output on the market will expand; price will fall. The initial monopoly

---

1. See Israel Kirzner, *Competition and Entrepreneurship* (Chicago: University of Chicago Press, 1973), for a thorough discussion of the entrepreneurship role.

position, and hence the economic rent, of the innovator is eroded to the benefit of consumers generally. In the ultimate equilibrium, the consumers secure the full benefit of the new product. Rents received by producers are dissipated in the dynamics of competitive market adjustment. Resources come to be allocated efficiently between the production of the new commodity and other uses in the economy.

Freedom of entry is critically important in the generation of allocative efficiency in a developing, changing economy. If the entry of those producers who are attracted by the rents of the innovating entrepreneurs is effectively blocked, there will be no dissipation of rents, and, of course, no shift of resources toward the production of the new product. Output will not be forced above monopoly limits, and price will not fall.

Rent Seeking without Social Return

To this point, the analysis has been straightforward elementary economics. Where does "rent seeking" come in? We need only to modify the setting by postulating a particular type of entry restriction. We may do this with a simple, and historically factual, example. Suppose that, instead of discovering a new commodity or service or production process, an innovating entrepreneur discovers a way to convince the government that he "deserves" to be granted a monopoly right, and that government will enforce such a right by keeping out all potential entrants. No value is created in the process; indeed, the monopolization involves a net destruction of value. The rents secured reflect a diversion of value from consumers generally to the favored rent seeker, with a net loss of value in the process.

Suppose that a courtier persuades the queen to grant him a royal monopoly to sell playing cards throughout the kingdom. The courtier so favored will capture sizable monopoly profits or economic rents, and this will be observed by other persons who might like to enter the industry. But their entry is effectively prevented by enforcement of the royal monopoly privilege. What the queen gives, however, the queen may take away, and the potential entrants are not likely to sit quietly by and allow the favored one among their number to enjoy his differentially advantageous position. Instead of passive observation, potential entrants will engage actively in "rent seeking." They will invest effort, time, and other productive resources in varying attempts to shift the queen's favor toward their own cause. Promotion, advertising, flattery, persuasion, cajolery—these and other attributes will characterize rent-seeking behavior.

The contrast between the unintended consequences of this behavior and that which characterizes profit seeking in the competitive market process is striking. Rent seeking on the part of potential entrants in a setting where entry is either blocked or can at best reflect one-for-one substitution must generate social waste. Resources devoted to efforts to curry the queen's favor might be used to produce valued goods and services elsewhere in the economy, whereas nothing of net value is produced by rent seeking. In the competitive market, by comparison, resources of potential entrants are shifted directly into the *production* of the previously monopolized commodity or service, or close substitutes; in this usage, these resources are more productive than they would have been in alternative employments. The unintended results of competitive attempts to capture monopoly rents are "good" because entry is possible; comparable results of attempts to capture artificially contrived advantageous positions under governmentally enforced monopoly are "bad" because entry is not possible.

Rent seeking, when used in this book, refers to the second model in all of its varieties, to activity motivated by rent but leading to socially undesirable consequences.

Rent Seeking and Governmental Action

At the beginning of this chapter I stated that rent seeking continues to gain importance in modern political economy because institutions have changed and are continuing to change. So long as governmental action is restricted largely, if not entirely, to protecting individual rights, personal and property, and enforcing voluntarily negotiated private contracts, the market process dominates economic behavior and ensures that any economic rents that appear will be dissipated by the forces of competitive entry. Furthermore, the prospects for economic rents enhance the dynamic process of development, growth, and orderly change. If, however, governmental action moves significantly beyond the limits defined by the minimal or protective state, if government commences, as it has done on a sweeping scale, to interfere piecemeal in the market adjustment process, the tendency toward the erosion or dissipation of rents is countered and may be wholly blocked. Rents must remain, however, and the signals emitted to potential competitors remain as strong as they are under standard market adjustment. Hence, attempts will be made to capture these rents, and resources used up in such attempts will reflect social waste, even if the investments involved are fully rational for all participants. Rent-seeking activity is directly related to the scope and range of governmental activity in the economy, to the relative size of the public sector.

The more apparent opportunities are those modern examples most closely analogous to the royal grant of monopoly introduced illustratively above. If supply is arbitrarily restricted and price is allowed to rise to market-clearing levels, rents accrue to those who secure the "rights" to engage in the activity. Governmental licenses, quotas, permits, authorizations, approvals, franchise assignments—each of these closely related terms implies arbitrary and/or artificial scarcity created by government. Whether such scarcity is reasonable governmental policy is not my concern here. Regardless of reason, such scarcity implies the potential emergence of rents, which, in turn, implies rent-seeking activity. Persons will invest genuinely scarce resources in attempts to secure either the initial assignments of rights to the artificially scarce opportunities or replacement assignments as other initial holders are ousted from privileged positions. In either case, and despite individually rational investments ex ante, valuable resources will be wasted in the process.

Few questions will be raised concerning the emergence of rent seeking when governmental action creates and supports monopoly positions and effectively prevents entry. Rents emerge because prices are not allowed to be brought down to competitive levels by expanding supply through the entry of new producers. Rent seeking of a different, but still wasteful, sort emerges, however, when governmental action interferes with markets in order to keep prices below rather than above competitive levels. With simple monopoly, and with the familiar examples noted above, rents emerge because *genuine* supply price falls below the actual price charged, with demand price being allowed to adjust to the latter in order for the market to clear. The surplus, the rent, accrues to the seller, the person who possesses the "rights" to market the commodity or service. Consider, however, the obverse setting, where the *genuine* demand price lies above the actual demand price authorized to be charged, with supply price being allowed to adjust to the latter in order for the market to clear. As in the obverse case, the wedge between the genuine demand price and the genuine supply price, both of which reflect opportunity costs to buyers and sellers, respectively, generates rents. In the second case, the rents accrue, not to sellers (who may, here, be competitively organized), but to purchasers or buyers who hold the artificially scarce "rights" to enter the market on the demand side. In the first case, the potential entrants who are thwarted are on the supply side, potential producer-sellers who will, unless constrained, enter and drive price down, hence dissipating rents. In the second case, there are potential entrants on the demand side, potential buyers who will, unless constrained, enter and drive prices up, hence dissipating rents. The analysis, as such, is fully symmetrical. The assignment of a "right to buy" something at, say, $1,000 below what would be a competitively determined price, has the same value as the assignment of a "right to sell" something at $1,000 above a competitively determined price. The signals transmitted are comparable in the two cases, and they will generate comparable if not identical rent-seeking behavior.

If allowed to function within a set of laws and institutions that protect individual property rights and enforce contracts, markets will allocate resources among alternative uses so as to ensure tolerably efficient results. But economists have concentrated far too much attention on efficiency and far too little on the political role of markets. To the extent that markets are allowed to allocate resources among uses, political allocation is not required. Markets minimize resort to politics. Once markets are not allowed to work, however, or once they are interfered with in their allocative functioning, politics must enter. And political allocation, like market allocation, involves profit seeking as a dynamic activating force. It would be absurd to conceive of a market process in which resources are either permanently locked in particular allocations or in which entrepreneurs are not continually searching for more profitable opportunities. Although it is perhaps less apparent, it would, nonetheless, be equally absurd to think that a politically determined allocation of resources could be frozen once and for all and that resource owners and entrepreneurs would not continually seek more profitable opportunities in politics as in markets. The motive force of profit seeking, or rent seeking, does not vary across the two institutional forms. The difference lies in the unintended results. Political reallocation, achieved via rent seeking, does not reduce or eliminate contrived scarcity. In politics, rent seeking, at best, replaces one set of rent seekers with another.

Political Allocation without Rent Seeking?

Earlier I associated the level of rent-seeking activity in a society with the size and scope of government activity in the economy. This proposition can be tested empirically, and the results of such a test would, I think, corroborate the relationship suggested. Such a test would necessarily draw data from the real-world actions of governments rather than from idealized constructions of what governments and politics might be. However, for completeness if for nothing else, I should examine the possibility that direct political allocation might take a form such that rent-seeking activity would not take place.

Rent seeking emerges under normally predicted circumstances because political interference with markets creates differentially advantageous positions for some persons who secure access to the valuable "rights." From this fact, we may derive a "principle." If political allocation is to be undertaken without the emergence of wasteful rent seeking, the differential advantages granted to some persons as a result of the allocation must be eliminated. This principle in turn suggests that all persons in the community must be allowed equal access to the scarcity values created by governmental intervention in the market economy. For example, if government decides to restrict the production or sale of a commodity, thereby creating the opportunity for economic rents, each person in the community must be granted an *equal* share in the prospective rents. If this sharing is announced in advance and becomes generally known, it will not be rational for anyone to invest resources in trying to secure differential advantages. Even this scheme is not certain to eliminate rent seeking, however, since, if it is known that government can assign equal shares, it might also be predicted that unequal shares could be assigned. Only if the equal-sharing rule could somehow be permanently implemented in each-and-all-possible scarcity-value distributions could we predict the total absence of rent seeking, even at the most basic level.

A more plausible means of assigning "rights" to contrived scarcity values would be for government to distribute such "rights" randomly in each situation. In this setting, all persons have equal expected values of rights, and they have little or no incentive to engage in rent seeking. Once again, however, some persons may predict a possible departure from the random distribution process until and unless the process itself becomes widely accepted as an untouchable rule or procedure for all political allocation.

Once we recognize that, under either of the two procedures suggested, much of the political motive for governmental interference with markets would disappear, the presumption of the validity of the empirical proposition relating rent seeking to size of government is strengthened.

Three Levels of Rent Seeking

Rent-seeking activity may occur at several levels, and I shall introduce a single example to indicate this prospect. Suppose that, for whatever reason, a municipal government decides to limit the number of taxicabs. (Whether this decision itself is desirable or undesirable need not concern us here.) If the valued licenses are to be distributed among potential entrants by bureaucratic authority, rent seeking of the most familiar sort previously discussed will, of course, take place. Suppose, however, that, after having settled on the number of taxicab licenses to be issued, the municipal government auctions those valued "rights" among prospective entrants. This procedure will directly and immediately convert the licenses into private property rights, which, we may also assume, are to be fully marketable. No rent seeking of the basic sort previously discussed will take place.

The government will secure the full values of the contrived scarcity, however, and the presence of rents at the level of the municipal budget suggests that rent seeking may shift to a second level. Potential political entrepreneurs may now seek to enter, not the taxicab industry directly, but the set of political-bureaucratic positions or occupations with access to the receipts of the auction. Both politics and the "civil service" will become differentially productive employments if rents are allowed to remain available to those persons fortunate enough to occupy the rent-access positions.

Let us extend our example further, however, to indicate that yet a third level of rent seeking may emerge. Suppose that government officeholders can expect to secure competitively determined salaries and perquisites. Suppose that there are no rent components present in any of the personal rewards to those who hold positions in government. In this setting, the economic rents that arise because of the contrived scarcity, transferred initially to government via the auction procedure, must be returned to all taxpayer-beneficiaries in the community. Unless, however, these rents are returned or passed through the budget in some nondifferential or random manner, rent-seeking activity at a third level will be aimed at securing differential shares in the total values. Suppose that the taxicab licenses are auctioned and that government officeholders are competitively paid, but that funds are returned to citizens in some inverse relationship to income and/or wealth. Even in such a highly restricted model, rent seeking may take a form of attempts on the part of persons to shift into activities that do not generate the type of income or wealth measurable for purposes of qualifying for receipt of rents.

The taxicab example is useful in illustrating at least three levels where rent seeking can occur once a contrived scarcity is created by governmental action. If the "rights to recover" rents are not distributed equally or randomly among all persons and are not auctioned, prospective entrants will engage in rent seeking through efforts to persuade authorities to grant differentially advantageous treatment. The familiar figure of the Washington lobbyist offers the illustration here. Most of the early work on rent seeking involves analysis of this sort of activity. In a broader sense, however, the second level of rent seeking may even be more important. If the salaries and perquisites of government positions contain elements of economic rent, if salaries and perquisites are higher than those for comparable positions in the private sector, prospective politicians and bureaucrats will waste major resources in attempts to secure the favored posts. Excessive education and training (notably, perhaps, among lawyers who are aiming at political office), excessive spending on political campaigns—these offer rent-seeking examples of this second type. Quite apart from the two primary levels at which rent seeking can take place, activity at the third level involves attempts by persons and groups to secure differentially favorable treatment or to avoid differentially unfavorable treatment, defined, not in terms of particular opportunities, but in terms of treatment by the governmental fiscal process. Faced with a prospect of differentially favorable or differentially unfavorable tax treatment by government, a person or group may (1) engage in lobbying effort; (2) engage directly in politics to secure access to decision-making power; and/or

(3) make plans to shift into or out of the affected activity. Resources may be wasted at all three levels simultaneously, despite the rational motivation to engage in such activity at each stage.

Conclusions

As the introductory examples have suggested, analysis of rent seeking is little more than applied price theory of the traditional variety. Such analysis does, however, turn much of modern economics inside out. The latter tends to commence with the presumed structure of an ordered market, and its analysis tends to be concentrated on spinning out even more elegant and rigorous "proofs" or "theorems" about the idealized model of the competitive process. But let us be honest. How much more do we know about market process than Adam Smith knew that is of practical relevance?

The analysis of rent seeking, as the contributions in this book indicate, shifts attention to interactions and to institutions outside of and beyond the confined competitive market process, while applying essentially the same tools as those applied to interactions within the process. The analysis of rent seeking is, therefore, properly designated as *institutional economics* in a very real sense. The analysis also falls within *public choice,* especially if the latter is defined methodologically as the extension of the basic tools of economics to nonmarket interaction. Indeed, the previously used rubric, "theory of nonmarket decision making," allows rent seeking to be included directly under its umbrella. As many critics, both friendly and unfriendly, have noted, public choice theory and the economic theory of property rights have several affinities. Rent-seeking analysis can readily be incorporated within the property-rights approach, and, as with public choice, the theory of rent seeking can be interpreted as an appropriate extension.

The primary purpose of this book is to collect the most relevant contributions to the analysis of rent seeking and by so doing to call more attention to the opportunities for further inquiry. As the contents of this book suggest, the subject remains new, and opportunities for productive and relevant research seem almost unlimited. The book contains the early bits and pieces of a line of inquiry that can be, should be, and will be extensively expanded. In the process, additional institutional and historical detail will be elaborated;

additional empirical tests will be conducted; additional rigor will characterize the formal analysis. We shall come to know much more about rent seeking. As, when, and if we do, we may hope that some contribution may be
made in shifting public attitudes toward constitutional reform that will reduce rather than continue to expand rent-seeking opportunities in our society.

PART THREE

Public Finance and Democratic Process

The Pure Theory
of Government Finance
A Suggested Approach

I

A framework for the pure theory of government finance may be erected on either of two political foundations, which represent, in turn, two separate and opposing theories of the state. Since neither construction is entirely appropriate when applied to all the problems faced in the fiscal area, the proper methodological procedure seems to be the setting-up of alternate theories.

In the first, or what may be called the "organismic," theory, the state, including all individuals within it, is conceived as a single organic entity. In the second, the state is represented as the sum of its individual members acting in a collective capacity. The individual and the state are fundamentally opposing forces in the latter concept, while in the organic view the state, or general interest, subsumes all individual interests. The theory of government finance based upon the second concept of the state may be called the "individualistic" one.

These two approaches have not been clearly separated or distinguished in the literature of government finance. Some variant of the organismic theory normally has been applied to the public expenditure side, while the individualistic theory has been predominantly employed in considering the distribution of the tax load. Fiscal marginalism has been extended to define the

From *Journal of Political Economy* 57 (December 1949): 496–505. Copyright 1949 by The University of Chicago. All rights reserved. Reprinted by permission of the University of Chicago Press, publisher.

optimum allocation of public expenditures among alternative uses, that is, in the pure theory of budgeting. The allocation of total tax burden among alternative sources, has, on the other hand, traditionally been discussed in terms of the relative tax pressures imposed upon individuals.[1] Such asymmetry, while perhaps appropriate in practical application, does not appear formally complete. It seems desirable to develop the two theories independently at the outset.

II

In the organismic theory the state is considered as a single decision-making unit acting for society as a whole. Presumably, it seeks to maximize some conceptually quantifiable magnitude. A major difficulty is apparent in the determination of what is to be maximized. What is the common denominator to which the alternative goals of the collective entity may be reduced for comparative purposes, analogous to the equally vague, but less elusive, "satisfaction" or "utility" for the individual? A common denominator is necessary as a starting point in order that any one "configuration of the economic system" may be regarded as better or worse than any other, or indifferent.[2] This general end of society may be called "general welfare" or "social utility"; the name is not important.

"Social utility" is a function of many variables. The maximizing process will include the manipulation of many factors which lie outside the scope of fiscal theory. The structure of the whole social organization is itself a property subject to change. Many of the variables are noneconomic; and, even among those which can be classified as economic in nature, a relatively small proportion can be embraced in fiscal theory. The nonfiscal variables, there-

1. There have been, of course, certain elements of each approach present in most competent works. The individual benefits from public expenditures have never been entirely overlooked, nor have the social effects of taxation been completely neglected. The work of Hugh Dalton is representative of a complete organismic approach, with certain qualifications (*Principles of Public Finance*, 9th rev. ed. [London: George Routledge & Sons, 1936]). The theory presented by the Italian school best represents the individualistic approach (cf. Antonio de Viti de Marco, *First Principles of Public Finance*, trans. E. P. Marget [London: Jonathan Cape, 1936]).

2. P. A. Samuelson, *Foundations of Economic Analysis* (Cambridge: Harvard University Press, 1947), 221.

fore, must be accepted as parameters for the smaller system, and "social utility" must be maximized, subject to the constraints imposed. The variables to be determined in the fiscal process fall into two groups—the expenditure variables and the tax variables. The amounts of public expenditure allocated to each use comprise the expenditure variables. The amounts of tax load imposed upon each economic entity or tax source (individuals, business units, estates, etc.) comprise the tax variables. There are as many variables in the fiscal system as there are expenditure outlets and tax sources. Any allocation of the total tax load represents a solution for the whole set of tax variables. Any distribution of public expenditure among competing uses indicates a fixing of values for all the expenditure variables. Included in the setting of these values is the determination of total tax load and total public expenditures.

It is the function of the "fiscal brain" to select the values of these many variables which will maximize social utility. The maximizing process consists of a simultaneous determination of all the variables on both sides. The necessary condition for a maximum is produced when the partial derivatives vanish or when a dollar's tax load upon each economic entity deducts from social utility an amount equivalent to that added by a dollar's expenditure in each line.

It is important to note that the optimum values for the tax variables cannot be determined independently except for given values for the expenditure variables. The allocation of the tax load which will maximize social utility or, in this case, minimize deductions from utility will be different for each separate distribution of total expenditure. Similarly, the distribution of expenditure which will maximize welfare will be a function of the tax variables. The relative additions to social utility provided by the offering of public services to particular groups will be dependent in part upon the relative tax loads imposed.

The principle of taxation which is appropriate in this theoretical framework is that of the Edgeworth-Pigou variety. The relevant criteria of comparison are reductions from social welfare or utility; the "least-aggregate-sacrifice" approach is the correct one. The principle of equimarginal "sacrifice" or, better, "subtraction," if values are given for the expenditure variables, provides an acceptable rule for the apportionment of the total tax burden. For each allocation of public expenditure the satisfaction of this principle will define an apportionment which will minimize the subtraction from social utility. It should be emphasized, however, that subtraction can be used only with reference to a social, not an individual, concept of utility.[3] For each given distribution of public expenditures the necessary condition for the optimum allocation of the tax load is reached when a dollar's tax upon each economic entity deducts an equivalent amount from aggregate social utility. The economic entities for such tax comparisons may or may not be individuals in this analysis.

Symmetrically, given values for the tax variables, an allocation of total public expenditure among alternative uses can be found which will maximize social welfare. This is also given by the application of the economic principle, or here the principle of "equimarginal addition." The necessary condition for the optimum is reached when a dollar of expenditure yields the same return, in addition to social utility, in each line. This allocation is independently determinate only for fixed values of all the tax variables. For each change in the apportionment of the tax load, a new optimum allocation of expenditure must be found.

Little more can be included in the framework of the organismic theory. Vague and general terms, such as "social utility" and "social welfare," are of little use in the discussion of policy problems. The theoretical steps in the maximizing of social utility offer little or no direct guidance to governmental fiscal authorities. As was mentioned earlier, this approach has been utilized largely in the theory of budgeting. Here it can provide a primary frame of reference, within which issues may be discussed, policies formulated, and decisions reached. Even in this limited usage, however, the functional interdependence of the whole fiscal system must not be overlooked.

III

The focus is completely shifted in the individualistic theory. The individual replaces the state as the basic structural unit. The state has its origin in, and

---

3. In this sense the principle of equimarginal sacrifice implies nothing about the ultimate equalization of incomes as a result of its application. This implication arises only when individuals are considered as the basic fiscal entities and when some assumption is made about the identities of individuals as pleasure machines.

depends for its continuance upon, the desires of individuals to fulfil a certain portion of their wants collectively. The state has no ends other than those of its individual members and is not a separate decision-making unit. State decisions are, in the final analysis, the collective decisions of individuals.

The income of the state represents payment made by individuals out of their economic resources in exchange for services provided. In the provision of these services the state is, in most cases, in a perfectly monopolistic position. However, it does not seek to maximize net revenue. Services are offered at cost. The supply curve of public services is an average-cost curve, not a marginal-cost curve. This applies, of course, only to the aggregate of all public services considered in the abstract as some sort of homogeneous magnitude. In no way does it imply that each particular service is "sold" to individuals at the average cost of provision. In the social-service state many services are offered free; others at marginal-cost prices. In very few cases (the particular services provided in return for fees being the major exception) is there much connection between payments made to government by individuals and the special benefits enjoyed. But, when the aggregate of all public services is considered, the attempt is made to cover total cost. In effect, if public services are categorized, the "losses" to the government resulting from the provision of some services must be balanced by "profits" accruing from the provision of others.

The extent and range of public services are determined by the collective willingness of individuals to purchase them. Services will be extended as long as the aggregate benefits are held to exceed the costs.[4] For the total of all public services, aggregate benefits should approximately equal total costs in terms of sacrificed alternatives. Ideally, the fiscal process represents a *quid pro quo* transaction between the government and all individuals collectively considered.[5] The benefit principle must be applicable in this sense.

Each individual is subjected to some fiscal pressure; his economic resources are reduced by the amount of tax that he bears. His real income is increased by the benefits that he receives from government services. The al-

---

4. Cf. Edward D. Allen and O. H. Brownlee, *Economics of Public Finance* (New York: Prentice-Hall Book Co., 1947), 19.

5. The "pure" theory should be formulated on the assumption of stability in the economic system and thus balance between the two sides of the fiscal account. "Functional" finance precepts can be fitted into the framework at a second theoretical level.

location of total tax load among individuals must be combined with the distribution of benefits from publicly provided services in any complete theoretical framework. However, in this approach the imputation of specific benefits to individuals has been almost entirely glossed over in the orthodox literature. Overwhelming attention has been devoted to the allocation of the tax burden.

The practical omission of the benefit side can be attributed in part to the erroneous foundations of the benefit theory of taxation. In the legitimate rejection of the benefit principle as the universal norm for the distribution of the tax burden, too much was thrown out. This principle, widely accepted in the seventeenth and eighteenth centuries[6] and reintroduced in a more sophisticated form in the 1880's,[7] is based upon the premise that there should exist a *quid pro quo* fiscal relationship between the individual and government. The principle has been overthrown for two basic reasons. First, there appears no precise manner of imputing shares of the aggregate common benefit from public services to specific individuals. A significant portion of public funds is expended for the "general welfare," not to benefit particular persons or groups. Second, it is recognized that the underlying *quid pro quo* ideal is not at all acceptable in the modern state.[8]

But these two basic objections to the benefit principle are of fundamentally different natures. The first is a technical or an administrative difficulty, which prevents the principle from having direct applicability to policy. The second rests upon a rejection of the ethical premise that there should be an individual *quid pro quo*. If we accept the *quid pro quo* ideal, the benefit principle is correct in the abstract; and the problem of individual imputation of benefits is a technical, not a theoretical, problem. De Viti de Marco recognized this and therefore accepted as a working hypothesis the return of benefits roughly in proportion to incomes. Thus, adopting the ethical standard of the benefit principle, he justified a system of proportional taxation. In such a theoretical framework the apportionment of the tax load is directly depen-

6. For an excellent short history of the early benefit theories see Erik Lindahl, *Die Gerechtigkeit der Besteuerung* (Lund: Gleerupska Universitets-Bokhandeln, 1919), 118 ff.

7. In the works of Pantaleoni, Sax, and de Viti de Marco.

8. Wagner clearly pointed out that, once the government began to provide social services, the benefit theory became completely inapplicable (Adolph Wagner, *Finanzwissenschaft* [Leipzig: C. F. Winter, 1890], 2:431–42).

dent upon the benefit hypothesis formulated. If benefits were assumed to accrue equally per head, de Viti de Marco would have held a system of poll taxation to be appropriate.[9]

The rejection of the benefit theory of taxation should rest not upon the difficulty of individual isolation of specific benefits but upon the unacceptability of the ethical ideal of the individual *quid pro quo*. Once this commutative fiscal relationship of the individual with government is thrown out as the norm, is there any value to be gained from attempts at surmounting the technical problem of individual-benefit imputation? In orthodox fiscal theory the implied answer to this question has been "No," with the result that benefit considerations have been seriously neglected. The whole expenditure side of the fiscal account has been given little attention. In the individualistic approach, both the total amount of public expenditure and its allocation among uses have been assumed to be fixed outside the pale of fiscal theory.

Fiscal analysis has proceeded as if all taxes were net subtractions from social income, never to be returned. J. B. Say's dictum that "the value paid to government by the taxpayer is given without equivalent or return"[10] has been implicitly accepted, although lip service has been paid to its inherent fallacy. It is evident that such a limitation leaves the body of theory incomplete and inadequate. If benefits from public services accrue to individuals as a group (and this is impossible to deny), it follows that specific benefits are received by particular individuals, regardless of the technical difficulty of dividing the common benefit among them. Aggregate benefits must be in the nature of a quantitative magnitude and thus subject to conceptual divisibility. Benefits simply cannot be forgotten. Wicksell very clearly pointed out that the procedure of leaving out the benefit side amounts to concluding that each individual actually gets no benefit whatsoever from the government services provided him.[11] And, since the addition of any number of zeroes yields a zero

9. Thus Graham says: "Since the value of most governmental services to the individual members of a community cannot be accurately assessed, nor can one take or leave them as he will, it could with some reason be contended that the ideal principle of allocation of the burden of taxation is neither progression nor proportionality but uniformity, that is, that all members of the community should pay the same amount" (Frank D. Graham, *Social Goals and Economic Institutions* [Princeton: Princeton University Press, 1942], 234).

10. *A Treatise on Political Economy,* trans. C. R. Prinsep (Philadelphia: J. B. Lippincott & Co., 1855), 413.

11. Knut Wicksell, *Finanztheoretische Untersuchungen* (Jena: Gustav Fischer, 1896), 82.

result, the aggregate benefit must also be zero if such an omissive assumption is made.[12] On this basis no public expenditure is theoretically justified. Furthermore, if no individuals in the social unit receive any benefit, it is apparent that no funds will be granted for the support of government. No tax bills could ever be passed by an elected representative assembly.

Only if individual shares of the aggregate benefit from public services are held to be roughly equal can the concentration of analysis on the allocation of tax burden alone be theoretically justified. It seems likely that this is the assumption made by some writers.[13] If phrases such as "chargeable against the whole community"[14] and "throughout the population"[15] can be interpreted as containing the implication that the benefits from most public services are shared equally among all citizens, then the approach has been internally consistent. If individual shares in the common benefit are considered equivalent, the real problems in fiscal theory are limited to the tax side, since equals would cancel equals when benefits are included in comparing the fiscal positions of individuals.

This necessary condition for the practical omission of benefit considerations should be clearly stated and its applicability empirically tested in so far as is possible. The dependence of the validity of the orthodox approach upon this rather narrow assumption was recognized by Kaizl and by de Viti de Marco.[16] But a general theoretical framework should not be so limited, even if this condition is made explicit.

---

12. Ibid.: "Ist jener Nutzen für die einzelnen Mitglieder der Gesamtheit gleich Null, so wird auch der Gesamtnutzen nicht von Null verschieden sein können."

13. For example, compare the following statements by J. S. Mill and Bastable:

"If a person or class of persons receives so small a share of the benefit as makes it necessary to raise the question, there is something else than taxation which is amiss, and the thing to be done is to remedy the defect, instead of recognizing it and making it a ground for demanding less taxes" (J. S. Mill, *Principles of Political Economy* [Boston: C. Little & James Brown, 1848], 2:354).

"But from the difficulty of discrimination it seems better to adhere to the general rule of distributing taxation without direct reference to the results of expenditure on different classes. Injustices of this kind ought to be corrected not by the redistribution of taxation but by alterations of outlay" (C. F. Bastable, *Public Finance*, 2d ed. [London: Macmillan & Co., 1895], 312).

14. Henry C. Simons, *Personal Income Taxation* (Chicago: University of Chicago Press, 1938), 31.

15. Allen and Brownlee, *Economics*, 192.

16. ". . . das fundamentale Corollar der heutigen Auffassung der Steuergerechtigkeit

The difficult problem of individual-benefit imputation must be squarely faced. It is impossible to speak of the "burden of taxation" without considering, at the same time, the benefits from expenditure made out of such taxation.[17] Even the setting-up of untested explicit hypotheses concerning benefit accrual is preferable to omission altogether.[18] The most realistic hypothesis might well be that of equal per head sharing,[19] but alternative ones should be considered and tested if possible.

The final economic position of the individual after his relationship with the "fisc" can be expressed in the form of a balance between the two sides of the fiscal account. (If we accept the *quid pro quo* premise, this balance will always be zero.) This balance can be called the "fiscal residuum."[20] If an individual's tax burden exceeds the value of benefits received from government services, he will have a positive residuum. He will pay a net tax. If the value of the share of public benefits which he enjoys exceeds the value of the contributions which he makes to government, the residuum will be negative. The individual will receive a net benefit. Only by a comparison of the residuums of individuals can the total effects of a fiscal system be analyzed and evaluated. Tax-burden comparisons alone are likely to yield quite different and perhaps misleading conclusions.[21]

... dass nicht nur die Last der Steuer gerecht vertheilt werde, sondern dass auch die Vortheile und Emolumente der öffentlichen Institutionen gleich vertheilt werden, dass sie Allen gleich zugänglich seien" (Kaizl, *Finanzwissenschaft*, 2:200, cited by Lindahl, *Die Gerechtigkeit*, 133).

"Thus one may abstract from the service of providing public security, if one assumes, and if the assumption corresponds to the facts, that the amount of security provided is equal for all productive enterprises that exchange their products. Thus, it is as if one were to cancel a common term in two terms of an equation" (de Viti de Marco, *First Principles*, 52).

17. Tibor Barna, *Redistribution of Income through Public Finance in 1937* (London: Oxford University Press, 1945), 3.

18. Ibid.

19. The use of this hypothesis has been found to yield important results in some areas. I have applied this to the theory of intergovernmental fiscal adjustment in a federal state and have been able to work out a determinate system of transfers without reference to particular tax burdens or particular service standards.

For another example of application to a similar problem see J. R. and U. K. Hicks, *Standards of Local Expenditure* (London: Cambridge University Press, 1943), 3.

20. The concept of a fiscal balance or residuum was utilized by Wicksell in a different sense (*Finanztheoretische*, 81).

21. The comparative study of the burdens of state and local taxes in New York and

This approach enables a general classification of fiscal systems to be made, comprising three major groups. First, those systems which tend to increase the inequality in the distribution of real income among individuals can be classified as "aggravative."[22] This type of system would be indicated if low-income individuals showed positive residuums, i.e., taxes in excess of benefits, while the high-income receivers showed negative residuums. Some systems of the sixteenth and seventeenth centuries which collected revenues from large elements of the population in the main for the support of the royal household and the nobility would perhaps be characteristic.

Second, those fiscal systems which tend to return to all individuals approximately the equivalent of their contributions and thus to have no net effect on the prevailing distribution of real income can be classified as "status quo" systems. This type would be indicated if a calculation of the fiscal residuums for individuals in all income brackets yielded roughly zero results. This type is perhaps best represented in the fiscal systems of the early nineteenth century, when a large share of revenue was collected from levies on property and a major portion was expended in the provision of protection, internal and external.

Third, those fiscal systems which tend to redress the prevailing distribution of real income toward more equality can be classified as "equalitarian" or "redistributive." If people in the low-income groups receive more in benefits than they pay in taxes and the upper-income groups contribute more than they receive in benefits, this type of system is indicated. This is, of course, the type which is characteristic of the modern state. A large share of revenue is derived from the proceeds of progressive income taxes, and a ma-

---

Illinois for 1936, published by the Twentieth Century Fund in *Studies in Current Tax Problems* (New York, 1937), can be used as an example. On the basis of tax-load comparisons alone, the tax load was found to be heavier in New York than in Illinois on eight out of the ten hypothetical families studied (p. 34).

By making the assumption of benefit accrual equally per head, and including New York and Illinois state and local expenditures in addition to the computed tax-load figures, it was found that the results were significantly changed. Where only two New York families out of ten were found to be in advantageous positions when tax burdens alone were considered, seven New York families became favored in fiscal treatment when the benefit side was included.

22. The use of the word "aggravative" here, of course, indicates the egalitarian "bias" of the writer.

jor portion of expenditures in peacetime is devoted to the provision of social services.

As was stated earlier, regardless of the kind of fiscal system, there should exist the *quid pro quo* relationship between government and all individuals taken together. This is represented by a balancing of the net taxes paid by certain individuals against the net benefits received by others in the first and third classifications. Only in the second type of system does the collective equalization of benefits and taxes imply that each individual receives in benefits the approximate equivalent of contribution made.

This simple classification represents nothing new.[23] It seems essential, however, that it be employed as the primary frame of reference within which more specific problems may be placed. One should bear in mind that the classification refers to fiscal systems, not to tax systems. Tax systems have been traditionally classified as regressive, proportional, and progressive, based upon the ratio of tax burden to income at different income levels. These terms are useful in describing the nature of a tax system, but they do not describe the fiscal system, as would appear to be the case in ordinary usage.

Progressive taxation has been justified because it leads to a more equal distribution of income among individuals. Standing alone, the statement that progressive taxation does redistribute real income is not true. It can be true only on the basis of certain assumptions about the other half of the fiscal system. If individual shares in the common benefit from public expenditures are all equal or approximately so, then progressive taxation will lead to a more equal distribution. But so will proportional taxation on the same basis.[24] Without considering the imputation of individual benefits, all that may be stated categorically is that progressive taxation will produce a more equal distribution of income than would proportional or regressive taxation. One cannot say that it will produce a redistribution; it may or may not.[25]

---

23. Cf. W. J. Shultz and C. L. Harriss, *American Public Finance*, 5th ed. (New York: Prentice-Hall Book Co., 1949), 104.

24. The statement that progressive taxation will redistribute incomes but that proportional taxation will not implies that benefits are returned to individuals in proportion to incomes and wealth.

25. The emphasis upon the redistribution effects of the tax side alone is indicated in

If a major share of governmental expenditures were allocated to provide protection to the property rights of the wealthy classes, then even a progressive tax system might not prevent the fiscal system from increasing real income inequality. On the other hand, if benefits were wholly in the nature of social services, poor relief, unemployment compensation, etc., then a *regressive* tax system might well be a part of a *redistributive* fiscal system.[26] Conversely, public expenditures made for the benefit of low-income groups may be financed by taxes on those same or even lower-income groups.[27] Certainly, if a significant tax increase or change in the structure of the tax system of any kind is proposed, the ultimate manner in which the proceeds are to be expended should, in part, determine the nature of the change. The same amount of redistribution may be as well accomplished by the levy of a sales tax to provide expanded social services as by an increase in the higher-bracket income-tax rates to finance additional defense expenditure. Since redistribution is only one goal of responsible social policy in the modern state, fiscal policy should reflect such possible alternatives.

The ratio of tax burden to income at various income levels should be separated from any underlying ideas concerning final distributive effects. Owing to the connotation which has caused them to be so sharply categorized with such distributive implications, perhaps it would be better if the terms "regression," "proportion," and "progression" were discarded.

The theoretical framework in the individualistic approach does not include the specification of a single fiscal system to be adopted by the society.

---

the following quotation for the *Annual Economic Report* submitted to the President by the Council of Economic Advisers in January, 1949: "The federal personal income tax has reduced somewhat the concentration of income. In 1947, for example, the lowest three-fifths of families received 29 per cent of total money income before tax compared to 31 per cent after tax, while the share of the upper one-fifth was reduced by taxes from 48 to 46" (reprinted in *United States News and World Report,* January 14, 1949, 72).

See also R. A. Musgrave and Tun Thin, "Income Tax Progression, 1929–48," *Journal of Political Economy* 56 (1948): 498–514.

26. In 1947 a state-wide general sales tax was imposed in Tennessee, with most of the proceeds earmarked for expenditure in the provision of educational services. It can plausibly be argued that the collection of the tax and the expenditure of the proceeds taken together are redistributive.

27. The British case seems applicable here. Should not the "redistributive" effects of the food subsidies be carefully scrutinized, considering the enormous levies on tobacco and liquor?

The ends to be served by the fiscal system are determined by political decisions. The framework does, however, enable the fiscal specialist to indicate the alternate distributions of tax burdens and public expenditures which will yield the desired results. If, for example, the society desires a fiscal system which will not affect the prevailing distribution of real incomes, any number of fiscal structures, tax-burden and expenditure allocations, can be formulated which will approximate it. Further, if this status quo ideal, plus an allocation of public expenditures, is given, the single most appropriate tax structure can be outlined.

A similar approach is suggested for other than status quo norms. The redress of the prevailing income distribution toward greater equality has been accepted as one of the fundamental purposes of the fiscal system in the modern state. The fiscal scientist can provide policy-makers with practical guides to action in several ways. If the desired degree of redistribution is known, the alternate pairs of tax-burden and public-expenditure allocations which will yield this result can be indicated. If this, plus the existing public-expenditure pattern, is known, it is possible to set up the tax system, assuming in this case that attainment is possible under the given conditions. On the other side, given the degree of redistribution and the apportionment of the tax load, the expenditure pattern can be established.

Society, however, does not normally make concrete decisions concerning the amount of redistribution desired. Rather, it determines an allocation of expenditures among uses and a distribution of the tax load which will, when combined, cause the fiscal system to be redistributive. The role of the fiscal scientist qua scientist in this situation is clear. With these properties he can determine roughly the amount of redistribution of real incomes actually accomplished through the fiscal process.[28] He is then able to indicate alternative tax and expenditure allocations which would yield approximately equivalent redistribution results, some of which might result in significantly different effects upon the economy. It is perhaps in the area of estimating the amount of redistribution carried out by the fiscal system that the most productive empirical work in the whole field of government finance can now be carried on. The traditional difficulty encountered in the attempt to impute specific shares of the benefits from public services to individuals, even upon

---

28. This is the approach taken in the path-breaking work of Barna (*Redistribution*).

the recognition of the communal nature of the aggregate benefit, should not be deterrent. It will not be, once it is fully comprehended that the benefit side cannot be left out and any sort of generalized theoretical framework set up. It must be recognized that the omission yields results equivalent to those based upon even more arbitrary assumptions than the heroic ones admittedly required concerning the incidence of public expenditures. With the expansion of government activity toward the provision of social services, and services to particular economic or social groups, the problem should present less of a dilemma. For example, the individual benefits from farm price supports can be more readily estimated than those from defense expenditures.

IV

In both the organismic and the individualistic approaches to fiscal theory, the paramount need is that the interdependence of the two sides of the fiscal process be clearly understood. Both approaches require parallel consideration to be given to the determination of the expenditure allocation and the apportionment of tax burden. In neither theory can either side be analyzed in isolation.

The organismic framework gives a much more complete normative behavior pattern for the fiscal authority. Since the government is the basic entity, the fiscal theory reduces to a statement of an applied maximization problem. The major obstacles lie in the attempts at translation of the theoretical guides to action into a realistic approach to practical policy. It becomes extremely arduous, if not impossible, to fill in the theoretical framework with empirical content.

In the individualistic approach the government represents only the collective will of individuals and cannot be considered the originator of action in an abstract sense. The fisc cannot be assumed to maximize anything. The fiscal system exists as one channel through which certain collective desires may be accomplished. The content of theory becomes the setting-up of a structural framework to enable the results of policies to be evaluated.

Taxation in Fiscal Exchange

Methodologically, the fiscal exchange paradigm is superior to its alternatives. This is demonstrated by the use of a simplified example. Difficulties arise when political processes force departures from basic exchange. Traditional equity norms can be viewed as constitutional protections against undue fiscal exploitation. In a broader perspective, the exchange paradigm remains applicable at the constitutional level. There are major philosophical advantages in remaining within the constitutional-contractarian framework.

1. Introduction

In his paper, "Reflections on Tax Reform," delivered as the C. Harry Kahn Memorial Lecture at Rutgers in 1972, Professor R. A. Musgrave acknowledged that the weakest part of the Simons tradition in tax reform policy discussion is its neglect of the expenditure-benefit side of the fiscal account. To assign a predominant role to equity criteria in assessing alternative tax instruments independently amounts to an implicit assumption that taxation represents a net withdrawal of resources from the social economy, a setting which Luigi Einaudi labeled as that of the "imposta grandine," literally the "tax as hailstorm." Much the same criticism can be levied against the independent analysis of alternative taxes in terms of their comparative efficiency properties, whether in the older excess-burden form or in the modern and more sophisticated optimal taxation framework.

From *Journal of Public Economics* 6 (1976): 17–29. Copyright 1976. Reprinted with permission from Elsevier Science.

I am indebted to my colleagues Gordon Tullock and Richard Wagner for helpful comments.

Even within their acknowledged normative realms of discourse, these conceptions of taxation are seriously incomplete. Even if the objective is limited to advising the social decision-maker, whomever this might be, on the implications of a consistent application of either equity or efficiency norms, the two-sidedness of the fiscal account must be incorporated into the discussion. If a more positive approach is taken, if the objective is that of explaining the emergence of tax institutions in a political setting that is, itself, preferred in an explicitly normative sense, an exchange model becomes a necessary starting point for meaningful analysis. Those who pay taxes and those who receive benefits from services financed by these taxes are members of the same political community; all persons may simultaneously be taxpayers and public-goods beneficiaries.

My purpose in this paper is to examine the implications of applying the fiscal exchange paradigm. I shall demonstrate that only this paradigm offers a fully consistent approach to taxation, and one that is sufficiently flexible to allow both equity and efficiency norms to be incorporated readily into the explanatory framework if and as these are appropriate. To the extent that the political decision-making structure remains "democratic," in any legitimate rendering of this term, only the exchange paradigm offers prospects for the derivation of refutable hypotheses about both the initial selection and the stability of tax instruments. In this treatment, I shall not advance the discussion much beyond that of Wicksell.[1] But modern public finance theory would indeed make great strides if the Wicksellian level of analysis and understanding could finally be achieved.

In section 2, I shall construct a highly simplified example that is deliberately designed for the simple application of both the equity and efficiency norms for taxation, conceived in the orthodox sense. These norms take on a different cast when an exchange setting is imposed. In section 3, I shall attempt partially to bridge the awesome gap between the idealized results of abstract analytical models and the real world. Section 4 is devoted to a discussion of the fiscal transfer process, an apparent aspect of fiscal reality that seems impossible to bring within the exchange conception under orthodox assumptions. In section 5 these assumptions are modified, and the "fiscal constitution" is distinguished from period-to-period budgetary changes. Sec-

---

1. K. Wicksell, *Finanztheoretische Untersuchungen* (Jena: Gustav Fischer, 1896).

tion 6 discusses some of the implications of the normative framework for prevailing public attitudes toward political process.

2. Simplified Illustration

Consider the simplest possible setting in which two persons (families), *A* and *B*, live side by side in a community. By all objectively measurable standards, *A* and *B* are identical; both receive the same incomes; both hold the same claims to assets. Further, revealed information about their potential behavior suggests that *A* and *B* react similarly to the unilateral imposition of taxes, regardless of the form these might take.

The tax-policy adviser to the government who has been reared on the familiar slogans will dust off the precepts of horizontal equity, equal treatment for equals, and he will recommend that *A* and *B* be taxed alike. Such equality in tax treatment is imbedded in American constitutional law and, considered in isolation, it seems to reflect a plausible extension of the basic norm of legal equality. To introduce differences in tax liability here would seem to be arbitrarily discriminatory. Regardless of revenue requirements, therefore, *A* and *B* would seem to qualify for equal tax treatment, whether the tax be levied on a per-head, income, consumption, wealth, or some other basis.

Suppose, now, that the government asks an economist to advise it concerning the "optimal" means of imposing fiscal charges on *A* and *B*. This expert would initially suggest resort to lump-sum levies, and if he introduces a welfare function that assigns an equal "social marginal utility" of income to each person in identical observable economic circumstances, he would suggest that these lump-sum charges be imposed in equal amounts.

In this grossly simplified example, the orthodox equity criterion and the optimal taxation criterion coincide, and the equal treatment of *A* and *B* seems to raise little objection, regardless of the revenue needs of the community. But this last proviso, in itself, suggests that the fiscal system remains open in a choice-making context. Neither criterion, as applied here, allows us to say anything at all about the amount of total revenue to be raised, about the quantity of public goods to be provided. This was noted by Wicksell, and this was the basis for his argument that the benefits side must be brought into account in any meaningful discussion of tax-burden distribution.

In our example, we were careful not to assume that *A* and *B* are identical in *all* respects. Suppose, now, that despite the range of identical characteristics, *A* and *B* are distinctly different in their demands for public goods and services, with *A* placing a higher evaluation on such services over all of the relevant levels of possible provision. For illustration, think of a single public service, police protection, and assume that *A* and *B* assess the subjective probabilities of criminal damage to life and property differently, despite the equality of objective economic circumstances.

If this difference in preferences should exist for a single privately-marketed good or service, it would be reflected in differing quantities purchased, with *A* and *B* separately adjusting quantities to correspond to their relative evaluations. For the public service, however, such individual quantity adjustment is not possible. Either because of the technology inherent in the service itself (jointness efficiency and/or nonexcludability) or because the institutional setting requires uniformity of provision, both persons will tend to receive the same quantity of the service.

Assume that, despite the postulated differences in evaluation of the public service, taxes are imposed in accordance with the equity and/or optimal taxation criterion outlined above; hence *A* and *B* are subjected to equal taxes, imposed in a lump-sum fashion. We may discuss this situation under two distinct models for budgetary decision-making. In the first, which we can call the planning model, we assume that decisions on the size of the budget, and hence on total tax revenues, are made by an external chooser who is able omnisciently to read individual preference functions. In the second, or public choice model, we assume that budgetary outcomes emerge from the interactions of citizens themselves, operating under some designated decision rules.

2.1. Planning model

If the planner can read individual preference functions, he can simply set the budgetary level so as to satisfy the necessary Samuelson conditions for public-goods efficiency, the equality of summed marginal evaluations with marginal cost of production.[2] The prior selection of a specific tax-sharing

---

2. I assume that the planner is "individualistic" in the sense that he incorporates individuals' own utilities in his decisions, rather than his own.

scheme, in our example one that produces equal tax shares, has the effect of designating a "social welfare function" or, more correctly, that of specifying a unique distribution of the post-tax, post-benefit fiscal surplus among persons. Under the conditions we have postulated, with equal taxation, both inframarginally and marginally, and with differing marginal evaluations, both persons, *A* and *B*, are forced out of "individual equilibrium" at the efficient budget level, but there would be no mutuality of gain to be secured from any change. The solution would, therefore, lie on the Pareto optimality surface.

Let us now suppose that the planner no longer feels constrained to impose equal taxes on *A* and *B*, and that he shifts the tax structure so as to make it conform more closely with public-goods preferences, simultaneously shifting, if and as required, the size of the budget to maintain the satisfaction of the Samuelson marginal condition. He imposes the Lindahl solution, which insures that individual marginal evaluations correspond precisely to individual tax-prices. Behaviorally, he now observes that both *A* and *B* agree on the budgetary level chosen; both persons are in "individual equilibrium."

The post-tax, post-benefit distribution of realizable fiscal surplus is different from that attained under the regime of equal tax shares, and the quantity of public goods may be different. It is necessary to keep in mind the precise definition of the Lindahl solution. In a behaviorally relevant sense, "taxes" have been replaced by "prices." The Lindahl solution converts the public-goods exchange into its closest possible equivalence to private-goods exchange. Individuals are confronted by "prices" (which differ from one person to another), and they are expected to "choose" preferred quantities in a manner that is psychologically equivalent to ordinary market behavior. The "price" of the public good (or public-goods bundle) that an individual faces is invariant with respect to his own behavior. There is no way that a person can modify the "price" with which he is confronted. In this sense the Lindahl price is identical to a lump-sum tax per unit of the public good.[3]

The genuinely omniscient planner could, of course, impose any indicated fiscal charges as lump-sum levies, whether he chooses to do so equally per head or as Lindahl-related to evaluations on the public good. If, for purposes of analysis, we assume lump-sum taxes are infeasible, even in this planning

---

3. For further discussion, see D. B. Johnson and M. V. Pauly, "Excess Burden and the Voluntary Theory of Public Finance," *Economica* 36 (1969): 269–76.

model, the required revenues, in either case, may be raised through the use of some standard tax base. Any departure from lump-sum taxes will necessarily introduce "inefficiency," when measured against some idealized criterion. However, given this assumed institutional constraint, either solution qualifies as efficient or optimal.

The shift from the regime of equal tax shares to the regime of Lindahl prices may be interpreted simply as the replacement of one "social welfare function" by another, both of which are, in one sense, "individualistic." A normative argument for the shift toward the Lindahl solution may be based on the presumption that individual utility is influenced by public as well as by private goods and that differences in evaluations placed on public goods are relevant in determining relative tax shares. This suggests that one of the two central attributes of a fiscal-exchange model may be incorporated without difficulty into a nondemocratic decision setting. The two-sidedness of the fiscal account (taxes and benefits) may be fully embodied in the "social welfare function" that informs the planner's decisions. There is no requirement that externally-derived norms for tax-sharing be defined independently of predicted or postulated distributions of spending benefits.

2.2. THE PUBLIC CHOICE MODEL

The second attribute of fiscal exchange cannot be accommodated in the nondemocratic setting, that which accentuates the voluntary nature of exchange itself. What if no planner exists, and even if one could be invented or imported, would we accept such an implied delegation of decision-making authority? The fiscal exchange approach is derived from Wicksell, who quite explicitly rejected the planning model, even as an instrument for analyzing fiscal alternatives. It is clearly wasteful to devote intellectual resources in proffering advice to a nonexistent decision-maker. No "social welfare function" exists independently of the mutual adjustment process itself. Regardless of how these may be defined, "equity" and "efficiency" will characterize observed results only as they are embodied in the choices made by individual participants.

For such participants, taxes are necessarily treated as "prices," as payments that are required for the financing of jointly-consumed goods and services provided through governments. If participants make no linkage between the tax and benefit sides of the account, taxes would simply never be observed. In this decision setting, it becomes methodologically absurd to lay down norms for tax-sharing independently from the distribution of benefits.

Let us return to the two-person example and apply a Wicksellian or public choice analysis. As before, we postulate that A and B are identical in all objective economic circumstances, but that they differ in their evaluations of the single public service that is under consideration. Through some Wicksell-Lindahl type of bargaining process, in which marginal adjustments in tax-prices as well as in public-service quantities take place, gains-from-trade will tend to be eliminated and a position reached that will satisfy the requirements for Pareto optimality. At this "trading equilibrium," individual marginal tax-prices will equal individual marginal evaluations, a set of equalities which, in turn, insures the satisfaction of the aggregative condition which requires summed marginal evaluations to equal marginal cost. There is nothing in this model of decision-making, however, which allows us to specify the distribution of total tax shares.[4] Any one of a possible subinfinity of distributions of the total fiscal surplus may be achieved in an unrestricted bargaining adjustment, bounded only by the constraint that each party must secure net benefits from public-goods provision, or, in the limit, must undergo no net loss. As the distribution of fiscal surplus changes, income effect feedbacks may, of course, modify somewhat the quantity of public good or service, the budgetary size, that will be Pareto optimal.

Because the distribution of total tax shares may vary widely over inframarginal ranges, one possible outcome of a Wicksellian process is that A and B, in our example, pay equal total tax bills, despite the differences in marginal tax-prices that are required in order that the bargaining process converge toward the Pareto optimality frontier. To say that this outcome *may* emerge as one from among many possible outcomes of the adjustment process, however, does not imply that such a specific outcome may be "plugged in" as a constraint at the outset, under the expectation that the Pareto frontier will tend to be achieved. To show this, suppose that A and B are now constrained in their bargaining behavior by the requirement that, at any pos-

---

4. If Lindahl tax-prices are interpreted to require the uniformity of marginal tax-price over varying quantities to each person, the bargaining adjustment need not converge toward the Pareto frontier.

sible budgetary level, total tax shares must be equal. Since the quantity of the public service to be selected is not known, but must instead emerge from the mutual adjustment itself, this requirement amounts to saying that tax shares must be equal for any possible budget size. This, in its turn, is equivalent to setting marginal tax-prices to each person at one-half of marginal cost. Because individual evaluations differ, the bargaining adjustments in this decision setting may stop short of capturing the full gains-from-trade, of attaining the efficiency frontier.

To the extent that the Wicksellian adjustment process reaches an equilibrium, which would be indicated by an end of efforts to make further bargains, this equilibrium is clearly Pareto optimal. From this it follows that there would be no rearrangement of tax shares which could command unanimous consent, even when the possibility of making the payments is allowed. The Wicksellian model requires that potential taxpayers reveal, through their behavior, evaluations on the public good or service, even when the strategic motivations for misrepresentation of these evaluations are fully acknowledged. In the fiscal exchange paradigm, the necessary condition for efficiency is present when marginal tax-prices equal marginal evaluations, but this condition tells us nothing at all about the division of total tax shares.

3. Toward Fiscal Reality

I have deliberately employed the simplified two-person example because it presents the exchange paradigm in its most favorable and persuasive setting. As we move away from such grossly simplified constructions, however, and as we try to incorporate empirical observations into our analysis, the advantages of adopting the fiscal-exchange perspective seem less apparent. A possible role for using equity and/or optimal taxation norms in shaping tax structure independently of the expenditure side may emerge, even within a democratic decision model.

The political unit contains many persons, many potential voters-taxpayers-beneficiaries, and fiscal decisions are made through a very complex political process which involves parties, pressure groups, political entrepreneurs, periodic but sometimes infrequent elections, legislative assemblies operating under complicated rules and with ordered committee structures, and bureaucratic hierarchies. The bridge between taxes paid and benefits received, which seems direct in the small-number illustration, may all but disappear in the calculus of the citizen. If taxpayers do not, in fact, make any connection between tax payments and benefits enjoyed, there seems to be a rationale for introducing independent norms. As Wicksell implied, however, the presence of any semblance of democratic decision-making requires that, in some ultimate sense, citizens do construct the bridge. Legislatures are observed to approve the imposition of taxes, however reluctantly, something which could not take place if voting constituencies sensed no return of public service benefits.

In the strict Wicksellian framework, however, decisions are made by general contractual agreement among all citizens, as illustrated in our two-person example above. In political reality, the democratic process rarely requires general agreement, even at the level of the legislative assembly. Less-than-unanimity rules are observed empirically operative in the so-called democratic structures. This departure from the pure exchange paradigm is perhaps more serious than the failure of the individual citizen to construct the bridge between the two sides of the fiscal account. In a real sense, the absence of a unanimity rule implies that, for members of some groups, there need be no connection at all between taxes paid and benefits received. Consider a political community in which two coalitions exist, J and K, with each being represented proportionately in the legislative assembly. J is the majority coalition; K is the minority. If the members of J can succeed in imposing all taxes on members of K, while, at the same time, securing for themselves all of the benefits from public services provided through government, there is no fiscal exchange. A member of the majority coalition can secure benefits without paying taxes, and a member of the minority must pay taxes without reckoning on any return of benefits.

Once this aspect of political reality is acknowledged, the equity norm for the distribution of tax burdens can be viewed as a constitutional standard designed to prevent the exploitation of minorities through the fiscal process. Under almost any version of the equity norm, taxes should be levied generally on all members of the political community, or on some basis that is considered to be nondiscriminatory. If taxes are levied generally on all persons, there are limits to the degree of fiscal exploitation, even if the majority coalition secures all of the benefits from public spending. The political entrepreneurs representing the majority will extend the size of the budget only to the point where marginal benefits to the majority are estimated to equal marginal taxes on the majority, and not to the point at which the majority reaches satiation with respect to public-goods provision.

In this perspective, there is no basis for the traditional application of the equity precepts to the tax side alone. The extension of equity norms to public spending, to the distribution of benefits among persons, can even further limit the degree of exploitation that the fiscal process generates. If taxes are imposed only in accordance with general standards, and if public spending is limited to goods that guarantee general benefits to all persons and groups, the power of the majority coalition to secure distributional gains at the expense of the minority may be confined within relatively narrow limits. Differences in evaluations placed on the public goods contained in the budgetary bundle may of course exist, and the majority may be able to insure that its own preferences are more fully reflected in the budgetary mix and levels chosen than are those of the minority. As the earlier two-person example suggested, incorporation of the equity norms into the fiscal structure may prevent the attainment of the Pareto frontier in many cases. But this degree of possible inefficiency may be relatively small when compared with the potentiality for fiscal exploitation that departures from the unanimity rule for decision-making might generate absent such constraints.

If, in fact, there should exist some reasonably close correspondence or relationship between the individual evaluations for public goods and the general bases for taxation which consistent application of the equity norm might suggest, there might seem to be relatively little conflict between the idealized Wicksellian exchange results and that which democratic process constrained by equity precepts would generate. If, in fact, income or wealth, properly measured, should prove to be a good surrogate for relative evaluations of public goods, the general taxation of personal income and/or wealth might seem to be both tolerably equitable and tolerably efficient in the Wicksellian fiscal exchange sense.

The practical achievement of this possible result depends critically, however, on the presumed absence of significant differences in behavioral responses. In reality, the ideally-efficient lump-sum taxes are infeasible, and tax liabilities are necessarily related to a base that is subject to some control by taxpayers. This ability to modify the base for tax liability through changing behavior need not introduce a significant problem if all persons are roughly similar in response patterns. Pre-adjustment income may provide a reasonable proxy for public-goods evaluation or demand, and relative tax-prices need not change greatly because of the necessary computation of tax liabilities on the basis of post-adjustment incomes. If, however, individuals should differ significantly in their adjustments to the tax, relative tax-prices in the post-adjustment setting may differ sharply from those anticipated in the pre-adjustment or planning stage of decision-making. Persons whose tastes and opportunities allow them readily to shift away from the base for taxation, for example measured money income, and toward nontaxable substitutes, for example leisure, are able to secure differential benefits. In this setting, the tax-rate structure applied to post-adjustment incomes that would be required to reflect, even if roughly, a possible outcome of a Wicksellian bargaining process might look much different from the tax-rate structure that might be selected on the grounds of orthodox equity norms. Even here some rapprochement is possible through appropriate redefinitions of the tax base, of "income," in the direction of greater generality.

4. The Fiscal Transfer Process

The reluctance of many tax-reform advocates to accept the exchange paradigm may be based on their unwillingness to abandon the explicit, normative argument supporting what they consider to be at least a subsidiary, if not the primary, function of the fiscal process, namely the *transfer* of real income and wealth among persons and groups within the political community. The taxing and spending process seems to offer a means through which the distributional results of the market may be modified in the direction of results that command more ethical legitimacy.

At one level of analysis, the introduction of a specific distributional role for the fiscal process requires a departure from the exchange paradigm. If real income is to be transferred from one set of persons to another, there is no exchange, save in the limited degree allowed by utility interdependence. And the distributional role assigned to the fiscal process in this tax-reform discussion is not that which may emerge from positive predictions about the workings of less-than-unanimity rules for collective decision-making, which may be designated as "imperfect" fiscal exchange. As envisaged by participants in this discussion, the distributional objectives of the fiscal process must be laid down from outside the decision structure itself, presumably by the benevolent despot against whom Wicksell raised such formidable objections.

Let us isolate the pure distributional or pure transfer aspects of the fiscal process from both the allocational aspects and from those transfers which might plausibly be explained by the existence of utility interdependence. For the pure transfer aspects, the decision process becomes fully analogous to a zero-sum game which players must continue to play. In this context, political equality, as signalled by the universality of the voting franchise, will generate predictable transfers, but these need not be heavily weighted in favor of the "very poor" as envisaged in the tax-reform discussions.[5] In recognizing this, as they must, what do the distributionally-motivated tax reform advocates consider themselves to be doing? Are they trying to persuade citizens to incorporate the utility of others into their preference functions? Are they advising political entrepreneurs to take up positions that are contrary to those reflected in their constituency interests?

I do not think that these reformers are consciously engaging in persuasion of this sort. They consider themselves to be articulating value judgments that "should" be universally held by all informed persons. But what is the basis for such an attitude? Here we must, I think, examine the fundamental conception of society and the place of individuals relative to each other in the society. In its short-term context, the fiscal exchange paradigm is based on the presumption that persons are well-defined entities, defined in terms of rights encompassing spheres of allowable and enforceable activities, both with respect to each other and to physical objects. In one sense, the exchange paradigm requires an acceptance of the status quo distribution of rights. An unwillingness to attribute "justice" or "equity" to the status quo may suggest grounds for a rejection of the exchange paradigm for the fiscal process. There has been, and remains, much ambiguity here which is again absent from Wicksell's discussion which contains a categorical distinction between the distribution of rights and the complex exchange which the fiscal process represents.[6] Whether at the level of intellectual discourse or of political reality,

5. I have examined some of the implications of universality in franchise for fiscal transfers in J. M. Buchanan, "The Political Economy of Franchise in the Welfare State," in *Essays in Capitalism and Freedom*, ed. R. Selden (Charlottesville: University Press of Virginia, 1975).

6. For my attempts to explore the questions concerning the basic distribution of

attempts to force the fiscal process into the dual roles of redressing differences in endowments and capacities among persons and of implementing complex exchanges for public goods among persons with defined rights can only create confusion. Even in the purest model of fiscal exchange, the Wicksellian unanimity setting, there exists individual motivation for strategic behavior, for the investment of resources in socially-wasteful attempts to secure relatively large shares of the gross gains-from-trade. As we depart from the unanimity rule setting, the motivation for behaving strategically falls, but this is offset by incentives offered for successful fiscal exploitation of minorities by majorities, even if no direct transfers are made. If, appended to and mixed up with this complex political exchange, the fiscal process is viewed by participants, and by political entrepreneurs, as an instrument for effecting direct transfers of incomes and wealth, the resource wastage involved in attempts to capture and to control collective decision-making may swamp the potentially realizable surplus that may be promised by public-goods provision. Furthermore, as suggested above, there is no assurance at all that the net transfers which would take place in such a setting would come close to those dictated by ethical precepts of "justice."

5. The Fiscal Constitution

In the earlier discussion of the equity norm as a possible constraint on the political exploitation of minorities, there was an implicit distinction made between constitutional rules and decision-making under defined rules. In much the same manner, we can now reinterpret the exchange-contractarian approach in a way that will account for observed fiscal transfers. To accomplish this, however, it is necessary to shift away from the implicit assumptions underlying the several orthodox models of the fiscal process. These proceed from a setting in which individual claims to income flows and/or asset values are well-defined.

Once we recognize, however, that the assignment or distribution of endowments and capacities among persons has some time dimension, and that identification of any person's specific position in future periods can be predicted only under uncertainty, it becomes possible to discuss the conceptual

---

rights, see J. M. Buchanan, *The Limits of Liberty* (Chicago: University of Chicago Press, 1975).

emergence of fiscal institutions in a contractarian framework, which is equivalent to the exchange framework save for the level of decision. In earlier work, I have referred to this level of collective decision as "constitutional," as opposed to collective choice under conditions when the distribution of rights is fully specified, a choice which I have referred to as "post-constitutional."

Fiscal institutions may be analyzed in a constitutional setting. The distinguishing feature of genuine constitutional choice lies in the recognized permanent or quasi-permanent nature of the alternatives that are considered. The individuals who participate in such choices are necessarily uncertain, at least to some degree, about their own roles during the periods through which the chosen alternative will remain operative. To the extent that such uncertainty exists, they will be led to select among alternatives in accordance with generally-applicable criteria of "fairness," "equity" and "efficiency," rather than fully-identifiable self-interest. Uncertainty about income and wealth positions in future periods can produce a general contractual agreement on a set of fiscal institutions, a fiscal constitution, that may incorporate protection against poverty and which may seem, when viewed in a short-term perspective, to produce pure transfers among individuals and groups.[7]

The philosophical advantage of the contractarian-constitutional approach

---

7. This insurance approach to fiscal redistribution, based on a contractarian model, was developed in some detail in J. M. Buchanan and G. Tullock, *The Calculus of Consent* (Ann Arbor: University of Michigan Press, 1962). There is an obvious affinity between this and the basic contractarian approach taken by Rawls, both in his earlier papers and in his book (*A Theory of Justice* [Cambridge: Harvard University Press, 1971]). One difference lies in our imposition of genuine uncertainty regarding individual positions as the device that insures motivation for a person to adopt the attitude required. Rawls, by comparison with this, suggests that even when an individual's own position is clearly defined, a person should act as if he is choosing behind the "veil of ignorance." A second difference in the two approaches lies in Rawls' attempt to describe specifically the distributional principle that would tend to emerge from the original contract, namely the difference principle. By contrast, in our view, the contractarian framework must allow for the possible emergence of many alternatives; and indeed the emphasis must be placed on the process rather than on the specific outcomes. This contractarian approach to distribution is fully consistent with, and possibly complementary to, Musgrave's analytical separation between the allocation and distribution branches of the budget (*The Theory of Public Finance* [New York: McGraw-Hill, 1959]). The contractarian approach suggests the possible advantages of formal institutional separation, with quite differing temporal perspectives informing the political deliberations in the two cases.

lies in the fact that it enables us to derive fiscal institutions from individual choices independently of externally-imposed ethical criteria. There is no logically necessary contradiction between pure fiscal transfers and democratic choice procedures, provided that the latter are bounded by constitutional constraints. Whether or not the pure transfers that we do seem to observe represent some embodiment of such a constitutional choice calculus is, of course, strictly an empirical question, along with the determination of the genuine exchange content in the observed provision of public goods and services. These are questions worthy of research effort, but they can scarcely be examined until and unless there is first some understanding of the necessity for making the constitutional–post-constitutional distinction. This distinction tends to be blurred in political reality when long-range structural reforms which may properly be classified as "constitutional" are discussed simultaneously with period-to-period allocative decisions.

6. Conclusions

Critics may properly object by suggesting that the exchange-contractarian paradigm, as I have interpreted it here, may be used to "explain" everything and, hence, to predict nothing. To a limited extent, this objection has merit, although testable implications of the approach may readily be derived. But the purpose of here presenting the exchange-contractarian model of the fiscal process is not primarily to facilitate the making of scientific predictions. The charge of nonoperationality may be levied, much more effectively, against the alternative approaches to taxation under consideration, those which embody either the traditional equity objectives or the efficiency-optimality norms. In my interpretation, we are examining alternative paradigms of the fiscal process, different "windows" through which the actual institutions which exist and those which might exist are viewed. The methodological alternative that is selected will determine both the predictive hypotheses to be derived and tested and, perhaps more importantly, the evaluative judgments to be made concerning prospects for "improvement."

In my view, and it is one that I think was shared by Wicksell, the exchange-contractarian paradigm is the only one that is wholly consistent with what we may legitimately call "democracy" or with a social order that embodies "democratic values." The alternative visions of fiscal order depend, in some ultimate sense, on the presence of a decision-maker *for* individuals in the community, and reform proposals are aimed at modifying *results*. Observed outcomes are evaluated against normative criteria that apply to outcomes. For example, a tax system is given low marks if it is "regressive." By contrast, the normative evaluation that emerges from the exchange-contractarian paradigm applies to *process* rather than to results. In this approach, it matters relatively little whether a tax system is "regressive" or "progressive." What does matter is whether or not the tax structure, along with the pattern of budgetary outlays, is generated through a decision-making process that reflects, even if imperfectly, individual values in a regime where all persons are given roughly equal weights.

This difference in perspective leads to differing objects or targets for improvement. The traditional proponent of equity objectives worries about the erosion of the income tax base, for example, evaluating what he sees in political reality against his idealized general income tax. The exchange-contractarian, on the other hand, finds relatively little to disturb him in the presence of tax loopholes, per se, if he conceives these to reflect plausible outcomes of a political bargaining process that he evaluates to be the "least bad" among possible decision structures. He is much more likely to get exercised about the inflation-induced increases in real rates of income tax, which reflect departures from explicitly legislated rate structures, and which foster rather than dispel fiscal illusion.

Finally, the differences in approach to tax and fiscal institutions are important for the promulgation of attitudes of citizens, as ultimate voters, taxpayers, and beneficiaries of public outlays. The exchange framework tends to promote a constructive attitude toward governmental process, an attitude that accentuates the cooperative aspects, that underlines the prospects for mutuality of gain for all citizens. The alternative framework may lead citizens and their political spokesmen to accentuate the profit-and-loss aspects of political competition, to promote a willingness on the part of a dominant coalition to impose its will on its minority opposition, and conversely, to generate in the minority an acceptance of a quasi-Marxist and exploitative view of governmental process. These public attitudes become more significant as the size of the public or governmental sector grows relative to the national product. To this point in American history, the relatively limited scope of overt fiscal exploitation can, I think, largely be explained by a generalized and widely-shared sense of fiscal exchange which has informed pub-lic thinking about both the constitutional and post-constitutional decision processes. To the extent that the fiscal process, and politics generally, comes increasingly to be viewed as a source for profit opportunities, unrestricted by constitutional precepts, we must predict decreasing fiscal equity along with further departures from efficiency, almost regardless of how these objectives are defined.

Public Debt, Cost Theory,
and the Fiscal Illusion

I. Introduction

To what extent does the presence or absence of a "public debt illusion" affect the temporal location of debt burden? This question is important in itself, but in exploring it I hope also to clarify some of the points that remain obscure in the recent literature. Puviani in his unique and highly original work on the fiscal illusion specifically included public debt as one institution through which such illusions may be generated.[1] In the more recent discussion, Vickrey and others have explicitly made reference to a "public debt illusion," and, at least to some extent, the phenomenon of postponing debt burden through time is held to depend on the presence of some illusion.

Clarification of the term "illusion" is needed at the outset. Following normal usage, illusion will be used here to refer to a phenomenon that appears to be what it is not, at least to some of the persons who encounter it. By implication, errors in behavior may arise because of the presence of illusion, errors that could be avoided by more complete knowledge. Economists are, of course, familiar with the "money illusion," a phenomenon that causes

From *Public Debt and Future Generations,* ed. J. M. Ferguson (Chapel Hill: University of North Carolina Press, 1964), 150–63. Reprinted by permission of the publisher.

This paper was written in its original form during the academic year, 1961–62, and it was presented as lectures at both the London School of Economics and at the University of Frankfurt. It has been substantially modified from its original version. In undertaking this revision, in 1963–64, I have benefited from several discussions with my colleagues James Ferguson and Emilio Giardina.

1. A. Puviani, *Teoria dell'illusione finanziaria* (Palermo, 1903).

people to interpret money values as real values. Presumably, the introduction of a monetary calculus has the effect of "hiding" or "distorting" the underlying real values of the alternatives that are confronted for choice. Men could be predicted to behave differently from the way they do behave were this illusion not present.

A public debt illusion may be defined similarly. It is, or may be, a phenomenon, inherent in the institution of public credit, that causes some men in the political group to behave differently from the way that they would behave in the absence of any illusion. Two different, but related, forms of an illusion will be discussed; these are considered in Sections II and III. I shall demonstrate that the presence or the absence of an illusion does not modify in any essential respects the elementary proposition that the real cost of public expenditures that are financed through debt tends to be shifted forward in time.

II. Undervaluation of Future Tax Liabilities

Vickrey suggests the most familiar form of a public debt illusion when he says: "if we assume a 'public debt illusion' under which individuals pay no attention to their share in the liability represented by the public debt ..." (p. 133).[2] This prompts the question: What is an individual's share in the liability that an issue of interest-bearing public debt represents?

I should specify, first of all, that I am concerned here with the individual as he participates, directly or indirectly, in a collective decision-making process where the creation of public debt is one among several fiscal alternatives. In short, I concentrate on the role of the individual as "voter-taxpayer-beneficiary." I shall assume that public debt, if chosen, will be issued independently of tax payments in subsequent time periods. In such a model, debt is serviced from general governmental revenues that are not earmarked in advance. Under such circumstances, the voter-taxpayer, if he is wholly free of illusion, will recognize that the contractual terms upon which debt is created embody claims upon his income, or that of his heirs, in future account-

---

2. William Vickrey, "The Burden of the Public Debt: Comment," *American Economic Review* 51 (March 1961): 132–37.

ing periods, claims that the government will implement through some ordinary taxing process. These claims may be discounted and some present value estimated.

If present values, so computed by each individual, are summed over all members of the political group, the aggregate liability so expressed need not be equal to the value of the public debt that is marketed. A divergence may appear between these two magnitudes because of the limited time horizons upon which individual plans are made. Individuals do not expect to live forever, and they may not treat their heirs as linear extensions of themselves for economic decisions. It does not seem appropriate to define as illusory behavior that stems from mere limitations on time horizons. However, I do not want to introduce here the many problems of "rational" behavior that the limitations of human life impose. I shall, therefore, examine the public debt illusion under the simplifying assumption that all persons act "as if" they expect to live forever. Even in this model, the single individual will find it difficult to determine his own particular share in the liability represented by public debt. The distribution of taxes required to service the debt will be independently chosen in each time period, in the absence of tied sources. This political fact requires that the individual consider a probability distribution of outcomes for his own share. Again, however, we assume that he does carry out the necessary calculations, and that each person arrives finally at a certainty equivalent for his own expected tax liability. In this highly rarified model, the sum of the present values separately estimated for all individuals should approximate the value of the debt that is to be issued.

No public debt illusion exists in this model. There is no net undervaluation of the future tax obligations that the debt represents. The question now is one of determining the difference in behavior between this model and one in which an illusion is explicitly assumed to be present. Is it correct, as Vickrey suggests, to say that "elimination of this factor eliminates the shifting to the future entirely . . ."?[3] Is the "burden of public debt" wholly concentrated on the "present generation," in the "here and now" of the initial period, in the absence of an undervaluation illusion?

The answer to each of these questions is, I think, negative. And the failure of economists to recognize this is based, in part, on an elemental, but near-

3. Ibid., 135.

universal, confusion in the theory of costs.[4] The presence or absence of an illusion, defined in the sense of some failure to discount properly future tax liabilities, is irrelevant to the question of "shifting" a burden of debt to the future periods. The illusion is important, and relevant, only in its effects on *decisions* made at the moment of the original debt issue or creation. Its presence or absence at this moment determines the individual's estimate of the *subjective cost* that a decision to finance public expenditures with debt issue involves. The illusion has no bearing on the distribution of the *objective cost* of this decision *over time*.

Before elaborating this point, it is useful to clarify the distinction between subjective cost and objective cost in a more general setting unrelated to public debt. Many economists overlook this difference, despite repeated warnings.[5] Subjective cost is the obstacle to decision; it consists in the alternative that is foregone *at the moment of choice*, an alternative which can, because it is rejected, never be attained or realized. This cost is wholly within the "mind" of the individual chooser, and it can never be measured by an external observer. It exists temporally only in the moment preceding an act of choice, if it can be dated at all. It results from the sense of anticipating enjoyments that must be foregone. All subjective cost is anticipatory in this sense; hence, conceptually, there is no distinction between an alternative foregone immediately subsequent to decision and one foregone years afterward. Both are, once and for all, given up once a positive choice is made. For this reason, the subjective cost involved in debt issue, as conceived by the voter-taxpayer who is "choosing," must be concentrated in the moment of decision, despite the fact that this cost arises wholly from some current expectation of *future*

4. In my own earlier writings on public debt, I shared this confusion; hence, my failure to be more explicit concerning the meaning of "burden" in my whole analysis (*Fiscal Theory and Political Economy: Selected Essays* [Chapel Hill: University of North Carolina Press, 1960], especially pp. 51–59; *Public Principles of Public Debt* [Homewood, Ill.: Richard D. Irwin, 1958]).

5. Notably by G. F. Thirlby, "Economists' Cost Rules and Equilibrium Theory," *Economica* 27 (May 1960): 148–57, and "The Subjective Theory of Value and Accounting 'Cost,'" *Economica* 13 (February 1946): 32–49; but also by F. A. Hayek, "Economics and Knowledge," *Economica* 4 (February 1937): 33–54; L. Robbins, "Remarks upon Certain Aspects of the Theory of Costs," *Economic Journal* 44 (March 1934): 1–18; and J. Wiseman, "Uncertainty, Costs, and Collectivist Economic Planning," *Economica* 20 (May 1953): 118–28.

tax liabilities. The debt illusion that Vickrey mentions has to do with the individual's estimation of this subjective cost. If illusion exists, there may be some undervaluation of the alternative with which debt issue is compared, and, because of this, errors may be made which would, in the absence of illusion, be avoided.

Subjective cost need not be equal to what is here called objective cost, if equality is meaningful at all between these two magnitudes. The fact that, in competitive equilibrium, the ability of the buyer-seller to adjust his behavior to a set of uniform market-determined prices converts subjective costs into an objectively-measurable quantity does not imply that, in nonequilibrium situations of choice, any equality need hold. Objective cost is defined as actual resource services that are "given up" or "paid out" to attain the alternative that is chosen. Conceptually, objective cost can be measured by some person external to the decision maker; a real flow of resource services can be observed. Objective cost is *never* realized until *after* decision. The nature of time itself prevents the simultaneity of choice and consequence that is assumed in so much of economic analysis. For many purposes, of course, this temporal gap between the incurring of subjective cost at the moment of definitive choice and the incurring of objective cost subsequent to choice may be ignored. But the distinction clearly cannot be neglected in any discussion of debt, public or private, since the essence of debt is the postponement of objective cost in time.[6]

It is, of course, the objective cost of the public project that is debt financed which is shifted to the future or postponed. Subjective cost or "burden," that which serves as an obstacle to decision, cannot be shifted, by the fact of decision itself, and it is this cost that is affected by illusion. The resource services that are actually committed upon a decision to borrow, to create debt, that actually must be "paid out" or "given up" in exchange for the benefits

6. The failure to see that *two* costs are associated with any act of choice, a subjective cost and an objective cost, has plagued much of the recent discussion on public debt, including my own. Note, especially, how the recognition of this point clarifies the ambiguity raised in footnote 1, page 746, in Franco Modigliani's paper "Long-Run Implications of Alternative Fiscal Policies and the Burden of the National Debt," *Economic Journal* 71 (December 1961): 730–55. Among the recent contributors, only Tibor Scitovsky seems to note a distinction, but he erroneously labels objective costs as "social" and, because of this, misinterprets its meaning ("The Burden of the Public Debt: Comment," *American Economic Review* 51 [March 1961]: 137–39).

of the debt-financed collective services can be dated at the time that resource services are transferred from individuals to the fisc, to the extent that these are drawn from current consumption.[7] This transfer takes place in periods subsequent to debt issue as interest and amortization charges come due. This is as true for private debt as for public debt. There is no conceptual difference between the two other than the greater likelihood that the illusion herein discussed will be present under public rather than under private debt due to the complex probability calculus that is necessary to determine individual liability. To the extent that the illusion arises in public debt, more mistakes are likely to be made, but no difference in the temporal location of objective cost is generated.

In the complete absence of illusion, the sacrifice of resources may have been fully anticipated when the initial decision to borrow was made. This does not modify the conclusion, however, that, had the project been tax financed and debt not issued, resource services in the amount of current interest-amortization charges could remain in the possession of the individual during those periods when debt service is necessary.

The concepts of national income accounting, when combined with the failure to distinguish properly between subjective and objective cost or "burden," have been largely responsible for the widespread acceptance of the fallacious idea that there is no postponement of cost involved in the creation of internal public debt. If we look at the fiscal operation from an aggregative or "social" point of view, resources are, of course, "given up" during the time period in which the public expenditure project is undertaken. The members of the group who bear this objective cost, who suffer this "burden" in terms of sacrificed potential consumption in the period of debt creation, *are not* the "purchasers" of the public project, the voters-taxpayers-borrowers-beneficiaries. Those who bear this initial-period objective cost are, instead, those members of the group who choose to buy the government securities that are offered for sale in a wholly private, voluntary, noncollective transaction. These persons will also suffer a subjective cost upon their deci-

---

7. If the taxes levied for the purpose of servicing the public debt should cause individual taxpayers to draw down capital rather than consumption funds, the objective costs of the collective services are postponed even farther into the future. See the discussion on this point below.

sion to lend current resources to the collectivity. And the objective cost which they bear arises when they "pay out" current purchasing power, current command over resources, to the public treasury in exchange for the bonds. Their exchange is not, however, for the benefits of the project that is being financed through the fiscal process but is, instead, for the future income stream that inheres in the debt instruments, the government securities. The central feature of public credit lies in its facilitation of this dual exchange between the taxpayer-borrower and the bond purchaser-lender. Two decisions are involved, as there must be in any exchange, since two parties to the exchange are present, and each decision has associated with it both a subjective and an objective cost element. The theory of public debt that I have called elsewhere the "new orthodoxy" is based on an oversight of these embarrassingly simple facts.

III. Failure to Distinguish Owned and Non-owned Assets

Puviani stressed a slightly different, although related, form of public debt illusion from that which has been discussed above. Let us begin with the familiar Ricardian equivalence between a debt obligation, which embodies the levy of an annual tax in perpetuity, and an extraordinary tax, which collects the full capital sum in the initial period. In such an equivalence, any illusion of the Vickrey type is absent, and, also, the model remains at the level of individual decision. To introduce the standard numerical example, the individual is confronted with the choice of paying a tax of $2,000 once and for all, or paying the sum required to service a debt of this amount through an annual levy of $100 in perpetuity, assuming a discount-interest rate of 5 per cent. Puviani suggested that, even here, the individual will not be indifferent between these two alternatives, but that he will tend to choose the annual tax in perpetuity. He will do so, not because he undervalues future tax obligations, but because he will not treat the acknowledged claims as diminution in the value of his owned assets in the same way that he would treat the once-and-for-all current tax alternative. In the first case, argued Puviani, the individual knows that he will continue to administer the same total assets, undiminished in productive power. The fact that the debt, as embodied in the annual tax in perpetuity, alienates a certain share of these assets will not be fully appreciated even though, in strict balance-sheet terms, the tax liability is fully capitalized. In this sense, therefore, a "public debt illusion" may exist.[8]

This argument applies to debt generally; there is no particular difference between public and private debt in this respect. When a decision to borrow is made, alternatives are, as of that moment, foregone. If we assume that loan contracts are enforced, the moment of decision to borrow and spend removes, once and for all, any opportunity that the individual or group may have for utilizing a certain share of income during subsequent time periods. This remains true independently of the rationality of the borrowing-spending decision. As suggested earlier, the subjective cost, which exists solely in the anticipation of foregone opportunities, is present only at the moment of choice when, to any external observer, nothing actually "happens." Resources are only "paid out" by the borrower to the lender as interest and amortization charges come due over time. This pay-out does have a temporal sequence that may be observed. And this pay-out always reduces potential consumption opportunities below what they would be otherwise, but this need not impose any "burden" in the subjective or "felt" sense. Psychologically, however, the alienation that would be required to eliminate all subjective burden here becomes almost impossible to imagine. At the moment of a borrowing decision, it is conceivable that the individual could "chop off" or "earmark" a sufficient portion of his total capital value, produced by discounting his future earnings stream, so that the servicing of the debt could take place "outside" his internal calculus. He could, in this way, simply treat this portion of his "assets" *as if* it were owned by his creditors. Or, in the extreme, he might actually implement a transfer of title. Note, however, that human as well as nonhuman capital must be included in total assets here, and, both institutionally and behaviorally, it is difficult to think of a transfer of ownership of human capital assets.

If such a complete alienation is not made, however, there will appear to be a "burden" of debt, in some genuinely subjective sense. If the borrower retains what we may call psychological or behavioral ownership of assets, even when these are offset by liabilities, he will "receive" income and then "transfer" this to his creditors. He will, as Puviani implies, suffer some "bur-

8. See the citation from Puviani contained in M. Fasiani, *Principii di scienza delle finanze*, vol. 1, 2nd ed. (Torino, 1950), chap. 3.

den" here, a feeling of deprivation, even though he has no alternative open to him. That is to say, he is confronted with no choice; hence, the subjective burden that he suffers here is not analogous to the subjective cost of decision, previously discussed, which arises precisely because he does have alternatives for choice. Indirect evidence of this Puviani-type of asset illusion is to be found in common or ordinary language where reference is universally made to the "burden" of carrying debt, public or private. By contrast, when an individual is observed to have purchased ordinary commodities, we do not find reference to his suffering a "burden of potatoes."

The temporal aspects of life itself make a Puviani-type illusion plausible. The individual who lives in the moment subsequent to choice is not the same person who has chosen, at least in all respects. The individual who inherits the consequences of past commitments, even those made by himself, in some physical sense of continuity, will always consider "what might have been," and the alternatives as seen retrospectively must look different from those contemplated at the time of choice.[9] The institution of debt, public or private, makes this attitude especially likely to arise since the individual debtor must, in an objectively observable sense, transfer resource services to creditors, resource services that he "might have" retained had not the borrowing commitment been made at some earlier point in time.

Thus, the Puviani hypothesis implies that the individual, when faced with a pure Ricardian choice, will prefer the debt–annual tax alternative, but also that in subsequent periods, despite the full discounting of future taxes that is inherent in the Ricardian equivalence, he will "feel a burden of debt." This should not be taken to suggest that there exists any shifting of the subjective cost of the debt-issue decision to future periods. It is possible that the subjective cost at the time of decision can be accurately estimated (as it is in the Ricardian equivalence), that no Vickrey-type illusion exists at all, and yet there may remain a subjective "burden" during periods of resource transfer. The fallacy to be avoided here is that of assuming that subjective or "felt" burden need add up to any particular sum. "The coward dies a thousand deaths."[10]

9. For an interesting treatment of the intertemporal inconsistency of decision, see the paper by R. H. Strotz, "Myopia and Inconsistency in Dynamic Utility Maximization," *Review of Economic Studies* 23 (1956): 165–80.

10. The analysis developed in this section has much in common with that discussed by

A contrast between debt issue and capital consumption illustrates the Puviani illusion. Analytically, an act of borrowing is not different from "using up" or "eating up" capital. In either case, the subjective cost, the negative side of the account that is relevant for decision, the rejected alternative, is represented in the mind of the chooser by some present value of an income stream over subsequent time periods, an income stream which will come into being if a debt-creation or capital consumption decision is not made, but which can never come into being at all if a positive option for either debt creation or capital consumption is exercised. The objective cost appears to be different in the two cases, but this apparent difference is due strictly to the institutional realities that reflect the presence of the Puviani illusion. The effective transfer of resource services, in the case of capital consumption as well as debt, occurs in future periods. By definition, capital, as capital, embodies potential consumption in future periods. Converting capital into current consumption potential represents a transfer of resource services away from potential consumption in the future. But capital, once consumed, once "eaten up," appears to be consumed. The alienation of assets appears to be made immediately after decision despite the fact that current consumption is no different here than it would be under borrowing. The individual living in periods after capital is overtly consumed has no sensation of "owning" assets that have already been destroyed in some "eating up" process, or of transferring income (potential consumption) from these nonexistent assets to "creditors." Hence, the presence of a "felt" burden of past decisions is much less likely to exist under capital consumption than under debt. In any time period, a person's income is, of course, in part the consequence of past decisions on the accumulation and decumulation of capital, private and public, human and nonhuman. But one does not, normally, feel overburdened by these past decisions. What is done is considered to be done, and that is that.

This attitude is in evident contrast to that which arises when debt obligations are outstanding. As suggested, the objective cost stream is identical in the two cases. Borrowing does not, however, carry with it the same alienation

---

James Ferguson, included elsewhere in this volume. Although these treatments were developed independently in the initial stages, I think that there now exists substantial agreement between us on the relevant issues in the controversy.

of claims to assets that capital consumption does. Assets are not really "destroyed" for the individual in the same behavioral sense under these two institutional operations.

In their recent contributions to the debt-theory discussion, Modigliani[11] and Vickrey[12] have stressed the point that taxation, insofar as it impinges on capital formation, involves a shifting to the future of the objective cost of the public project that is financed. Insofar as the taxpayer chooses to meet his current obligation by drawing down his rate of capital formation instead of restricting consumption, he is, of course, reducing his income over future periods. The objective cost of the project is, to this extent, effectively shifted forward or postponed. Where Modigliani, Vickrey, and, also, Musgrave[13] err is in their suggestion that public debt issue involves such a postponing of objective cost *only if, in the aggregate,* the rate of capital formation in the economy is less than it would be under the tax alternative. This extension of an argument that is basically correct represents a lapsing back into a sophisticated version of the national accounting fallacy that has distorted the more naïve discussions of public debts. Even if those persons who purchase the bonds should do so wholly out of funds otherwise destined to current consumption, the public debt, as such, still involves a shifting of objective cost to future periods, by the individual members of the political group, considered in their role as "purchasers" of the debt-financed public project, that is, as taxpayers-borrowers. The fact that, in the aggregate, the expanded public utilization of resources on behalf of these persons, or persons acting as taxpayers-borrowers-beneficiaries, is just offset by the reduction in resources devoted to consumption by the lenders—bond purchasers, or persons acting in this capacity, has no relevance for any fiscal decision. It is both meaningless and misleading to talk here in terms of "social" or "global" aggregates. For the individuals, as taxpayers-borrowers, as purchasers of the desired collective goods project, the issue of public debt is a *means of consuming* capital. That is to say, the operation is for them analytically equivalent to the imposition of a capital

11. "Long-Run Implications."

12. "Burden of the Public Debt."

13. Richard A. Musgrave, *The Theory of Public Finance* (New York: McGraw-Hill Book Company, 1959), chap. 23.

levy upon themselves to finance the same project, assuming away distributional differences and the Vickrey-type illusion. The capital levy is not normally considered for reason of the Puviani illusion.

As a taxpayer-borrower, the individual's income stream (his potential consumption) in future periods is reduced by the full amount of the debt service charges that are imposed upon him. He could prevent this only if, when the debt is initially created, he should set aside resources and *create capital* sufficient to generate an income equivalent to that necessary to meet future debt service charges. The individual, as taxpayer-borrower, could, in this manner, convert the future objective cost into a current-period objective cost. If, however, the model of political choice is assumed to be a voluntaristic one, the "representative" taxpayer-borrower could accomplish this purpose far more simply by accepting current tax financing rather than debt financing for the public project. Just as capital consumption is the analytical equivalent of debt creation, so capital creation is the analytical equivalent of debt retirement. Hence, capital creation designed to offset the temporal effects of debt creation can occur only if the debt creation is imposed on the individual externally, and not chosen by him.

The point to be emphasized is that whether or not the bond purchaser draws funds from his own consumption or from investment during the initial period is wholly irrelevant to the taxpayer-borrower, except in a remote and indirect way. The aggregate rate of capital formation in an economy is, of course, affected by the source of the funds used to purchase public debt instruments. This rate is a meaningful datum for some purposes. But such an aggregate rate of investment does not directly affect or influence the decisions of individuals as they participate in fiscal decisions made on behalf of the whole collectivity. In this capacity, individuals recognize only that public debt, regardless of the source of funds, will impose an objective cost upon them that is represented by a necessary transfer of resources away from them in future periods. If they do not want to incur this temporal pattern of resource pay-out they will not choose to create debt in the first place.

The fact that the totality of the saving-investing decisions in the whole economy acts to insure that the rate of capital formation shall be such-and-such cannot, directly, modify the essential elements in debt creation as a fiscal operation.

IV. Conclusion

Public debts probably generate fiscal illusions of both the Vickrey and the Puviani sort. Individuals, for many reasons, probably do undervalue the future tax liabilities that an issue of debt embodies, and, even if they do not, they should probably still prefer debt to the current tax alternative. The analysis of this paper has demonstrated, however, that the presence or absence of illusion does not affect the temporal pattern of resource payment which debt issue must involve. The presence of a Vickrey-type illusion may affect the subjective cost estimates involved in making a decision to borrow, and, because of this, it may produce errors in the behavior of individuals as they participate in collective choice processes. Once a decision is made, however, the objective cost of the debt-financed project can be located only in time periods following that in which the debt is created and the funds expended for the provision of collective services.

The Puviani illusion acts to create a behavioral distinction between capital consumption and borrowing, despite the analytical equivalence between these two institutions. This distinction allows us to explain the "felt" burden of debt, even when future tax liabilities have been fully and accurately capitalized in the estimate for subjective cost at the time of decision. A recognition of this analytical equivalence also leads to the conclusion that taxation, insofar as individuals draw down capital funds to meet current tax obligations, can also involve a postponement of objective cost in time. Here, as in the case of debt, the relevant conversion decisions are made by individuals, and serious confusion can result from an undue concentration on "social" aggregates, considered apart from individual choices. Individuals, as taxpayers-borrowers, who are observed to choose public debt as a fiscal alternative, will confront an objective cost in future income periods. This remains true independently of the sources from which the funds that are used to finance the public project are originally drawn.

ADDITIONAL REFERENCES

Bowen, William G., Richard G. Davis, and David H. Kopf. "The Burden of the Public Debt: Reply," *The American Economic Review* 51 (March 1961): 141–43.

————. "The Public Debt: A Burden on Future Generations?" *The American Economic Review* 50 (September 1960): 701–6.

de Viti de Marco, Antonio. "La pressione tributaria dell'imposta e del prestito," *Giornale degli economisti* 1 (1893): 38–67, 216–31.

Elliott, James R. "The Burden of the Public Debt: Comment," *The American Economic Review* 51 (March 1961): 139–41.

Lerner, Abba P. "The Burden of Debt," *The Review of Economics and Statistics* 43 (May 1961): 139–41.

Meade, James E. "Is the National Debt a Burden?" *Oxford Economic Papers* 10 (June 1958): 163–83.

————. "Is the National Debt a Burden: A Correction," *Oxford Economic Papers* 11 (June 1959): 109–11.

Miller, H. Lawrence, Jr. "Anticipated and Unanticipated Consequences of Public Debt Creation," *Economica* 29 (November 1962): 410–19.

Ricardo, David. *Principles of Political Economy and Taxation, Works and Correspondence* (Royal Economic Society, 1951), 1:244–46.

Shoup, Carl S. "Debt Financing and Future Generations," *The Economic Journal* 72 (December 1962): 887–98.

Tullock, Gordon. "Public Debt—Who Bears the Burden?" *Rivista di diritto finanziario e scienza delle finanze* 22 (June 1963): 207–13.

Keynesian Follies

No one can challenge the proposition that John Maynard Keynes exerted a major influence on the ideas and events of this century. For me the Keynesian difference carries a negative sign because I retrospectively predict an alternative history that "might have been," a sequence of events that is normatively superior to the history that we experienced. Any such retrospective prediction is, of course, beyond the reach of scientific falsification. Objectively measurable imputation of the effect of any person, whether negatively or positively valued, remains an impossible exercise.

I have chosen my title, "Keynesian Follies," carefully. *Folly* is defined as (1) lack of good sense or of normal prudence, (2) inability or refusal to accept existing reality or to foresee inevitable consequences.[1] Both of these definitions convey something of the policy stance that I associate with the term *Keynesian*. I have put "follies" plurally in my title in order to suggest that several separate but related elements are involved, and, also, to hint that, to an extent, the whole historical episode has theatrical aspects of its own.

The Art and the Science of Political Economy

Keynes states explicitly that the central purpose of the book, the half century's life of which we celebrate at this conference, was to change the percep-

From *The Legacy of Keynes,* Nobel Conference XXII, ed. David A. Reese (San Francisco: Harper & Row, 1987), 130–45. Copyright 1987 by HarperCollins Publishers. Reproduced by permission of the publisher.

I am indebted to William Breit, Hartmut Kliemt, Charles Rowley, and Viktor Vanberg for comments on an earlier draft. I should also express my appreciation to the participants in a July 1986 seminar at the Research Department, Federal Reserve Bank of Richmond.

1. *Webster's Third New International Dictionary, Unabridged* (Springfield, Mass.: G. and C. Merriam, 1966), 883.

tion of his fellow economists, his peers among the academic scribblers. In this statement, Keynes indicated his own respect for the influence of ideas on events, and he set out deliberately to modify the mind-set of those whose chief business it was to impose intellectual order on a highly complex social process. He succeeded; by the middle years of the 1940s, economists almost everywhere had become "Keynesians" in their conceptualization of the macroeconomy. They had quickly learned to look at their world through the Keynesian window.

Perception of a reality is not, however, equivalent with reality itself, and the Keynesian follies find their source in the matching failures. Once having taken on the Keynesian mind-set, the Keynesians proved to be notoriously reluctant to change their perception of macroeconomic and political reality even in the face of accumulating empirical evidence throughout the 1940s, 1950s, and 1960s.

Keynes was the consummate artist, and his macroeconomic abstractions were comparable in boldness with those of his painter, poet, and composer peers in the world of high culture that he inhabited. Because his acknowledged purpose is to change perception rather than to explain, the artist must acknowledge the existence of competing perceptions.[2] Further, when perception is used instrumentally for more ultimate purposes, as it was used by Keynes, there would necessarily be some allowance made for appropriately timed switches among alternative perceptions of that which is. But while Keynes may be interpreted as an artist, his economist peers were scientists. His work was not taken as offering a situationally constrained perception of economic reality appropriate to the 1930s but as embodying a generalizable scientific paradigm. Neither Keynes nor any of his early disciples was aware of this fundamental difference that emerges naturally between the artist and the scientist.

This theme perhaps deserves further clarification. The scientist's research program, and any policy implications based on that program, is based squarely on a uniqueness postulate. That which is to be explained is the ob-

---

2. I have been influenced by Professor William Breit, Trinity University, in suggesting that the competing perceptions notion may apply to economics. For a preliminary statement of his position, see William Breit, "Galbraith and Friedman: Two Versions of Economic Reality," *Journal of Post-Keynesian Economics 7* (Fall 1984): 18–29.

jective reality that exists, and this reality by its very objectification excludes alternatives. The scientist's research program yields hypotheses that may be falsified, and a sufficiently robust bundle of rejected hypotheses may lead, at some point, to a genuine revolution, the replacement of one research program by another. At any moment, there exists for any scientist only one research program, one of a set of mutually exclusive alternatives. By contrast, the artist offers a personal perception of reality, a perception that is not directly falsifiable. Even within the mind of the individual artist, there may exist alternative perceptions, several "windows" through which reality may be examined. And as among several artists, a multiplicity of competing perceptions is necessarily acknowledged.

Considered as an artist's perception, the Keynesian model of the macroeconomy takes its place alongside alternative perceptions. It is neither "true" nor "false," neither "right" nor "wrong," since these are descriptive attributes that simply do not apply. The Keynesian perception offered original insights that may have been helpful in interpretations of the macroeconomy of the 1930s. As many who knew him have suggested, the perception might have been replaced by others in response to the shift in the economic and political environment.[3]

The Keynesian follies emerged only when the perceptions of Keynes as artist were falsely interpreted as a research program of Keynes as scientist. In the sections that follow, I shall discuss several elements in this scientistic ossification of the basic Keynesian perception. Matters of money, full employment, functional finance, fine-tuning, political process—these are subjects that require separate treatment. I hope to show that each of these areas of inquiry may be viewed in a somewhat different light when placed in the context of the artist-scientist comparison that I have suggested.

---

3. Keynes wrote explicitly for the purpose of changing the perception of his economist peers. This instrumental motivation of his whole enterprise may allow critics, who accept my artist designation, to array Keynes-as-artist alongside those artists whose efforts are pursued within the context of an inclusive ideology, whether voluntarily or under coercion. In this sense, Keynes-as-artist would be quite distinct from the artist who seeks only to discover "truth" in his perception. For my part, I am willing to take it as given that Keynes was himself writing within his own current perception of reality rather than utilizing his intellectual resources to play upon the naivete of his peers.

Matters of Money

The Keynesian model, that presented in *The General Theory of Employment, Interest and Money*,[4] was subjected to very early and continuing criticism on the grounds of its relegation of money and monetary institutions to secondary importance in the operation of the real macroeconomy. In the interpretation I have advanced above, Keynes himself may be defended from these charges. In earlier works, he had presented alternative perceptions of the workings of the macroeconomy that embodied a central role for money in stabilization of the macroaggregates. The new book was deliberatively different; it was a new canvas upon which was placed a model aimed to draw attention toward nonmonetary relationships. So interpreted, the folly lies not in the initial Keynesian presentation of the alternative model but in the scientistic inference that the model represented—indeed, a revolutionary switch between research programs. Admittedly here my argument suffers from the rhetoric of Keynes himself, since this rhetoric seems to have been explicitly intended to convey the mutual exclusiveness between the new model and the old. In any case, rhetoric or no, the scientistic interpretation was placed on the effort. Keynes was read as having advanced the falsifiable hypothesis that money matters little if at all, a hypothesis that was clearly rejected by events as early as the middle 1940s.

A more important implication for the political economy of policy was the shift of attention away from monetary institutions as the potential targets for change. Interpreted as advancing the hypothesis that money matters little if at all, Keynesian economics tended to support an acquiescence in the sometimes jerry-built monetary regimes that were in existence in the 1930s. The rational constructivism of the Keynesians was directed toward alternative targets that were much less amenable to feasible reform.

As noted above, the inefficiency of money as a relevant macroaggregative variable in early Keynesianism was quickly recognized, and attempts were made to reckon with this apparent gap in the analysis. The shift in perception had been so total, however, that these attempts were almost universally car-

---

4. John Maynard Keynes, *The General Theory of Employment, Interest and Money* (New York: Harcourt, Brace & Co., 1936).

ried out *within* the basic Keynesian framework of analysis rather than in the form of substitution of an alternative perception of the macroeconomy. This emphasis on a single model of the macroeconomy was directly traceable to the scientistic mind-set of the Keynesian advocates. There seemed to be little or no appreciation of the possible side-by-side existence of alternative models of economic process, each one of which might yield helpful insights, and each one of which might prove more or less appropriate in differing situations. The artist claims no monolithic legitimacy for his own perception; the scientist, by contrast, brands as heresy any perception that does not seem consistent with the prevailing research program. The whole mid-century history of economics and political economy might have been quite substantially different had economists proved more willing to tolerate the simultaneous existence of competing models of reality. Rather than "money does matter and can be readily incorporated in the basic Keynesian research program," we might have had the Keynesian real-variable models in existence alongside the non-Keynesian monetary theories of the business cycle. The disciplinary dominance of the Keynesian program, even as the relevance of money came to be incorporated within the models, ensured the continued neglect of basic reform in monetary institutions, a neglect that need not have occurred in the alternative competing programs scenario suggested. It seems, therefore, fully appropriate to label this institutional neglect as having resulted, in part at least, from "Keynesian folly."

Full Employment

Keynes is largely responsible for elevating employment (and/or output) to a position as an explicit objective for policy. As I have emphasized, Keynes sought to change the basic perception of the economic process; he sought to bring employment, as such, onto center stage as a variable subject to direct manipulation. He sought to overthrow the classical model of market equilibrium in which employment is determined only as an emergent result or consequence of the interaction among the demand and supply choices made by market participants.

Once again in this respect, Keynes was too persuasive. By elevating full employment to explicit consideration as a policy target, and thereby generating neglect of both monetary and market institutions, the Keynesian emphasis ensured the eventual stagflation that we experienced in the 1970s. The scenario might have been quite different if the Keynesian effort had been recognized for what it was rather than for what it was not.

The folly of full employment can best be discussed with reference to an early Chicago-based criticism of the theory of Keynesian macroeconomic policy. Attributed initially to C. O. Hardy, but taught to many of us by Henry Simons, the criticism was to the effect that a market economy (closed) could be characterized by any two of the following three conditions, but that all three conditions could not be met simultaneously: (1) full employment of the labor force; (2) stability in the value of the monetary unit; (3) noncompetitive labor markets. There need be no inconsistency between the satisfaction of the first two desired conditions if labor markets are competitive, but until and unless competitive wage adjustments are observed, either (1) or (2) must be violated. Concentration on (1) as a macroeconomic target must, therefore, ensure that (2) is not satisfied.[5]

Keynes himself would not have denied the elementary validity of this central Chicago proposition, interpreted as a set of mutually inconsistent equilibrium conditions. What Keynes argued was that the macroeconomy of the 1930s could not be and should not be perceived in terms of the classical market-clearing research program that the Chicago proposition embodies. In this respect, the long-continuing debate over whether the Keynesian analysis is an equilibrium or a disequilibrium theory seems to have missed the mark. The Keynesian analysis is an equilibrium theory, but it is one that is *constrained in its temporal setting of the 1930s.* That environment embodied an expectational chaos in which existing monetary arrangements seemed to have lost all equilibrating pressures toward the downside satisfaction of (2). The "animal spirits"[6] were cautious to an extreme, and the simplistic model of a highly elastic aggregate supply function did indeed capture a feature of that economy that was.

The economy that was in the 1930s, however, was not the economy that was in the 1940s and beyond. Hard evidence was available as early as 1946 to

5. This framework for presenting the policy conflict may be interpreted as a mid-1940s version of the Phillips curve relationship. The discussion implicitly presumed that full employment might be achieved by sacrifice of monetary stability. There was no hint of the post-Phillips notion of a natural rate of employment.

6. Cf. Keynes, *General Theory,* chap. 12, particularly p. 162.

the effect that the supply function sloped upward. As with money, however, the Keynesian success had proved to be so sweeping that the accumulating supply-side evidence was incorporated within the aggregative Keynesian model of the macroeconomy as opposed to the restoration of a competing classical program. In terms of policy targeting, the Phillips curve trade-off of the late 1950s and 1960s replaced the more naive full employment objective that had been earlier advanced. Only with the natural-rate hypothesis of the late 1960s did most economists finally discard the basic Keynesian research program. For the best part of three decades, therefore, economists tried to use a perception designed to isolate features of a macroeconomy in deflationary expectational chaos to look at a macroeconomy in postwar boom. The supreme folly of the Keynesians was perhaps the genuinely held but arrogant opinion to the effect that the surge in employment and output was itself a consequence of the application of the Keynesian policy tools.

Functional Finance

The policy instrument used to generate employment-output expansion in the Keynesian blackboard construction (or in the hydraulic machine model displayed widely in both Britain and the United States in the early postwar years) is government spending, the G in the simplified algebra. An exogenous increase in G adds to aggregate demand and directly or indirectly creates new employment and additional output. But how can government spending be increased exogenously? Governments, like persons or firms, must finance their spending. There are three alternatives available: (1) taxation, (2) money creation, and (3) borrowing.

In retrospect, it seems surprising (in 1986) that any attention at all was devoted to (1), that is, to the macroaggregative effects of tax-financed increments to rates of government outlay. Nonetheless, books as well as articles were devoted exclusively to analyses of balanced-budget multipliers that attempted to compare the expansionary effects of incremental governmental spending with the offsetting contractionary effects of incremental taxation. Given the level of expositional simplicity involved, the commonly stated value of unity for the balanced-budget multiplier is not to be criticized. What remains surprising, however, is the apparent failure of the economists who worked with these models to recognize that, within the structure of the models necessary to generate the unit value result, there is no normative argument for the levy of positive taxes. In order to produce a value of unity for the multiplier, the share of the tax dollar that would otherwise have gone into personal or corporate saving must represent a net drainage from the economy's spending stream. But the value of the multiplier can be increased severalfold by the simple expedient of spending without taxing. Were the analyses here subconsciously motivated by a desire to increase the relative size of the public or governmental sector, quite apart from macrostabilization objectives? Some such motivation combined with the underlying prediction that the macroeconomic objectives called for continuous expansionary stimulus rather than contraction may have been present. Once government spending was introduced as an instrument for the achievement of employment and output targets, attention was necessarily diverted from the allocative decision between the private and public sector that must always be made through some collective choice process.

The center of attention in the whole Keynesian theory of economic policy was, of course, on unbalanced rather than on balanced budgets. From the outset, the emphasis was placed on the use of government spending to expand employment and output, with this spending financed from nontax sources. The Keynesian approach to policy was, and has continued to be, associated with deficit financing. Formally, the models require that a budgetary regime involving deficits and surpluses be utilized, but the underlying predictive thrust is on the need for employment-output expansion, and, hence, on budgetary deficits. The increase in G is to be financed by (2) or (3).

It is at precisely this point that I have been mystified by Keynesian policy discourse, a mystification that has continued for forty years and that is shared by all Chicago-trained economists of my generation. Why have the Keynesians concentrated their policy analysis on the financing of spending by government borrowing rather than on the money issue alternative? Why has the textbook thrust of Keynesian policy embodied the bond financing of either expanded spending rates or reduced tax rates? Note that the superiority of money issue to finance deficits does not depend in any way on the relevance or irrelevance of money, as such. We can remain within the simplest of early Keynesian models, in which only rates of aggregate spending matter, and still conclude that money issue dominates government borrowing as a means of financing spending. This result follows so long as any share of the funds borrowed might have entered the spending stream. The money financing of budget deficits is superior even if attention is exclusively concentrated on the efficacy of the instruments in securing the employment-output objectives.

Among the many Keynesian economists, only A. P. Lerner consistently recognized the distinction between money creation and borrowing as the means of financing deficits, and his idealized regime of functional finance embodied compensatory budget adjustments accompanied exclusively by the required issue or destruction of money, and, hence, neither net government borrowing nor government debt retirement for macrostabilization purposes.[7] Had other Keynesian advocates followed Lerner in this respect, another Keynesian folly might have been avoided because the subject matter need never have emerged as relevant to the macropolicy debates.

The Keynesian emphasis was, however, placed on the *debt* financing of budget deficits. As a result, Keynesians felt it somehow obligatory to demonstrate that the creation of public debt, generally and apart from any particulars of macroeconomic policy, involved no temporal displacement of payment for the public spending that is so financed. Further, the Keynesians felt obliged to argue that public borrowing is categorically different in effect from private borrowing. The network of intellectual-analytical confusion in the elementary theory of public debt was the direct target of one of my first books, and I shall not devote space here to a repetition of old arguments.[8] The Keynesian intellectual "fog," for that is what the whole discussion surely reflected, was motivated, in part, by the underlying purpose of securing widespread public and political acceptance of an activist fiscal policy regime. To convince the noneconomist public to abandon the classical precepts of fiscal prudence, the Keynesians felt that they needed to show that public debt did not matter because, after all, "we owe it to ourselves." How simple it would have been to make the straightforward Lerner-Keynesian argument to the effect that *neither* taxation *nor* debt is an appropriate means of financing the deficits called for by an activist fiscal policy regime. The classical analysis

7. See Abba P. Lerner, *The Economics of Control* (New York: Macmillan, 1944), especially pp. 305–10.

8. See James M. Buchanan, *Public Principles of Public Debt* (Homewood, Ill.: Irwin, 1958).

of public debt could have remained within the filing cabinet labeled public finance orthodoxy.

The introduction of an activist fiscal policy regime of budgetary adjustment did require that the classical precepts of fiscal prudence be abandoned, and specifically that budgetary balance be dethroned as a central and overriding policy constraint (I shall defer discussion of this displacement until later). The activist regime of fiscal policy did not require any shift in the classical analysis of public debt, either positive or normative. Because of the widespread failure of economists to make the appropriate distinction between budgetary imbalance on the one hand and the means of financing such imbalance on the other, an unnecessary source of confusion, ambiguity, and argument was introduced.

We can go a bit further in this speculation about the "might have beens" if the Keynesians should have followed Lerner's lead in making the clear distinction between debt issue and money creation. The questionably productive research program engendered by Robert J. Barro's 1974 paper entitled "Are Government Bonds Net Wealth?"[9] might have been avoided. Following up Martin Bailey's earlier suggestion,[10] Barro sought to demonstrate the inefficacy of a fiscal policy shift from tax to bond financing of government outlay. The Bailey-Barro effort was directly stimulated by the claims of the Keynesians of the 1960s to the effect that the tax-to-bond shift was expansionary in the macroeconomic sense.

If the Keynesians should have adhered consistently to Lerner's norms for functional finance in their treatment of policy, there would never have been cause for the Bailey-Barro reaction, at least in the same form that it took in the 1970s. Even the most zealous of the rational expectation theorists could scarcely make a counterclaim to the Keynesian argument that an unanticipated tax-to-money shift is expansionary.[11]

---

9. Robert J. Barro, "Are Government Bonds Net Wealth?" *Journal of Political Economy* 82 (November 1974): 1095–1117.

10. Martin Bailey, *National Income and the Price Level* (New York: McGraw-Hill, 1971).

11. The rational expectation theorists have developed the distinction between anticipated and unanticipated changes in money creation as a part of the general argument that any systematic policy program must incorporate money issue responses that may be anticipated. This distinction is, however, quite different from the Barro-Ricardo argument concerning the nonexpansionary effect of the substitution of debt for tax finance. In this

Fine-Tuning

My discussion of the folly of fine-tuning can be brief, since this deficiency in the Keynesian theory of macroeconomic policy has been more widely recognized than any of the others that I examine in this paper. Indeed the very concept of "fine-tuning" the economy through compensatory budgetary adjustment is antithetical to the initial thrust of the Keynesian model, as advanced by the Cambridge master. In the macroeconomic environment of the 1930s, the model did yield useful insights, and policy implications may be gained from the modified perception of the economic reality that then existed. The compensatory budgetary adjustments called for by the initial Keynesian perception reflected "broad-tuning," rough-and-ready, catchall, revolutionary shifts in any parameters deemed subject to immediate political control. The folly lay with the post-Keynesians who converted the broad strokes of the master with the implied time-constrained shifts in budgetary flows into a highly sophisticated, if naive, analytical structure from which idealized budgetary adjustments were derived in apparent independence of the expectational setting. To have believed sincerely that budgetary fine-tuning (even in the absence of the political realities to be discussed later) would have been efficacious for stabilizing employment and output over the possible swings of ordinary economic cycles seems, in retrospect, beyond the limits of academicized isolation. Yet, such was the state of the Keynesian intellectual epoch.

Ordinary Politics

The most significant folly that has been widely attributed to Keynes and the Keynesians involves the presumed neglect of the workings of ordinary politics and political institutions in the implementation of any activist stabilization policy, and notably any use of spending and taxing as instruments. In his biography of Keynes, R. F. Harrod refers to the "presuppositions of Harvey Road," which he defines as the attitudes toward politics and government

---

case, even if the switch from tax to bond financing is completely unanticipated, the Barro argument carries through due to the alleged ability of persons to capitalize fully future tax obligations embodied in debt.

held by the Keynes who wrote *The General Theory of Employment, Interest and Money* in 1936.[12] These attitudes embodied a disregard for ordinary politics, based on a belief that Keynes's own powers of persuasion were indeed such as to ensure that any government would follow his lead, along with those of his economist peers, in policy matters.

This stance of Keynes can, on the one hand, be directly interpreted as a reflection of the isolated intellectual elitism that was characteristic of Cambridge early in this century. And there seems no question but that elements of such elitism were present; Keynes was no small-*d* democrat, despite his early philosophical liberalism. On the other hand, a somewhat more favorable interpretation may be placed on this characteristic of Keynes himself when we recognize that his work was aimed at changing the economic perception of his colleagues in extraordinary times, when the politics as well as the economics might have been expected to be nonusual, nonordinary. We need only to recall our own U.S. history in this respect. When Franklin Roosevelt assumed office in early 1933, the ordinary institutions of politics were, in effect, suspended. The checks and balances ceased to function, so extreme were the times, and politicians stood ready and willing to implement sweeping changes almost without regard for consideration of the permanent consequences and with little apparent regard to the special interests of their constituencies. Keynes had not, of course, published the book by 1933, but he may have had something like the early New Deal setting in mind as an idealization, modified, as appropriate, for the political structure of his own country.

If we interpret Keynes as the artist who sought to change perception with broad-brush abstractions in the environmental parameters of depression, there need be no inference concerning the extension of the perception to the workings of the economy or the polity in ordinary times. Once again, this interpretation suggests that the folly lies with the Keynesians, who imposed the scientistic straightjacket too readily on Keynes's work, and who failed to sense that the word *general* in the title of the book should not have been understood to convey the notion of an unchanging economic-political environment.

In any case, whether we attribute the folly here directly to Keynes or to the

12. R. F. Harrod, *The Life of John Maynard Keynes* (London: Macmillan, 1951), 192–93.

Keynesians who followed, the record is there to be observed. Ordinary politics in democracy prevents implementation of the policy norms emerging from the Keynesian theory of macroeconomic management, independently of the analytical difficulties that have been previously noted. That is to say, even if there should be no problems inherent in the Keynesian explanatory model, the attempt to stabilize the macroeconomy by compensatory budgetary adjustment would have failed. In ordinary times, political decision makers, ever responsive to constituency pressures, are driven by a natural proclivity to expand rates of spending and to reduce rates of taxation. The Keynesian policy model seemed to offer an intellectual-moral argument for expanded public spending financed by debt (or money). But ordinary politics fails almost totally when the other side of the Keynesian policy norms are required for macroeconomic purpose. Political decision makers cannot increase taxes so as to generate compensatory budgetary surpluses. The bias toward deficits emerges directly from the most elementary application of public choice principles.[13]

In this context, the net contribution of the whole Keynesian half century must be evaluated negatively. It is represented best by the regime of massive and continuing budgetary deficits that we observe, deficits that bear no relationship to any alleged macroeconomic purpose, and that are almost universally acknowledged to have adverse consequences for the economy as well as for the moral bases of modern society. These deficits emerged because the Keynesian impact was to dislodge almost totally the precept of budget balance from the effective fiscal constitution. Once the budget was introduced as an instrument of policy adjustment, there was no means of avoiding the non-Keynesian consequences. Even here, however, the negative impact would have been severely constrained if the Lerner norms had been adopted. It seems unlikely that even the irresponsibilities of the fiscal politics of the 1970s and 1980s could have been achieved by money financing of deficits of the magnitudes observed.

13. For extended discussion of the material of this whole section, see James M. Buchanan and Richard E. Wagner, *Democracy in Deficit: The Political Legacy of Lord Keynes* (New York: Academic Press, 1977). See also James M. Buchanan, Charles Rowley, and Robert Tollison (eds.), *Toward the Political Economy of Deficits* (Oxford: Basil Blackwell, forthcoming).

Conclusions

The Keynesian follies that I have discussed—matters of money, full employment, functional finance, fine-tuning, ordinary politics—these summarize familiar criticisms of the whole Keynesian enterprise. What I have tried to do in this paper, however, is to incorporate these criticisms in an interpretation of the Keynesian effort that may offer an insight into the intellectual history of the half century. My theme is that Keynes was essentially an artist, offering others a new perception of the economic reality of his time, a perception that he may have deemed necessary to draw out inferences for the dramatic policy action that he felt governments should undertake. The economic reality need not have been presumed invariant over time, and in this respect my interpretation is fully consistent with that of Shackle, who has always emphasized the subjectivist element in Keynes's vision.[14] The economic reality of the 1930s, characterized by expectational chaos, could not be understood properly modeled as if it were an economy in periods of expectational stability.

Argument may, of course, be joined over whether or not Keynes, even if interpreted as suggested, failed to foresee the consequences of the widespread acceptance of his own time-constrained perception. Indeed we may go so far as to suggest that the elementary folly of Keynes lay largely in his presumption of too much intellectual sophistication on the part of those whom he sought to convince and/or too much arrogance concerning his

---

14. See G. L. S. Shackle, *The Years of High Theory* (Cambridge: Cambridge University Press, 1967). See particularly pp. 129–34. The Shackle statement excerpted below comes close to the general interpretation I have tried to develop in this paper.

Keynes's whole theory of unemployment is ultimately the simple statement that, rational expectation being unattainable, we substitute for it first one and then another kind of irrational expectation: and the shift from one arbitrary basis to another gives us from time to time a moment of truth, when an artificial confidence is for the time being dissolved, and, we, as business men, are afraid to invest, and so fail to produce enough demand to match our society's desire to produce. Keynes's *General Theory* attempted a rational theory of a field of conduct which by the nature of its terms could only be semi-rational. *But sober economists gravely upholding a faith in the calculability of human affairs could not bring themselves to acknowledge that this could be his purpose.* They sought to interpret the *General Theory* as just one more manual of political arithmetic. (p. 129; italics supplied)

own powers of repersuasion, particularly posthumously. But the Keynesian follies emerged, for the most part, from the failure of those who followed the master to sense the critical dependence of the whole perceptual apparatus on the presumption of fixity in the reality that was being perceived.

This is not the place for extended treatment of the differences between the natural and the human sciences, or of the differences between the science of economic behavior, on the one hand, and the science of the macroeconomy, on the other. The nonfalsified propositions in economics are, at best, very few in number, only in part due to the familiar difficulty in setting up controlled experiments. As I have suggested elsewhere,[15] men are like rats only in some aspects of their behavior. To the extent that they are not ratlike, their behavior is unpredictable. At best, imaginative economists, whose interests transcend the boredom of rat-maze experimentation, can hope to isolate and abstract elements of uniformity in particularized expectational-institutional circumstances.

I end with a simple question: In an imagined economy characterized by an effectively operating commodity-based monetary standard would the Keynesian enterprise have been a part of our intellectual history?

15. See James M. Buchanan, "The Domain of Subjective Economics: Between Predictive Science and Moral Philosophy," in Israel Kirzner (ed.), *Method, Process, and Austrian Economics: Essays in Honor of Ludwig von Mises* (Lexington, Mass.: D. C. Heath, 1982), 7–20.

Socialism Is Dead
but Leviathan Lives On

I appreciate the opportunity to give this John Bonython Lecture, and especially to follow in that very distinguished succession of previous lecturers, all of whom are friends of mine.

More than a century ago, Nietzsche announced the death of God. Behind the drama of its presentation, this statement was intended to suggest that the omnipresence of God no longer served as an organising principle for the lives of individuals or for the rules of their association, one with another. If we can disregard the revival of fundamentalism, notably in Islam, we can refer to this century as one "without God." And, indeed, many of the horrors that we have witnessed find at least some part of their explanation in the absence of human fear of a deity's wrath.

I want to suggest here that, since Nietzsche, we have now passed through an interim period of history (roughly a century) during which, in one form or another, the God pronounced dead was replaced in man's consciousness by "socialism," which seemed to provide, variously, the principle upon which individuals organised their lives in civil society. And I want to match Nietzsche's announcement with the comparable one that "socialism is dead." This statement seems much less shocking than the earlier one because it has been and is being heard throughout the world in this year, 1990. I suggest, further, that the gap left by the loss of faith in socialism may, in some respects, be equally significant in effects to that which was described by the loss of faith in the deity. In a very real sense, the loss of faith in socialism is more dra-

The John Bonython Lecture, CIS Occasional Paper 30 (Sydney: Centre for Independent Studies, 1990), 1–9. Reprinted by permission of the publisher.

matic because it is at least traceable to the accumulation of quasi-scientific evidence. The god that was socialism took on forms that were directly observable; there were no continuing unknowns waiting to be revealed only in another life. And the promised realisation of the socialist ideal could not be infinitely postponed in time. In other words, the god that was socialism is *demonstrably dead;* there could have been no comparable statement made subsequent to Nietzsche's announcement.

These are strong claims, and I intend them as such. Socialism promised quite specific results; it did not deliver. It failed in the straightforward meaning of the word. And those of us who are in positions to think about ideas and their influence can only look back in amazement at the monumental folly that caused the intellectual leaders of the world, for more than a century, to buy into the "fatal conceit" that socialism embodied—"fatal conceit" being the wonderfully descriptive appellation recently introduced as the title of F. A. Hayek's last book (*The Fatal Conceit: The Errors of Socialism,* 1988). How did we, as members of the academies and intelligentsia, come to be trapped in the romantic myth that politically organised authority could direct our lives so as to satisfy our needs more adequately than we might satisfy them ourselves through voluntary agreement, association and exchange, one with another? I suspect that, literally, thousands of man-years will be spent in efforts fully to answer this question. I shall return to the question briefly later in this lecture. But first I want to emphasise that the "fatal conceit" was almost universal. Let us now beware of current attempts to limit acceptance of the socialist myth to those who were the explicit promulgators and defenders of the centrally planned authoritarian regimes of the USSR and its satellites. There were socialists among us everywhere, in all societies, at all levels of discourse, and, even in the face of the evidence that continues to accumulate, there are many who still cannot escape from the socialist mind-set. And even for those of us who have, somehow, shifted away from the mind-set of socialism, and who acknowledge, however begrudgingly, that the socialist god is dead, there may not have emerged any faith or belief in any non-socialist alternative. We may accept socialism's failure; we may not accept the alternative represented by the free market or enterprise system, even as tempered by elements of the welfare or transfer state.

Socialism and Individualism

I shall, first, try to define socialism, lest we allow those who enjoy the exploitation of our language to shift the meaning of terms before we realise what is happening. Socialists everywhere, confronted with the evidence that economies organised, wholly or partially, on socialist principles cannot deliver the goods, are now making desperate efforts to redefine the term "socialism" to mean something quite different from its received meaning, either in its historical development or in modern reality. To counter all such efforts at the outset, we can perhaps do no better than to consult the source books. The entry on "socialism" in *The New Palgrave: A Dictionary of Economics* (Macmillan: London), and published as recently as 1987, is by Alec Nove, a distinguished British scholar, who is himself a socialist. Nove's definition is as follows:

> Let us provisionally accept the following as a definition of socialism; a society may be seen to be a socialist one if the major part of the means of production of goods and services are not in private hands, but are in some sense socially owned and operated, by state, socialised, or cooperative enterprises. (p. 389)

As Nove emphasises, the key elements in this definition are summarised in the shortened statement that "the means of production . . . are not in private hands." Socialism, as a guiding principle for organisation, is opposed directly to "individualism," which could be summarised in the statement that "the means of production are in private hands." A more extended definition would include the corollary statement that the means of production, the resource capacities to produce that which is ultimately valued by persons, are *owned* by individuals, that is, *privately,* and that such ownership carries with it the liberty, and the responsibility, to make the relevant choices as to how, when, where and to what purpose these resource capacities will be put.

Only in an economy that emerges out of the complex exchange interrelationships among persons who privately own and control resource capacities can the incentives of resource suppliers be made compatible with the evaluations that persons as final demanders place on goods and services; only in such an economy can the resource suppliers, separately and independently, fully exploit the strictly localised information that emerges in the separate but interlinked markets; only in such an economy can the imaginative potential of individuals to create that which other persons may value be allowed to operate.

It is now, in 1990, almost universally acknowledged that such an economy "works better" than a socialised economy in which decisions on resource use are made non-privately, that is, by state or cooperative agencies. And the meaning of "works better" is quite straightforward: the private-ownership, individualised economy produces a higher valued bundle of goods and services from the resource capacities available to the individuals in a politically organised community. The only proviso here is that the value scalar, the measure through which disparate goods and services are ultimately compared, must be that which emerges from the voluntary exchange process itself. If the value scalar is, itself, determined by the centralised socialist planners, there is, of course, no reason to think that the private-ownership economy will "work better" in generating more "value" along this measure.

Classical Political Economy

It is sometimes too easy to overlook the simple principles in our headlong rush to get into the complexities. Let me pause, therefore, to emphasise what I have already said here. The private-ownership, market economy "works better" than the socialised economy; it produces more goods. But, and at the same time, it allows individuals more liberty to choose where, when and to what purpose they will put their capacities to produce values that they expect others to demand. Should we be surprised, therefore, when our history texts tell us about the genuine excitement that the discovery of the principles of classical political economy generated? Only with the philosophers of the 18th century did it come to be understood, for the first time, that the private-ownership economy could, indeed, make nations wealthy, but, at the same time, could ensure persons the liberty to make their own choices. These were heady ideas; it is little wonder that several generations of intellectual and political leaders were so aroused. Persons could be free from coercion by other persons and get rich at the same time, provided only that the state organised the legal-political framework for protection of private properties and for the enforcement of voluntary contracts. This discovery of the complementary values of freedom and well-being that the market order makes possible did indeed seem wonderful. And of course we know that this same complementarity is now being rediscovered all over again in so many lands.

Why, then, did the principles of classical political economy, which seemed so strongly to suggest the relative superiority of a market or free enterprise economy, lose their persuasive powers so quickly? Why did the intellectual leaders and social philosophers abandon *laissez faire* from roughly the middle of the 19th century and throughout most of this century?

Socialism Triumphant

We must, I think, appreciate the rhetorical genius of Marx in his ability to convert arguments advanced in support of market organisation into what could be made to appear to be support for a particular distributional class, the capitalists. By clever substitution of emotion-laden terminology, the market system became "capitalism," and the search of every person for his own advantage became the profit-seeking of the greedy capitalists. This rhetorical genius, coupled with totally erroneous economic analysis embedded into pseudo-scientific jargon about the laws of history, was highly successful in elevating the distributional issue to centre stage, to the relative neglect of the allocational and growth elements that were central in the classical teachings. And, further, the whole Marxian-socialist challenge was introduced into the political arena in the middle of the post-Hegelian epoch, during which the state was conceptualised only in a romantic vision completely divorced from the observable reality of politics.

(Let me pause to say here that I do not intend to present the socialist defence in caricature. I speak as one who shared fully in the socialist mind-set, from which, thanks to Frank Knight, I escaped relatively early in my career. But I appreciate the appeal of the Marxist-socialist ideas even if, now, I cannot explain it.)

There is no need to review in detail the history of the socialist century-and-a-half. Governments everywhere resumed their natural proclivities to interfere with the liberties of persons to make exchanges, and now supported by arguments that politicised control of economic decisions was necessary to correct market failures.

Lenin exploited the chaos of Russia to introduce the first fully socialist system of organisation, the consequences of which we now know too well. But recall that during the early decades, the Soviet Union was held out as paradise by socialists in the West, both in Europe and America. After World War II, socialism reigned triumphant; Eastern Europe was absorbed into the Soviet political orbit; countries in Western Europe socialised their economies, to greater or lesser degrees. Even where economies were largely allowed to remain free of politicised interferences, Keynesian-inspired macromanagement was supported by arguments about the tendency of capitalism to generate massive unemployment.

Socialism in Retreat

The triumph of socialism, either in idea or reality, was never complete. There were isolated residues of understanding of classical political economy, and some markets were allowed to remain free from politicised direction, and particularly in Western countries. Nonetheless, it remains accurate to describe the central and generalised thrust of politics as "socialist" up to and including the decade of the 1950s and early 1960s.

Between the early 1960s and today, the early 1990s, socialism became ill and died. What happened? There were two sides to the coin, which may be succinctly summarised as "market success" and "political failure." The accumulation of empirical evidence must ultimately dispel romance. And the evidence did indeed accumulate over the three decades to demonstrate that free market economies performed much better than politically directed or planned economies. The German *Wirtschaftwunder* should not be overlooked in this potted history. The economic reforms that Erhard implemented were based on an avowed acceptance of the principles of a market economy, and the principles were demonstrated to work. Germany achieved economic recovery rapidly in the 1950s and 1960s. By contrast and comparison, the socialist experiments tried out in Britain in the late 1940s and early 1950s proved to be demonstrable failures. Nationalisation did not produce the goods that had been promised. The Sputnik showpiece that seemed to suggest rapid Soviet development proved to be just that, a showpiece and nothing more. Honest evaluation suggested that the centralised economies of the Soviet Union, China and East European countries were not successful in producing goods and services. In the United States, the extended over-reaching of the welfare state in the 1960s set off predictable citizen reaction.

Ideas also matter. And here the record of the academic economists remains, at best, a very mixed bag. The great debate about the possible efficiency of the centrally planned economy, the 1930s debate over socialist calculation, between Mises and Hayek on the one hand and Lange and Lerner on the other, was judged by economists to have been won by the socialist side. Furthermore, the theoretical welfare economists of the early and middle decades of this century were primarily, indeed almost exclusively, concerned with demonstrating the failures of markets, with the purpose of providing a rationale for political interferences.

But the public-choice revolution in ideas about politics, and political failures, was also sparked primarily by academic economists. When the very elementary step is taken to extend the behavioural models of economics to apply to public choosers, to those who participate variously in political roles, as voters, politicians, bureaucrats, planners, party leaders, etc., the romantic vision that was essential to the whole socialist myth vanishes. If those who make decisions for others are finally seen as ordinary persons, just like everyone else, how can the awesome delegation of authority that must characterise the centralised economy be justified? I do not suggest here, in any way, that public choice theory set off the reaction against politicisation, socialism and other variants of the controlled economy. The reaction, which has now extended over the whole world, was surely triggered directly by the many decades of the observed record of political failures. Public choice, as a set of ideas, was, I think, influential in providing an intellectual basis which allows observers to understand better what it is they can directly observe. Political failure was everywhere observed; public choice supplied the explanation as to why the observations were valid.

The Absence of Faith

I stated earlier that there were two sides to the coin: market success and political failure. Both the observations and the ideas that have been developed over the period of socialist retreat have concentrated on the second of these, that is, on political failure. There now exists widespread scepticism about the efficacy of politics and political solutions to achieve economic results. Bureaucracies are mistrusted; politicians are not the heroes of legend. The socialist principle of organisation is not expected to work well. The faith in political and government nostrums has all but vanished, as a principle.

This loss of faith in politics, in socialism broadly defined, has not, however, been accompanied by any demonstrable renewal or reconversion to a faith in markets, the *laissez faire* vision that was central to the teachings of the classical political economists. There remains a residual unwillingness to leave things alone, to allow the free market to organise itself (within a legal framework) in producing and evaluating that which persons value. We are left, therefore, with what is essentially an attitude of nihilism toward economic organisation. Politics will not work, but there is no generalised willingness to leave things alone. There seems to be no widely shared organising principle upon which persons can begin to think about the operations of a political economy.

The Natural Emergence of Leviathan

It is in this setting, which does seem to be descriptive of the era into which we are so rapidly moving, that the natural forces that generate the Leviathan state emerge and assume dominance. With no overriding principle that dictates how an economy is to be organised, the political structure is open to maximal exploitation by the pressures of well-organised interests which seek to exploit the powers of the state to secure differential profits. The special-interest, rent-seeking, churning state finds fertile ground for growth in this environment. And we observe quite arbitrary politicised interferences with markets, with the pattern of intervention being dependent strictly on the relative strengths of organised interests.

This setting, which I have referred to as Leviathan, has much in common with the mercantilist-protectionist politics that Adam Smith attacked so vehemently in his great book in 1776. Hence, in two centuries we seem to have come full circle. The selfsame barriers that Adam Smith sought to abolish are everywhere resurging, as if from the depths of history. And the selfsame arguments are heard in the land, both in support and in opposition. The arguments for Leviathan's extensions are not versions of the socialist's dream;

they are, instead, simple efforts to claim a public interest in a single sector's private profit.

Towards Constitutional Limits

There will be no escape from the protectionist-mercantilist regime that now threatens to be characteristic of the post-socialist politics in both Western and Eastern countries so long as we allow the ordinary or natural outcomes of majoritarian democratic processes to operate without adequate constitutional constraints. We have learned to understand interest-group politics; we no longer have a romantic vision as to how the state operates. If we have not rediscovered, and do not rediscover, and understand the precepts of *laissez faire,* as organising principles, it will be necessary to address that which we do know and have learned. If we know that politics fails and that its natural proclivity is to extend its reach beyond tolerable bounds, we may be led to incorporate constraints into a constitutional structure. Depoliticised economic order is within the realm of the politically-constitutionally possible, even if the accompanying faith in market organisation is not fully regained. We can protect ourselves against the appetites of the monster that the Leviathan state threatens to become without really understanding and appreciating the efficiency-generating properties of the market.

A threshold was crossed in the 18th century when we learned how the rule of law, stability of private property and the withdrawal of political interference with private choices, could unleash the entrepreneurial energies that are latent within each of us. The modern age was born. Humankind seemed near to the ultimate realisation of its socially organised potentiality only to have this future threatened and in part forestalled by the emergence of the socialist vision, a vision that has now been shown to be grounded in romance rather than in scientific understanding. The central flaw in the socialist vision was its failure to recognise the limits of politicised organisation.

Recognising the limits in order to avoid harm is as important as recognising the potential that may be achieved within those limits. The organised polities of the nation-states, and the associations among those states, must be kept within constitutional boundaries. The death throes of socialism should not be allowed to distract attention from the continuing necessity to prevent the overreaching of the state-as-Leviathan, which becomes all the more dangerous because it does not depend on an ideology to give it focus. Ideas, and the institutions that emerge as these ideas are put into practice, can be killed off and replaced by other ideas and other institutions. The machinations of interest-driven politics are much more difficult to dislodge. Let us get on with the task.

PART FOUR

The Economist and Economic Order

Positive Economics, Welfare
Economics, and Political Economy

Economic theory, as we know it, was developed largely by utilitarians. Admitting the measurability and interpersonal comparability of utility and accepting the maximization of utility as an ethically desirable social goal, neoclassical economists were able to combine an instinctively human zeal for social reform with subjectively satisfactory scientific integrity. The positivist revolution has sharply disturbed this scholarly equilibrium. If utility is neither cardinally measurable nor comparable among persons, the economist who seeks to remain "pure" must proceed with caution in discussing social policy. The "positive" economist becomes an inventor of testable hypotheses, and his professional place in policy formation becomes wholly indirect.

Milton Friedman has provided the clearest statement of the positivist position,[1] and he has called for a distinct separation between the scientific and the non-scientific behavior of individuals calling themselves economists. But economics, as a discipline, will probably continue to attract precisely those scholars who desire to assist in policy formation and to do so professionally. The social role of the economist remains that of securing more intelligent legislation, and the incremental additions to the state of knowledge which "positive" economics may make seems to shut off too large an area of discussion from his professional competence. Does there exist a role for the po-

From *Journal of Law and Economics* 2 (October 1959): 124–38. Copyright 1959 by The University of Chicago. Reprinted by permission of the publisher.

1. M. Friedman, *Essays in Positive Economics* (1953), 3–43.

litical economist as such? This essay will examine this question and suggest an approach.[2]

I. The New Welfare Economics

The "new" welfare economics was born in response to the challenge posed by the positivist revolution. The intellectual source of this subdiscipline is Pareto, whose earlier attempts to introduce scientific objectivity into the social studies led him to enunciate the now-famous definition of "optimality" or "efficiency." This definition states that any situation is "optimal" if all possible moves from it result in some individual being made worse off. The definition may be transformed into a rule which states that any social change is desirable which results in (1) everyone being better off or (2) someone being better off and no one being worse off than before the change. This Pareto rule is itself an ethical proposition, a value statement, but it is one which requires a minimum of premises and one which should command wide assent. The rule specifically eliminates the requirement that interpersonal comparisons of utility be made. As stated, however, a fundamental ambiguity remains in the rule. Some objective content must be given to the terms "better off" and "worse off." This is accomplished by equating "better off" with "in that position voluntarily chosen." Individual preferences are taken to indicate changes in individual well-being, and a man is said to be better off when he voluntarily changes his position from A to B when he could have remained in A.

The theoretical work completed during the last twenty years has consisted, first of all, in a refinement and development of the Paretian conditions for "optimality." Much attention has been given to a careful and precise definition of the necessary and sufficient attributes of a social situation to insure its qualification as a Paretian P-point, that is, a point on the "optimality surface." The application of this theoretical apparatus has taken two lines of development. The first, which is sometimes more specifically called

---

2. The approach which will be suggested here involves an extension of some of Wicksell's ideas on fiscal theory to modern welfare economics. For a recently published translation of Wicksell's fiscal theory, see "A New Principle of Just Taxation," in *Classics in the Theory of Public Finance*, ed. R. A. Musgrave and A. T. Peacock (1958), 72.

the "new welfare economics," is an attempt to devise tests which will allow changes in social situations to be evaluated. This work, which has been associated with Kaldor, Hicks, and Scitovsky, includes the discussion of the "compensation principle" and the distinction between actual and potential increases in "welfare." The second line of development has been, in one sense, a critique of the Kaldor-Hicks approach. The ethical purity of the compensation tests proposed has been questioned, and additional ethical norms have been deliberately reintroduced through the device of a "social welfare function," which, conceptually, orders all possible states of society. With this, the problem of genuine choice among alternatives disappears, and the single "best" state of the world may be selected. This function may take any form, but its users have normally conceived the Paretian conditions to be relevant in defining a preliminary subset of social configurations. This approach, which is associated with Bergson, Samuelson, and Graaff, now appears to have more widespread support than the alternative one. Its supporters, notably Samuelson, argue that the Kaldor-Hicks efforts were "misguided" and erroneous[3] and that only the "social welfare function" construction offers real promise of further development. In the latter, allegedly, "the foundation is laid for the 'economics of the good society.' "[4]

II. Omniscience and Efficiency

Welfare economists, new and old, have generally assumed omniscience in the observer, although the assumption is rarely made explicit, and even more rarely are its implications examined.[5] The observing economist is considered able to "read" individual preference functions. Thus, even though an "increase in welfare" for an individual is defined as "movement to a preferred position," the economist can unambiguously distinguish an increase in welfare independent of individual behavior because he can accurately predict

3. Samuelson, "Comment," in *A Survey of Contemporary Economics*, vol. 2, ed. Haley and Ellis (1952), 37.

4. Samuelson, "Social Indifference Curves," *Quarterly Journal of Economics* 70 (1956): 22.

5. J. de V. Graaff, in his book *Theoretical Welfare Economics* (1957), p. 13, makes the assumption explicitly, but after one short paragraph proceeds with his argument.

what the individual would, in fact, "choose" if confronted with the alternatives under consideration.

This omniscience assumption seems wholly unacceptable. Utility is measurable, ordinally or cardinally, only to the individual decision-maker. It is a *subjectively* quantifiable magnitude. While the economist may be able to make certain presumptions about "utility" on the basis of observed facts about behavior, he must remain fundamentally ignorant concerning the actual ranking of alternatives until and unless that ranking is revealed by the overt action of the individual in choosing.

If a presumption of ignorance replaces that of omniscience, the way in which "efficiency" as a norm enters into the economist's schemata must be drastically modified. No "social" value scale can be constructed from individual preference patterns, since the latter are revealed only through behavior. Hence "efficiency" cannot be defined independently; it cannot be instrumentally employed as a criterion for social action. Discussions of "ideal output" and "maximization of real income" become meaningless when it is recognized that the economizing process includes as data *given ends* as conceived by individuals. Ends are not *given* for the social group in any sense appropriate to the solution of problems in political economy, and the normally accepted definition of the economizing problem is seriously incomplete in not having made this clear.

"Efficiency" in the sense of maximizing a payoff or outcome from the use of limited resources is meaningless without some common denominator, some value scale, against which various possible results can be measured. To the individual decision-maker the concept of an "efficiency criterion" is a useful one, but to the independent observer the pitfalls of omniscience must be carefully avoided. The observer may introduce an efficiency criterion only through *his own estimate of his subjects' value scales*. Hence the maximization criterion which the economist may employ is wholly in terms of his own estimate of the value scales of individuals other than himself. *Presumptive efficiency* is, therefore, the appropriate conception for political economy.

The relationship of the *presumptive efficiency* criterion to the Paretian construction remains to be clarified. Given the assumption of ignorance, Paretian "efficiency" cannot be employed in aiding a group in choosing from among a set of possible social policy changes. A specific change may be judged to be Pareto-optimal or "efficient" only after it has, in fact, been proposed and the individual preferences for or against the change revealed. Nevertheless, in discussing proposals before individual preferences are revealed, the economist may utilize a *presumed efficiency* notion which retains the Paretian features. In diagnosing a specific proposal, the economist makes a judgment as to its "efficiency" on the basis of *his own* estimate of individual preferences. The Paretian elements are retained in the sense that the observer makes no attempt to do other than to "translate" what he considers to be individual preferences. He accepts these preferences, or tastes, as *he thinks they exist.* He does not evaluate social alternatives on the basis of individual preferences as he thinks they should be.

This characteristic behavior of the political economist is, or should be, ethically neutral; the indicated results are influenced by his own value scale only insofar as this reflects his membership in the larger group. Conceptually, the economist may present a social policy change as "presumed Pareto-optimal," the results of which are wholly indifferent to him as an individual member of society. The propositions which the economist is able to develop through the procedure outlined are operational in the modern sense of this term. The presentation of a policy shift is a hypothesis concerning the structure of individual values and is subject to conceptual contradiction. The failure of recent methodological discussion to recognize this operational aspect of political economy appears to be based on an attempt to place the practitioner in a false position in the decision-making complex. The political economist is often conceived as being able to *recommend* policy A over policy B. If, as we have argued above, no objective social criterion exists, the economist qua scientist is unable to recommend. Therefore, any policy discussion on his part appears to take on normative implications. But there does exist a positive role for the economist in the formation of policy. His task is that of diagnosing social situations and presenting to the choosing individuals a set of possible changes. He does not recommend policy A over policy B. He presents policy A as a hypothesis subject to testing. The hypothesis is that policy A will, in fact, prove to be Pareto-optimal. The conceptual test is *consensus* among members of the choosing group, not objective improvement in some measurable social aggregate.

Political economy is thus "positivistic" in a different sense from the more narrowly conceived positive economics. Both allow the expert to make certain predictions about the real world—predictions which are operationally meaningful. Propositions of positive economics find their empirical support or refutation in observable economic quantities or in observable market behavior of individuals. Propositions in political economy find empirical support or refutation in the observable behavior of individuals *in their capacities as collective decision-makers*—in other words, in politics.

Propositions advanced by political economists must always be considered as tentative hypotheses offered as solutions to social problems. The subjective bases for these propositions should emphasize the necessity for their being considered as alternatives which may or may not be accepted. But this is not to suggest that one proposition is equally good with all others. Just as is the case with positive economics, the skill of the observer and his capacity in drawing upon the experience which has been accumulated will determine the relative success of his predictions.

There are no fully appropriate analogies to this task of the political economist, but the role of the medical diagnostician perhaps comes closest. The patient is observed to be ill; a remedy is prescribed. This remedy is a hypothesis advanced by the diagnostician. If the illness persists, an alternative remedy is suggested and the first hypothesis discarded. The process continues until the patient is restored to health or the existence of no solution is accepted. While this analogy is helpful, it can also be misleading. In political economy the observer isolates an "illness" or rather what he believes to be an "illness" through his knowledge of the system. He presents a possible change. But this change is a "cure" only if *consensus* is attained in its support. The measure of "wellness" for the political economist is not improvement in an independently observable characteristic but rather agreement. If no agreement can be attained, the presumed "illness" persists, and the political economist must search for still other possible solutions. The political behavior of individuals, not market performance or results, provides the criteria for testing hypotheses of political economy.

III. Compensation and Externality

The "welfare economics" suggested here is simpler than that which assumes omniscience on the part of the observer. Much of the discussion in the subdiscipline has been devoted to two problems, both of which will be substantially eliminated in the approach suggested. First, the appropriateness or inappropriateness of compensation has been a central topic along with the discussion of the legitimacy or illegitimacy of certain tests. But, quite clearly, if the political economist is presumed to be ignorant of individual preference fields, his predictions (as embodied in suggested social policy changes) can only be supported or refuted if full compensation is, in fact, paid.[6] The potential compensation argument disappears, and the whole controversy over the appropriate tests becomes meaningless at this level of argument.

Many scholars have objected to the requirement that compensation be paid on the grounds that such requirement creates a serious bias toward the initial or status quo distribution of "welfare" among individuals of the group. This criticism seems misdirected and inapplicable if the purposes of compensation are conceived to be those outlined. Full compensation is essential, not in order to maintain any initial distribution on ethical grounds, but in order to decide which one from among the many possible social policy changes does, in fact, satisfy the genuine Pareto rule. Compensation is the only device available to the political economist for this purpose.

If the observing economist is assumed omniscient, the actual payment of compensation may seem unnecessary, and the requirement for payment may appear to introduce the bias mentioned. No additional information about individuals' preference fields is needed, and none can be revealed by behavior. A proposed change is no longer a hypothesis to be tested, and the relatively neutral ethics imposed by the Pareto rule may prove too restrictive. And, if the observer does not move in the direction of the Bergson-Samuelson welfare function, he may attempt to devise tests for potential compensation. In this way the whole debate about the Kaldor-Hicks-Scitovsky criteria for improvement has arisen. This approach constitutes a distortion of the Pareto rule. If ethical evaluations on the part of the observer are to be introduced, there is no place for the Pareto rule. This rule is designed for use in situations where individual values must count, not because they possess some inherent ethical superiority (which is quite a different point), but be-

---

6. There are two distinct meanings of the word "compensation." In ordinary discussion, compensation is conceived as an objectively measurable quantity; this conception has no relevance for welfare economics. Compensation must be defined in terms of the individual choice process, and it becomes measurable only through an observation of choices made. Full or adequate compensation is defined as that set of payments required to secure the agreement of all parties to the proposed change.

cause individual action provides the only guide toward acceptable collective action.

The full-compensation requirement need not imply—indeed, it will not normally imply—the maintenance of the status quo in the distribution of either income or welfare. Presumably, if a given social change is approved by all parties, each must be better off in absolute terms. Therefore, at the simplest level of discussion, there is more "welfare" to go around than before the change. To be sure, the relative distribution of "welfare" may be modified significantly by a fully compensated change. This is true because the order of presentation will determine the final point chosen from among a whole subset of acceptable points. The political economist cannot, however, say anything concerning the relative merits of the separate points in this subset. This amounts to saying that the political economist's task is completed when he has shown the parties concerned that there exist mutual gains "from trade." He has no function in suggesting specific contract terms within the bargaining range itself.

An additional simple, but often overlooked, point on compensation needs to be made. The requirement of full compensation as here interpreted need not imply that the measured incomes of individuals or groups may not be reduced by acceptable social policy changes. "Welfare" is defined as that which is expressed by individual preference as revealed in behavior. And individual behavior may be fully consistent with a reduction in measured personal income or wealth. For example, a policy which combines progressive income taxation and public expenditure on the social services may command unanimous support even though the process involves a reduction in the measured real incomes of the rich. The existence of voluntary charity indicates that individuals are, in fact, willing to reduce their own incomes in order to increase those of others. And the peculiar nature of collective choice makes support for collective or governmental action perhaps even more likely. Many individuals may find themselves saying: "I should be willing to support this proposal provided that other equally situated individuals do likewise." Thus collective action may command relatively widespread support, whereas no purely voluntary action might be taken in its absence.[7]

7. This point has been stressed by W. J. Baumol in *Welfare Economics and the Theory of the State* (1952).

A second major problem which has concerned theorists in welfare economics has been the possible existence of external effects in individual consumption and production decisions, sometimes called "spillover" or "neighborhood" effects. But this annoying complication also disappears in the approach to welfare economics suggested here. If, in fact, external effects are present, these will be fully reflected in the individual choices made for or against the collective action which may be proposed. External effects which are unaccounted for in the presumptive efficiency criterion of the economist and the proposal based upon this criterion will negate the prediction of consensus represented in the alternative suggested. The presence of such effects on a large scale will, of course, make the task of the political economist more difficult. His predictions must embody estimates of a wider range of individual preferences than would otherwise be the case. The compensations included in the suggested policy changes must be more carefully drawn and must be extended to include more individuals who might otherwise be neglected.[8]

Both the compensation and the externality problems may be illustrated by reference to the classical example of the smoking chimney. The economist observes what he considers to be smoke damage and discontent among families living adjacent to the smoke-creating plant. Using a presumptive efficiency criterion, he suggests a possible course of action which the group may take. This action must include, on the one hand, the payment of some tax by the previously damaged individuals who stand to gain by the change. On the other hand, the action must include some subsidization of the owners of the firm to compensate them for the capital loss which is to be imposed by the rule of law which states that henceforward the full "social" costs of the operation must be shouldered. Some such tax-compensation–smoke-abatement scheme will command unanimous consent from the group which includes both individuals living within the damaged area and the owners of the firm. The problem for the political economist is that of searching out and locating from among the whole set of possible combinations one which will prove acceptable to all parties. If the smoke nuisance is a real one, at least

8. The discussion of this paragraph assumes that the membership in the group making the collective choice is at least as large as the "neighborhood" defined by the presence of external effects.

one such alternative must exist. If no agreement of this sort is possible, the economist can only conclude that the presumptive efficiency criterion was wrongly conceived and the hypothesis based upon it falsified.[9]

IV. The Scope for Political Economy

To this point, the behavior of the political economist has been the primary topic of discussion. The argument has been that the political economist, as such, has no contribution to make to the discussion of uncompensated changes but that a "positive" political economy, involving fully compensated changes, can be defined. From this argument, the inference may be drawn that full compensation is desirable in all cases, and the requirement for compensation may appear to stultify much "desirable" social policy.

The appropriateness or inappropriateness of compensation must be explicitly discussed quite apart from the methodology of political economy. The main point to be made is that the principle of compensation, and, thus, the scope for political economy, is restricted to those social changes that may legitimately be classified as "changes in law," that is, changes in the structural rules under which individuals make choices. Compensation is desirable here because only through the compensation device can appropriate criteria for "improvement" be discovered. This is merely to put in somewhat different language the classical liberal conception of democracy itself.

Within the structure of existing law, no grounds for the payment of com-

---

9. Objections will be raised to the procedure suggested here because its acceptance seems to leave the door open to exploitation of some parties to the contract by other unscrupulous parties. The owners of the smoke-creating firm may refuse to agree to any scheme except the one which grants them compensation equal to the full benefits of the proposed change. This possibility, or its converse, exists. But, in refusing to agree to any proffered compensation equal to or above the estimated value of the capital losses undergone, the owners must recognize that such opportunities might not recur.

As a second point, if the distributional results of a change are significantly important, this fact alone may reduce the extent of the bargaining range. Even though the objectively measured "income" of the previously damaged group were demonstrably increased by the adoption of the tax-compensation–smoke-abatement plan, this group might not agree if the owners secured the predominant share of the total benefits. They might veto the plan on distributional grounds, thereby preventing unanimity.

pensation exist. This point may be illustrated by reference to the theft example used by Stigler in his critique of the new welfare economics.[10] Could not the "real income" of society be increased by bribing potential thieves instead of hiring policemen? This question is irrelevant. Presumably, those individuals who are thieves at any moment have supported laws which are designed to prevent theft. Stealing is a recognized violation of existing law and, as such, deserves punishment without compensation. Quite clearly, no consensus could be expected on a proposed change in the law that would involve bribing all future thieves. The suggestion that such a change might increase "real income" implies some objective definition of real income which is independent of individuals' behavior.

A more practical example involves the government's prosecution of monopoly. The capital losses which are imposed upon firms successfully prosecuted should not, normally, be offset by compensation. This is because such action involves, in principle, no lawmaking. By contrast, the removal of a long-existing and specific exemption to the law should be accompanied by the appropriate compensating action.

There are, of course, difficult problems involved in distinguishing between changes in the law and the enforcement of existing law. But such problems are no different from those normally faced in the everyday definition of property rights, which are, of course, enormously difficult. The whole issue here may well be put in terms of property rights. The political economist in the specific role here discussed is concerned with social or collective action that modifies in some way the structure of legitimate property rights. Compensation is required for the reasons suggested above. On the other hand, law enforcement may modify the structure of actual property right, but, in principle, it does not disturb legitimate rights.

Political economy, therefore, applies to only one form of social change, namely, that which is deliberately chosen by the members of the social group acting in their collective capacities. Changes may occur for many reasons, and the set of possible changes that constitutes the domain for political economy is a relatively small subset of the total. Therefore, the requirement of compensation necessary to insure consensus or unanimity is not open to the

10. Stigler, "The New Welfare Economics," *American Economic Review* 33 (1943): 356.

commonly voiced objection that all progress involves social disturbance and that some individuals must be injured and some benefited by any significant social upheaval.

Changes may occur through shifts in tastes, introduction of new techniques, or growth in the supply of basic resources. These are normally considered to be the means through which an economy "progresses" or "grows." Changes of this nature are, however, different, philosophically, from those which are deliberately imposed through collective action. And this distinction is important. The free-market economic order is organized on the assumption that shifts may occur in the fundamentally exogenous variables. Imperfections of knowledge about the possible shifts in these underlying variables are incorporated with the appropriate offsetting entrepreneurial rewards and punishments. Any attempt to secure compensation for all losses would surely destroy the system. But changes imposed by collective action are different, and the uncertainty involved in attempts to predict such action cannot be discounted or offset in the ordinary market structure.[11]

V. The Social Welfare Function

The approach to political economy suggested in this essay may be compared with the Bergson-Samuelson approach which deliberately introduces ethical evaluations in the form of the "social welfare function." Both approaches aim at establishing a role for the economist qua scientist beyond positive economics narrowly defined. The differences between the two approaches lie in the treatment of individual values.

The "social welfare function" is an explicit expression of a value criterion. It incorporates fully the required information concerning the relative importance of conflicting aims, including the relative importance of separate in-

11. Some of the points made in this section may be clarified by the use of the game analogy, an approach to political economy that has been thoroughly developed by my colleague, Rutledge Vining. Political economy is concerned exclusively with the modifications of the rules of the game, and this branch of the discipline has no place in the discussion of strategic action taken by either side in the game itself. The compensation requirement suggests only that all players agree on the rules before continuing the game. Changes made within existing law are analogous to the enforcement of agreed-on rules, and changes arising from the strategic contest itself are fully analogous to the changes taking place by a shift of the exogenous variables of the economic order.

dividuals within the social group. The function orders all possible social situations and allows an external observer to select one as "best." Presumably, this "best" point will lie on a "welfare frontier" which contains a sub-infinity of possible points. But the precise meaning of this "welfare frontier" is not entirely clear. If social situations are to be ordered *externally,* the "individual welfare scales" embodied must be those akin to those which enter into the presumptive efficiency criterion discussed above. Individual preferences, insofar as they enter the construction (and they need not do so) must be those which *appear to the observer* rather than those revealed by the behavior of the individuals themselves. In other words, even if the value judgments expressed in the function say that individual preferences are to count, these preferences must be those presumed by the observer rather than those revealed in behavior.

Several questions may be raised. Unless the relevant choices are to be made by some entity other than individuals themselves, why is there any need to construct a "social" value scale? There would seem to be no reason for making interpersonal comparisons of "welfare" based on hypothetical individual preferences except for the purpose of assisting in the attainment of *given ends* for the group or some subgroup. This central feature of the approach seems, therefore, to be contrary to one of the presuppositions of the free society. The function may be useful as a device in assisting the decision-making of a despot, benevolent or otherwise, an organic state, or a single-minded ruling group. But, once this limitation is recognized, individual preferences, even as presumed by the observer, need not enter into the construction at all except insofar as it becomes necessary to consider predicted individual reaction to coercively imposed changes. The Pareto conception of "optimality" loses most of its significance.

The approach adopted here is based upon the idea that no "social" values exist apart from individual values. Therefore, the political economist, instead of choosing arbitrarily some limited set of ethical norms for incorporation into a "social welfare function," searches instead for "social compromises" on particular issues. His proposals are hypotheses about individual values, hypotheses which are subjected to testing in the collective choice processes. Actual values are revealed only through the political action of individuals, and consensus among individual members of the choosing group becomes the only possible affirmation of a "social" value. The order which is present among "social" decisions, if indeed there is one, is revealed in the decision process itself, not external to it. Whereas the "social welfare function" approach searches for a criterion independent of the choice process itself, presumably with a view toward influencing the choice, the alternative approach evaluates results only in terms of the choice process itself.

VI. Consensus among Reasonable Men

In developing the argument of this essay, I have assumed that the social group is composed of reasonable men, capable of recognizing what they want, of acting on this recognition, and of being convinced of their own advantage after reasonable discussion. Governmental action, at the important margins of decision, is assumed to arise when such individuals agree that certain tasks should be collectively performed. To this extent, my argument rests on some implicit acceptance of a contract theory of the state. Since it is carried out only after general agreement, collective action is essentially voluntary action. State or governmental coercion enters only insofar as individuals, through collectively imposed rules prevent themselves from acting as they would act in the absence of such rules.

I am aware of the limitations of this conception of society, and I can appreciate the force of the objection that may be raised on these grounds. Societies in the real world are not made up exclusively of reasonable men, and this fact introduces disturbing complications in any attempt to discuss the formation of social policy.

In outlining the structure of a possible non-evaluative political economy, I am suggesting that we proceed on an *as if* assumption. Despite our knowledge that some men are wholly unreasonable, we assume this away just as we have done in the organization of our whole democratic decision-making processes. Insofar as "antisocial" or unreasonable individuals are members of the group, consensus, even where genuine "mutual gains" might be present, may be impossible. Here the absolute unanimity rule must be broken; the political economist must try, as best he can, to judge the extent of unanimity required to verify (not refute) his hypothesis. Some less definitive rule of relative unanimity must be substituted for full agreement, as Wicksell recognized and suggested.

This necessary modification does not materially reduce the strength of the argument presented. But it does place an additional responsibility upon the political economist. He is forced to discriminate between reasonable and unreasonable men in his search for consensus. This choice need not reflect the introduction of personal evaluation. Relatively objective standards may be adduced to aid in the discrimination process. Reflection from everyday experience with groups which use unanimity as the customary, but not essential, means of reaching decisions should reveal that the genuinely unreasonable individual can be readily identified. This reduction of the unanimity requirement to some relative unanimity does not suggest that "unreasonable" as a characteristic behavior pattern can be determined on the basis of one issue alone. And it should be emphasized that in no way whatsoever does continuing disagreement with majority opinion suggest unreasonableness.

VII. Majority Rule, Consensus, and Discussion

The hypotheses which the political economist presents are tested by the measure of agreement reached, qualified only by the relative unanimity requirement introduced in the preceding section. But there remain two major practical difficulties to be confronted at this testing stage. These make the empirical testing difficult and, in some cases, impossible. First, collective decisions in democratically organized societies may be, and normally are, made on the basis of some variant of majority rule rather than consensus or unanimity, even if the latter is qualified to rule out limited "antisocial" dissent.

The economist, employing his presumptive efficiency criterion, presents for consideration a policy change which embodies the hypothesis that the adoption of this change will constitute "improvement" in the "welfare" of the group in accordance with the Pareto rule. This proposal is then voted upon, either by all individuals in a referendum or by their representatives in a legislative body. If a majority rejects the proposal, the economist's hypothesis is clearly refuted, and alternatives must be sought. The hypothesis is equally refuted if a minority dissents, but the proposal may be carried on the basis of majority decision. This adoption tends to preclude the presentation of alternative hypotheses more acceptable to the minority. Majority rule, considered as a final means of making decisions, has the effect of closing off discussion and of thereby limiting severely the efforts of the political economist.

This result of majority rule places before the political economist a great temptation and also places upon him significant responsibility. Knowing that collective decisions are made by majority rule, he will be tempted to present social alternatives which may command majority support rather than consensus. Adequate compensations for damaged minorities may be omitted in the proposals suggested with a view toward making the majority more receptive. Deliberate attempts in this direction would violate the neutral position outlined for the political economist here, but, given the inherently subjective basis for the presumptive efficiency criterion at best, the proposals presented may tend to reflect majority-oriented biases quite unintentionally. The danger that this bias will occur places upon the practitioner the responsibility of insuring that suggested proposals do, in fact, include compensations to damaged minorities estimated to be adequate and, contrariwise, do not include overcompensations to damaged majorities.

The probability that decisions will be made without consensus being attained adds responsibility to the economist's task. Much greater care must be taken with the construction and application of the presumptive efficiency criterion. Again the analogy with the medical diagnostician may be helpful. Majority rule tends to place the political economist in the position of the diagnostician who may propose a fatal dosage if his diagnosis should prove incorrect. Hence he must be more careful than otherwise in proposing alternative remedies.

The practical difficulties introduced by majority rule may not be great if there exists consensus that all collective decisions reached in this way are temporary or provisional and are subject to reversal and modification. If majority rule is understood to be, not a means of making final decisions, but rather as one of making provisional choices while discussion continues, the possibility remains that alternative hypotheses can be presented subsequent to a favorable majority vote. No barrier to discussion need be introduced by majority rule conceived in this way.

But if majority rule is conceived as merely a step in the discussion process leading toward final agreement, a second major problem of practical importance arises. The whole process of discussion which characterizes the democratic idea implies that, insofar as their behavior in making collective decisions is concerned, individuals do not have explicitly defined ends of an instrumental sort. If they do, discussion is bound to be fruitless, and an initial disagreement will persist. The purpose of political discussion is precisely that of changing "tastes" among social alternatives. The political economist, therefore, in constructing and applying his presumptive efficiency criterion, must try to incorporate the predicted preferences of individuals, not as they exist at a given moment, but as they will be modified after responsible discussion. In other words, he must try to predict "what reasonable individuals will reasonably want" after discussion, not what they "do want in a given moment" before discussion or what they "ought to want" if they agreed in all respects with the observer.

This recognition that individuals do not have *given ends* which can, at any moment, be taken as data by the observer appears to blur the sharp dividing line between "positive" political economy as here outlined and "normative" political economy which allows the observer to introduce his own ethical evaluations. This makes it more important that the attempt be made to test propositions in terms of expressed individual values instead of first attempting to estimate such values as a basis for decision.

VIII. Conclusion

Positive science is concerned with the discovery of "what is"; normative science, with "what ought to be." Positive economics, narrowly conceived, overly restricts the "what is" category. Political economy has a non-normative role in discovering "what is the structure of individual values." The political economist, in accomplishing this task, can remain as free of personal value judgment as the positive economist. To be sure, the objectivity of the political economist is more difficult to preserve, and his behavior in departing from it more difficult for observers to detect. His hypotheses must take the form of policy propositions, and these may tend to appear as recommendations rather than hypotheses. And, since such hypotheses must be based on some presumptive efficiency criterion, an element of subjectivity is necessarily introduced. But the presence of subjective evaluation of the outside world (which includes the preference fields of other individuals) does not imply the infusion of an individual value judgment concerning the "goodness" of the proposal presented.

In a sense, the political economist is concerned with discovering "what people want." The content of his efforts may be reduced to very simple terms. This may be summed up in the familiar statement: *There exist mutual gains from trade.* His task is that of locating possible flaws in the existing social structure and in presenting possible "improvements." His specific hypothesis is that *mutual* gains do, in fact, exist as a result of possible changes (trades). This hypothesis is tested by the behavior of private people in response to the suggested alternatives. Since "social" values do not exist apart from individual values in a free society, consensus or unanimity (mutuality of gain) is the only test which can insure that a change is beneficial.

In his diagnosis and prescription, the economist must call upon all the skills and resources which he possesses. These include the traditional "efficiency" tools, but, in utilizing these, he must beware of slipping into the easy assumption of omniscience. The individual preference patterns which he incorporates into his models must be conceived as presumed or predicted, and the changes which are based on these must always be considered tentative hypotheses to be subjected to testing in the polling places. The economist can never say that one social situation is more "efficient" than another. This judgment is beyond his range of competence. He presents a hypothesis that one situation is "presumed Pareto-efficient," and he allows the unanimity test (appropriately modified) to decide whether his prediction is correct or incorrect. From this it follows that all his proposals must embody estimated full compensations.

The role of the political economist as outlined here may be quite limited. The applicability of political economy is inversely related to the rate at which majoritarian conceptions of the democratic process replace the classical liberal conceptions. Even in a world seemingly dominated by majoritarian views, however, the approach outlined here can be useful in establishing some norms for scientific objectivity. Beyond the area of "positive" political economy, there may be room for the individual to serve in a normative capacity as an especially well-informed citizen. Here his own ethical evaluations may be explicitly introduced, and he may choose to utilize certain welfare function constructions in this task. But this behavior must be sharply distinguished from his professional role, either as positive economist or as political economist.

Perhaps this essay may best be summarized by the consideration of a single example: the removal of a long-established tariff. The positive economist can predict that imports of the commodity will increase, that domestic prices of the commodity will fall, that exports will increase, that resources will be shifted from the domestic to the export industries, etc. The "positive " political economist, building on the fundamental theorems of positive economics, attempts to devise a proposal or proposals which will remove or reduce the tariff and be approved by an overwhelming majority of the whole social group. He advances a proposal which embodies a tariff reduction, along with estimated full compensation to the damaged industries financed out of a tax imposed on benefited groups. This proposal is advanced as a hypothesis. If the proposal is accepted by the whole group, the hypothesis is not refuted. If it is rejected, or approved by only a majority, the political economist should search for alternative schemes. In all this, as an observer, he is ethically neutral. His own evaluations of the alternatives considered do not, and should not, influence his behavior in any way other than that necessarily arising out of his membership in the group.

If complexities of the collective decision-making process arise to prevent a genuine testing of the hypothesis, the economist may, if he desires, discard his "scientific" cloak. He may introduce his own ethical evaluations and state openly and frankly that he thinks tariff reductions would be "good" for the whole group.

It seems useful that these three types of behavior of individuals calling themselves economists be separated and classified, even if practical politics reduce the second type to relative insignificance.

The Relevance of Pareto Optimality

I. Introduction

In his basic paper, "On Welfare Theory and Pareto Regions,"[1] Professor Ragnar Frisch has properly emphasized the necessity for specifying carefully the constraints that confine the "Pareto Region," that region within which the Pareto criterion for classifying positions is to be employed. As he demonstrates, the region will depend upon the nature of the constraints introduced, and the set of points or positions that may be classified as "optimal" will vary with these constraints. I propose here to discuss the nature of the appropriate constraints in a somewhat different manner and from a different philosophy than that of Frisch. His view, which is that "social value judgments" must be introduced in order to determine the form of constraints, leaves the relevance of the whole Paretian construction up in air since, by implication, any change in the set of "social value judgments" employed will change the definition of optimality. By contrast, I shall try to demonstrate that meaningful criteria may be used to delineate the "appropriate" Pareto region, and the notion of Pareto optimality may, in this way, be rescued from the almost meaningless state to which any usage of "social welfare functions" or "social value judgments" seems to reduce it.

In the discussion that follows, I shall show that the Pareto criterion is of

From *Journal of Conflict Resolution* 6 (December 1962): 341–54, copyright 1962 by Sage Publications, Inc. Reprinted by permission of Sage Publications, Inc.

The ideas developed in this paper emerge from a continuing "community of discourse" in which several persons have participated at various times. The contributions of each cannot be isolated, but Ronald Coase, Otto Davis, Francesco Forte, Gordon Tullock, and Rutledge Vining should be especially mentioned. All errors remain my own.

1. See Ragnar Frisch, "On Welfare Theory and Pareto Regions," *International Economic Papers* 9 (1959), 39–92.

little value when employed solely to classify "results" defined with respect to the orthodox economic variables, inputs and outputs of goods and services possessed by different persons in the social group. I shall, instead, argue that the criterion must be extended to classify social rules which constrain the private individual behavior that produces such results. When the discussion of "optimal" rules is introduced, it may be shown that such rules produce results that, themselves, may be "nonoptimal." This apparent paradox will be illustrated in each of three separate cases, each one of which has relevance for policy issues.

II. The Rules of the Game

Frisch separates the conditions or constraints confining Pareto regions into two groups which he labels *obligatory conditions* and *facultative conditions.* The first group includes those conditions that are exogenous to the group, taking the form of technical and physical limitations to production. These conditions are, of course, familiar, and they serve as part of the environment for any problem of choice, whether this is confronted by the individual or the group. Indeed, without these conditions no choice problem should ever arise. I shall not, in the argument of this paper, be concerned directly with this set of physical constraints. The second group of constraints are those that the group chooses to impose upon itself. They constitute, so to speak, the "rules of the game" within which individuals of the group make decisions and organize activity. The discussion will be devoted largely to this set of conditions or constraints. It is this set that has been largely neglected by welfare economists who have used the Pareto criterion, with the result that much of the analysis has been empty of content.

In discussing this second set of conditions, I shall depart from Frisch's terminology and from his analysis. Henceforward, I shall refer to these conditions or constraints as *rules,* considered as standards of conduct applicable to all the members of the social group. Frisch chooses to define facultative conditions in terms of what I call result variables, inputs and outputs of goods and services assigned to individuals. He then separates the *selection* problem from the *realization* problem. By the former, he means the classification of positions within the broad region defined by both the obligatory and the facultative constraints. In the *realization* problem, he asks whether or not there exists a "régime" or "régimes" which will produce these Pareto-optimal positions. Frisch's approach, in this respect, seems both cumbersome and misleading. It tends to direct attention away from the basic choice issues that members of the group confront. In a free society (the only society for which Pareto construction seems at all relevant), the group chooses or decides collectively upon the *rules* that are to be mutually imposed upon the behavior of its members. As Professor Rutledge Vining has stressed, the game analogue is quite close here. Members of the group may, of course, choose among different rules and sets of rules on the basis of predictions concerning the results expected from the operation of these rules, but, explicitly, the group makes a choice only among rules. Thus, the issues facing the group are solely those of *realization,* to use Frisch's terminology. The selection problems do not arise explicitly.[2]

At any particular moment of time, there must exist a set of rules, either legally imposed and enforced by some collectively organized agency or conventionally honored, and these rules serve to constrain the behavior of the members of the group as they act in their capacities as private individuals. The first point to be made is that, given *any* such set of rules, *any* position reached by the group is Pareto-optimal provided only that individual members of the group are both fully informed and fully rational.

The set of rules serves to define a "Pareto region," described as the set of all possible positions or points attainable under both these social rules and the physical constraints that are present. Each of these positions may be defined, formally, as a vector in the "welfare space" so limited, components of this vector being inputs and outputs of goods and services assigned to each

---

2. To Frisch a facultative constraint is illustrated, for example, by the requirement that the share of the national income going to workers shall not fall below a certain proportion of the total. His selection problem then becomes that of determining whether or not positions exist that can satisfy this condition along with the obligatory conditions. Only after this is done, does Frisch pose the realization problem which involves the question as to whether there exist social rules for individual behavior that will produce the "optimal" positions selected. My difference with Frisch here is that I suggest that social groups rarely, if ever, impose facultative conditions of this sort explicitly. Instead the group actually chooses laws, and modifications in existing laws, which produce certain predicted results. Thus, the set of rules in existence at any moment of time becomes the facultative conditions which serve to confine the Pareto region.

person in the group. Any change in the rules governing private behavior will change the structure of the region. Once a region is defined, however, the Pareto criterion may be employed to classify all points or positions into two sets, those that are "optimal" and those that are "nonoptimal." In a region so strictly confined, however, *any* position finally attained will be in the Pareto-optimal set of positions, except for ignorance and irrationality in the behavior of some or all individuals in the group. No paradox is involved here when it is recognized that each individual, if rational and fully informed, will maximize his expected utility within the constraints imposed on his behavior by the existing social rules. If each individual does this, there is no change, within the existing rules, that can make anyone better off. The Pareto criterion, in this situation, has relevance only insofar as it provides some assistance in dispelling areas of ignorance or in removing certain barriers to rational behavior. This application of the criterion is not without usefulness; the observer may be able to assist persons by demonstrating the presence of "gains" that can be made, even within the rules. The tax lawyer, without knowing it, is applying the Pareto criterion in this sense.

It seems clear, however, that welfare economists have not intended that the Pareto criterion be used only in so limited a fashion. In the models that have been generally employed, individuals are assumed to be both rational and fully informed. In such models, therefore, all positions attained are, by definition, Pareto-optimal, and, hence, the Pareto criterion loses all relevance. But the Pareto scheme has been directed explicitly toward assistance in the formation of *policy,* that is, toward changes in the existing set of rules that constrain the private actions of individuals. Once this is admitted, however, the question that immediately arises concerns the extent to which rules changes are to be allowed.

Most of the actual discussion among welfare economists has concerned a rather well-defined "region," but almost no attention has been given to the requirement that, to be relevant at all, this region must be defined by "constitutional" limits placed on changes in social or organizational rules of the game. If, by contrast, the situation is assumed wholly open in this respect, with only obligatory constraints applying, the Pareto criterion becomes almost as meaningless as in the strictly confined case in which no rules changes are allowed at all. Should we allow a change in the rules such that, if he is able, one man could make all his fellow citizens his slaves? Positions could still be classified as "optimal" and "nonoptimal," but, obviously, the content of the classification scheme becomes relatively empty.

Meaningful use of the Pareto criterion, for classifying positions or states, must, therefore, be limited to "regions" that allow for *some* but not *any and all* changes in an existing set of social rules. In Section IV, I shall argue that the requirement of consensus or unanimity among members of the group on such "constitutional" changes does provide the appropriate limits to their relevant Pareto region. Before this, however, I shall, in Section III, present a simple illustration of the analysis of this section.

III. Illustration

Let us assume a very simple two person–two goods world. The two individuals differ in their capacity to produce the two goods, although each person can, to some extent, produce some of each good. Production possibilities confronting each individual are shown in Figure 1, and, for simplicity only, production possibility curves are assumed linear.

We may first examine the strictly confined case discussed in Section II. Assume that there exist rules which wholly prohibit trade between the two

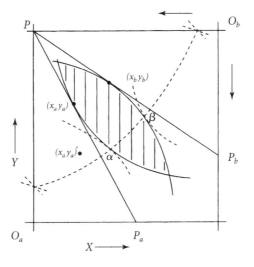

Figure 1. Pareto point-sets under varying rules

persons. Within this set of rules, each individual will act so as to maximize his expected utility. Individual A, who is highly skilled in the production of good Y relative to X will reach a position of individual equilibrium at (x_a, y_a); similarly, Individual B will reach a position of individual equilibrium at (x_b, y_b). The final position of the "group," which may be defined by the quantities $(x_a y_a)$ $(x_b y_b)$, is Pareto-optimal, within the relevant Pareto region. The region in this case is that set of points or positions that might be attained by the movement of the two individuals within the production possibility frontiers (PP_a) and (PP_b), and without trade. Thus, for example, the position defined as, $(x_a y_a)'$ $(x_b y_b)$, is within the region defined, and it is classified as a nonoptimal position. Any such position, however, can be departed from upon a realization of the individual of his own opportunities. If A, in this instance, is rational and informed, he will not, of course, remain at the nonoptimal position.

Let us now examine the second case. Assume that existing social rules allow the two individuals to cooperate through specialization and exchange, but that mutually respected rules enforce sanctions against deliberate exploitation through fraud, robbery, subjugation, and murder. These restrictions convert our model into one that is familiar to economists. Individual A will specialize in the production of good Y; Individual B will specialize in the production of good X. Individual shares in total production are shown at P. After trade, a position of "equilibrium" is attained along the contract locus $\alpha\beta$. The Pareto region in this case becomes the whole set of positions that were potentially attainable in the first case, without trade, plus that set of points shown by the lightly shaded area in Figure 1. (Only the second group of these may be represented in Figure 1 by single points since only with trade is the whole "box" utilized.) Within this well-defined Pareto region, the set of points falling along the locus $\alpha\beta$ is the Pareto-optimal set. Note that, through changing the form of the constraints imposed, the Pareto region is expanded, and the set of optimal positions is changed. In this instance, note that the whole of the Pareto region in the first, strictly confined case, is contained within the Pareto region appropriate to the second case, that in which trade is allowed to take place. There is no intersection, however, between the Pareto-optimal set of positions in the first case and the Pareto-optimal set of positions in the second case.

We may now consider the third case, that in which *no* restrictions are placed on the behavior of individuals. No "rules of the game" are respected by members of the group. Trade can, obviously, take place, but, also, one individual can defraud the other, can rob the other of his possessions, can even make the other his slave if he is able to exert sufficient physical force. In this extreme model, only the external obligatory constraints confine the Pareto region. All positions that may be represented as points within the area of the Edgeworth box of Figure 1 are contained in this region, plus, of course, those that are within the region relevant to the strictly confined case. This unconditional Pareto region of the third case, which we may call the unconstrained, includes within it the appropriate regions of the first and second cases. The Pareto-optimal set of positions in this third case is defined as those points falling along the locus $O_a \alpha \beta O_b$. Note here that, should A be the strong man in the two-man group, he could make B his slave and move to a position in the vicinity of O_b, provided that we neglect, for purposes of this model, the pure subsistence requirements of B. The position on the locus in the vicinity of O_b would be defined as Pareto-optimal, despite B's complete exploitation. Note here that there does exist an intersection between the Pareto-optimal sets in the second and third cases. Those positions that are Pareto-optimal under the more loosely defined Pareto region and which fall within the more closely defined region must also be Pareto-optimal in the second region.[3]

IV. The Unanimity Criterion

The illustrative model presented above suggests that welfare economists have normally assumed, implicitly, that the second case describes the situation when they have applied the Pareto classification scheme. The first, or strictly confined, case, in which the Pareto criterion is useful only in dispelling ig-

3. This proposition, in general terms, is one of the important relationships that Frisch stresses. ("On Welfare Theory," 59.) Note, however, that the method introduced here does not support Frisch's proposition that the Pareto-optimal set of positions in the more closely confined region is more *inclusive* than the subset of the Pareto-optimal set of the loosely confined region contained within the closely confined region. It is not appropriate to develop the differences in conclusions here. These differences arise from the fact that the constraints employed here are treated in terms of rules.

norance or irrationality is not the implicit model upon which the new welfare economics has been constructed. Nor is the third case, in which only the physical or obligatory constraints serve to inhibit the private behavior of individuals, the relevant one. Almost all discussions relating to the Edgeworth-box type of diagram limit the set of Pareto-optimal positions to those defined by some contract locus. This limitation to a "contract" locus amounts to the placing of additional constraints on human behavior, constraints that can only be interpreted in the form of mutually accepted rules and regulations.

What are the characteristics of these additional constraints, which are purely facultative, to employ Frisch's term? As the analysis above demonstrates, these constraints cannot be wholly described by any existing set of social rules within which private behavior takes place. To be at all relevant for discussions of policy, the Pareto criterion must be applied to the classification of positions that may be attained through *changes* in the existing set of social or organizational rules. But the analysis has also demonstrated that the criterion loses much of its meaning if all changes in rules are permissible. How is an effective limit to be placed on the admissibility of rules changes, to modifications in the "constitution"?

One answer to this question is provided by the Wicksellian unanimity criterion. Given any existing set of social rules, changes in these rules are permissible to the extent that all members of the group agree. By permissible here, I mean only that the effective Pareto region is assumed to be limited by the extent of such unanimously approved changes. Welfare economists have not explicitly accepted this unanimity principle for limiting constitutional changes, but this principle is implied in much of the analysis.

An analogy with voluntary games is helpful here. In discussions of changes in the rules, through which a game is defined, it is normally assumed that each individual player retains the alternative of withdrawing from play. This constraint serves to limit the set of possible rules changes. Within this "constitutional rule," a region of optimal and nonoptimal positions becomes possible and this region may be described and the Pareto criterion employed in making the relevant classification. Coerced games, those in which the individual is forced to play, quite independently of his possible preference for withdrawing, have not been fully discussed. The "prisoners' dilemma" can be considered as a coerced game, but the mere fact that game theorists have treated this as an exceptional or peculiar case illustrates the overwhelming emphasis that has been placed on voluntary games.

The unanimity criterion for changes in the set of rules that govern individual behavior allows a unique, and generally applicable, Pareto "region" to be defined. This approach requires, of course, that a start be made from an existing set of rules. Meaningful analysis must, however, always "start from" some base or reference position. This does not sanctify the *status quo* or elevate it to any position of special respect. The approach rests, instead, on the elemental proposition that changes must be made on some existing situation, and meaningful limitations must be placed on the sort of changes that are to be allowed. Unless the unanimity principle is applied to constitutional changes, we are left with the necessity of introducing "social welfare functions" of which there are as many as there are individuals in the group.

Accepting the Wicksellian approach, the Pareto criterion can be applied at two levels. First, within the existing set of rules, the classification may be helpful in dispelling ignorance and irrationality as noted previously. Secondly, the criterion may be used to classify positions, unattainable under existing rules, but which, conceptually, may be attained through the adoption of rules which, themselves, can be agreed upon by all members of the group. It should be noted that this application and use of the Pareto criterion is not subject to the charge made by Frisch that it amounts to saying that "free competition is the best of all possible régimes in the class of régimes which consists of the régime of free competition."[4] The unanimity principle for constitutional change will allow departures from free competition, free trade, when the necessary side conditions are not satisfied. The existence of interactions among individual utility functions or among individual production functions may reflect the existence of "mutual gains from trade" that may be secured through changes in the rules, either through the collectivization of activities or through the restricting of certain types of human behavior.[5] The introduction of the unanimity principle does emphasize an element of the

---

4. "On Welfare Theory," 67.

5. For a more complete discussion see James M. Buchanan, "Positive Economics, Welfare Economics, and Political Economy," *Journal of Law and Economics* 2 (October 1959): 124–38.

competitive or market process that has, however, been seriously neglected. As Professor Frank Knight has suggested, much of the support for the market form of organization arises from the simple fact that it is the only form of organization upon which men seem able to agree.

V. The Notion of "Optimal" Rules

Through the use of the single constitutional constraint suggested, a determinate Pareto region is defined, given the obligatory constraints. Changes that do not fall within this limited set may, of course, be made, that is, changes upon which all members of the group do not agree. This suggests that changes in the organizational rules, themselves, may be classified into two sets, those that are Pareto-optimal and those that are nonoptimal. As we shall demonstrate, the Pareto classification may prove more relevant in such a classification of changes in rules than in the discussion of results or outcomes.

If all members of the group *always* benefit from changes in the rules, it seems obvious that such changes would be carried out. And any failure to make such generally beneficial changes must reflect, at a different level from that previously discussed, the presence of ignorance concerning the results of the changes proposed. Even at the level of rules changes, therefore, the Pareto criterion can be helpful only insofar as it assists in dispelling ignorance and irrationality. But the ignorance about the working out of social rules is clearly a more pervasive phenomenon than that concerning the availability of individually attainable alternatives. Changes in social rules involve the necessity of making predictions of a considerably more sophisticated nature than those involved in changes in individual habits or modes of conduct. For example, it is probably much easier for me to predict the consequences of changing my own working hours than to predict the consequences that might result from a general change in the working hours of the whole community. The Pareto criterion, as employed by the political economist, can serve a useful function in demonstrating the mutuality of gain to be expected from proposed rules changes.

Few problems arise, however, in the simple cases postulated here, that is, those that produce results that are *always* beneficial to all members of the relevant social group. For an illustration, return to the first case discussed in connection with Figure 1. Existing social rules prohibiting all trade between the two individuals would obviously be modified to allow trade which would, in the model, produce results that would, in each instance, be mutually preferable to both parties, or, at the limit, preferred by one and indifferent to the other.

Many situations are not so simple. A change in any existing rule need not produce results that will, in every case, be beneficial to all members of the group. But note that this need not imply that the unanimity principle for constitutional changes is inapplicable. The members of the group may be observed to agree on changes in the rules that produce "results" that, when classified by the orthodox Pareto criterion, are clearly "nonoptimal"; in other words, "optimal rules," *defined as those that cannot be changed by general agreement,* may generate results that may be classified as nonoptimal. Note that this definition of "optimal rules" is identical with the standard definition for the optimality of a position or point.

VI. The Enforcement of Competition

I propose now to examine three separate situations, in each one of which the operation of organizational rules accepted by general consensus, and, thus, "optimal," may be predicted to produce results which, if independently classified within the region as proposed above, seem clearly nonoptimal.

That is to say, there may exist no means of securing agreement among all members of the group on any change in the rule, despite the fact that observed results may be classified as nonoptimal by the orthodox usage of the Pareto criterion. Three separate situations are discussed because the reason for the apparent paradox is different in each one. Numerous illustrations may be introduced in each situation, but I shall confine the discussion largely to three important issues of policy.

The most familiar situation is that presented when the results produced by the operations of a constraining rule are, to some degree, indeterminate. Predictions must be made about the pattern of some probability distribution of results, with some elements in this pattern being mutually beneficial to all parties while others are harmful to some members of the group, beneficial and harmful being defined here relative to the situation produced under some alternative state of affairs. In this situation, any rule must produce results that, on occasion, are nonoptimal and which, if independently considered, could be improved upon in such a way as to secure mutual gains to all members of the group. As Professor Ronald Coase has pointed out, each time a driver is forced to stop at a road sign or signal in an isolated no-traffic situation, Pareto-optimality is violated. Clearly, the driver could be made better off and no one else made worse off should the sign or signal be removed, for that particular moment. Nevertheless, we observe such traffic signals in profusion, and few persons would choose to see them abolished. The implication is that, somehow, predictions are made to the effect that the costs to the group stemming out of all instances of nonoptimal results are more than offset by the benefits occurring in those, perhaps few, cases when the signals do insure optimal results. A comparison of costs and benefits is necessary, or, more broadly considered, a comparison of alternative institutional arrangements or social rules over a whole sequence of possible results.

Are there economic analogues to the traffic signal situation? Communities are observed to adopt rules that prohibit certain business practices with the aim of preserving or enforcing competition. Among such rules are those that prevent separate firms in an industry from entering into wholly voluntary agreements on prices, market shares, and mergers. For members of the specific industrial subgroup, such rules are equivalent to prohibitions on trade or exchange. For this subgroup, changes that remove this constraint would clearly be mutually beneficial to all parties. But the Pareto construction is rarely, if ever, applied at this level. Presumably, for some larger social group, which includes the firms in question, the restrictive rules may be optimal. If such rules are to be judged optimal, however, the logical basis for their support requires examination. Why should the inclusive social group impose upon its own members rules that prohibit the reaching of wholly voluntary agreements? Any such rule must be predicted, on occasion, to produce nonoptimal results.[6]

The standard response here is that the predicted presence of external

6. For an interesting group of papers that suggest the development of economists' attitudes in this direction, see those by M. A. Adelman ("The Antimerger Act, 1950–60," *American Economic Review* 51 [May 1961]: 236–44); Almarin Phillips ("Policy Implications of the Theory of Interfirm Organization," *American Economic Review* 51 [May 1961]: 245–54); Donald Dewey ("Mergers and Cartels: Some Reservations about Policy," *American Economic Review* 51 [May 1961]: 255–62). Dewey, especially, explores the possible conflict between the restriction on freedom of contract and the orthodox criteria for economic efficiency.

(spillover, neighborhood) effects can dictate the imposition on such constraints on private behavior. Firms within an industrial subgroup may, if allowed freedom of action, reach agreements that will damage members of the more inclusive group who are not party to these agreements, consumers, or potential rivals. This familiar explanation begs more questions than it answers, however, for it is evident that such prohibitive rules are not imposed in *all* cases where voluntary agreements among members of a subgroup exert some effects on the utility of those external to the agreements. The marriage contract may be cited as one that would surely be prohibited under such a rigid application of the externality principle. What is required here is obviously some comparison, some balancing off, between the operation of a rule that prohibits voluntary agreements exerting effects and the situation that would prevail in the absence of such a role.

Such a comparison is more difficult than it might appear. How can third parties be injured by voluntary contractual arrangements among others? Provided freedom of contract is present, and provided that the costs of organizing voluntary agreements can be neglected, there is no damage that may be inflicted on third parties. Hence, there is no justification of the rule prohibiting "trade," regardless of the presence of externalities. No rules prohibiting mergers, for example, could be supported in this case. If firms in a specific industry should find it advantageous to merge, and if the threatened result should portend injury to consumers, then surely the organizational arrangement that would emerge under the conditions postulated would be that of a consumers' cooperative, large enough to secure the full efficiencies of scale but without monopoly exploitation. If the organization of agreement is costless, the capital value of the assets of the firms in question will always be as great to consumers as to the existing owners. A "bargaining range" will exist, and trade will tend to take place.

The optimality or efficiency of any rule prohibiting voluntary agreements can only be demonstrated in those cases where some external effects are present *and* where there is some asymmetry in the costs of organizing different voluntary arrangements.[7] Of course the reaching of voluntary agree-

---

7. The importance of organizational costs in determining the institutional structure has been seriously neglected by economists. There are indications, however, that the problems in this area are beginning to be recognized and that significant modifications in

ments is not costless, and the costs of reaching agreement are not identical for all possible arrangements. When this is recognized, the comparison of alternative rules that govern human behavior takes on different aspects. Rules that serve to restrict the reaching of wholly voluntary agreements among members of the group can be justified if predictions suggest that certain types of voluntary arrangements are, relatively, costly. In the particular example here, that of industrial combinations, the required asymmetry does seem to be present. Firms that are party to an agreement or to a potential agreement are fewer in number than consumers and potential consumers of almost any final product or service. The costs of reaching agreement increase significantly as the size of the group required to agree is expanded.[8] From this it follows that the firms, faced with the lower costs of agreeing or combining, may enter into agreements that will significantly damage consumers without these consumers being able to enter into the appropriate offsetting agreements. Under such conditions as these, it becomes rational for the members of the larger and more inclusive social group to adopt a general rule or set of rules that may prohibit, or severely restrict, voluntary agreements within an industrial group. The benefits to be secured from the operation of this rule may be expected to outweigh the costs, when a whole sequence of events is considered.

The important conclusion for purposes of our analysis here is that, in any particular application, observed results from the operation of such a rule may seem to be clearly nonoptimal. Firms may be observed to be too small to take full advantage of efficiencies of scale. Pareto optimality in the stan-

---

economic theory, and in welfare economics especially, may result. For an early recognition of the importance of these factors, see Ronald Coase, "The Nature of the Firm," *Economica* 4 (1937): 386–405; reprinted in American Economic Association, *Readings in Price Theory* (Homewood, Ill.: Richard D. Irwin, 1952), 331–51. For essentially the same line of reasoning applied to the Pigovian welfare calculus, see Coase, "The Problem of Social Cost," *Journal of Law and Economics* 3 (1961): 1–45.

In this connection also, see Buchanan, "Positive Economics," especially pp. 130–31; and, also James M. Buchanan and Gordon Tullock, *The Calculus of Consent* (Ann Arbor: University of Michigan Press, 1962). Also, see Otto Davis and Andrew Whinston, "Externalities, Welfare, and the Theory of Games," *Journal of Political Economy* 70 (June 1962): 241–62.

8. This relationship is central to the analysis contained in Buchanan and Tullock, *Calculus of Consent*, which is, essentially, an analysis of the choice among political decision-making rules.

dard sense involved in the measurement of results is violated. Yet the rule prohibiting firms from merging into units of "optimal" size may itself be "optimal" in the sense that, even with full compensations, there may be no way of securing consensus on any change. Thus, the mere demonstration of some violation of Pareto optimality in the orthodox classification of *results* may not be sufficient to suggest that some change in *policy* is dictated. Such a demonstration will, of course, always remain a necessary condition before any change in policy is to be considered.

VII. Rules versus Authorities

The familiar debate over "rules versus authorities" in monetary policy may be introduced as an illustration of a second type of situation where optimal rules, those from which no changes may be made by unanimous consent, may operate so as to produce nonoptimal results. When attention is concentrated on particular events, as these may be described by the relevant variables, a strong case can always be made for the superiority of an administrative authority or authorities over any rule or set of rules prescribing action in advance. A monetary authority, endowed with wisdom and prudence, can take full advantage of the information peculiar to the particular event. Such an authority, empowered to act independently of specific constraining rules, should be able to insure a closer attainment of the "Pareto frontier" than would the operation of any automatic or quasi-automatic general rule for policy action.

The specific decisions or actions that an authority will take cannot, however, be predicted in advance, at least to the same degree that the operations of an automatic rule can be predicted. When the beneficial effects expected to result from predictability *per se* are significant, some general rule may be more acceptable than the loosely confined authority, even with the expectation that particular results from the operation of the rule will be less than optimal in many instances. The foreknowledge that the rule will be followed can modify behavior in such a manner as to make the rule, over an expected sequence of events, more desirable than the authority. If, in adjusting their behavior to a predictable rule for monetary action, private individuals and firms eliminate much of the need for such action, the rule may be preferred over even the most efficient authority which must, by definition, remain more unpredictable in its own actions than the constraining rule. In each and every particular event, considered in isolation, the authority could, conceptually at least, produce more desirable results for *all* members of the social group. But these results are produced within a framework governing private decisions that is different under the presence and absence of the rule. It may become largely irrelevant, therefore, to compare the efficacy of the authority and some alternative rule in terms of the specific results that would be produced under a single framework.[9]

There are numerous noneconomic examples of this situation where the alternative institutional arrangements exert important differing effects on the pattern of human behavior. Perhaps the most familiar discussion is found in the debates over capital punishment. Those who argue in support of capital punishment do so largely on the grounds that a "rule" requiring punishment will deter potential criminals, whereas those who argue for the abolition of executions do so on the grounds that, in each particular case, little is to be gained by the execution of the condemned prisoner.

The Pareto classification of "results" into optimal and nonoptimal sets is less relevant in this situation than in the first type that was discussed in Section VI. There the rule, to be optimal, must be predicted to produce both optimal and nonoptimal results, with the former events outweighing the latter on balance. In this second situation, by contrast, particular results could, conceptually, be nonoptimal in each particular instance while the rule producing these results remains an optimal one.

VIII. Collective Decision-Making

An example of a third situation where nonoptimal results are produced from the operation of rules that may embody general consensus is provided in the institutions for collective decision-making. A constitutional rule may, for in-

---

9. Even if, over the course of historical experience, a hypothetical rule for monetary policy could be shown to have worked badly, relative to the actual operations of an authority, this would tell little about the relative desirability of the rules since the whole framework of private decision-making would have been different had the rule been in operation instead of the authority. Similarly, empirical studies such as those carried out by Warburton, and Friedman, suggesting the superiority of nonexistent rules can, at best, be broadly illustrative, nothing more.

stance, dictate that group decisions on specific matters shall be made upon agreement among some designated proportion of the total population, or its representative assembly. Simple majority agreement is a familiar device in democratic societies, although the range of institutional arrangements for collective decision-making is extremely wide. The slightest observation reveals that group action on many issues may be concluded upon agreement among members of some subgroup smaller than the total group.

In each such arrangement, results will surely be nonoptimal on many occasions. To insure that each position obtained through the process of collective decision-making should qualify as Pareto-optimal, all decisions would have to be reached through the unanimous consent of all members of the inclusive group, not some proportion of this number. This need not imply, however, that a constitutional rule dictating the institutional arrangements for ordinary collective decision-making need be nonoptimal. It may prove quite impossible, even granted the full utilization of compensation, to secure the general consent of all members of the group on a constitutional change toward more inclusive voting agreements.

A specific illustration may prove helpful. Assume that the constitutional rule dictates that ordinary group decisions are to be made by simple majority voting. Assume a three-man group, and assume that each member of the group possesses assets valued at $100. Let us neglect purely redistributive transfers and assume that the group, through the exercise of majority decision, can choose to utilize resources to produce or consume "collective" goods. Is there any assurance that the projects approved will, in fact, be equally or more productive than the sacrificed private investments? Let us suppose that, with a general tax of $33 levied on each member of the group, a project can be constructed that yields only $70 worth of benefits, but that these are uniquely concentrated so as to benefit solely B and C. In this case, with simple majority controlling, B and C can carry the decision and insure the expenditure of public funds on the project in question. The result must be classified as nonoptimal. All members of the group could be made better off by some return to the position prior to the approval of the project.[10]

---

10. One additional, and constraining, rule must be present to insure these results. If there are no restrictions on vote buying and selling, the political analogue to side payments, those members of a threatened minority could always bribe the members of the

Must it be concluded in this case that the constitutional rule that allows majorities to carry group decisions is, itself, nonoptimal? Or is it possible that the group may agree, through an explicit failure to approve any change, on such a rule? Once the costs of reaching agreement are incorporated into the calculus here, there is no necessary contradiction or paradox. The attainment of unanimity in ordinary day-to-day collective decisions may prove to be extremely costly. Rather than undergo this cost, members of the group may decide, in the constitutional process, to accept the departures from Pareto optimality that less-than-unanimity voting rules may produce. Majority voting is, of course, only one of the many arrangements that might be made.[11]

Other illustrations of what is essentially the same situation may be drawn readily. In ordinary exchange processes, potential traders may actually refrain from trading if the costs of bargaining and negotiation promise to be prohibitively high. Or, alternatively, they may choose to adopt conventions, rules, that are, in themselves, arbitrary as a means of reducing bargaining costs. In advanced economies, it is a conventional rule that the seller of goods shall set the price. This reduces the costs of higgling and bargaining, but, as in the majority voting example, it surely produces nonoptimal results on many occasions, as these results have been traditionally classified by welfare economists using the Pareto classification.

IX. Conclusions

The preceding discussion has demonstrated that the application of the Pareto criterion to organizational rules introduces complexities in prediction and in analysis that have been neglected in the concentration on particular results. The standard procedure, which involves the examination of a position (e.g., an "allocation" of resources) with a view to determining whether

---

majority to refrain from undertaking "wasteful" projects. In this case, only purely redistributive transfers would be made through majority voting, and, of course, Pareto optimality would not be violated. We observe, however, that generally accepted ethical and legal rules prohibit the making of such side payments, that is, vote buying and selling.

11. This discussion of collective decision rules is necessarily brief. For the reader who is interested in a further elaboration and development of the ideas sketched here, see Buchanan and Tullock, *Calculus of Consent*.

or not moves from that position are possible that will benefit at least one member of the group without damage to another, is seriously incomplete. When examined in isolation, many particular positions may be nonoptimal in this narrow sense. And, if a single, isolated move could be made, the preferences of all members of the group might, conceptually, be revealed through an agreement to make the indicated change to an optimal position. But group decisions cannot be made in terms of single cases, and for several reasons. Collective decisions must be made in terms of organizational rules or constraints that are expected to prevail over a sequence of results. Nonoptimality in a single instance does not imply potential consensus on a change in the organizational rules.

This emphasis on the extension of the Pareto classification to organizational rules does not suggest that the orthodox usage in the classification of final positions or results is without value. Surely, the operation of alternative rules can only be evaluated in terms of predicted results, and the Pareto construction can be helpful in this process. At the level of application to the social constitution, to the evaluation of the "rules of the game," the Pareto criterion serves, however, a function that it cannot possibly serve in the more standard usage. Unless the observing economist is assumed to be omniscient, his classification of a final position as nonoptimal can never be more than a conjectural hypothesis that is impossible to test. If members of the group do not explicitly choose among final positions in the appropriately defined welfare space, the hypothesis that some members of the group can be made better off by a change remains empty. By contrast, the classification of an organizational rule as nonoptimal can be considered as a hypothesis that is subject to conceptual testing. If a presumed or apparent nonoptimal rule cannot be changed through agreement among members of the group, the hypothesis stating that the rule is nonoptimal is effectively refuted.

The contrast between the approach suggested here and the more familiar usage of the Pareto construction by the welfare economists should not be overemphasized. As suggested earlier, the standard usage has, implicitly, defined the Pareto region as that which is limited by the constitutional constraint inherent in the unanimity principle. In addition, the concentration upon final results or positions need not be misleading in those cases where the correspondence between rule and result is reasonably complete. In most cases of economic policy, the demonstration of inefficiency in an allocation of resources does imply that there exists some change in the organizational rules upon which all members of the group could agree. Nevertheless, as the situations discussed above have shown, the correspondence need not be present in this sense, and possible errors can always be prevented by an emphasis on the choice among alternative sets of social rules or constraints.

Starting from any existing set of rules, combined with the external or obligatory constraints arising out of technical limitations, the economist has a well-defined Pareto region within which he can bring all of his analytical skills into play. All possible changes in the constitutional structure become admissible so long as these rules changes may, conceptually, be approved by general agreement. The unanimity principle for changes in the "social constitution" provides the only appropriate facultative constraint.

The alternative approach is, of course, that which involves the introduction of "social welfare functions" or "social value judgments." However, even as the proponents of this alternative approach admit, the economist is no more able to dictate such judgments than is any other citizen. By introducing his constraints in the form of social value judgments, the economist may leave the major part of his appropriate task undone. He may remove himself all too quickly from the area in which he does, in fact, possess some special competence. Rather than closing off discussion through the introduction of such judgments, the economist's function is that of keeping discussion open. He must utilize his skills in presenting to the social group hypotheses in the form: "I think that a change from current policy to policy X is one upon which all members of the group can agree." He must try to formulate alternative social compromises as means of testing alternative hypotheses. In slightly different terms, the economist's task is simply that of repeating in various ways the admonition, "there exist mutual gains from trade," emphasizing the word "mutual," and forever keeping in mind that "trade" need not be confined to the exchange of goods and services in the marketplace.

Welfare economics can make real progress through such a change in approach which, quite literally, may be called the introduction of "constructive institutionalism."

Politics and Science
Reflections on Knight's Critique of Polanyi

I. Introduction

Knowing of my admiration for both men, a colleague recently called to my attention Frank Knight's 1949 critique[1] of Michael Polanyi's *Science, Faith, and Society* (1946).[2] The reissue of the latter monograph[3] in 1964 contained a new introduction by the author, but no reference was made to Knight's fundamental criticism. Because the issue raised by Knight seems too important to be ignored, there is perhaps some justification in my attempt to restate the differences between these two scholars in my own terms. This justification is strengthened by the continuing relevance of the issue at stake, especially with reference to the general methodological setting for modern "political science."

As Knight notes at the outset of his review, Polanyi's implied equation of science and social order represents an interesting inversion of the more familiar, and hopefully discredited, view that sociopolitical problems are similar to scientific problems in that "scientific method" is required for their "so-

From *Ethics* 77 (July 1967): 303–10. Copyright 1967 by The University of Chicago. All rights reserved. Reprinted by permission of the University of Chicago Press, publisher.

I am indebted to Craig Roberts for several helpful suggestions, although our continuing disagreement on several points in the paper should be stressed.

1. Frank Knight, "Virtue and Knowledge: The View of Professor Polanyi," *Ethics* 59 (July 1949): 271 84.

2. Michael Polanyi, *Science, Faith, and Society* (Riddell Memorial Lectures, University of Durham [London: Oxford University Press, 1946]).

3. Michael Polanyi, *Science, Faith, and Society* (with a new Introduction; Chicago: Phoenix Books, University of Chicago Press, 1964).

lution." For Polanyi, orthodox scientific method, as many persons think and talk about it, does not characterize scientific process. Scientific problems, as well as social problems, or indeed all problems, involve *personal evaluation*. Knight offers his normally persuasive, "yes, but . . ." type of criticism to this elevation of intuitive perception (as opposed to observation) to a predominant role in scientific discovery. Within limits he broadly accepts Polanyi's theory of scientific progress.

The differences between these two social philosophers which this paper discusses are indeed profound, but any treatment of such differences would be misleading if it were not prefaced by an emphasis on their agreement on many issues. Knight accepts, again within limits, Polanyi's eloquent defense of freedom in the scientific community. More importantly, for purposes of this paper, both Knight and Polanyi assign a major role to the spontaneous co-ordination process represented by market exchange broadly conceived in the social constitution for their "good societies." Both generally and in particulars they share an avowed opposition to the authoritarian state, and both openly support individual freedoms defined in the terms of classical liberalism.

What is at issue between Knight and Polanyi is the legitimacy of the *same* defense of freedom in science and in the political order. Is social like scientific organization? Can norms or principles for organization that seem demonstrably appropriate for the community of science be extended by analogy and analysis to the social or political order? Both directly and by implication if not by major emphasis Polanyi's answer to these questions is affirmative. Knight's response is an emphatic negative. In essence, Polanyi seems to say: "Have respect for truth, and you shall be free." Knight seems to respond by saying: "But sociopolitical questions cannot be answered by 'true' or 'false.' Things are not nearly so simple as that." Michael Polanyi, the optimist, confronts Frank Knight, the pessimist. They look at political process through quite different "windows."

The waning prospects for advancing toward the social order that both Knight and Polanyi seek (or even preserving the achievements made) may depend critically on some reconciliation of their opposing views, or if not reconciliation at least mutual understanding. Modern liberalism advances, and confusedly oversteps itself, often on the basis of arguments that are at least akin to Polanyi's. Classical liberalism retreats and reduces itself to negativism in the process, often on the basis of arguments that may be interpreted as inarticulate expressions of the Knightian conception of social order.[4]

II. The Jigsaw Puzzle

To Polanyi, a distinguished physical scientist in his own right, science is analogous to the continual filling in and expansion of a gigantic, never-ending jigsaw puzzle.[5] No single scientist need know what the "final" picture may look like, and the prevailing interpretation of the big picture may change progressively through time. Scientific effort consists in searching out pieces or shapes that fit from among an infinite variety of possibilities, and a scientific discovery consists in the initial intuitive perception of a relevant shape or pattern. On this vision of scientific process, Polanyi bases his argument for the freedom of individual scientists to seek out and look for shapes and patterns as their own professional consciences dictate. The jigsaw analogy is indeed convincing, and its organizational implications are clear. The most efficient means of organizing many persons in the solving of a single puzzle is to allow each one to conduct his own private search among the whole jumble of pieces. Planning from above in such puzzle-solving is obviously nonsensical. And, although the analogy must be used with some caution, much the same can be said for the organization of science and scientific endeavor. The planned or centrally-directed organization of science aimed at accomplishing specific "social goals" can only stifle the general progress of science itself.

III. Truth in Science

There is no important difference between Knight and Polanyi on the latter's argument in defense of scientific freedom or even on the broad conception

---

4. It must be emphasized here that neither Polanyi nor Knight is responsible for the extensions suggested, directly or indirectly. In fact the very reasonableness of each of their own positions is helpful in providing a base for reconciliation of the more rigid extremes.

5. For an explicit discussion of this analogy, see Michael Polanyi, "The Republic of Science" (lecture delivered at Roosevelt University, January 11, 1962 [Chicago: Roosevelt University, 1962]), 6–8.

of what scientific progress represents. Slight difference arises, however, in their implied conceptions of "truth" in science, and this, in turn, becomes important, indirectly, in the extension of the reasoning to political order. To Polanyi, "truth" is derived from an existential reality, remaining to be discovered even if it is outside the scientist's current perception, and progress in science takes place through ever-improving glimpses of this reality. In its fullness or completeness, this reality may never be grasped, and scientific development may modify existing conceptions, even to the extent of discarding old prints and replacing these by new ones. In the process, however, there is an avowed faith in the existence of the reality which any picture or model more or less successfully represents.[6]

In an instrumental sense, Knight's view of scientific "truth" is similar, but, conceptually, there seems to be an important difference. Although he remains far from accepting a purely relativistic position, Knight refrains from either asking or answering the question concerning the existence of some ultimate and unchanging reality. "Truth" is measured only by agreement or consensus among informed persons, despite the acknowledged questions that this definition begs. Whether or not there is reality behind the models becomes essentially an irrelevant question. In this Knightian context, the pictures, the models of science, are "true," at any given epoch, within the relatively absolute limits defined by general agreement among the informed. These models, these pictures, change through time, sometimes dramatically and ofttimes slowly. "Truth," as such, changes in the process, and there is no finality in revelation, even in some utopian future state. On balance, this Knightian position, if I have interpreted it correctly, depends critically on the emergence of "relatively absolute absolutes" in scientific truth as in everything else. Despite the convergence of the two positions in a practical sense, the tolerance limits are somewhat broader in the Knightian than in the Polanyi conception of truth. To Polanyi, progress toward the unveiling of a yet-undiscovered reality is shown to be more efficient if individual scientists are allowed freedom of search, of exploration. One of his provocative lectures is

6. "The first step is to remember that scientific discoveries are made in search of reality—of a reality that is there, whether we know it or not. The search is of our own making, but reality is not" (Michael Polanyi, "The Creative Imagination" [Oxford, April 1965, mimeographed]).

entitled "A Society of Explorers," a title that is, in itself, revealing. The defense of scientific freedom becomes *instrumental;* ultimately, the aim is efficiency in science, in discovery of truth itself. By contrast, Knight's position must produce, finally, a defense of scientific freedom that is grounded on the ever-present relativism of even the most widely acknowledged "truths." Pragmatically, as suggested above, both scholars agree on the organization of science. Both agree that science "works better" if it is organized on the basis of free individual decisions.

IV. Truth in Politics

My attempted summary sketch of the Knight-Polanyi differences in the conception of scientific truth is perhaps sufficient to introduce their more profound differences in the conception of political "truth." These latter are, of course, the main subject of Knight's paper. Only by some general understanding of the role that truth plays in their conception of scientific process can the widely differing assessments of these two respected philosophers for the prospects for political freedom be appreciated.

What is political decision? Presumably, like all decisions, it results from a choice among alternatives, a choice that must be binding on all members of the body politic. How can this be compared with a scientific decision (explanation)? Presumably, in science, a decision results from a choice among alternative explanations of phenomena, and this decision is not considered to be final until all, or substantially all, qualified members of the scientific community accept it. Once this stage is reached, the chosen explanation becomes "binding" in the paradigmatic sense. The similarities as well as the differences between the two cases become clear in this summary. One difference arises immediately. In politics, decisions are made, and implemented, *before* general agreement is attained. Results are binding by force of the decision, not by prior agreement by force of reasoned argument. Nonetheless, the similarities are also striking, provided that the underlying alternatives for choice are themselves comparable in the two cases. If, in point of fact, a political decision can be represented as a choice among alternative "explanations" of "reality," there will be, ex post, one "best" alternative, which, within limits, can be appropriately labeled to be the "true." Given this classical conception of politics, which continues to dominate a large part of modern political science, the Polanyi extension is helpful and revealing. Political choices are essentially "truth judgments," and the rules for choosing among alternatives are, or should be, based on norms for efficiency in arriving at "truth" in some quasi-scientific sense of this term. Free and open discussion, toleration of dissenting opinion, these become but features of a total process of producing political "truth" efficiently.

The truth-judgment model of politics need not be accepted. There may be no "best" alternative upon which all members of the group should agree, even given full knowledge. The question of politics may remain one of *choice*, and individuals may differ in their evaluations of the alternatives. These differences may be inherently *personal, subjective,* and they may be irreducible to agreed-on objective standards. Political choice, in this alternative vision, becomes a necessary means of reconciling different individual-group evaluations, not a means of producing "truth" at all. Hopefully, or better, ideally, general agreement can be attained after sufficient discussion, exchange, compromise. But even should full unanimity be observed in support of some multidimensioned outcome, a "true" judgment cannot be said to have been produced. The terms are simply not applicable in the realm of discourse that we use to discuss politics.

If politics is not aimed at the discovery of "truth" in any sense comparable to science, agreement among individuals cannot be expected to emerge as a result of free and open discussion. Enlightenment does not necessarily produce unanimity, and it is essentially a false hope that so elevates sweet reason. Politics becomes the process through which divergent interests are compromised. Politics is the collective counterpart to individual choice and nothing more. As an individual, I may choose to paint my house either white or red. There are certain physical constraints within which my choice must lie, but given these I can choose among alternatives in accordance with my own tastes or values. It becomes highly questionable, if not improper, to say that my selection of white as the color for my house is "true" while the alternative red is "false." This usage of terms would be equally questionable even if all of my neighbors, as well as the architectural color consultants, agree that white is aesthetically the more satisfying color. The analogy used here threatens to open up the age-old issue of "truth in art" which I do not choose to and shall not consider.

Politics, in this interpretation which I attribute to Knight and which I share with him, becomes the collective counterpart to my choice of paint color. There are some things that men must do collectively rather than individually for simple efficiency reasons. Group choices must be made. Once we confront group choice, however, we encounter the prospect of individual disagreements on the ordering of alternatives. Is the collective "house" to be painted red or white? It is likely that some members of the group will prefer one color and some the other. Politics is the process through which the initial preferences are expressed, discussed, compromised, and, finally, resolved in some fashion. Resolution may, however, amount to an overruling of some preferences in favor of others. Political order or stability requires, of course, that those whose preferences are overruled acquiesce in the collective outcome. It does not require that their "tastes" be modified so as to prefer the chosen outcome, or that, once they fully understand the alternatives, they will necessarily prefer what is chosen for them. Indeed, it is precisely the presence of dissent in the face of decision that separates genuinely democratic politics from that of the brainwashing variety.

Individuals differ, one from the other, even if equally informed. Economists summarize this by saying that utility functions differ. Individuals rank "goods" ("bads") differently. But "goods" ("bads") can be either private or public. In my own utility function, a biennial trip to Europe stands much higher than the biennial purchase of a new automobile. In the utility function of my colleague, this order is reversed. We are different. In my own utility function, federal government outlay on the space program stands higher than federal outlay on the poverty program. In the utility function of my colleague, this order is reversed. There seems to be little, if any, difference in these two cases, except that which dictates that we both accept some politically determined result in the latter public-goods mix. Acceptance does not, however, imply agreement, and no particular mix emerges as the "true" one.[7]

---

7. The discussion here is confined to political issues upon which disagreement can be interpreted in the two alternative ways suggested. Much the same analysis can be extended to issues in normative ethics, and, indeed, the discussion of disagreement by Charles L. Stevenson closely parallels that presented here. See his *Ethics and Language* (New Haven, Conn.: Yale University Press, 1944). Stevenson's distinction is between disagreement in *belief* and disagreement in *attitudes*. Essentially, Stevenson sought to clarify the ambiguities arising when this distinction was not made explicit, and, on balance, he

In the politics as discussed here, Knight's basic criticism of Polanyi's position seems surely to be correct. Contrast the sketch of political choice advanced here with scientific choice. In the latter, alternative explanations are possible for a single set of phenomena, and, at the initial stages of inquiry, scientists may express wide disagreement. The process of scientific discovery is, in itself, a narrowing of the areas of this disagreement. Possessing a common reference system and acknowledging common standards for evaluation, scientists are engaged in a continuously developing process of rejecting "false" explanations and replacing these with "true" ones. Here "truth" is appropriately measured by agreement, and here the term is, in itself, meaningful. This is not, of course, to deny that there does not remain "taste" or "valuation" in science, at all levels. Scientific disagreements are not, however, primarily disagreements on values. These are disagreements on facts, on analysis, in interpretation—disagreements that will progressively disappear as the field of knowledge widens. Pragmatically, science proceeds "as if" its practitioners are explorers discovering existential reality, and the metaphysical questions about this reality itself need not be raised at all.

V. Justice and the Good Society

A part of politics is surely the grubby, quasi-corrupt, day-to-day settling of intergroup, interpersonal claims. It is, and must be, pressure-group politics with the pork-barrel and the wheeler-dealers as vital elements. But is this all there is to politics? Is there not some place left for the classical quest after "justice," after the organizing principles of the "good society"?

Some reconciliation of the Knight and Polanyi positions becomes possible if attention is shifted to the different politics embodied in these questions. Earlier, politics, as implicitly defined, involved the production of public goods. But we can define another stage of political choice. Politics can be considered as the choice of *rules* by which men live together. We are deep in the cardinal sin of using the same word "politics" to mean two quite different things, and, indeed, this has been one of the major sources of modern con-

---

took what would be, in the argument of this paper, a position close to that advanced by Knight, as I have interpreted the latter.

fusion. I shall, from this point, refer to this higher-stage, rule-making politics as "constitutional." This will appropriately distinguish it from the mundane stage of politics in the ordinary meaning. It is one of the many tragedies of twentieth-century liberalism that the importance of distinguishing these two stages has now been almost wholly forgotten.

Consider now constitutional politics, the problems of choice among rules. Here the alternatives are rules or institutions within which both private-goods and public-goods choices shall be made by persons acting singly or in groups. Constitutional rules constrain both private individual choice behavior and collective political behavior. Rules prohibiting theft prevent my taking my neighbor's property; and rules prohibiting arbitrary discrimination prevent my being taxed for public goods while my neighbor goes scot-free.

What can we say about the process through which such rules are chosen? Does this process resemble science? Or is it, at an admittedly different level, similar in kind to the ordinary operational choice of public "goods" already discussed?

The appropriate location for genuine constitutional choice seems to be somewhere between the limits imposed by the choice among scientific explanations on the one hand and the choice among alternative publicly supplied goods on the other. There may be differences in individual evaluations of alternative rules, differences that may, in one sense, reflect basic value orderings. To this extent, agreement will not be produced by open discussion. Something more than evaluation is involved in many cases, however. Individual differences may be based, to a large extent, on differing predictions about the working properties of the alternative rules under consideration. Within these limits, meaningful discussion and analysis can take place, and the careful assessment of alternative models can closely resemble scientific process of the standard sort.

The useful analogy for constitutional choice is found in the choice of rules for a standard parlor game. Prospective players engage in a discussion of these rules, before play actually starts, and, after play has commenced, this discussion continues concerning possible changes in the rules adopted. In such a context, what is the purpose or objective sought by the players? It is not, and cannot be, the advancement of their own differential interests, the single player's own preferred "good," because, when the rules are chosen, there must remain great uncertainty as to how particular rules will advance particular interests. The inherent uncertainty that surrounds constitutional choice among rules makes individual behavior necessarily different from that which may be observed in situations where private interests are readily identifiable. The individual, as a prospective player, will prefer that set of rules which he predicts will make for a "better" game, a game that is "fair," "efficient," "interesting." These terms reduce to the same descriptive content in this particular choice setting.

Consider now the problem of reaching group agreement on a set of rules, a set that applies to all participants in the game. Different persons will initially possess somewhat differing versions of their "ideal game." Discussion can proceed, however, and disagreement can be narrowed, because argument can be based not on personal values but on predicted working properties of alternative rules. Such discussion, to the extent that it is open and free, can squeeze out major areas of discord: Disagreement may remain, after full discussion, but this will be scarcely different from science since basic value differences remain even in the consensus that the latter seeks, and secures, as it progresses.

The shift of attention from the level of operational decision to that of constitutional decision restores, to an extent, Polanyi's analogical tie between science and the social order. Care must be taken at this point, however, to keep the major differences that remain clearly in mind. Let us limit consideration to genuine constitutional decisions, the choices among alternative political rules. As suggested, there are important elements of similarity between the process of discussion, selection, and agreement on such rules, and the process of free scientific discovery. But there are also important differences, and these are based in the fundamental objectives that are implicit in each of the two processes. Science represents a process of discovery, of exploration, and success is measured by agreed-on criteria of "truth." Pragmatically, we are convinced by the force of scientific argument. Scientific proof can be established; propositions can be refuted. Within limits that can be defined in advance and with reasonable precision, radiation treatments can retard cancer. Christian Science cannot do so, within equally defined limits.

Compare this with the choice of a set of rules for political order, a constitution. Can this process be considered, at any level, as one of discovery or exploration seeking the "true"? Admittedly, this has been the conception of political philosophers throughout the ages. The "good society" has been sought as if it were unique. But is this conception legitimate, or is it wholly misleading?

It seems clear that feedback effects of error cannot work comparably in constitutional politics and in science. Assume, for current argument, that there does exist one uniquely best set of rules for organizing social interaction and that general agreement on this set as best would, in fact, be attainable in some ex post global settling of accounts. Rules must be chosen, however, without a vision of this final best constitution, and choice must be made among several alternatives. Suppose that an error is made and that, initially, rules are chosen that are inconsistent with those that should be embodied in the "good society." How will this error make itself known to those individuals, of necessarily limited vision, who must live by the rules that they have chosen? What external observations can reveal to persons that they are involved in a game that is being played under a second-best or n-th best set of rules? Contrast this position with that faced by the reasonably intelligent savage engaged in a rain dance. The latter can, by using his senses, observe that the dance does not bring the rain. Of course, such distinctions and comparisons should not be pushed too far; but their existence must be recognized.

The "best" social order is simply that which works "best." However, only one set of rules can be tried at one time, and experiments must be long-range to be at all revealing. No alternative explanations are, therefore, likely to be directly observable, unless we allow for cross-cultural comparisons on the one hand and historical observations on the other. Again by contrast, the rain-maker's dance can be observed alongside the cloud-seeding experiments of the trained meteorologist. Alternative scientific experiments are possible within the limited observation pattern of individuals, and choice can be made among these on the basis of such observation, and not on the basis of a mere comparison of conceptual alternatives.

VI. Is There One "Good Society"?

A more fundamental difference between "politics" and "science," even at the level of selection among constitutional rules, involves the uniqueness of solution. The issue relates to the conception of scientific truth, discussed earlier, but additional complexities are also present. In one sense, science is discovery, and this, in itself, implies the uniqueness of that which is found, the object of search. Pragmatically, the issue of truth in science can proceed as if the underlying reality is unique.

When these conceptions are extended from science to social order, to politics, however, major questions arise. If politics, at the constitutional level, involves a process of discovery and exploration analogous to that of science, must we assume that there is a unique "explanation," a unique set of rules that define the elements of good society which, once discovered, will come to be generally accepted by informed and intellectually honest men? But is there such an end to the rainbow in political philosophy after all? Is there a single best set of rules for organizing men politically, a set that can be continually if never completely discovered like the big jigsaw puzzle of science, provided only that there is maintained a free and open discussion of alternatives and that allowance is made for provisional trial and error, for experiment, for science transferred to social systems?

To some omniscient being of a different and higher order of intelligence than man, to a being who can view man's interactions, one with another, solely in terms of his own evaluative criteria, the answer may be in the affirmative here. But to man himself, the existence of such singularity in solution seems highly dubious. Values would seem to differ, and perhaps widely, even among enlightened men, and different men will tend to value different rules. My ideally "good society" need not be identical with yours in general or its particulars, even if we fully agree on the working properties of the alternative rules under discussion.

Polanyi, the distinguished physical scientist, seems to opt for an affirmative answer. This is, perhaps, understandable. In science, man becomes as God in his vision of the natural universe. By extension, God, observing man, can see the reality of social order. And, notably, Polanyi allows God a role, and it is not distorting his approach to say that he conceives discovery in the political-social realm as the revelation of God's design. In relatively sharp contrast here, Knight remains highly dubious about God, and he is unwilling to go beyond man's own competence to judge on the basis of his own criteria. And, at this level, men place values on different things. "Science" and "politics" remain poles apart, even when we have reduced politics, to the maximum extent that is possible, to the long-range continuing search for a set of constitutional rules.

VII. "Political Science"

If I have interpreted them correctly, the differences between Knight and Polanyi seem to be intrinsically important, but their relevance to social thought generally is much wider than specific concentration on the ideas of these two scholars alone might suggest. At issue, finally, is the whole conception of political process. Throughout the ages, political philosophers have taken the Polanyi side of the argument, and this includes even those who have been the most vociferous in their denunciations of "science" in politics, as such. The Polanyi conception belongs squarely in the idealist tradition of political philosophy, a tradition from which modern political science, as a discipline, is only now beginning to emerge. For the most part, politics has been conceived as a process of arriving at truth-judgments. This is well illustrated by a recent argument of a leading American political scientist. In a volume devoted to "rational decision," Professor Harvey C. Mansfield, Jr., suggested that "rational decision" tends to be prevented from emerging in politics because of the necessity for compromise of divergent interests.[8]

This truth-judgment conception of politics may be accompanied, as in the case with Polanyi, by an eloquent defense of individual freedom, based on the continuing and inexhaustible processes of discovery, on the provisional nature of all truth that is found, and upon the efficiency in exploration that only such freedom can insure. Unfortunately, however, the truth-judgment conception need not carry such a defense of individual freedoms as its accompaniment. The conception lends itself, more or less naturally, to what amounts to an attitude of basic intolerance on the part of those who hold that certain political "truths" have already been discovered.[9] Implicitly, these persons claim the "right" to impose "truth" on those who refuse, with apparent ignorance, stubbornness, or blindness, to recognize error. Members of the recalcitrant minority, those who reject the "truth" that politics

---

8. Harvey C. Mansfield, Jr., "Rationality and Representation in Burke's 'Bristol Speech,'" in *Rational Decision, Nomos VII*, ed. Carl J. Friedrich (New York: Atherton Press, 1964), especially pp. 197 f.

9. Polanyi seems to recognize this point in quite a different context: "On the grounds of the discipline which bound him to the quest of reality, he (the scientist) must claim that his results are universally valid. . . . To claim universal validity for a statement indicates merely that it *ought* to be accepted by all" ("The Creative Imagination," 19).

reveals, become first cousins of the rain-maker, and they tend to be treated with similar scorn. This attitude of intolerance seems especially to characterize the modern American left-liberal who dominates the academic setting and to whom there must always exist a set of prevailing "truths," politically determined, and from which open dissent becomes, somehow, "immoral."

The philosophical gap between this idealist conception of politics and the alternative conception, here attributed to Knight, is wide indeed. Politics, in the latter, becomes at best some attempt to compromise issues among individuals and groups with admittedly different values. There are no "truths." The implicit tolerance that this position must embody is self-evident. The defense of individual freedom is here non-instrumental. It is based, finally, on a recognition and acceptance of the value of individual values.

Order Defined in the Process
of Its Emergence

Norman Barry states, at one point in his essay, that the patterns of spontaneous order "appear to be a product of some omniscient designing mind" (p. 8). Almost everyone who has tried to explain the central principle of elementary economics has, at one time or another, made some similar statement. In making such statements, however, even the proponents-advocates of spontaneous order may have, inadvertently, "given the game away," and, at the same time, made their didactic task more difficult.

I want to argue that the "order" of the market emerges *only* from the *process* of voluntary exchange among the participating individuals. The "order" is, itself, defined as the outcome of the *process* that generates it. The "it," the allocation-distribution result, does not, and cannot, exist independently of the trading process. Absent this process, there is and can be no "order."

What, then, does Barry mean (and others who make similar statements), when the order generated by market interaction is made comparable to that order which might emerge from an omniscient, designing single mind? If pushed on this question, economists would say that if the designer could somehow know the utility functions of all participants, along with the constraints, such a mind could, by fiat, duplicate precisely the results that would emerge from the process of market adjustment. By implication, individuals are presumed to carry around with them fully-determined utility functions, and, in the market, they act always to maximize utilities subject to the constraints they confront. As I have noted elsewhere, however, in this presumed

From *Literature of Liberty* 5 (Winter 1982): 5. Reprinted by permission of the publisher.

A note stimulated by reading Norman Barry, "The Tradition of Spontaneous Order," *Literature of Liberty* 5 (Summer 1982): 7–58.

setting, there is no genuine choice behavior on the part of anyone. In this model of market process, the relative efficiency of institutional arrangements allowing for spontaneous adjustment stems solely from the *informational* aspects.

This emphasis is misleading. Individuals do not act so as to maximize utilities described in *independently-existing functions*. They confront genuine choices, and the sequence of decisions taken may be conceptualized, *ex post* (after the choices), in terms of "as if" functions that are maximized. But these "as if" functions are, themselves, generated in the choosing process, not separately from such process. If viewed in this perspective, there is no means by which even the most idealized omniscient designer could duplicate the results of voluntary interchange. The potential participants *do not know until they enter the process* what their own choices will be. From this it follows that it is *logically impossible* for an omniscient designer to know, unless, of course, we are to preclude individual freedom of will.

The point I seek to make in this note is at the same time simple and subtle. It reduces to the distinction between *end-state* and *process* criteria, between consequentialist and nonconsequentialist, *teleological* and *deontological* principles. Although they may not agree with my argument, philosophers should recognize and understand the distinction more readily than economists. In economics, even among many of those who remain strong advocates of market and market-like organization, the "efficiency" that such market arrangements produce is independently conceptualized. Market arrangements then become "means," which may or may not be relatively best. Until and unless this teleological element is fully exorcised from basic economic theory, economists are likely to remain confused and their discourse confusing.

Natural and Artifactual Man

I claim no competence in ethology, and I am fully aware that there are numerous attributes that have been adduced to make the categorical distinction between the human and higher animal species, attributes such as language, sense of death, ability to think in complex fashion, etc. I want to concentrate here on a single attribute that does make men categorically different from even the higher animals, an attribute that seems to me to be too much neglected in modern economics.

We know that we could examine the behavior of my dog scientifically. We could set up experiments, and we could, I am sure, derive a utility function from such experiments, much as the economists who work with rats have done at Texas A&M. This exercise might be useful in many respects. On the basis of the utility function so derived, we might be able to predict with reasonable accuracy just how my dog would behave if his opportunity set were modified in various ways. This accuracy in prediction could be increased if we extended the experiment, and the predictions, to apply to a large-number, or representative, setting rather than to a single behaving unit.

How would this procedure differ if we experimented with and made predictions about man, either as individual men and women, or as representative members of a large group? Once I pose the issue in this way, the response, and my emphasis here, should be evident to you. Our predictions about man must always be less accurate than our predictions about animals. But why is this so? What does man do that animals do not do? Clearly, the standard attributes called upon to categorize man differently from his fellow

From *What Should Economists Do?* (Indianapolis: Liberty Fund, 1979), 93–112. Reprinted by permission of the publisher.

This chapter was initially presented as a lecture at a Liberty Fund Series Conference in Blacksburg, Virginia, in July 1978.

mammals will help us little here. We need to do better than this; man does not become less predictable because he uses language.

What I am getting at is that a central difference between my dog and any one of us lies in his lack of any sense of becoming different from what he is. This is to be contrasted with your sense of "becoming" as a central part, indeed probably the most important part, of life itself. As human beings, we know that we are going to die; perhaps my dog does not know this about himself. But we, as human beings, also know that we can, within limits, shape the form of being that we shall be between now and the time of death, even when we fully reckon on the stochastic pattern of life expectancy.

For my purposes, I shall call my dog a "natural" animal, and I shall call any one of us a "natural and artifactual" animal, or, perhaps preferably, an artifactual animal bounded by natural constraints. We are, and will be, at least in part, that which we make ourselves to be. We construct our own beings, again within limits. We are artifactual, as much like the pottery sherds that the archaeologists dig up as like the animals whose fossils they also find.

A digression is necessary at this point in order to forestall possible misunderstanding. My title, and my general discussion in terms of the dichotomy between "natural" and "artifactual" man, does not imply that I equate "natural" wholly with biological or genetic elements. I accept the importance of what Hayek calls the "culturally evolved man," which, in a sense, is neither "natural" nor "artifactual." For my purposes, to the extent that individuals are rigidly bound by culturally evolved rules of conduct or modes of behavior, these elements would make up part of "natural man," or, better stated, "nonartifactual man." On the other hand, to the extent that culturally evolved rules of conduct exist but require an act of choice by persons to accept or to reject adherence, these elements of behavior would be artifactual, in my terminology here. My emphasis is concentrated on the simple distinction between that part of man's behavior that is "programmed," and hence "predictable scientifically," and that which is not.

There is, of course, nothing new or even novel in what I am saying here, and you should have no difficulty in accepting my statements. But I am trying to develop this argument for a purpose, which is one of demonstrating that modern economic theory forces upon us patterns of thought that make elementary recognition of the whole "becoming" part of our behavior very difficult to analyze and easy to neglect.

Let me begin by offering a brief and only partial catalog of what I think are misleading directions. First, consider human capital theory. I do not deny the productivity of insights gained by looking at education and training as investment in human capital, nor do I reject out of hand the usefulness of attempts to measure rates of return on such investment along with comparisons of rates on ordinary investment outlays. As you know, the human capital approach has been criticized, by Jack Wiseman among others, because it tends to neglect the direct consumption attributes of the apparent investment process, and notably in education. I have no quarrel with such criticism, but it is quite different from what I want to advance here. A good part of education can be modeled appropriately neither as capital investment nor as consumption of final services. Instead it must somehow be modeled as "spending on becoming"—on becoming the person that we want to be rather than the one we think we might be if the spending is not made in this way. (This purpose of education is, of course, clear when we think of education for children as determined by parents and by society rather than by the children themselves. We do not educate children primarily to produce income streams or even utility streams; we educate them to make them over into persons "better" than and different from those they would be without the educational process. At least this is our intent.) But let me return to "self-investment." The activity is investment in a sense because life through time is reckoned. But it is not investment in any life-cycle sense, which might be deemed akin to that of the squirrel that accumulates nuts for winter, yet with no conception of itself as something other than the squirrel it is and will remain. I am not proposing to deny that there is a lot of squirrel in each of us, to our credit perhaps. I am, instead, saying that there is much more to apparent "investment behavior" (defined as nonconsumption) than squirreling. (And I should add more to it than the Ricardian extension of the life-cycle model to intergenerational linkages.)

The metaphor of "capital" investment seems misplaced when we think of a person's outlay of time and money on information, on knowledge. A person is not investing with the aim or purpose of increasing the size of an objectively measured income stream in perpetuity, a stream that may be converted or potentially converted into consumption by the selfsame person or his heirs. He is investing in becoming the different person that he must become as he acquires knowledge and wisdom; he cannot do otherwise than become different. And as he does so, he must embody a different "utility function," if we choose to carry around this baggage of the economist with us. Hence, he must choose differently if he should be confronted with the same constraints as before, which is in itself a logical impossibility because of the nature of time itself. As you can see, even to talk about present values of future income streams, about rates of return, is of questionable worth in analyzing such behavior as I am trying to identify here.

As a second example, let us consider the Stigler-Becker proposition to the effect that economists should proceed on the assumption that utility functions are stable through time and invariant as among persons.[1] Introspectively and observationally, we may want to reject this notion out of hand. But my interest does not lie in the empirical validity or invalidity of the invariance assumption itself. Instead, my interest lies in the thought pattern or mind-set that the Stigler-Becker hypothesis imposes on anyone who tries to analyze behavior seriously.

Consider their own example of music and music appreciation. The individual's preference function, which is unchanging, contains music as a basic component. Music now is produced by current inputs and time, and music in future periods is, in part, produced by current-period investment in music appreciation and in time spent on current consumption. Hence, music becomes cheaper to produce relative to other consumption or end items as time progresses; a person is, therefore, predicted to purchase more inputs to produce music as costs fall. There is no need to resort to the notion that tastes or preferences have shifted.

But what does this approach imply with respect to the basic commodity or service in the preference function, music? There is no change possible in the *quality* of the service purchased in their model; music appreciation cannot induce a shift from rock to classical, yet is this not precisely what we should expect to observe? It seems impossible, in the Stigler-Becker world, to invest in becoming more appreciative of music or of anything else. This restriction tends to shut off or to foreclose whole aspects of behavior from analysis and examination.

My purpose, however, is not to criticize particular areas of concentration,

---

1. George J. Stigler and Gary S. Becker, "De Gustibus Non Est Disputandum," *American Economic Review* 67, no. 2 (March 1977): 76–90.

but to advance a broad criticism against economic theory generally. If I may resort to philosophical terms, what I am objecting to in modern economic theory is its *teleological* foundations, its tendency to force all analyzable behavior into the straitjacket of "maximizing a utility or objective function under constraints." In one way, I am suggesting that the utilitarian origins of nineteenth-century political economy may have come to haunt us and to do us great damage.

Let me try to put my argument positively. It is useful to think of man as an imagining being, which in itself sets him apart from other species. A person sees himself or herself in many roles, capacities, and natures, in many settings, in many times, in many places. As one contemplates moving from imagination to potential behavior, however, constraints emerge to bound or limit the set of prospects severely. One might, for example, imagine himself living in any age of history, past or imagined future. But as action is approached, the constraint of the here and now impinges. One imagines an ability to fly unaided through space, to walk on water, to live on love. But one faces up to the reality of the limits imposed by the laws of science before the real replaces the romantic. One can imagine himself to be of the opposite sex until the physical structure of his own body is allowed to intervene. One can think of what he might have been with different sets of genes.

Once all of the possible constraints are accounted for (historical, geographic, cultural, physical, genetic, sexual), there still remains a large set of possible persons that one might imagine himself to be, or might imagine himself capable of becoming. There is room for "improvement," for the construction of what might be. Further, in thinking about realizable prospects, a person is able to rank these in some fashion, to classify members of the set as "better" or "worse."

Constrained by the several "natural" limits (which, as noted above, include the cultural), an individual is further constrained by his own construction of himself in past periods. But recognizing the possible prospects that remain open to him through his remaining life span, and ranking these prospects in some way, the individual remains capable of achieving the prospect that he chooses. To make such choice, the costs of the alternatives must be reckoned along with the anticipated benefits. But here I lapse too closely into standard economists' terminology, which is precisely the trap I want to avoid in this lecture. I should emphasize that the relationships between the prospects that might be achieved and the costs of achieving these may not be at all clear, indeed they could not be.

Nonetheless, the prospects of becoming are sufficient to channel action, to divert resources away from the automatic routine that utility maximization, as normally presented, seems to embody. And choices made in becoming a different person are irrevocable, regardless of their productivity, when viewed *ex post*. We move through time, constructing ourselves as artifactual persons. We are not, and cannot be, the "same person" in any utility-maximization sense. There is nothing in personal behavior akin to Adam Smith's "discipline of continuous dealings" to enable us to undo or to correct past sins of omission or commission.

Much of what I have said to this point is probably broadly acceptable to you, at least as warning against pushing our formalizations in economics too far. I have done little more than stress what Frank Knight spent much time discussing, namely, man's tendency to want to want better things, to become a better man. This theme is fully developed in the essay "Ethics and the Economic Interpretation," the first essay in *The Ethics of Competition*.[2] More recently, Burt Weisbrod[3] has explicitly discussed the possibility of investment in securing "better" sets of utility functions. What I have done is to marry this discussion of man's desire to modify his own being, with what may be called a subjective or even neo-Austrian theory of time and choice. In the latter, I have been influenced by G. L. S. Shackle, whose difficult but idea-packed book *Epistemics and Economics*[4] I have been struggling to get through this summer. I have also had access to Shackle's 1976 Keynes lecture to the British academy, "Time and Choice."[5] Further, I have had occasion to read Jack Wiseman's paper, "Costs and Decisions."[6] You will also recognize that much of my discussion of choice in this paper is related to my earlier treat-

2. Frank Knight, "Ethics and the Economic Interpretation," *The Ethics of Competition* (Chicago: Midway Reprint, 1967), 19–40.

3. Burt Weisbrod, "Comparing Utility Functions in Efficiency Terms or, What Kind of Utility Functions Do We Want?" *American Economic Review* 67, no. 5 (December 1977): 991–95.

4. G. L. S. Shackle, *Epistemics and Economics* (Cambridge: At the University Press, 1972).

5. G. L. S. Shackle, "Time and Choice," *Proceedings of the British Academy* 62 (1976): 306–29.

6. Jack Wiseman, "Costs and Decisions" (University of York, 1978, mimeographed).

ment in *Cost and Choice.*[7] To the philosophical cognoscenti, much of my discussion probably embodies the influence of Whitehead, albeit indirectly since I had never read Whitehead before completing the draft of this lecture.

We could, I suspect, have an interesting discussion if I stopped at this point. But there is more to my purpose than merely to raise some of the issues of general approach or method. I want to argue that our failure to allow for any accounting of the sort of choice behavior involving investment in becoming something different has inhibited our ability to understand as well as our willingness to try to understand some of the problems of our time, both individual and social. By implicitly refusing to consider man as artifactual, we neglect the "constitution of private man," which roughly translates as "character," as well as the "constitution of public men," which translates into the necessary underpinning of a free society, the "character" of society, if you will.

Let me take care at this point not to be misunderstood. I am not calling for the return of some romantic image of man that transcends "human nature," an image of man that you and I cannot even recognize as our fellow in plausibly imagined social order. I am not calling for some idealized person who might be imagined independently of the very real constraints of "natural man." I have used the term *artifactual* here precisely for the purpose of allowing some recognition of the basic constraints of human nature while, at the same time, allowing for wide areas of choice within these constraints, areas within which we can, and do, construct ourselves as individuals, from the base largely constructed for us by our forebears. Artifactual man, along with his institutions of social order, was embodied in the wisdom of the eighteenth century, a wisdom that modern man has seemed in danger of losing altogether.

How can the prevailing orthodoxy account for such a simple act as that by a person in quitting smoking, an example that was discussed at some length by Tom Schelling[8] at the New York meetings? Or going on a diet? If the person's utility function is unchanged, and if the constraints faced do not change, how can we account for such behavior?

---

7. James M. Buchanan, *Cost and Choice* (Chicago: Markham Publishing Co., 1969).
8. T. Schelling, "Altruism, Meanness, and Other Potentially Strategic Behaviors," *American Economic Review* 68, no. 2 (May 1978): 229–30.

The explanation falls into place readily if we allow for some recognition that persons imagine themselves to be other than they are and that they take action designed to achieve imagined states of being. A smoker can surely imagine himself or herself freed of the habit, with a transformed set of preferences that would not include any desire to smoke. Reckoning on such a prospect as within the realm of the possible, a person sacrifices current enjoyment in the uncertain quest for the state of being that he can imagine. A person may undertake such renunciatory behavior voluntarily and spontaneously through a whole sequence of periods, or such behavior may take the form of the adoption of some quasi-permanent rule that will effectively impose constraints on predicted lapses into the satisfaction of "natural" desires. A smoker may carry cigarettes with him and face up to the temptation of his desires each and every time that these arise. Or a smoker may throw out all of his cigarette inventory and impose upon himself a strict rule against further purchases. Or, he may even go much further and authorize others to coerce him against indulgence of his desires.

As the smoker abstains, or as he is forced to abstain by the operation of an internal or an external constraint, he will find that he does become different from the person that he was. His preferences shift; he becomes the nonsmoker that he had imagined himself capable of becoming. The costs of having achieved such a transformation, when viewed *ex post*, may seem to have been trivial or even nonexistent, whereas the benefits may seem immense. But how could these costs and benefits, measured *ex post*, be of value in informing the calculus of the "other" person at the stage of the initial decision?

This example of the smoker is simple and straightforward, but I should emphasize its generality in the context of this paper. The behavior examined is not restricted to addicting goods and services, as some critics might immediately suggest. Almost the same analysis can be applied to any aspect of human behavior that represents "civility" in the larger meaning of this term. I refer here inclusively to manners, etiquette, codes of conduct, standards of decorum, and, most important, morals. A person conducts himself, within the natural limits available to him, and the artifactual person he becomes does, at any moment, maximize utility subject to constraints. But constraints on his own behavior imposed in past periods have shaped the form of his utility function, perhaps out of all recognition in some primitivistic sense. I may cite Frank Knight at this point. From the longer excerpt that George

Stigler put on his calendar, I cite only the following: "Insofar as man is wise or good, his 'character' is acquired chiefly by posing as better than he is, until a part of his pretense becomes a habit."[9]

I cannot fully articulate my worries to the effect that modern economic theory leads us away from any appreciation of artifactual man, but I was highly sympathetic to a statement made by C. W. Griffin in a letter to *Business Week* in response to an earlier article on the intrusion of genetics into economics. Griffin said: "From the naively optimistic eighteenth-century view of man as a potentially rational God, we have plunged to the naively pessimistic extreme of viewing man as an individual ant."[10]

We find statements everywhere to the effect that modern man has lost the faith in progress that was pervasive in the post-Enlightenment period, the eighteenth and nineteenth centuries, and most of this century. J. B. Bury entitled his classic little book *The Idea of Progress*,[11] implying by this title that the idea may be more important than the reality. This implication is surely correct in the normative sense of exerting influences on behavior. The hopes for man, individually and collectively, held out by the post-Enlightenment social philosophers may have been naive, especially when viewed from the perspective of our age. But the lesson to be drawn is surely and emphatically not one of resignation to man's fate as a natural animal.

We shall indeed revert to the jungle if we continue on our present course, whether in our private behavior patterns, or in our collective-governmental-institutional dynamic, aided and abetted by the make-work of the so-called social sciences. If we twiddle around with our "scientistic" economics and political science, if we remain so enraptured by esoteric puzzles, if we place exclusive faith in empirical demonstrations or in evolutionary processes, we are contributing to the process of deterioration.

Individually, persons must recapture an ability to imagine themselves capable of becoming "better" persons than they are. But the ranking of prospects requires valuation. "Push-pin is not as good as poetry." The role of education is to provide persons with both an array of imagined prospects

---

9. Frank Knight, "The Planful Act: The Possibilities and Limitations of Collective Rationality," in *Freedom and Reform* (New York and London: Harper & Brothers, 1947).

10. C. W. Griffin, Letter, *Business Week*, May 8, 1978, 6.

11. J. B. Bury, *The Idea of Progress* (New York: Dover Publications, 1932).

and some means of valuation. Modern education is, as we know, failing dismally in both parts of this role, but perhaps more seriously in the second than in the first. There is little or no transmission of the cultural-value heritage of the historically imagined American dream in which individuals were able to hold out images of themselves and their society in accordance with generally accepted standards of "betterness." We could, of course, discuss such matters at length, but my emphasis in this paper is on other aspects of the modern dilemma. In particular, I want to concentrate on the role that political economists might play in promoting rather than holding back the good society of free and responsible men and women, a society that we all should seek. By general agreement, the economist has little or no business teaching morals or ethics, and no justification for building his theories on romantic notions of man that will not stand empirical test.

Lest I should become too confused, and become too confusing to you in the process, let me begin at the beginning, and tell you what prompted this whole effort. I did not set out with any intent of preparing a general methodological disquisition. But I was led to the sort of inquiry that my early remarks suggest by an attempt to explain satisfactorily to myself just why attitudes that seem so natural to me seem so difficult for others. Note carefully that I refer to "attitudes" here, not to ideas. In particular, I sought to understand why the "constitutional attitude" seems so foreign to so many of my fellow economists, to understand why this central aspect of what was a part of the conventional wisdom of our Founding Fathers now seems so elusive. My usage of the word *artifactual* is borrowed directly from Vincent Ostrom, who has repeatedly emphasized the necessity of considering the political constitution as an artifact, to be categorically distinguished from an evolved legal order.[12] The American experience, perhaps unique in history, has embodied the attitude that we *create* the institutions within which we interact, one with another, that we construct the rules that define the game that we all must play. But we can never lose sight of the elementary fact that the selection of the rules, "constitutional choice," is of a different attitudinal dimension from the selection of strategies within defined rules.

I was led to ask, however, whether persons who do not and cannot con-

12. See his "David Hume as a Political Analyst" (Indiana University, 1976, mimeographed).

ceive themselves to be artifactual (even if, in fact, they are and must be), can easily conceive of artifactual social institutions, artifactual rules of the game, to be chosen apart from the simple selection of strategies to be played in the complex interaction process defined by the rules of order. Does the manner in which men model their own behavior affect, and perhaps profoundly, the way that they model the social institutions under which they live? If individuals conceive themselves in the teleological image of modern economics, can they shift gears to a nonteleological image of a community?

We know that the utilitarians were unable to make this leap, at least consistently and without much ambiguity and confusion, which plagues us still. We know also that modern economics has become more, not less, teleological. In the post-Robbins era, we define our subject matter as the study of the allocation of scarce means among alternative ends, and the idea of maximization under constraints becomes central to all that we do. In the wake of methodological consensus, the theoretical welfare economists, having been forced to abandon naive utilitarianism, played teasingly with the Pareto criterion (which is not at all teleological, at least in the way that I interpret it), only to abandon this in favor of the "social welfare function." In so doing, they were explicitly extending the teleological model of the individual maximizer to that for the community or collectivity as a unit. To those economists who made such an extension, Arrow's impossibility theorem was a genuinely shocking revelation. A "social welfare function" must be constructed in order to allow for some modeling of the collectivity in teleological terms, but such a function becomes a logical impossibility under plausible conditions. What to do? What to do? I need not say that the welfare economists, among whom I should surely include Kenneth Arrow himself, are, to this day, groping for answers.

As you can recognize I am on familiar territory here, but partial corroboration for much of my argument lies in the chilling neglect of my own attempts, over a quarter-century, to secure general acknowledgment that no problem exists. Why should anyone have ever tried to model a community of *separate* persons teleologically, as if somehow "social states" could be, or should be, arrayed in some order of ascendancy, in terms of a single maximand? To me, as I stated in 1954,[13] such an effort has seemed misguided from

---

13. James M. Buchanan, "Social Choice in Voting and the Market," *Journal of Political Economy* 62 (August 1954): 334–43.

the outset, even absurd. But why do most of my colleagues persist in their efforts? What is the difference between me and them?

These questions are in the background of my exploratory remarks in this lecture (the appropriate place to be exploratory). Perhaps we should have been examining more closely the models for individual choice, and the images conveyed in those models, rather than unduly concentrating attention on the amalgamation of separate individual choices into collective results. Perhaps the nonteleological elements of individual choice have been too much neglected by us all. If each one of us is defined by an unchanging and invariant utility function, the Benthamite challenge remains ever present. Conceptually, the adding-up problem beckons, and this objective, once achieved, leads us back to the implied authoritarianism of Bentham's progeny, the practicing social democrats of our time.

But what happens to this progression once we so much as recognize that individuals do not maximize anything that remains stable for more than the logical moment for analysis. The maximization calculus may remain highly useful as a logic of choice, but only to the extent that its severe limits are explicitly acknowledged. Heraclitus noted that man does not step into the same river twice, first, because the stream has passed, and, second, because man too has moved forward in time. Choice is, and must be, irrevocable, and a person is constructed by the choices he has made sequentially through time, within the natural and the artifactual constraints that have limited his possibilities. The rational ideal eliminates choice, as Shackle emphasizes. Choice requires the presence of uncertainty for its very meaning. But choice also implies a moral responsibility for action. To rationalize or to explain choices in terms of either genetic endowments or social environment removes the elements of freedom and of responsibility. "Natural man," in the model of some behavioral responder to stimuli, akin to my dog, contradicts both the notion of individual liberty and that of individual responsibility for the consequences of the choices made. Man must bear the responsibilities for his own choices because of his artifactual nature, because he has available to him alternative "choosables," to use Shackle's term, because man makes his own history.

If individual man is to be free, he is to be held accountable, he is to be deemed responsible for his actions. But at the same time he is allowed to take credit for his achievement. Who can claim credit for results that could have been predicted from nature? From a knowledge of his genetic endowment or his social environment, or both? But once man is conceived in the image of an artifact, who constructs himself through his own choices, he sheds the animalistically determined path of existence laid out for him by the orthodox economists' model. A determined and programmed existence is replaced by the uncertain and exciting quest that life must be.

If man can envisage himself as a product of his own making, as embodying prospects for changing himself into one of the imagined possibilities that he might be, it becomes relatively easy for him to envisage changing the basic rules of social order in the direction of imagined good societies. In doing so, however, nothing teleological can be introduced since man must recognize that even within his own private sphere of action there is no maximand. Individually, man invests in becoming that which he is not. Collectively, men agree to modify the artifactual rules within which they interact one with another so as to allow individualized pursuit of whatever men may choose.

A felicific calculus becomes absurd in this setting, as does all talk of such things as "national goals," "national priorities," or even such familiar things as "university objectives." Traditionally, many of us who have been critical of such talk remark that "only individuals can have goals." But I am here advancing the more radical notion that *not even* individuals have well-defined and well-articulated objectives that exist independently of choices themselves. Introspectively, we must realize that we do not. My plea is that we begin to temper our analytical-explanatory thought patterns to allow for what we know to be real, regardless of the havoc wrought to our aesthetically appealing logical structures.

Out of all this there emerges a strong defense of individual liberty that cannot readily be advanced by the modern economist, influenced as he is by his utilitarian heritage. The modern economist can introduce time into his models only if he treats individuals as squirrels, to return to my earlier example. The squirrel's behavior can be interpreted as maximizing the present value of his utility stream. Given his constraints, and his utility function, the squirrel is not, and cannot be, concerned with the size of his "choice" set, with the existence or nonexistence of his rejected alternatives. A dramatically different attitude emerges, however, in the conception of the artifactual man that I have sketched out here. A person chooses, as Shackle stresses, from among many imagined futures, and he remains necessarily uncertain as to how that which he chooses will work out. He has a clear interest in seeing that the choice set, the set of alternative imagined futures, remains as open as is naturally possible, and, if constrained, that the constraints be also of his own choosing. The deliberate closing off of future options by the introduction of apparently irrelevant constraints, externally imposed, must damage the individual who knows that he must choose among uncertain prospects continually through time.

Consider, for example, an urban dweller who does not, in the orthodox analysis, embody an argument for privacy in his utility function. Within the corpus of formal analysis, such a person cannot be much concerned about the introduction of zoning restrictions that effectively force a higher concentration of persons in space. By contrast, consider the same urban dweller in the image suggested in this paper. He does not, and cannot, predict that person he may want to become in subsequent periods. He wants to "keep his options open," because he can imagine himself to be someone quite different from the person he now is. He does not, let us say, choose to leave the urban center today, tomorrow, or next week. But he can imagine himself becoming the person who could make a future choice to move to the suburbs or the country. He seeks to hold all such options open, even if his behavior, viewed in retrospect, indicates no exercise of the options in question. The building of the Berlin Wall harmed every person living in East Berlin. This is a simple statement of fact that orthodox economists would find difficult to interpret by means of their prevailing analytics.

Man wants liberty to become the man he wants to become. He does so precisely because he does not know what man he will want to become in time. Let us remove once and for all the instrumental defense of liberty, the only one that can possibly be derived directly from orthodox economic analysis. Man does not want liberty in order to maximize his utility, or that of the society of which he is a part. *He wants liberty to become the man he wants to become.*

Rights, Efficiency, and Exchange
The Irrelevance of Transactions Cost

I. Introduction

Economists commence analysis with utility functions and production functions as defining attributes of choosing-acting entities. Interdependencies among utility and production functions of separate persons and units provide the origins of exchanges, which become the central subject matter for economists' attention. Interdependencies that remain outside exchanges, uncompensated transfers of positive and negative values, become externalities in the economists' lexicon. One of the contributions of the property-rights, law-economics research of the last three decades has been the focus of economists' attention on the necessity of including legal-institutional constraints along with resource constraints in any analysis of economic interaction.

Lawyers commence analysis with legal rights assignments as defining attributes of potential litigants. Differential evaluation of rights by separate persons and units gives rise, in the legal setting for analysis, to exchanges in rights, which are equivalent to the exchanges that the economists analyze. Predation or invasion of rights, whether actual or potential, gives rise to appeals to the protective capacity of the state, or, with uncertainty in rights definition, to potential litigation.

Note that the economists' conception of externalities bears no direct relation to the legal invasion of rights. Persons may impose economic harms

From *Ansprüche, Eigentum und Verfügungsrechte* (Berlin: Duncker and Humblot, 1984), 9–24. Reprinted by permission of the publisher.

I am indebted to A. J. Culyer, David Levy, Viktor Vanberg, and Karen Vaughn for helpful comments on an earlier draft.

or benefits, without payment or exaction of compensation, while confining behavior within spheres of legally defined rights. Lawyers, as well as economists, have come to recognize, however, that well-defined rights can facilitate exchanges.[1]

Ambiguity remains on the question as to whether or not legally-permissible impositions of harms (and/or benefits) of a person (persons) on another (others) generate inefficiency in resource utilization in a setting where rights are well-defined and contracts are enforced and in which all persons can enter into voluntary exchanges. In such a setting, *will resources necessarily move toward their most highly valued uses?*

The central argument in Coase's seminal 1960 paper, "The Problem of Social Cost,"[2] is that voluntary exchange in well-defined rights provides a sufficient condition for allocative efficiency. Coase amended this central proposition by what has been widely interpreted as a "zero-transactions costs" qualifier, which, as I shall demonstrate, weakened the force of his argument.[3] Robert Cooter raised the question explicitly in his 1982 paper, "The Cost of Coase."[4] He argued that allocative efficiency is guaranteed by voluntary exchanges of rights only in fully-competitive environments, and that strategic bargaining behavior will emerge as a source of potential resource wastage in noncompetitive interactions. In the absence of some externally-imposed rule for dividing the purely-distributional gains, there is no assurance that exchanges in rights will shift the economy toward the Pareto efficiency frontier and maintain a position on the frontier once reached.

My purpose in this paper is to exorcise the ambiguity here, an ambiguity that emerges from confusion on elementary conceptual principles, and a confusion that is shared, at least to some degree, by the Coasians as well as

1. A by-product of law-economics analysis has been the proposition that the definition of rights "should" reflect some underlying economic efficiency norm. I shall not discuss this norm here, but my analysis suggests that the norm enters the analysis quite differently under the conception of efficiency herein advanced.

2. R. H. Coase, "The Problem of Social Cost," *Journal of Law and Economics* 3 (October 1960): 1–44.

3. Coase did not refer to transactions costs, as such. The qualifying statement that has been interpreted in zero-transactions cost terms is as follows: "and the pricing system works smoothly (strictly this means that the operation of a pricing system is without cost)" (p. 2).

4. Robert Cooter, "The Cost of Coase," *Journal of Legal Studies* 11 (January 1982): 1–34.

their critics. I shall demonstrate that consistent application of a *subjectivist-contractarian* perspective offers genuine clarification along several dimensions of the law-economics intersection.[5]

II. A Contractarian Reconstruction of the Coase Theorem

Coase was primarily interested in showing, through a series of both hypothetical and historical examples, that freedom of exchange and contract will insure that resources are allocated to their most highly valued uses, that if the assignment of rights is clear, parties involved in actual or potential interdependence will have incentives to negotiate among themselves and exchange rights to the disposition over resources so long as differential evaluations are placed on those rights of disposition. Put in externality language, Coase was essentially arguing that all Pareto-relevant externalities would tend to be eliminated in the process of free exchange-contract among affected parties.[6]

It is unfortunate that Coase presented his argument (through the examples) largely in terms of presumably objectively-measurable and independently-determined harm and benefit relationships. In his formulation, these relationships become *identical* in the perception of all parties to any potential exchange of rights.[7] Hence, the unique "efficient" (benefit maximizing or loss minimizing) allocation of resources exists and becomes determinate conceptually to any external observer. The efficacy of free exchange of rights

5. I have elaborated this perspective in earlier writings. See, in particular, my *Freedom in Constitutional Contract* (College Station: Texas A&M University Press, 1978).

6. This sentence summarizes the central argument made in James M. Buchanan and Wm. Craig Stubblebine, "Externality," *Economica* 29 (November 1962): 371–84. In writing that paper, Stubblebine and I considered ourselves to be developing an argument that was wholly consistent with Coase's, even if we also recognized that our approach was basically contractarian, whereas his was not explicitly defined. Coase, who had been a colleague at the University of Virginia, did not, however, like the Buchanan-Stubblebine paper, presumably because he strenuously objected to any usage of the term, "externality." Also, however, his objection may have stemmed from the ambiguity in perspective that I emphasize in this paper.

7. For an analysis of a setting in which potential traders differ in their evaluation of benefits and/or harms, see James M. Buchanan and Roger L. Faith, "Entrepreneurship and the Internalization of Externality," *Journal of Law and Economics* (March 1981): 95–111.

in attaining the objectively-determined "efficient" outcome becomes subject to testing by observation. The exchange process, in this perspective, is itself evaluated in terms of criteria applied to the outcomes that the process is observed to produce. There are values inherent in allocations that exist quite independently of the means through which these allocations are generated.

Despite his own earlier contribution to what may be called the subjectivist theory of opportunity cost,[8] Coase's position on the independent determinacy and existence of an "efficient" allocation of resources is not clear. Both his use of the numerical examples and his introduction of the transactions-costs proviso suggest that Coase was, indeed, applying outcome criteria to results of the exchange process rather than limiting his attention to the process itself. To the extent that Coase does apply outcome criteria for allocative efficiency, however, his whole analysis, along with that of his many favorable interpreters, becomes vulnerable to the critique mounted by Cooter and others, who suggest that elements of confusion have been introduced by thinking that transactions costs involve only communication-information difficulties. In fact, parties to bargains in small-number settings with distributive as well as allocative implications have strategic reasons to conceal their preferences and, in large-number settings, all parties may have free-rider motivations, independently of any communication-information failures. In both of the latter cases, voluntary exchange would not seem to guarantee the attainment of the Pareto efficiency frontier, and for reasons not well defined within the transactions-costs rubric. Interpreted in terms of satisfying outcome criteria for efficiency, the Coase theorem fails in noncompetitive settings; free exchange and contract among parties does not necessarily generate an allocation of resources to their most highly valued uses. "Social value" is not necessarily maximized; "Externalities" that are Pareto-relevant may remain in full trading equilibrium.

The Coasian, who remains at the same time an objectivist for whom an "efficient" resource allocation exists independently of the process of its generation, will have difficulty responding satisfactorily to the critique advanced by Cooter and others who make similar arguments. Parties to potential ex-

---

8. See R. H. Coase, "Business Organization and the Accountant," in *L. S. E. Essays on Cost*, ed. James M. Buchanan and G. F. Thirlby (New York: New York University Press, 1981), 95–134. Revised version of materials written and published initially in 1938.

changes who are rational maximizers of expected utilities may fail to reach the presumed objectifiable Pareto efficiency frontier. "Gains from trade" may remain after the parties conclude their bargaining sessions; resources may remain in uses that yield relatively lower values than they might yield in alternative uses.

If, however, the whole Coase analysis is interpreted in subjectivist-contractarian (or, if preferred, Austrian-Wicksellian) terms, the critique can be shown to be without substance. If the only source of valuation of assets or resource claims is the revealed choice behavior of parties to potential exchanges, there is no means through which an external observer can determine whether or not trade, as observed, stops short of some idealized norms. If a person, A, is observed to refuse an offer of $ X for asset, T, that person, A, must be presumed to place a value on T in excess of $ X. That asset, in A's usage, must be yielding a value or benefit more than $ X. The fact that some portion of the imputed subjective value of T, to the current owner, A, may be based on his estimates as to the real preferences (valuations) of B, the potential purchaser, is totally irrelevant. In the institutional setting implicitly postulated here, in which A and B are isolated parties to potential exchange, the absence of a consummated exchange of the asset, T, demonstrates that this asset remains in its most highly valued use. "Efficiency" in resource use, *given the institutional setting,* is insured so long as A and B remain free to make the exchange or to refuse to make it.

Note that the invariance version of the Coase theorem is *not* valid in this perspective. The contractarian approach suggests that free exchange among parties will guarantee that resources remain in their most highly valued uses, but it does imply that the ownership or liability patterns, the assignment of legal rights, may affect the allocation that emerges in small-number settings, and quite apart from the acknowledged relevance of income effects. A switch in the assignments of ownership rights in my example, from A to B with respect to the initial ownership of the asset, T, may well result in the retention of the asset by B, and, therefore, in a usage different from that to which A might have put the asset with the earlier ownership assignment.

III. Is What Is Always Efficient?

The contractarian reconstruction of the Coase theorem outlined in Section II may seem, at the outset, vulnerable to the charge that, so interpreted, the theory becomes a tautology.[9] If there is no objective criterion for resource use that can be applied to outcomes, as a means of indirectly testing the efficacy of the exchange process, then so long as exchange remains open and so long as force and fraud are not observed, that upon which agreement is reached is, by definition, that which can be classified to be efficient.[10] In this construction, how can inefficiency possibly emerge?

In an early paper, published initially in 1959,[11] I suggested that agreement is the only ultimate test for efficiency, but that the test need not be confined in application to the allocative results or outcomes generated under explicitly existing or defined institutional-structural rules. The agreement test for efficiency may be elevated or moved upward to the stage of institutions or rules, as such. Agreement on a change in the rules within which exchanges are allowed to take place would be a signal that patterns of outcomes reached or predicted under the previously-existing set of rules are less preferred or valued than the patterns expected to be generated under the rule-as-changed. Hence, the new rule is deemed more efficient than the old. The discussion and agreement on the change in the rules here is analogous to the trade that takes place between ordinary traders in the simple exchanges made under postulated rules.

With a change in the rule or institution, however, the pattern of outcomes reached through within-rule trades or exchanges would be expected to be different from that attained under the rules that existed prior to the change. This suggests only that any allocation of resources that is to be classified as "efficient" depends necessarily on the institutional structure within which

---

9. Cooter, "The Cost of Coase," 14–15.

10. Note that this statement does not require any presumption about the knowledge possessed by potential participants in the interaction process. An alternative formulation of the Coasian perspective may be advanced in which the presumption of shared knowledge of institutional results is critical to the allegedly tautological character of the Coasian propositions. In his interesting paper, which ties together several strands of modern theory, T. K. Rymes seems to advance this alternative formulation. See T. K. Rymes, "Money, Efficiency, and Knowledge," *Canadian Journal of Economics* (November 1979): 575–89.

11. See my "Positive Economics, Welfare Economics, and Political Economy," *Journal of Law and Economics* 2 (October 1959): 124–38. Reprinted in my *Fiscal Theory and Political Economy* (Chapel Hill: University of North Carolina Press, 1960), 105–24.

For recent papers that deal with the general topic under discussion in this section, see David Levy, "Is Observed Monopoly Always Efficient?" (Center for Study of Public Choice, 1982, mimeographed); A. J. Culyer, "The Quest for Efficiency in the Public Sector: Economists versus Dr. Pangloss" (University of York, September 1982, mimeographed).

resource utilization-valuation decisions are made.[12] This implication creates no difficulty for the subjectivist-contractarian who does not acknowledge the uniqueness of the resource allocation that is properly classified to be efficient.

The position I am advancing here may be clarified by reference to the familiar prisoners' dilemma. The contractarian is not put in the role of denying that such dilemmas exist. Indeed his diagnosis may suggest that such dilemmas characterize many areas of social interaction. Consider, then, how the contractarian-subjectivist would approach the prisoners' dilemma. Take the most familiar, and original, example, where there are two prisoners presented with the classic alternatives, and allowed no communication with each other. Here, the outcome predicted, and possibly observed, to emerge may be classified as "presumably inefficient" for the set of prisoners considered as a group because they are not allowed to make explicit exchanges. If they are, instead, allowed to communicate, one with another, and to make *binding-enforceable contracts,* they would never remain in the "both confess" trap. They would exchange binding commitments not to confess, and this result, as observed, would be classified properly as "efficient," again for the set of prisoners treated as the relevant group.

The dilemma, as such, may, however, be an efficient institution for forcing prisoners to confess. That is to say, the subset of the population made up of prisoners only may not be the set relevant for a political-collective evaluation of the institution. In the more inclusive community, the test for whether or not that institution which removes the option of binding contracts among prisoners is efficient would depend on the attainment or nonattainment of community-wide consensus on change to some alternative institution.

IV. Transactions Costs

I have not introduced transactions costs as a possible barrier to the attainment of allocative efficiency through voluntary exchanges anywhere in the

12. On this point, see W. C. Stubblebine, "On Property Rights and Institutions," in *Explorations in the Theory of Anarchy,* ed. Gordon Tullock (Blacksburg: Center for Study of Public Choice, 1972), 39–50. Also see my paper, "The Relevance of Pareto Optimality," *Journal of Conflict Resolution* 6 (December 1962): 341–54. Reprinted in my *Freedom in Constitutional Contract,* 215–34.

above discussion. And, as I noted earlier, the thrust of Coase's argument is weakened by the insertion of the transactions costs qualification or proviso. There is no meaning of the term "allocative efficiency" in an idealized zero-transactions costs setting under the subjectivist-contractarian perspective. Such "efficiency" assumes meaning only if an objectivist conceptualization of resource use is implicitly postulated. Resources will, of course, be differently allocated by voluntary exchanges of rights in differing institutional settings, as noted above, but to say this is to do nothing more than to say that persons will behave differently under differing constraints.

To the extent that trade is free to all parties in an interaction, and all parties have well-defined rights, resources will move toward their most highly valued uses without qualification. To the extent that potential traders are coerced, either by prohibitions on their ability to make enforceable contracts or by the imposition of noncompensated transfers, no conclusions about value maximizing resource use can be drawn because the rules permit no test.[13] The only criterion available, that of prior agreement on the transfers of value, is explicitly replaced as a decision rule, although it remains as the valid test.

In this Section, I propose to discuss three broadly-defined categories of problems that are often placed in the transactions costs rubric, and I shall show how these putative barriers to allocative efficiency are readily incorporated into a coherent subjectivist-contractarian argument.

Information-communication constraints

Transactions costs are perhaps most familiarly discussed as arising from some failure of parties to potential exchange to attain access to information on proffered terms of trade or to communicate their own offers effectively to other traders. Hence, or so the orthodox argument might run, if potential traders could be better informed and be made better able to communicate one with another, now-unconsummated trades might be worked out, generating increments in value, insuring greater efficiency in resource use. If "efficiency" is defined as that pattern of resource use reached through vol-

---

13. Interpreted in these terms, the Coase qualifying statement, cited in footnote 3 above, should have been "the pricing (exchange) system works without interference."

untary exchanges *after* the new information-communication setting is in place, then, of course, the prior-existing allocation is *now* "inefficient." But in the postulated initial setting, there was a different information-communication environment. Given the then-existent constraints under which traders behaved, the prior allocation was "efficient."

Whether or not a shift in information-communication constraints is, in itself, an efficient or Pareto-superior change can be determined only by applying some criterion that remains *internal* to the set of potential traders. If the initial constraints are deemed to be "inefficient," potential traders will, themselves, find it advantageous to invest resources in efforts to shift them.

Consider a simple example. There are two totally isolated villages, Adam and Smith, with no communication with each other. In one village, two deer exchange for one beaver. In the other, two beaver exchange for one deer. In the setting of isolation, the allocative results are efficient provided that trade is free in each village. If the isolation between the villages is not itself efficient, it will be to the advantage of a trading entrepreneur in one village or the other to seek out means of breaking the trading barrier. Profits from arbitrage will attract such behavior as will be required to remove differentials in the terms of trade and to generate differing patterns of resource use, if the shift is such as to confer net benefits. It is misleading to suggest that the initial setting of isolation prevented efficient resource utilization because of the transactions cost barrier. Voluntary exchange must be defined to include entrepreneurial trading effort which will emerge to insure that all gains-from-trade in breaking down information-communication constraints are exhausted.

To the extent that the constraints that exist are *artificially* imposed, via the auspices of political-governmental agency, the activities of entrepreneurial traders that might otherwise generate an optimal breakdown of barriers may be prevented or inhibited. In the presence of observed artificial constraints the allocative patterns can be labeled as "presumably inefficient," since trade is not allowed to take place.

FREE-RIDER CONSTRAINTS

The question of the possible efficacy of removing existing governmental-political constraints, or of imposing new ones, shifts analysis to the second familiar source of alleged barriers to resource utilization, a source that is often swept within the transactions-cost qualification, but is more specifically discussed under the "free rider" rubric. In large-number settings, the individual participant has little or no incentive to initiate action designed to yield benefits for all members of the community, to secure information about alternatives, and to be concerned about enforcement of community-wide agreements. There may exist complex exchanges that might be agreed to by all participants, but it is to the advantage of no single person or small group to assume the leadership role in the design and implementation of such potential agreements.

This setting differs from that discussed under the information-communication rubric in that individual entrepreneurial efforts cannot here be depended on to search out productive shifts in institutional arrangements due to the absence of residual claimancy. In my 1959 paper, I suggested that the proper role for the normative political economist was that of discovering potential rules changes that might yield general benefits and then of presenting these changes as *hypotheses* subject to the Wicksellian contractual-consensus test. If, when presented a suggested change in rules, agreement among all potentially interacting parties is forthcoming, the hypothesis is corroborated. The previously existing rule is proven inefficient. If disagreement emerges on the proposed rules change, the hypothesis is falsified. The existing rule is classified as Pareto-efficient. And, given this institutional setting, any outcomes attained under free and open exchange processes are to be classified as efficient.

It is useful at this point to introduce the classic externality case from welfare economics, the setting in which ordinary economic activity within well-defined legal rights imposes noncompensated damages on a sufficiently large number of persons so as to insure failure of a bargained solution due to free-rider motivation.[14] Can "uncorrected" outcomes in this setting be labeled to be efficient? Consistent application of the contractarian perspective must attach the efficiency label here, so long as all members of the relevant community remain free to make intervening offers and bids to those traders whose activity is alleged to generate the spillover harms. There is no overtly

---

14. For an analysis of this setting in a more general context, see my "The Institutional Structure of Externality," *Public Choice* 14 (Spring 1973): 69–82.

coercive overriding of individual claims. The fact that, given the institutional structure postulated, outcomes are reached through an exchange-contract process open to all entrants is the criterion for efficiency of those outcomes, the only one that is available without resort to some objectivist standard.

Note, however, that this classification of such "noncorrected" outcomes in the alleged large-number externality situation as "efficient" is not equivalent to taking some Panglossian attitude toward the set of arrangements that generates such outcomes. The institutional structure may *not* be efficient, and the political economist may hypothesize that general agreement can be secured on some realignment of rights (including required compensations to those who might be asked to give up valued claims) that will allow potentially damaged parties in the interaction to possess rights of veto over specified in-market activity of the ordinary sort.

In the contractarian perspective, to say that free and open exchange tends to insure that resources flow to their most highly valued uses means only that such uses are relevant to the institutional structure in being. It is not to say that the unfettered market under any and all assignments of rights is the most "efficient" institution. These are two wholly different propositions that have become confused because of the failure to make the distinction between the objectivist and the subjectivist perspective on allocative processes.

It is necessary to distinguish carefully between agreement or unanimity as a *test* for an "efficiency-enhancing trade" and unanimity as a *decision rule.* This distinction tends to be neglected in analyses of simple exchanges organized through market processes, largely because the decision rule that effectively operates coincides with the ultimate test for the results of that rule. Within a specific legal order, if entry is free, market exchanges are made under an implicit rule of unanimity.[15] If A and B voluntarily agree to an exchange, and if C remains free to offer possibly differing terms to either party, there is no outcome that does not pass the consensus test. The outcome attained can be classified as "efficient" because it reflects agreement among all parties, and the decision rule or institution that allows such outcome pat-

---

15. On this point, see my paper, "Individual Choice in Voting and the Market," *Journal of Political Economy* 62 (August 1954): 334–43. Reprinted in my *Fiscal Theory and Political Economy* (Chapel Hill: University of North Carolina Press, 1960), 90–104.

Also see Ludwig von Mises, *Human Action* (New Haven: Yale University Press, 1949), 312.

terns to be generated can be classified to be "efficient" if there is no consensus to be reached on any possible change.

With "public good" or "public goods" in the standard meaning, however, it may be impossible that market exchanges, made voluntarily within well-defined assignment of rights, will generate patterns of results that are preferred by participants. Given the assignment of rights, and given the institution of exchange, the outcomes reached may still be classified to be "efficient." But the institution of voluntary exchange, as ordinarily understood, may not, in this case, be "efficient" because there may emerge general agreement upon a change in institutional structure. Explicit political or governmental decision rules may be accepted by all parties as being preferred to the decision rules of the market. That political-governmental decision rule upon which agreement is reached, however, may *not* require consent of all parties to reach particular outcomes, either explicitly or implicitly. That is to say, the "efficient" decision rule may be such that specific outcomes need not meet the consensus test.[16]

Consider an example. Suppose that there is general agreement upon a constitutional rule that specifies that police services shall be politicized and that decisions on the organization and financing of these services shall be made by majority voting rules in an elected legislature. By the fact of general agreement, this *institution* is efficient. There is no change upon which everyone affected might agree. Within the operation of the rule or institution, however, there is no basis for presuming that particular outcomes are "efficient" in the contractarian perspective. A majority coalition may impose its preferences on the members of the minority. And, given the legal order which may prohibit side payments, resources may well be allocated to uses that are valued less highly than they might be in alternative uses. There is simply no means of making the required test for efficiency or inefficiency within the rule or institution as it operates.

The majority-rule setting here is analogous to that discussed earlier under the prisoners' dilemma. For the inclusive community, a rule that places captured prisoners in isolation and prevents binding contracts, may be "efficient," despite its evident presumed inefficiency to the subset of prisoners

---

16. For elaboration, see James M. Buchanan and Gordon Tullock, *The Calculus of Consent* (Ann Arbor: University of Michigan Press, 1962).

themselves. With majority rule, or any less than unanimity rule, for political-governmental decisions, the decision structure may itself be "efficient" while at the same time the particular outcomes attained under the structure may be presumed inefficient, at least in some situations, for those who are directly coerced. To introduce "transactions costs" as a barrier to the attainment of efficiency in this generalized free-rider context seems to confuse rather than to clarify the complex set of issues involved.

Strategic behavior

The third source of alleged inefficiency in resource utilization, also sometimes included in the broadly-defined transactions-costs basket, is summarized under the rubric, *strategic behavior*. Cooter concentrated his critique of the Coase theorem on this element, in the sense previously noted.

The strategic-behavior setting differs from the two previously analyzed. As Cooter correctly indicates, the alleged barrier to possible agreement among potential traders or bargainers arises in small-number, noncompetitive settings not from any necessary informational or communication failure that might be profitably eliminated by arbitrage. And, since the numbers of potential interacting parties are small, there is no free-rider motivation for behavior. In this setting, how can criteria for improvement be derived internally from the parties?

Here there is a direct analogue to the large-number setting in the sense that any modification of the structure of interaction becomes a "public good" for all parties. Hence, in a strict two-person interaction where both parties expect to engage in a whole sequence of similar potential interactions, they may acknowledge the wastefulness of investment in strategic bargaining. In such a case, they would agree on an arbitration procedure or rule which might take the form of the appointment of an external or third-party adjudicator along with a commitment to accept the terms laid down. Again, as in all other settings, the test for efficiency in the institutional rule is agreement among affected parties.

In a more inclusive context, if all members of the relevant political community recognize that many of them will be placed in small-number bargaining settings on occasion, as either buyer or seller in potential exchanges, there may possibly emerge some general agreement on political-legal rules that reduce the potential profitability of strategic investment. Such rules may involve the promotion of competitive environments for exchanges of rights, since competition, actual and potential, dramatically restricts the scope for strategic behavior. Note, however, that such an agreement would not be based putatively on any perception that competition produces an objectifiably meaningful efficient allocation of resources. The agreement itself becomes the test as to whether or not competitive arrangements are more "efficient" than the alternative arrangements in being.

V. Competition as a Device or as a Determinant

As the last remarks suggest, there are two profoundly different conceptions of competition and the competitive process that emerge from the objectivist perspective on the one hand and from the subjectivist-contractarian perspective on the other. In the former, there exists an efficient allocation of resources independently of any process through which it is generated. From this supposition, it follows that institutional arrangements may be directly evaluated in terms of their relative success or failure in attaining the desired pattern of resource use. Normative argument in support of competitive institutions emerges, in this perspective, only because such institutions are judged to be relatively superior "devices," "instruments," or "mechanisms" in generating independently derived results. Where competitive institutions do not seem to exist, as defined by some independently derived structural criteria (e.g., number of firms in an industry, concentration ratios, etc.), there emerges a normative argument for direct intervention with voluntary exchange process as a means of moving results toward the externally derived allocative norm or ideal. Small-number bargaining settings (bilateral monopoly, isolated exchanges, locationally specific assets) necessarily fail to guarantee efficiency due to the presence of incentives for strategic behavior. Governmental action in monitoring the bargains struck in all such settings seems a normative consequence of the analysis.

In the subjectivist-contractarian perspective, "efficiency" cannot be said to exist except as determined by the process through which results are generated, and criteria for evaluating patterns of results must be applied only to processes. In this perspective, voluntary exchanges among persons, within a competitive constraints structure, generate efficient resource usage, which is determined only as the exchanges are made. Competitive institutions, in this perspective, are not instruments to be used to generate efficiency. They are, instead, possible structures, possible rules or sets of rules, that may emerge from generalized agreement. If such institutions do not emerge from a consensus operating via politically orchestrated exchanges, those alternative arrangements that may be observed to persevere must themselves be judged to be "efficient," and, within these structures, patterns of voluntary exchange outcomes may also be so classified.[17] The role of the political order, of law, or government, is to facilitate agreement on institutional arrangements, and to police rights assigned under such agreements. There is no role for specific governmental monitoring of bargains anywhere in the picture.

I should acknowledge at this point that it is difficult for anyone trained in economics in this century to hold consistently to the perspective that I have laid out in this paper. What is government's role, for example, in the case of natural monopoly, which operates "inefficiently" under the orthodox perspective and thereby seems to warrant political-governmental intrusion into the exchanges that might be made between the monopolist and his potential customers? No such normative inference can follow from a consistent application of the contractarian perspective. At best, the hypothesis may be advanced to the effect that consensus should emerge on a scheme to "buy out" existing owners of such monopolized resources (opportunities) and to replace their operation with governmental-political management, based on some cost-based pricing rules. But the subjectivist will also acknowledge that costs are not independently determinate, in which case such operating rules

---

17. I seek no quarrel at this point with the evolutionists who argue that institutions emerge from the historical process of development without any explicit constitutional-political agreement having been made. So long as rights are well-defined and enforced, the institutional evolution meets the criterion of implicit unanimity analogously to the market process more narrowly defined. And the continued acceptance of institutional forms itself suggests the presumption that these forms meet the efficiency test.

Wegehenkel has specifically related the process of evolutionary change in an economy to the transaction-costs discussion. While accepting the orthodox meaning of the Coase theorem, Wegehenkel argues that the evolutionary process, generated by entrepreneurial effort, pushes the economy continually in the direction of transactions-costs reduction. See Lothar Wegehenkel, *Gleichgewicht Transaktionskosten und Evolution* (Tübingen: Mohr, 1981).

become absurd. At best, the hypothesis must be for a scheme that would compensate the monopoly owners and replace them with governmental agents. Modern public choice theory has put the nod to "public interest" idealizations of the behavior of such agents. In some final analysis, the subjectivist-contractarian must be hypothetically pragmatic in all those cases that seem to have been the bread-and-butter of conventional normative political economy, welfare economics, and, now, law-and-economics. He may, with little fear of analytical ambiguity, strongly urge that alternative sets of rules be presented and tested in the political exchange process. And he may, of course, utilize his specialist talents in the design and predicted operation of such alternative arrangements. He should not, however, ever be allowed to take the arrogant stance of suggesting that this or that set of institutions is or is not more "efficient."[18]

VI. Conclusions

In this paper, I have tried to support the following propositions:

1. Given the institutions within which behavior is constrained, voluntary exchanges among traders in a legal market order tend to insure that resources flow to and remain in their most highly valued uses;
2. the most highly valued uses of resources depend on the institutional setting within which voluntary exchanges take place;
3. institutions are, themselves, variables subject to change, and agreement among persons who operate within institutional constraints is fully analogous to voluntary exchange within established rules;
4. the several so-called "transactions costs" barriers to "efficiency" in resource allocation can be more appropriately analyzed in the context of hypotheses about institutional reform;
5. the ultimate test for institutional reform remains that of agreement among affected parties.

18. It should be evident from my argument that there is no justification at all for judicial introduction of the putative efficiency norm, presumably to be imposed independently of the political process. On this, see my "Good Economics—Bad Law," *Virginia Law Review* 60 (Spring 1974): 483–92. Reprinted in my *Freedom in Constitutional Contract,* 40–49.

I have shown that these propositions follow consistently from a subjectivist-contractarian perspective on the behavior of persons within well-defined institutional structures as well as on their behavior in modifying such structures. The perspective allows a functional role for the political economist to be well defined. The propositions place the now-famous Coase theorem in a position that renders it much less vulnerable to its objectivist critics. At the same time, however, the implication that what is is always efficient is avoided.

Analysis must be based squarely on the recognition that persons are simultaneously "trading" at several levels. They are considering voluntary exchanges within institutional rules that they treat, for purposes of such within-rule calculus, as fixed. Given the institutions of the market or private sector, resources tend to be flowing to their most highly valued uses, although care should be taken here to state this proposition in terms of the continuously equilibrating properties of the system rather than in terms of any achieved equilibrium. At the same time, however, the same persons are engaged in nonmarket or political "trades," within the defined political order that exists. In this set of interactions, economic resources need *not* be moving toward their most highly valued uses because, under the decision rules of the political order, persons may be permitted to effectuate resource transfers without the voluntary agreement, explicit or implicit, of all affected parties. The political decision rule, as contrasted with the market decision rule, offers no test of the results that it acts to generate.

At the same time that they act within defined market and political rules, persons are considering "trades" that may involve changes in these decision rules, or institutional structures, themselves. There will be, at this level, forces generated by utility maximizing considerations that move the rules-structure toward that which is "efficient." The patterns of resource use generated under less-than-unanimity decision rules in the political order, which embody no presumption of value maximization for the reasons noted, may offer reasons for considering shifts toward the market order, which does generate results that may be presumed to be value-maximizing. However, other reasons may well dominate any such comparative institutional calculus. Consistency requires that the contractarian apply the same criterion for institutional efficiency that he applies to allocative efficiency within institutions. That which is efficient is that upon which all potentially affected parties agree, explicitly or implicitly. While the absence of the unanimity rule in politics does give some basis for the generalized hypothesis that, where they are substitutes, individuals would agree to replace politicized arrangements with market or market-like arrangements, this must remain strictly a hypothesis subject to the agreement test.

My whole analysis in this paper has been based in the presupposition that, in both the market and the political order, rights are well defined. With reference to constitutional reform in particular, however, basic uncertainties in the assignment of rights may inhibit agreement on rules changes. Persons who remain uncertain as to just what rights they do possess in a politicized economy cannot consider rationally-based plans for exchanges in these rights. Those members of politically-organized groups who seem politically-advantaged under existing rules will not agree to constitutional reform without compensation, and those who might otherwise be willing to pay such compensation may not do so because they do not acknowledge the rights of those to whom such payments would have to be made. It is in this whole area of potential political-constitutional "exchange" that the problems of modern Western societies are acute, and it is to the analyses of these problems that scholars in the broadly defined law-economics, property-rights, public-choice subdisciplines should turn increasing attention.

PART FIVE

Ethics and Economics

The Foundations
for Normative Individualism

What is the ultimate justification for regimes of social interaction that allow biologically defined members of the human species to choose separately among locational, occupational, associational, evaluational, life-style, production, and consumption alternatives? Why are such regimes deemed superior, in some relevant normative sense, to others that restrict, in some relative degree, the choice options of separate persons? Why is a liberal social order that is descriptively permissive of individual migration among many interlinked communities preferred to an order that defines and enforces the status of each person within the many communitarian dimensions? Social philosophers who are, at the same time, advocates of a liberal or free society embodying the maximal exercise of individual liberties have often neglected these basic questions, perhaps in some misguided presumption that answers are as unnecessary as they are obvious.

1. Epistemic Individualism

It is to Douglas Rae's credit that he has forced a consideration of such questions. At a June 1988 conference in Santa Cruz, California, Rae presented a paper entitled "Epistemic Individualism, Unanimity, and the Ideology of Liberty."[1] The subject matter of the first part of the three-part title, and the

From *The Economics and the Ethics of Constitutional Order* (Ann Arbor: University of Michigan Press, 1991), 221–29. Copyright 1991 by The University of Michigan Press. Reprinted by permission of the publisher.

1. Douglas Rae, "Epistemic Individualism, Unanimity, and the Ideology of Liberty: *The Calculus of Consent* Revisited" (paper presented at the Liberty Fund Conference, Santa Cruz, California, June 1988).

paper, directly addresses the justificatory questions and offers a provisional answer. Rae's claim is that the liberal tradition, from which *The Calculus of Consent*[2] emerges, rests upon what he calls *epistemic individualism* as its fundamental justification principle. The claim is that the liberal advocacy of free institutions, notably those of the market economy, find normative justification in epistemological considerations. In Rae's account, the epistemic individualism claim is that the individual is privileged as a choice maker because he or she knows better than anyone else what is "best" for his or her own well-being.

I do not challenge the descriptive relevance of Rae's presentation, and implied criticism, insofar as it applies to the normative justification for individualism, along with its institutional consequences, that informs the attitudes of many of my peers in economics and political economy. I want to reject, however, the descriptive accuracy of Rae's thesis in application to my own underlying philosophical perspective. My conceptual starting point, as expressed in *The Calculus of Consent* and other writings, is not based on the individualism that Rae labels to be "epistemic," either in its descriptive or its normative components.[3] In the discussion below I shall attempt to explain in some detail the fundamental ontological and normative assumptions that inform my position and also discuss how these differ categorically from the epistemic individualism attributed to me.

Although economists rarely pause to think about the philosophical foundations of their own constructions, when and if forced to explicit commitment most of them would accept the qualified utilitarian designation that their models descriptively incorporate. In these models, individual choosers-actors maximize utility by selecting a preferred combination of the feasible alternatives available, with the feasibility-set being determined by both natural and institutional limits. In these constructions, "utility," or more generally "that which is maximized," has a presumptive existence that is independent of any exercise of choice itself. An individual's utility function is described as a complete ordinal array of all potential alternatives, both those

---

2. James M. Buchanan and Gordon Tullock, *The Calculus of Consent: Logical Foundations of Constitutional Democracy* (Ann Arbor: University of Michigan Press, 1962).

3. I make no claim concerning the position of my coauthor, Gordon Tullock.

within and without the feasible set. There exists a unique utility-maximizing choice that can be located once the utility or preference function is specified along with the appropriate constraints.

As noted, implicit in this whole construction is the ontological assumption that there is "something"—whether called a utility function or not—that exists and can, at least conceptually, be objectified and separated from individual choice. If this assumption is made, then the relation between an individual's choice behavior and his or her utility function becomes a matter of fact. That is, there arises a factual question open to investigation concerning the correspondence between the choices made and the change in the individual's position as measured on the independent scalar. It becomes appropriate to classify certain choices as appropriate or even maximizing, as applied against the criteria provided by the utility function.

Only if this ontology—which I *do not* accept—is adopted, do the questions supposedly faced by epistemic individualism arise. And only within this ontology does the conflict between epistemic individualism and its potential alternatives assume relevance. Only if it is presumed that an individual's choice behavior and the utility function exist as conceptually separate things does it make sense to raise the question as to whether the individual or some third party or parties can most reliably identify the choices that are defined as "best" in terms of the given utility function.

If the well-being or welfare of the individual is equivalent to utility and is accepted as the ultimate normative objective, and if, further, the individual is presumed to possess superior knowledge of his or her own utility or preference function, there is an epistemic basis upon which arguments for extending the range of voluntary individual choices can be constructed, along with consequential arguments for the establishment and maintenance of institutions that maximally allow such choices. Conversely, there is a basis for arguments that call into question the normative legitimacy of institutions that restrict individual freedom of choice. Those institutions of an individualistic social order, and notably those of market exchange, derive their normative justification from the relative efficacy of these institutions in exploiting this epistemological privilege granted to participants. Conversely, those institutions that limit individual choice, and notably those of the state, derive their possible normative justification only upon the emergence of some effective demonstration that the epistemic privilege of participants is somehow more than offset by other considerations, or that, in other settings, participants do not enjoy such privileges at all.

2. Challenges to Epistemic Privilege

I propose to examine briefly three separate but related challenges to the legitimacy of social arrangements that embody maximal dependence upon individual choice, each one of which reflects an attempt to deny the epistemic privilege of individuals who participate in such arrangements.

BENEVOLENT PATERNALISM

Welfare economists often refer pejoratively to those persons who seek to impose their own "meddlesome preferences" on others whose conflicting preferences reflect differing life-styles. And the difficulty of separating attempted intrusions of genuinely meddlesome preferences from the attempted exercise of benevolent paternalism must be acknowledged. The existence of benevolent paternalism on the part of some persons cannot, however, be denied. Such persons genuinely seek to insure that others than themselves secure the highest level of well-being or utility that feasibility limits allow. The paternalists reject only the claim of epistemic privilege; they do not think that individuals know what is best or good for them. The paternalists advance the counter claim that they, as outsiders, as informed experts, know more about the ability of the relevant choice options to satisfy the ultimately desired objectives of the persons affected than those persons themselves who might otherwise make the choices in question. The paternalistic claim is that, in some final or ex-post reckoning, individuals must acknowledge their own initial unknowledge or tendency to err, and, thereby, must validate, ex-post, the limits that are imposed on their ability to make the "right" choices.

Note that the paternalists' claim can be exclusively epistemic. They need not replace individual utility maximization as the normative goal. And they need not introduce arguments reflecting some supraindividualistic "social" or "public" interest into the relevant functions. The claim is, quite simply, that someone knows better than the individuals themselves how to secure their own well-being.

"Scientific" socialism

Quite a different sort of challenge to the epistemic privilege of the individual under liberalism is mounted by the "scientific" socialists, especially of the classical Marxist-Leninist tradition. That which is "good" for individuals is to be determined by the objective laws of historical development. Mankind, rather than existing, empirically identifiable individuals, is the normatively relevant unit. Neither the voluntary participation of individuals, even as members of the proletariat, nor their ex-post approval, is required as any part of the justificatory exercise. "Social choices," in this construction, are not derived from "individual values" but are, instead, the implementation of mankind's recognized destiny.

The challenge of the "scientific" socialists to individualism remains epistemic, but in a much more intrusive sense than that of the paternalists. The ultimate objective, at least rhetorically, remains the welfare of individual participants in the political community, but this welfare is not measured, even conceptually, by individually separable indicators of utility. Individuals themselves are defined only as members of the community; they cannot, in principle, conceive of, much less have knowledge of, their separably identifiable well-beings.

Political idealism

A third criticism of the liberal social order in which persons are allowed wide scope for voluntary choice, particularly through the institutions of a market economy, can be interpreted in epistemic terms, although here it is the object of knowledge rather than the means of its attainment that assumes center stage in the argument. This criticism, which I call "political idealism," does not embody a conception of individuals seeking out or aiming for separately identifiable goals or objectives that assume meaning in other than communitarian terms. This feature is shared with the scientific socialists. But the goals or objectives of persons-in-community are now to be sought, not in some pretense of scientific inquiry, but rather in the Platonic summum bonum—the good, the true, and the beautiful—that can be defined for us by the philosophers. In this strand of criticism, those institutions that allow individuals to exercise private choices over wide ranges of action may tend to promote the vulgar and animalistic desires of ordinary humankind which then take priority over those higher values that can be revealed only to the select few who hold access to the founts of wisdom.

The three criticisms of the liberal order sketched here along with other variants—for example, technocracy—intersect, one with another, and each incorporates different epistemological presuppositions concerning both the inner knowledge of the means possessed by individuals and the "outer" knowledge of the ends that "should" provide the ultimate motivations for action. My purpose in this section has not been to examine any of these, or other, criticisms of liberalism in detail; my purpose is, instead, to suggest the potential vulnerability of any pure epistemic defense, whether to the arguments noted here or to others. A liberal order that is founded on epistemic justification remains open both to analytical and empirical deconstruction of its essential proposition.

3. Subjectivism: Epistemic Limitation and Normative Implications

My purpose in this short chapter is to suggest that the foundation for a normative individualism is not epistemic. In addition, I suggest that the criticisms of the liberal order that seek to exploit the vulnerability of the epistemic argument are not pertinent to the alternative justificatory argument that best describes my own position.

My own ontological presuppositions do not allow any conceptual separation or distinction between an individual's choice behavior and his or her utility function. My position is sometimes classified to be one of strict *subjectivism*, applications of which have been discussed in my book, *Cost and Choice* and other works.[4] From a subjectivist perspective, a "utility function," as such, does not exist which, even conceptually, could be observed and recognized independently of an individual's choice behavior. All there is are individual choices, and it is about these choices, not about some alleged relationship to some utility function, that we develop theories. We may, for example, observe that persons sometimes regret choices that have been

4. James M. Buchanan, *Cost and Choice: An Inquiry in Economic Theory* (Chicago: Markham Press, 1969).

made, and we may conjecture that some third person might have been able to predict that such regret would occur, post choice. And we may then hypothesize that this third person might have been able to offer "good" advice to the chooser, pre choice. But none of these theories about choices require the introduction of a choice-independent utility scalar.

The modern economist who models the individual as choosing among feasibly alternative bundles of goods to maximize a utility function that does exist independently of choice itself presents no evidence that such functions actually exist, and, if pushed, the economist would agree that "utility" is little more than a rhetorical artifice that is introduced as an aid in explaining choice behavior within an imposed rational choice reconstruction. While the issue of epistemic individualism is of relevance for this conception, it has no bearing on my ontological perspective; the individual chooses that which he chooses, and there need exist neither prior nor posterior "knowledge" that enables any choice to be classified as "correct" or "incorrect" against some criterion of well-being. At the moment of choice itself, the individual selects the alternative that is preferred, but this tautological proposition embodies no presumption about epistemic privilege.

Choice exercised by an individual involves self-creation along with the creation of constraints imposed on the choices of others. This reciprocal interaction takes place over a whole temporal sequence. The "individual," as described by a snapshot at any moment, is an artifactual product of choices that have been made in prior periods, both by himself or herself and others. If it is acknowledged that any person, post choice, is necessarily different from the person that made the choice, and that the difference is produced, in part, by the act of choice itself, it becomes absurd to apply criteria of "correctness" directly to choice, as such, including epistemic criteria.[5]

Knowledge concerns that which is, or that which is potentially, knowable by someone. Knowledge cannot, therefore, extend to the unknowable, which must contain *all* that takes place in the future, *including* choices that will be made. Neither the individual who may choose internally nor the paternalist

5. For an elaboration of my position here, see James M. Buchanan, "Natural and Artifactual Man," in idem, *What Should Economists Do?* (Indianapolis: Liberty Fund, 1979), 93–114. I have been influenced by the work of G. L. S. Shackle. For the most complete statement of his position, see G. L. S. Shackle, *Epistemics and Economics* (Cambridge: Cambridge University Press, 1972).

who may impose a selected alternative externally can claim epistemic privilege, since the selection among alternatives at t_0 will itself *create* a setting at t_1, from within which any evaluation of the t_0 choice must be made.

The distinction between the two ontological conceptions that I have tried to contrast has implications for justificatory arguments advanced in support or opposition to alternative social-organizational arrangements. As I have noted, epistemic individualism plays no role in my own ontological presuppositions, but this statement implies nothing directly about the justificatory argument.

The justificatory foundation for a liberal social order lies, in my understanding, in the normative premise that individuals are the ultimate *sovereigns* in matters of social organization, that individuals are the beings who are entitled to choose the organizational-institutional structures under which they will live. In accordance with this premise, the legitimacy of social-organizational structures is to be judged against the voluntary agreement of those who are to live or are living under the arrangements that are judged. The central premise of *individuals as sovereigns* does allow for delegation of decision-making authority to agents, so long as it remains understood that individuals remain as *principals.* The premise denies legitimacy to all social-organizational arrangements that negate the role of individuals as either sovereigns or as principals. On the other hand, the normative premise of individuals as sovereigns does not provide exclusive normative legitimacy to organizational structures that—as, in particular, market institutions—allow internally for the most extensive range of separate individual choice. Legitimacy must also be extended to "choice-restricting" institutions so long as the participating individuals voluntarily choose to live under such regimes.

For the justificatory construction here, epistemic features of choice are simply irrelevant. Individuals are to be allowed to choose among potentially available alternatives simply because they are the ultimate sovereigns. And this conclusion holds independently of the state of knowledge possessed about either means or ends. If individuals are considered the ultimate sovereigns, it follows directly that they are the *addressees* of all proposals and arguments concerning constitutional-institutional issues. Arguments that involve reliance on experts in certain areas of choice must be addressed to individuals, as sovereigns, and it is individuals' choice in deferring to experts-agents that legitimizes the potential role of the latter, not some external assessment of epistemic competence, as such.

4. Application

I have opposed a subjectivist to an epistemic foundation for normative individualism. The discussion has indicated the central differences between these two philosophical frameworks. I have not yet examined the implications of the two foundations in any practical application. It is, I think, relatively easy to show that the social philosopher who relies on epistemic privilege to defend individual freedom of choice and the institutions that allow this freedom to be exercised maximally faces a much more difficult burden of proof than the philosopher who rests his or her argument squarely on a subjectivist interpretation.

Consider the eighteenth- and early-nineteenth-century argument in defense of the institution of human slavery. Intellectually honest philosophers, from Plato through the nineteenth century, supported the institution of human slavery on epistemic grounds. Commencing from the presupposition that persons differ in their intrinsic epistemic capabilities, a presupposition that carries solid empirical support, even if not in terms of distinct groupings of persons, these philosophers, both classical and modern, supported attempts to construct and to maintain an institutional correspondence between epistemic capabilities and the ranges of voluntary choices allowed to individuals. These institutions are explicitly designed to allow those who are more capable epistemically to impose their will coercively upon those who are considered less capable. And this institutional correspondence is not, of course, limited to the explicit institution of slavery; it applies equally to all institutions that allow for differential access to the exercise of individual choice.

How does the epistemic individualist counter the sometimes persuasive argument of the elitist, which itself evokes epistemic standards? The response that the individual really does "know best" what is "good" for him or her may seem quite empty, and especially when the individual is observed to make choices that seem to guarantee hunger, deprivation, myopic prodigality, and addiction. Is it not preferred, on epistemic grounds, that the homeless alcoholic in the streets be made a slave (under the auspices of the modern state) for "his or her own good"?

The burden of argument placed on the epistemic individualist in all such cases may be contrasted sharply with that which the subjectivist confronts. The latter can remain appropriately deaf and blind to the entreaties of the elitist who claims supraindividualist status. The biological dividing line that separates members of the human species from other animals is surely easier to draw than any within-species line (even the no line limit) that the epistemic defense of individuality must trace out. I am not suggesting that all problems of identification disappear; qualification for membership as individuals in the human species that is relevant for the free exercise of choice cannot be met by children and the mentally incompetent. These problems seem, however, minuscule in comparison with those that arise in the alternative framework.

If "that which is best" for an individual exists independently of choice by that individual, the institutional arrangements within which choice may be exercised are not directly related to the definition of the objective. The problem for institutional-constitutional design is one of achieving "efficiency" in the attainment of the defined state of the world. By contrast, if "that which is best" for an individual does not exist independently of choice by that individual, the institutional structure must, at some level, facilitate such choice if, indeed, "that which is best" is accepted as the ultimate normative objective. "That which is best" is objectively meaningful only at the moment of choice itself. In the observed context of the institution of human slavery, it becomes absurd to refer, as Plato, to the superior knowledge of the master concerning "that which is best" for the individual slave. In directing the activity of the slave, the master is, at the moment of choice, selecting "that which is best for the master"; he or she could do nothing other than this.

The subjectivist argument requires, however, much more attention to the level of choice than the epistemic argument. As noted it is ontologically absurd to define the master's choice as selecting among alternatives "that which is best for the slave." On the other hand, "that which is best for the *individual as slave,*" determined only by the individual in question, may possibly involve voluntary agreement, as some level of contractual choice, to submit to the coercive authority of another person. Slavery, as an institutional arrangement, cannot be condemned as "not best" independently of its observed coercive establishment.

The alternative philosophical foundations for normative individualism, and for the structure of institutions that allow the exercise of voluntary choice, carry quite different implications for individual responsibility. The vulnerability of the epistemic defense of individualism to demonstration of incompetence on the part of some members of the political community lends itself readily to politicized corrections for such incompetence. Regardless of the institutional structure, which may itself reflect a generalized acceptance of normative individualism, the elite may express concern for those who do not demonstrate the capability of knowing what is really best for themselves, in the selection of either means or ends. The way is open for the modern welfare states, which combine elements of epistemic individualism with the elitism of those who defend the institution of human slavery. The normative individualist whose ontology is subjectivist operates on the presumption that, by their very being as individuals, members of humankind are and must be treated as responsible for their own choices. Individuals are not to be "protected from their own folly," even if this basic stance is tempered with ordinary compassion.

The Justice of Natural Liberty

I. Introduction

The 1976 bicentennial of the publication of Adam Smith's *The Wealth of Nations* occurs amid a still-accelerating discussion of the principles of justice, stimulated in large part by John Rawls. His catalytic book, *A Theory of Justice,* published in 1971,[1] has caused economists, along with other social scientists and philosophers, to devote more attention to "justice" in the first half-decade of the 1970s than in perhaps all of the preceding decades of this century combined. This discussion has been hailed as the return of political and social philosophy to its former status of intellectual interest and respectability. My purpose in this paper is to re-examine Adam Smith's norms for social order, notably for justice, and especially as these may be related to the modern post-Rawlsian discussion. I want, in particular, to evaluate Smith's "system of natural liberty" in terms of criteria for justice that are akin to those employed by Rawls.

In order to do this, it will first be necessary to define, as fully as is possible, Smith's underlying model or paradigm for social interaction, a paradigm that was influenced by the historical setting of Scotland in the 1770s. In addition, it will be useful to discuss briefly Smith's methodology. Once these steps are taken, we can outline Smith's ordering of the priorities for reform. From this we should then be able to suggest how a returned Adam Smith might view our society in 1976, and how his modern ordering of reform pri-

From *Journal of Legal Studies* 5 (January 1976): 1–16. Copyright 1976 by The University of Chicago. Reprinted by permission of the publisher.

I am indebted to my colleagues, Victor Goldberg, Nicolaus Tideman, Gordon Tullock, and Richard Wagner for helpful comments on earlier drafts.
1. John Rawls, *A Theory of Justice* (1971).

orities might differ from those two centuries removed. This imagined Smithian stance may then be compared and/or contrasted with that of John Rawls. In what may be surprising, and especially to those who are only casually familiar with the works of each man, I shall demonstrate that the similarities outweigh the differences. A returned Adam Smith would be a long distance from the modern libertarian anarchists, and even from the espousal of the minimal state described by Robert Nozick.[2] But John Rawls is also a long distance from the position which has been attributed to him, that of being a "defender of the liberal welfare state, somewhat modified in the direction of greater egalitarianism."[3] These philosophers would surely be closer to each other than either would be to the image that intellectual fashion has imposed upon him.

II. The Real and the Conceptual World of Adam Smith

Adam Smith was one of the leading figures of the Scottish Enlightenment, which suggests that his interests were in no way provincial. His intent in *The Wealth of Nations* was to offer a readily generalizable criticism of what he labeled the "policy of Europe." But he lived and worked, nonetheless, in eighteenth-century Scotland. Because his writings, and again notably *The Wealth of Nations*, retain so many elements of direct and current relevance, it is easy for the modern reader to neglect the necessary influences of time and place on his analysis as well as on his normative priorities.

What were the essential structural characteristics of the society that Adam Smith observed? Almost two centuries would elapse before a popular tract could condemn an "affluent society." The industrial revolution, with its technological counterpart, was in its very early and formative stages. Indeed its full achievements might never have become reality save for the impact of some of Smith's own ideas. The modern corporation was foreshadowed only in the government-sponsored international trading companies. Still largely agricultural, Britain was only becoming "a nation of shopkeepers."

The society that Smith observed was highly stable relative to that of our

---

2. Robert Nozick, *Anarchy, State and Utopia* (1974).
3. Marc F. Plattner, "The New Political Theory," *Public Interest* 40 (Summer 1975): 120.

own century. This society was also very poor by twentieth-century standards; Smith's analysis was applied directly to what we would now call a "developing" or an "underdeveloped" society. The expansion in material goods generated by the technological revolution of the post-Enlightenment era was not predictable in 1776. Most men were born to live, work, and to die in the same local community.

Some appreciation of this historical setting is helpful in any attempt to define Smith's working model for social interaction. Two central elements of this model or paradigm may be isolated here as important in understanding his conceptions of justice. The first of these involves what we should now call the utility of income to the individual. Smith did not use this terminology and he was not intellectually hidebound by the now-dominant orthodoxy which largely neglects basic questions about the meaning of utility itself and then proceeds to impose a particular form on the utility function. Instead, Smith carefully distinguished between that which drives men to action—the promised or anticipated utility from an increasing stream of real goods and services or from a growing stock of assets—and that which measures the actual satisfactions secured subsequent to the receipt of such incremental flows and stocks. Beyond a certain level of real income (a level which was, nonetheless, presumably out of reach for the average or representative member of the working class), the anticipated marginal utility of income to an individual exceeds the realized marginal utility. This divergence constituted, for Smith, the great deception that was essential in driving the whole system, which acted to insure that self-interest would, in fact, generate increasing prosperity and economic growth.[4]

In some sense, therefore, differentials in measured or received incomes among individuals and among social classes or groups were, to Adam Smith, considerably less important than to his counterpart who inhabits the modern welfare state. Smith was not nearly so ready to translate these into differences in achieved satisfaction, happiness, or well-being. And who is to attribute naiveté to Adam Smith in this respect? The balance is not on one side alone.

Smith expressed little or no normative concern with income differences

---

4. For the most direct statement on this, see Adam Smith, *The Theory of Moral Sentiments*, ed. E. G. West (1969), 263–65.

among persons; he was primarily concerned with the absolute levels of income generated, and with the differences in these levels among time periods, that is, with growth. He did infer a direct relationship between the aggregate income generated for the whole society and the well-being of the laboring classes.

There is a second element of Adam Smith's model of social interaction that is helpful in evaluating his conceptions of justice. Smith did not assume or postulate significant differentials in capacities among human beings. The differences between the "philosopher and the street porter" were explained largely in terms of upbringing, training, and education. In the current debates, Smith would find himself arrayed squarely on the side of those who stress environmental factors and who play down the relevance of genetic endowments. Smith was also writing before Cairns and Mill had developed the economic theory of noncompeting groups. In his conceptual model, individual income differences (at least as regards wage or salary incomes) were explained largely in "equalizing" terms. That is to say, in an operative "system of natural liberty" the observed differences would be those that would be predicted to emerge when all persons freely exercised their choices among occupations and employments. By implication, at least for the members of the laboring class, in such a system all persons would be equally advantaged at the onset of making career and occupational choices.

III. The Scottish Method

A. L. Macfie makes the distinction between what he calls the Scottish method, characteristic of Adam Smith's approach to problems of social policy, and the scientific or analytical method which is more familiar to modern social scientists.[5] In the former, the center of attention lay in the society as observed, rather than in the idealized version of that society considered as an abstraction. As I have suggested above, Smith did have an underlying model or paradigm for social interaction; he could scarcely have discussed reforms without one. But his interest was in making the existing social structure "work better," in terms of the norms that he laid down,

5. A. L. Macfie, *The Individual in Society: Papers on Adam Smith* 19 (1967).

rather than in evaluating the possible limitations of the structure as it might work ideally if organized on specific principles. Frank Knight suggested that critics of the free-enterprise system are seldom clear as to whether they object to the system because it does not work in accordance with its idealized principles or because it does, in fact, work in some approximation to these principles. There is no such uncertainty with respect to Adam Smith. He was critical of the economic order of his time because it did not work in accordance with the principles of natural liberty. He was not, and need not have been, overly concerned with some ultimate evaluation of an idealized structure.

Smith's methodology has been turned on its head by many modern scientists. The post-Pigovian theory of welfare economics has largely, if not entirely, consisted in a search for conceptual flaws in the workings of an idealized competitive economic order, conceived independently of the flawed and imperfect order that may be observed to exist. Partial correctives are offered in both the theory of the second-best and in the still-emerging theory of public choice, but the perfect-competition paradigm continues to dominate applied economic policy discussions.

This methodological distinction is important in our examination of Smith's conception of justice. In one sense, John Rawls' efforts in defining and delineating "a theory of justice" are akin to those of the neoclassical economists who first described the idealized competitive economy. (I am not, of course, suggesting that Rawls' attempt has had or will have comparable success or even that the basic subject matter is amenable to comparable analytical treatment.) By contrast, Adam Smith saw no need for defining in great detail the idealized operation of a market system and for evaluating this system in terms of strict efficiency criteria. Similarly, he would have seen no need for elaborating in detail a complete "theory of justice," for defining those principles which must be operative in a society that would be adjudged to be "just." In comparing Smith with Rawls, therefore, we must somehow bridge the contrasting methodologies. We can proceed in either one of two ways. We can make an attempt to infer from Smith's applied discussion of real problems what his idealized principles of justice might have embodied. Or we can infer from John Rawls' treatment of idealized principles what his particular applications of these might be in an institutional context. In what follows, I shall follow both these routes.

IV. Justice as Security

Adam Smith did not publish the book on jurisprudence that he had projected, although a student's notes from his lectures apparently include most of the material that might have been incorporated.[6] In these lectures, "justice" was listed as only one of the four great objects of law. In the section specifically on justice, Smith referred almost exclusively to the relatively narrow conception of security. "The end of justice is to secure from injury."[7] In this context, the treatment seems quite different from that of John Rawls, for whom "justice is the first virtue of social institutions."[8] But the difference can be exaggerated, even here. Smith explicitly calls attention to security as a necessary attribute of any well-functioning society, and he reflects commonsense usage of the term "justice" in his discussion. Rawls, two centuries later, takes this aspect of justice more or less for granted, and shifts his discussion to another level. He would, presumably, agree fully with Smith that any just society would also require security of person and property. Rawls' primary interest is "beyond justice" in the more restricted definition employed by Adam Smith.[9]

Their difference lies in the fact that Smith did not make a comparable extension. Distributive justice, in the modern meaning of this term, is largely neglected by Smith, at least in terms of explicit treatment. This is explained, in part, by Smith's underlying presuppositions about utility differences, noted above, and in part by the relatively greater importance appropriately assigned to economic development in the eighteenth-century setting. As I shall demonstrate, however, Smith's suggestions for policy reforms generate distributive results that may be reconciled readily with Rawlsian criteria. We need not accept Jacob Viner's interpretation that writers in the Scottish tradition were minimally interested in reform, in the modern meaning of this term.[10]

6. Adam Smith, *Lectures on Justice, Police, Revenue and Arms*, ed. Edwin Cannan (1896).

7. Ibid., 5.

8. Rawls, *A Theory of Justice*, 3.

9. Ibid., 7.

10. See Jacob Viner, *Guide to John Rae's "Life of Adam Smith,"* 112, published with John Rae, *Life of Adam Smith*, Reprints of Econ. Classics (1965).

V. Natural Liberty

Adam Smith explicitly rejected a contractarian explanation for the emergence of government and for the obligation of persons to abide by law, preferring, instead, to ground both on the principles of authority and utility.[11] Furthermore, he did not recognize the possible value in using a conceptualized social contract as a benchmark or criterion for evaluating alternative political structures. However, his device of the "impartial spectator" serves this function and is in many respects akin to the conceptualized contract. Smith's norms for social order were not strictly utilitarian, in the Benthamite sense, and justice was an important attribute, justice which embodied the security to person and property previously noted but extended beyond this when his whole structure is considered.[12] Beyond security, Adam Smith would have surely ranked "natural liberty" as his first principle of justice.

> To hurt in any degree the interest of any one order of citizens for no other purpose but to promote that of some other, is evidently contrary to that justice and equality of treatment which the sovereign owes to all different orders of his subjects.[13]

In several applied cases, he makes clear that violations of natural liberty are unjust.[14]

Before discussing these, however, it may be helpful to digress somewhat. Smith's great work, *The Wealth of Nations,* has been widely interpreted as being informed normatively by efficiency criteria. This emphasis is broadly correct, provided that the efficiency norm is not given exclusive place. Smith's purpose was that of demonstrating how the removal of restrictions on free market forces, how the operation of his "system of natural liberty," would greatly increase the total product of the economy and, more impor-

11. Smith, *Lectures,* 11–13.

12. For a good discussion on this, see Macfie, *The Individual in Society,* 68–71.

13. Adam Smith, *The Wealth of Nations* (Modern Library ed.) [hereinafter cited as *The Wealth of Nations*]. All subsequent references are to this edition. Note the similarity of this statement of Smith to John Rawls' definition of the principle of equal liberty, cited below.

14. See *The Wealth of Nations,* 121–22 (on apprenticeship requirements), 141 (on restrictions on migration), 497 (on entry restrictions), as examples.

tantly, how this would generate rapid economic growth, thereby improving the lot of the laboring classes. What is often missing from this standard interpretation is Smith's corollary argument, sometimes implicit, to the effect that this system of natural liberty would also promote his ideal of justice. Failure to allow individuals to employ "their stock and industry in the way that they judge most advantageous to themselves, is a *manifest violation of the most sacred rights of mankind.*"[15] There was, to Smith, no trade-off between "efficiency" and "equity," in the more familiar modern sense. As a general principle of social order, the freedom of individual choice would produce efficiency; but it would also be a central attribute of any social order that was just.

My emphasis in this paper is on this aspect of Smith's argument because I want to compare his first principle of "natural liberty" with Rawls' first principle of "equal liberty." Smith's method forces us to look at his examples rather than to expect to find any elaborated discussion of the concept per se. The examples suggest that Adam Smith was by no means an eighteenth-century Robert Nozick, who conceived natural moral boundaries to individuals' rights and who claimed that any invasion of these rights was unjust. The Smithean system of natural liberty is not anarchy, either the Hobbesian war of each against all or the more confined Rothbard-Nozick setting where individuals mutually respect the boundaries of each other. "Boundary crossings," to employ Nozick's helpful terminology here, violate Smith's natural liberty in some cases but such violations must be assessed in essentially pragmatic terms. Smith's sanctioned violations of natural liberty were not invariant to the environmental setting in which individuals might find themselves.

Almost by necessity, we look at Smith's treatment from the vantage point of modern welfare economics. When we do so, his limits to the exercise of natural liberty seem to coincide surprisingly with those extensions of potentially warranted collective action that might be laid down by a careful and sophisticated application of externality analysis. To Smith, there is clearly an unwarranted invasion of natural liberty if an individual's (any individual's) freedom of choice is restricted when there are no demonstrable spillover damages on others in the community. On the other hand, Smith sanctioned interferences with individual freedom of choices when the exercise of such

15. Ibid., 549 (italics supplied).

choices (for example, the building of walls that were not fireproof) "might endanger the security of the whole society."[16] Smith explicitly stated that such latter restrictions on individual choices may be "considered as in some respect a violation of natural liberty," but that such choices ought to be "restrained by the laws of all governments."[17]

Adam Smith distinguished between what we would now call pecuniary and technological externalities. His approved interferences with natural liberty extended only to those cases where genuine technological externality could be demonstrated, and he quite explicitly stated that possible pecuniary spillovers gave no cause for restrictions on trade.[18] It would, of course, be absurd to suggest here that Smith's final array of potentially justifiable interferences with the freedom of individual choices corresponds fully with that which might be produced by the modern welfare economist. Furthermore, his own array of examples of potentially warranted interferences with natural liberty would surely be different in 1976 from that of 1776. On balance, however, there seems no question but that Smith's implied analysis of potential restrictions on the freedom of individual market choices can be made reasonably consistent with modern efficiency analysis, utilizing Pareto criteria for meaningful improvement. That is to say, even if Pareto optimality or efficiency is held up as the only relevant norm, many of Smith's particular examples would qualify. What is important for my purposes, however, is that Smith sanctioned interferences only when efficiency criteria overweighed those of justice, conceived here not in distributional terms at all, but in terms of the value of natural liberty. If we leave aside considerations of administration and enforcement, modern economic analysis would suggest the introduction of restrictions when overall efficiency is enhanced, with no explicit recognition of the necessary trade-off with individual freedom of choice. With Adam Smith, by contrast, any restriction on the freedom of individuals "may be said . . . [to be] a manifest violation of that natural liberty, which it is the proper business of law, not to infringe, but support."[19] Possible effi-

---

16. Ibid., 308.

17. Ibid.

18. See, in particular, his discussion on page 342 of *The Wealth of Nations*, where he rejects imposing restrictions on entry into retailing trades even "though they [shopkeepers] may so as to hurt one another."

19. Ibid., 308.

ciency gains must, therefore, be reckoned against the costs in liberty, in "justice" in the broader sense here considered.

In evaluating his own work, there is some evidence that Adam Smith considered *The Wealth of Nations* to be a demonstration that the "system of natural liberty," which emerged more fundamentally from normative criteria of justice, could *also* meet efficiency criteria.[20] It is perhaps our relative overconcentration on his major treatise that causes modern interpreters to overlook the noneconomic, or more generally the nonutilitarian, foundations for the "natural system of perfect liberty and justice."[21]

VI. Rawls' Principle of Equal Liberty

Smith's principle may be compared with John Rawls' first principle of justice, that of "equal liberty," to which he assigns lexical priority over his second principle. These two principles or conceptions of liberty are, in practice, substantially equivalent although, strictly speaking, and perhaps surprisingly, Rawls must be classified as a more ardent *laissez faire* theorist than Smith. This is due to Rawls' lexical ordering of the principle of equal liberty as prior to his distributive precept. Smith, in contrast, inserts a threshold before marginal trade-offs can be considered, a threshold beyond which invasions of apparent natural liberty might presumably be sanctioned. But their positions are similar in that neither Smith nor Rawls is utilitarian in the sense that final evaluation is reduced to a single standard. To Smith, the "impartial spectator" would not condone piecemeal interferences with natural liberty even if aggregate social production was thereby maximized. To Rawls, the maximization of expected utility is rejected as the objective, even behind a genuine veil of ignorance.

The principle of equal liberty, as presented by Rawls, is stated as follows:

20. In Rae's citations from the notes of John Miller, one of Smith's best students, there is the following passage: "In the last of his lectures he examined those political regulations which are founded, not upon the principle of *justice* but that of *expediency*, and which are calculated to increase the riches, power, and prosperity of a state. Under this view he considered the political institutions relating to commerce, to finances, to ecclesiastical and military establishments. What he delivered on these subjects contained the substance of the work he afterwards published under the title of *An Inquiry Into the Nature and Causes of the Wealth of Nations*." See John Rae, *Life of Adam Smith,* 55.

21. *The Wealth of Nations,* 572.

> Each person is to have an equal right to the most extensive total system of
> equal basic liberties compatible with a similar system of liberty for all.[22]

In his discussion Rawls emphasizes the implications of this principle for political institutions (e.g., for equality of franchise, for freedom of speech and press), but he tends to neglect the comparable implications for economic institutions, which were, of course, central to Adam Smith's concern. In several places, Rawls does state that the principle of equal liberty suggests a market system, but he does not discuss particular examples or cases.[23] Nonetheless, any attempt to apply the Rawlsian principle must lead to a condemnation of many overt restrictions on individual choices that have been and may be observed in the real world. Particular interferences that would, in this way, be classified as "unjust" by Rawlsian criteria would correspond very closely to those which Smith classified in the same way. Consider only two of the most flagrant modern-day examples. The uniform minimum wage regulations imposed by the Congress under the Fair Labor Standards Act, as amended, would clearly be "unjust" under either Rawlsian or Smithean criteria. Mutually agreeable contractual terms between unemployed persons (notably teenagers) and potential employers are prohibited, with an absence of comparable restrictions on others in society.[24] Or, consider the regulations of the Interstate Commerce Commission in restricting entry into trucking, clearly an invasion of the natural liberty of those who might want freely to enter this business as well as a violation of the principle of equal liberty. The listing could be readily extended to such institutions as tenure in universities, restrictive licensing of business and professions, prohibition or sumptuary taxation of imports, subsidization of exports, union shop restrictions in labor contracts, and many others.

It is unfortunate that Rawls did not see fit to discuss more fully the application of his first principle to such institutions, especially since his treatise and general argument have attracted such widespread attention from social

---

22. Rawls, *A Theory of Justice*, 250.

23. "I assume in all interpretations that the first principle of equal liberty is satisfied and that the economy is roughly a free market system." Ibid., 66.

24. Minimum wage legislation would also be unjust by Rawls' second principle since the primary groups harmed are those who are least-advantaged, those with relatively low economic productivity.

scientists generally. Economists have continued to call attention to the inefficiency of these institutions, but, since Smith, they have rarely called attention to their fundamental injustice.[25] Had they, or Rawls, done so, these institutions might have proved more vulnerable to criticism than they have appeared to be.

Difficulties arise when we attempt to apply the Rawlsian principle of equal liberty to those restrictions on individual choices that might be plausibly defended on familiar externality grounds. As noted above, Smith's less constraining norm allows natural liberty to be violated under some circumstances, provided that the costs are properly reckoned. But Rawls' lexical ordering prevents this sort of trade-off, even with the insertion of an appropriate threshold. Consider, for a real-world example, the closing of the Saltville, Virginia, plant of the Olin Corporation in the early 1970s as a result of governmentally imposed water-quality standards. Local residents were left unemployed; long-term contractual agreements between these persons and Olin were terminated, clearly a restriction on liberties. Presumably, defense of this governmental action was based on the alleged benefits of improved water quality to the general population of the whole country. It does not seem possible to stretch Rawls' principle of equal liberty to cover such instances. The liberties of some persons were restricted for the alleged benefits of others, and without appropriate compensation. There was no trade-off with other liberties, as Rawls might have required; the defense could only have been advanced on utilitarian-efficiency grounds. To Rawls, this governmental action could only be classified as "unjust."[26]

Working from the principle of equal liberty alone, therefore, and keeping

---

25. In his treatise on liberty, F. A. Hayek does not represent liberty or freedom as an attribute of "justice," but rather as an independent "source and condition of most moral values." (p. 6) At one point (p. 99), however, he does suggest that justice requires something akin to the Rawlsian principle of equal liberty. F. A. Hayek, *The Constitution of Liberty* (1960).

26. I do not suggest that the idealized Rawlsian constitution could not allow for escapes from the genuine externality–public goods dilemmas that fully independent private adjustments might produce. Such a constitution would require that such escapes be accomplished through more inclusive contractual agreements, which would, of course, embody compensations to those who might be harmed by change. My point in the text here is to indicate that the Rawlsian principle of equal liberty would not allow for governmentally imposed changes without compensation, regardless of the benefit-cost ratios.

in mind the lexical priority assigned to this principle in his whole construction, we must conclude that John Rawls is far from the "defender of the liberal welfare state" that he has been made out to be, and, indeed, that his implied institutional structure for the economy closely resembles that which was first described by Adam Smith. Only a "system of natural liberty," a regime of effectively operating free markets, could meet Rawlsian requirements for "equal liberty," and, through these, for "justice."

VII. Distribution and Justice

Rawls has been misinterpreted in this respect because of his relative neglect in elaborating the implications of his first principle for economic institutions and, more importantly, because of his relative concentration on the second principle that he adduces, that which addresses the distribution of the social product. It is here that Adam Smith and John Rawls seem most apart, and Rawls explicitly discusses the system of natural liberty only to reject it in favor of what he terms the system of democratic equality.[27] But we need to see precisely wherein these two philosophers diverge. I shall try to demonstrate that, once their methodological differences are acknowledged and once their empirical presuppositions are fully exposed, there need be little variance in their assessments of reform priorities in a 1976 setting.

We can perhaps best commence by examining the distributional consequences of Adam Smith's system of natural liberty, under the empirical presuppositions that Smith himself adopted. In 1776, a very large part of the total population was made up of members of the laboring classes, and Smith did not think that inherent differences in capacities were significant. The economic position of an average or representative member of this group could best be improved by allowing markets freely to emerge and to operate, by removing all or substantially all restrictions on trade, and by eliminating all constraints on the flow of resources, human and nonhuman, among alternative uses. Such a system would predictably generate differences in incomes among different members of the laboring classes, but these would tend to equalize the relative advantages of different employments. Those who were not members of these classes, those employers who accumulated

27. Rawls, *A Theory of Justice*, 65–75.

capital and utilized it productively in hiring labor, would secure differentially higher incomes from profits. But Smith makes it clear that it is precisely the attraction of such incomes which drives the whole process, which insures that the economy grows and prospers. Even here, however, Smith raises some questions about the efficacy of exceptionally high incomes from profits, and he warns against the tendency toward profligacy that such excesses create.[28] Smith is not clear on the possible allocative role played by rental incomes secured by landowners. Given his pre- but quasi-Ricardian model of the economy, he probably would not have been opposed to taxes on land rent.

There are distributional consequences of Smith's system, but, strictly speaking, the *distribution* of product among social classes or among members of any one class is clearly secondary to production, to securing maximal national income. This was to be accomplished by the removal of disincentives throughout the economy. The overriding objective was to increase the economic well-being of the members of the laboring classes while adhering to the precept of justice which the system of natural liberty represented.

At first glance, Smith's system seems a world apart from the Rawlsian setting, where the emphasis is on distribution, with production being largely neglected. The difference principle of distribution, appended lexically to that of equal liberty, states that inequalities in access to primary goods are acceptable in the just society only insofar as they are shown to be advantageous to the least-advantaged members of the community. But, in the empirical setting postulated for Adam Smith, what would an application of this Rawlsian difference principle have implied? An argument for a tax on land value might have been produced, along with an argument for taxation of excessively high incomes from profits, with a redistribution of proceeds generally to members of the laboring classes. Perhaps more importantly, from his discussion of the favorable effects of less restrictive laws of land ownership and transfer in the English as opposed to the Spanish and Portuguese colonies, we may infer that Smith would have supported legal reforms designed to open up prospects for greater mobility of persons between the land-owning

---

28. This aspect of Smith's argument is stressed by Rosenberg. See Nathan Rosenberg, "Some Institutional Aspects of *The Wealth of Nations*," *Journal of Political Economy* 68 (1960): 557.

and nonowning groups.[29] Such reform implications of his system could have been readily accepted by Smith, who might, however, have treated such reforms as being of slight importance compared with the more fundamental steps which involved the removal of governmental constraints on individual liberty.

Rawls projects the distributional issue to center stage perhaps because he presumes, empirically, that there exists only a relatively remote relationship between the pattern of income receipts, and of asset holdings, in society and the aggregate size of the total product. Furthermore, he seems to assume that there exists a distribution of natural or inherent capacities among persons, a distribution which tends to generate nonequalizing income-wealth differentials that carry with them neither economic nor moral justification. In the Rawlsian paradigm, the philosopher is not merely an educated porter.

The "system of natural liberty" that Rawls explicitly discusses, and rejects, is not that of Adam Smith.[30] Rawls uses this designation to refer to a system that embodies economic efficiency (Pareto optimality) as its only objective, and his critical remarks suggest that he does not impose the constraints that are made quite explicit in Smith. Rawls does not examine Smith's system in itself, but from his more general discussion we may infer that his central objection would be focused on the dependence of distributional outcomes on initial asset holdings, or initial endowments. Before treating this point in some detail, I re-emphasize that Rawls does not criticize the market-determined distribution of product given the set of initial endowments, a source of much confusion in the continuing critique of social institutions.[31] His attention is concentrated, properly, on the pre-market distribution of endowments to which, contrary to Nozick, Rawls attributes no moral qualities.

Adam Smith did not discuss the distribution of initial endowments, but for his system of natural liberty to meet the Rawlsian precepts for justice in the postulated Rawlsian setting, two conditions would have to be met. First, any deliberately imposed change in the basic institutions of society designed

29. See *The Wealth of Nations*, 538–39.

30. Rawls, *A Theory of Justice*, 65–75.

31. For my own explicit discussion of this point, see James M. Buchanan, "Political Equality and Private Property: The Distributional Paradox" (prepared for a conference on Markets and Morals, Battelle Institute, Seattle, May 1974) (forthcoming in conference proceedings).

to bring about greater equality in initial endowments must be shown to worsen the position of the least advantaged. It does not seem likely that this condition could be fulfilled.[32] Even here, however, it should be recognized that the most glaring inequalities in initial endowments could scarcely arise in a genuine system of natural liberty. How many great family fortunes would exist had not the government employed its power to enforce and to police monopoly privileges? Secondly, there would have to be a direct relationship between the economic position of the least-advantaged members of society and the total income generated in the economy. This condition seems more likely to be met, regardless of how the "least-advantaged" members are to be defined, provided only that the difference principle is applied in a dynamic setting.[33] Institutional changes that tend to retard or to stifle economic growth seem likely to harm the position of the least-advantaged rather than to improve it, almost regardless of the motivation for such changes.[34]

I do not want to make Adam Smith and John Rawls seem to be more similar in their basic philosophical positions than a careful interpretation of their published works might warrant. Even when we take into account the historical and methodological distance between them, and even when we try to apply their criteria for justice in the converse empirical settings, we cannot legitimately infer a Smithean distributional interest comparable to Rawls. In 1976, a returned Adam Smith might or might not be an egalitarian of Rawls-

---

32. An argument to this effect could be plausibly advanced with respect to certain of the more obvious proposals. One such argument that might possibly be extended in this way relates to the confiscatory taxation of inheritances; see Gordon Tullock, "Inheritance Justified," *Journal of Law and Economics* 14 (1971): 465.

33. Critics of Rawls have pointed to the ambiguities that arise in defining "least-advantaged," and Rawls has acknowledged the difficulties involved when dynamic or intergenerational issues are introduced. Even if the "least-advantaged" are defined to be those members of society who are wholly nonproductive, growth-retarding policies will violate the difference principle if the intergenerational discount rate is sufficiently low. The indigent of the 1970s are in a better position than they would have been had a Rawlsian difference principle of justice been applied, without consideration of the intergenerational impact, in the 1870s.

34. The "quality of life" or environmental regulations that have now become widespread seem to offer the best examples. These institutional changes are acknowledged to have differentially harmed those who are in differentially disadvantaged economic positions. Quite apart from possible violations of the principles of equal liberty, these changes would have to be classified as unjust by the difference principle.

ian stripe. Because of his relative underemphasis on the relationship between material goods and human happiness, the most judicious evaluation suggests that Smith would not have been motivated to stress distributional inequities to the extent of Rawls. It also seems clear that, even in the affluence of 1976, Smith would have paid considerably more attention to the net benefits, measured in terms of both efficiency and justice, to be secured by a dismantling of restrictions on freedom of individual choices.

Finally I should note a possible difference in the implications of a commonly shared philosophical rather than empirical presupposition for normative discourse. Even if he should have recognized, empirically, that persons differ, and substantially so, in basic capacities, Adam Smith might well have argued that such inequalities have no place in, and in fact must be presumed away, in the process of designing a just and viable social order. The basic institutions of society must be based on the presumption that men are "equals" in some fundamental generic sense.[35] This is the attitude that clearly informs the United States Declaration of Independence, and the coincidence of dates between this and the publication of *The Wealth of Nations* is not merely historical accident. From this presumption or presupposition, undue concern with distributional outcomes might be considered to be, at base, aberrant. In this light, the onus would be on John Rawls to defend his concentration on the distributional principle as appended to the principle of equal liberty rather than on Adam Smith to defend his failure to make a comparable extension.

35. For a discussion of this presumption of fundamental equality, even in the context of empirical inequalities, see James M. Buchanan, *The Limits of Liberty: Between Anarchy and Leviathan* (1975), especially pp. 11–12.

Rawls, of course, accepts this presumption in his basic contractarian derivation of the principles of justice. The presumption is not at issue here. The possible difference lies in the implications of this presumption for distributional norms.

Care must be taken to distinguish a presumption of equality in some "original position" and/or in some basic philosophical sense, and the elevation of distributional equality as an ideal attribute of the just society. Rawls is somewhat vulnerable on this count, especially because he derives his principles of justice from "fairness" notions. In so far as "fairness" applies to the rules of games, by extension to ordinary games, it becomes questionable to speak of achieved or final equality as an ideal. This would amount to "condemning a footrace as unfair because someone has come out ahead." On this point, see Frank H. Knight, *The Ethics of Competition* (1935), 61.

VIII. Conclusions

I have had several objectives in this paper. First of all, I have tried to show that Adam Smith's system of natural liberty, interpreted as his idealized paradigm for social order, embodies justice as well as economic efficiency. Indeed Smith may well have conceived his masterpiece to be an argument to the effect that the system which was acknowledged to embody justice could also be efficient. Secondly, I have attempted to compare Smith's first principle of natural liberty with John Rawls' first principle of equal liberty. Although I have not tried to examine an exhaustive list of examples here, a straightforward application of either of these principles implies significant restrictions on the propriety of governmental-political interference with the freedom of individuals to make their own economic decisions. My ultimate, and perhaps most important purpose has been to use the timely discussion of Adam Smith's precepts for justice as a vehicle for correcting what has seemed to me a grossly neglected aspect of John Rawls' much-acclaimed and much-discussed book. Both Smith and Rawls are libertarians in that principles of liberty hold positions of priority in their orderings of objectives. Neither is utilitarian in the Benthamite or even in the more constrained Paretian sense of this term. The differences between Smith and Rawls lie in the fact that Smith's discourse is concentrated on the efficiency-producing results of natural liberty; the corollary attributes of justice are not stressed. And, for the several reasons noted, the distributional results are not explicitly evaluated against criteria of justice. On the other hand, Rawls treats liberty sketchily despite the lexical priority assigned to it, and he concentrates on the distributional qualities of an idealized social order. Translated into practical reform proposals, however, both philosophers accept an effectively operative market economy as a basic institution in any society that could be classified as just.

The differences in distributional emphasis are important, but I have showed that these are at least partially explained by differences in empirical and possibly philosophical presuppositions. One implication of the comparison should be that a libertarian position is not inconsistent with an egalitarian one, despite attempts to make these seem contradictory by both the libertarian-antiegalitarians and the collectivist-egalitarians. A strong defense of the liberties of individuals, which can only be secured in an operating market economy, may be joined with an equally strong advocacy for the reform of basic social institutions designed to produce greater equality among individuals in their initial endowments and capacities. This is how I interpret John Rawls' position, which comes close to that associated with Henry Simons,[36] whose explicit emphasis on free markets is clearly akin to that of Adam Smith. If my interpretation is accepted, the normative distance between Adam Smith and John Rawls is surely less than the sometimes careless comparisons of images would suggest.

36. See Henry Simons, *Economic Policy for a Free Society* (1948) and *Personal Income Taxation* (1938).

There are some ambiguities in Rawls which make my interpretation less persuasive than might appear. He does not seem to recognize the necessary relationship between an operative market economy and the dispersion of property ownership. For this reason, particular sections of his treatise may be interpreted as collectivist in flavor. (See, especially, Rawls, *A Theory of Justice,* 271–72.) On balance, these seem to me to represent failures to follow through carefully the full implications of the first principle of equal liberty.

Ethical Rules, Expected Values, and Large Numbers

I. Introduction

What influences an individual's choice among ethical rules? I shall demonstrate that the size of the group within which he consciously interacts is a critical determinant. Individual choice behavior, even at this fundamental level of ethical rules, may differ sharply between small groups and large groups. This hypothesis is corroborated by well-known and commonly observed experience. To my knowledge, however, ethical theorists have neglected the apparent importance of group size.[1]

In the remainder of this introductory section I relate my discussion to the standard questions in ethical theory. In so doing I am guided solely by the necessities of the argument that I want to develop. My lack of competence to discuss ethical theory per se will be fully apparent. In Section II I discuss the individual's choice among ethical rules in terms of an ordering of potential social states or situations. One particular ordering will be advanced as plausible, and its appropriateness will be defended. The individual's choice among ethical rules is shown to depend on this ordering along with his probability calculus concerning the ethical choices made by "others" in the rele-

From *Ethics* 76 (October 1965): 1–13. Copyright 1965 by The University of Chicago. All rights reserved. Reprinted by permission of the University of Chicago Press, publisher.

I am indebted to my colleague, Gordon Tullock, for several helpful conversations during the preparation of this paper.

1. M. G. Singer's argument comes close at one point to incorporating size as such, but in a context different from that of this paper (see his *Generalization in Ethics* [New York: Alfred A. Knopf, Inc., 1961], 137).

vant group. Section III examines the importance of group size for this probability calculus, and simple examples are introduced to show how the individual's decision can be modified solely by a change in numbers. The dilemma of the individual who finds himself a member of a critically large group is treated in some detail. Section IV develops comparisons with individual choice behavior in economic theory, where the relevance of group size has been recognized even if not sufficiently clarified. Finally, Section V briefly explores some possible implications of the critical size hypothesis for reforms in social institutions.

To avoid preliminary misunderstanding, let me state what this paper is not. It is not an essay in "ethics," by which I mean a discussion of what individuals should or should not do. Aside from this, as will be evident to informed readers, the paper is not designed to contribute to Kantian criticism, either in the traditional sense of discussing what Kant really meant or in the modern version of discussing the generalization principle of argument. I shall be concerned exclusively with an individual's choice among ethical rules and with the possibilities of *predicting* this choice. Any analysis of choice must involve some consideration of the alternatives, and it is here that I accept, without argument, the relevance of something akin to the Kantian distinction between the *moral law* and the subjective or *private maxim*. My concern is with a question similar to one put by Beck: "it is a question of what are the conditions, in a being like man, that make it possible for him to take an interest in the law and have the law as his incentive."[2] I am not directly interested in the individual's ability to make an appropriate distinction between that action dictated by the "moral law" and that dictated by the "private maxim," either universally or in specific instances. I simply accept that the generalization or universality principle can be applied in a sufficient number of cases to make my argument, which is restricted to those cases, worth developing.[3] The analysis requires only that the individual be assumed to confront a choice among ethical rules and that something loosely similar to the Kantian dichotomy describes the alternatives that he faces.

2. Lewis White Beck, *A Commentary on Kant's Critique of Practical Reason* (Chicago: University of Chicago Press, 1960), 219.

3. My reading of the literature is admittedly spotty. But within these limits I find my own position to be reasonably close to that stated by Warner Wick in his review paper, "Generalization and the Basis of Ethics," *Ethics* 72 (July 1962): 288–98.

In this setting I want to examine the possibilities of predicting this choice. Note that the choice to be analyzed is that between separate *rules* for behavior, not that between separate *acts* in particular circumstances. Much of my discussion can be applied directly to the latter choice, but, for reasons to be noted, there are advantages to limiting specific analyses to the choice between rules, which, once chosen, will serve to predetermine acts within the limits implied.

The individual is presumed to be facing the following question: What ethical rule shall I adopt as a guide to my behavior in subsequent actions? There are two alternatives before him. He can adopt a rule, which we shall call "the moral law," or he can adopt a rule which, loosely, we shall call "the private maxim." By selecting the first, the individual commits himself to act in subsequent situations on the basis of something like the generalization principle. That is, he will not act in ways other than those which allow his particular action to be universalized, regardless of the specific consequences. By selecting the second rule instead, he commits himself in advance to no particular principle of behavior. He retains full freedom to act on the basis of expedient considerations in each particular instance that arises. Note that, in terms of observed or revealed behavior in particular acts, there need be no difference in the results of these two ethical rules. The person who rejects the moral law as an ethical rule that effectively constrains his choices among acts may, nonetheless, fully accept the behavior dictated by this law in particular circumstances. For this reason, the choice that I am centrally concerned with should not be interpreted as one between "moral" and "immoral" rules.

II. The Ordering of Social States

As soon as the notion of generalization or universalization is introduced, individual behavior embodies social content. The choosing-acting party interacts with other parties, whose behavior in turn becomes a part of the necessary environment within which his own choices take place. In this respect much of the Kantian criticism seems to me to have been overly individualistic. The individual's decision as to whether he should adopt the moral law or the expediency criterion as an ethical rule surely depends upon his own predictions about the behavior of others and upon his evaluations of comparative states of society incorporating this behavior. The rules predicted to be chosen by others will be of importance in determining the descriptive characteristics of alternative social states or situations.

We want to examine now the individual's evaluation of separate social states or situations, and we can best do so in terms of an ordering that he places on alternative consequences or outcomes. These outcomes can be described in terms of two sets of ethical rules, his own and those of "others." Listed below in ascending rank is an ordering of six social states.

1. *The worst possible world.* The individual himself adopts the moral law, but almost none of his fellows does so. He should expect to be grossly exploited. This is clearly an undesirable state of affairs for other than a masochist.

2. *Mondo cane.* This second state is only slightly better than the first. Here the individual predicts that almost none of his fellow citizens will follow the moral law as an ethical rule. However, in this combination he, too, follows the criterion of expediency. He can, by following the dominant behavior pattern, prevent differential exploitation.

3. *Commitment in a mixed world.* This is a state in which the individual predicts that roughly one-half of his fellows will follow some version of the moral law and in which he also adopts this law as an ethical rule. Along with the other committed persons in the group, he will expect to be forced, on occasion, to behave contrary to the dictates of expediency.

4. *Expediency in a partially committed world.* This differs from the third state only in the individual's own choice of an ethical rule. Here he adopts the rule of following his own private maxims in determining particular acts. Clearly he will expect to experience, on some occasions, differentially favorable consequences from this retained freedom.

5. *The generalized world.* This state may, within limits, be called the idealized Kantian world. The individual who is making the ordering, along with substantially all of his fellows, adopts the moral law as a general rule for behavior. Mutual self-respect, honesty, duty: these make for a highly desirable social interaction process.

6. *Expediency in a duty-bound world.* In this state the individual himself retains the rule that allows him to act from his own private maxims whereas substantially everyone else in the group follows some version of the moral law. Clearly, this state is the most desirable for the individual. He retains

complete freedom to follow the dictates of expediency in particular actions as his own subjective attitudes may suggest, while also enjoying a wider freedom to act, if he so chooses, strictly in terms of the categorical imperative.

I suggest that the ordering presented above is a reasonable one for most individuals. It may be objected that this ordering of social states itself reflects the evaluations of an immoral person because it does not impute to the adoption of the moral law itself a positive component or value. An individual, it might be argued, "should," and if moral "will," prefer a world in which he himself acts in accordance with the moral law because of some intrinsic worth of morality itself. I do not propose to quarrel with those who might take this position, even were I equipped to do so. But the possible objection along these lines is not germane to my analysis, and it is precisely to cover myself in this respect that I have concentrated on the choice of ethical rules rather than on the choice of acts. The individual may, for reasons indicated, prefer to act in accordance with the moral law, even though he does not choose to adopt this law as his overriding ethical rule. If, however, he places any value at all on a widened area of choice, he will tend to rank the states where he retains such choice, all other things being equal, higher than the states where this choice is explicitly narrowed.

The suggested ordering was presented in a simple numerical listing, 1 through 6. Some numerical scale will be helpful in discussing the individual's choice of rules, but this scale is wholly arbitrary so long as the numbers stand in the same order one to another. For simplicity only, I shall use the numbers in the simple listing to indicate the relative evaluations that the individual might place on the several possible social states. Alternatively, any number of zeros could be added to each number, or, perhaps more realistically, there may be multiples placed between each subset of two in the listing. In the latter case the ordering might run, in ascending rank—1, 2, 30, 40, 500, 600—indicating wide differentials between the world of moral law as an ethical rule and the world of expediency. The point to be emphasized is, however, the essential arbitrariness of the particular numbers assigned. It is in part to emphasize this, as well as for simplicity, that the simple numerical listing will be used here.

We can summarize the individual's ordering that has been suggested in a simple 2-by-3 matrix (Table 1) in which the rows indicate the alternative rules that he may choose while the columns indicate the possible behavior patterns that he predicts for "others" in the interacting group. It is evident that there can be as many columns as desired, depending on the detail with which he might want to specify the individual's predictions about the choices of rules by others.

The information summarized in the matrix is not sufficient to enable us to predict how the individual will actually choose between the two ethical rules that he confronts. There is no indication to this point as to his estimates of the probabilities of the choice patterns of "others." Until we introduce such estimates, expected values for his own choice alternatives cannot be derived. We need to know what probability the individual assigns to each of the three possible behavior patterns of his fellows.

Let us suppose that he assigns a probability of 0.6 to the first pattern, 0.3 to the second, and 0.1 to the third. The matrix is rewritten in abbreviated form as Table 2, with the predicted or assigned probabilities in parentheses. Given the values in the ordering, along with the probabilities as assigned in Table 2, we can compute expected values for each alternative confronting the individual who must decide. As the right-hand column indicates, the expected value from following the moral law as a rule is less than that from adopting the rule of expedient behavior. Under the conditions depicted, the individual can be predicted to reject the moral law as an ethical rule, and to adopt instead a rule that will allow him to act in each case on his own subjective maxims.

Table 1

	"Others"		
	---	---	---
Individuals	*Almost None Follow Moral Law as Rule*	*About One-Half Follow Moral Law as Rule*	*Almost All Follow Moral Law as Rule*
Follow private maxims as rule	2	4	6
Follow moral law as rule	1	3	5

Table 2

Individual	"Others"			Expected Value
	None	*One-Half*	*All*	
Private maxim	2(0.6)	4(0.3)	6(0.1)	3
Moral law	1(0.6)	3(0.3)	5(0.1)	2

The expected values depend, of course, on the probabilities that the individual assigns to the various patterns of behavior for "others" than himself. Careful examination of the numerical example reveals, however, that a change in these probabilities will not modify the choice of a rule that is dictated. Suppose, for illustration of this point, that the probabilities are changed from (0.6, 0.3, 0.1) to (0.0, 0.4, 0.6). Clearly, under this new situation the expected value under either rule is increased; the individual simply lives in a "better" world. But note that, given the same rank ordering and same valuations, the expected value from adopting the moral law as a rule, which is now 4.2, remains less than that expected from the alternative-rule choice, which becomes 5.2. Hence, we conclude that in this model, regardless of the pattern of rule choice that the individual predicts on the part of his fellows, he will not be led to adopt the moral law as a binding ethical rule for his own behavior so long as his evaluation of comparative social states remains that indicated in the matrix illustrations.

Ethical theorists may object to the usage of any numerical scale to indicate the evaluations that the individual places on social states, and because I am an economist I may stand accused of introducing expected utility by the side door. I am, of course, tempted to call "that which the individual maximizes in his choice behavior" something like "utility," and the approach here stems from the expected utility analysis that is familiar in modern economics. It must be emphasized, however, that the numerical scale does nothing other than provide a helpful tool for analyzing individual choice among ethical rules, and any connection between this scale and "utility" in any connotation of "happiness" or "pleasure" can be quite explicitly rejected. Individuals choose what they choose, whether this be apples or ethical rules, and we can, in both cases, discuss their choices in terms of some ranking of "better" and "worse" results. If we could not do so, we should be unable to discuss choice at all. This is the only function of introducing the arbitrarily precise numerical ordering of social states. If this were the end of it, much of the matrix illustration would, of course, be almost wholly unnecessary baggage. As I shall demonstrate in the following section, however, the construction does enable significant conclusions to be reached.

III. The Relevance of Numbers

In a sense, the example presented above is deceptive because one assumption that is essential for the results has been deliberately left unmentioned. Recall that changes in the probabilities assigned to different rule choices on the part of "others" do not change the ranking of the expected values of the two alternatives for the individual who is trying to decide which rule to adopt for himself. But this is true only within the limits of the particular example, and it should have been noted that the reference individual was assumed to assign the *same* probability distribution to "others," *regardless of his own choice of an ethical rule.* In terms specifically of the matrix of Table 2, the same probability distribution was assumed applicable for each row. This assumption will be appropriate only in those situations where the individual predicts that his own choice of a rule in no way modifies or influences the similar choices of "others."

Consider, now, a sharply different setting in which only this one element is modified. The probability distribution in the first row of the matrix, which applies when he rejects the moral law as a rule, is assumed unchanged from that of Table 2. For the second row, which holds when he chooses to adopt the moral law as a rule governing future acts, let us introduce a different probability distribution, that which was previously used as the modification on our illustration. The matrix will then look as shown in Table 3. Note that in Table 3 the expected value for the choice represented in "follow the moral law" now exceeds that for the alternative "follow private maxims." There is no change in the individual's ordering of the social states or even in his presumed numerical evaluations.

The question is one of determining the conditions under which an individual's rational calculus will lead him to assign probabilities of one sort or another. When will he assign probabilities of the sort shown in Table 3 rather

Table 3

Individual	None	One-Half	All	Expected Value
		"Others"		
Private maxim	2(0.6)	4(0.3)	6(0.1)	3
Moral law	1(0.0)	3(0.4)	5(0.6)	4.2

than those of Table 2? The central hypothesis of this paper is that the size of the interacting group is one of the important determinants in this assignment. An individual who consciously interacts with only a small number of other persons in ethical relationships will tend to assign probabilities similar to those illustrated in Table 3, while the same individual, if he consciously interacts with a critically large number of other persons, will assign probabilities similar to those of Table 2. The precise numerical values are not, of course, important here. The only requirement is that there be some positive relationship between the individual's own choice of an ethical rule and the choices that he predicts for others.

The general validity of this hypothesis for the small-number model may be shown by reference to a simple, three-person example. There are three persons in an isolated setting, say, a desert island, and each person faces the choice among ethical rules when considering how to behave with his fellows. Clearly, any one of the three will tend to recognize that his own choice of a rule, and subsequent adherence to it, will to some considerable extent influence the similar choices to be made and followed by the other two members. Since we may assume that each of the three prefers to live in a setting of mutual self-respect, as shown by our ordering, the most likely outcome will surely be one where each and every person adopts, and follows, something that is akin to the Kantian categorical imperative.[4] His standard for behavior will be some version of the generalization principle.

This result will tend to emerge in a small group quite independently of

4. In the extreme, the analysis may be extended to the one-person group. Here the behavioral rule chosen or the action taken will necessarily be the one-person analogue to the generalization principle. It is essentially on these grounds that the Aristotelian defense of private property is based.

the individual's particular evaluations of the several possible social states so long as the suggested rank order holds. The differences in evaluation between the idealized Kantian world and that peopled by subjective maximizers may be great or small. The critical requirement is located only in the diagonally weighted probability assignments of the matrix. The upper-right-hand squares must tend toward zero in expected value because of the unlikely event of the indicated combinations of rules emerging in the social interaction process. In small groups, the individual simply cannot expect uniquely to enjoy a widened range of choice.

The small-group model can be contrasted with that which includes a large number of persons, and for which the matrix illustration of Table 2 applies. Here the individual considers his own choice of an ethical rule to exert no influence on the choices of rules made by others. In effect, the choices of others here are treated as a part of the natural environment, so to speak, and not dependent on the individual's own decision. In this limiting case, the individual must make probability assignments that are described in their critical characteristics by Table 2. An interchange between the rows in the matrix will not change the probability distribution of the choices of rules by others.

It is perhaps worth emphasizing that my argument is not the relatively familiar one that presents the plight of the potentially honest man who finds himself among thieves. In a group of critically large size, the individual will tend to adopt the rule of following the expediency criterion even if he thinks that *all* of his fellow citizens are saints, provided only that the suggested ordering holds. Numerically, this is clearly shown in the illustrations, but repetition of the point seems warranted. The conditions of individual choice are such that there will be a rationally based rejection of the rule, "follow the moral law," quite independently of predictions as to the ethical rules that may be chosen by others in the interacting group.

If the analysis is applicable for any one individual in the critically large group, it must, of course, be applicable to all. Because of this interdependence, each member (and hence all members) will find himself in a genuine dilemma. He may value the social state depicted by the combinations on the right-hand side of the matrix much higher than those on the left. But despite this, he will find that he ends up, necessarily, in the upper-left-hand square. Rationally, he cannot adopt the moral law as a principle for his own behavior. Neither can his fellows. Therefore, the predictable consequences of ethical choices are those characteristic of a world where all persons reject the moral law as a controlling rule, and, instead, follow their own private maxims. Each and every person may, of course, consider that he would be "better off," in terms of his own evaluation, in a different world where the moral law is widely accepted as an overriding ethical rule. But, privately and voluntarily, there is simply no means through which the single individual can choose to make this alternative state of the world more nearly realizable.[5]

The dilemma is a real one, and it is similar to, although not identical with, that which is commonly discussed in game theory as "the prisoners' dilemma." In the latter, each of two prisoners is led to confess by the conditions of the situation in which he is placed, despite the fact that both prisoners would be in a more desired position should they both refrain from confessing. The difference between the prisoners' dilemma and the large-group ethical dilemma discussed here lies in the fact that, as ordinarily presented, the former remains a small-group phenomenon. The results emerge because of the absence of communication between the prisoners and because of their mutual distrust. The large-number dilemma is a more serious one because no additional communication or repetition of choices can effectively modify the results.

There is nothing in the analysis that suggests the actual size that a particular group must attain before the individual choice calculus undergoes the relatively dramatic change that has been noted. It seems evident that the dividing line between the critically small and the critically large group will vary with many circumstances, and no attempt will be made here to list these. Similarly, it is also clear that the individual differences will make for important differences in ethical choices. Under identical external circumstances, some members of a group of a given size will tend to choose rules as if they are interacting in a critically small setting, while other members may choose rules as if the group is critically large.[6] The hypothesis does not require that

5. The large-number dilemma is apparently familiar to ethical theorists through numerous examples, but the relevance of large numbers per se has not been appreciated. For examples of situations in which the dilemma appears see Singer, *Generalization in Ethics,* 69–70, 86–87.

6. In an interesting recent study of individual voting behavior in American municipalities, James Q. Wilson and Edward C. Banfield have noted significant differences in patterns of choice among different ethnic groupings. They attribute these differences in

these distinctions be made. All that is necessary for the hypothesis to hold is that, for any given individual who may be observed to follow what may loosely be called the rule of moral law in his small-group interactions, there is some increase in group size that will cause him to modify his ethical rule and become a private maximizer.

When stated in this fashion, the numerous corroborations of the hypothesis in everyday experience are familiar. Volunteer fire departments arise in villages, not in metropolitan centers. Crime rates increase consistently with city size. Africans behave differently in tribal culture than in urban-industrialized settings. There is honor among thieves. The Mafia has its own standards. Time-tested honor systems in universities and colleges collapse when enrolments exceed critical size limits. Litter is more likely to be found on main-traveled routes than on residential streets. Even the old adage, "Never trust a stranger," reflects a recognition of this elemental truth, along with, of course, additional ethical predictions. Successful politicians organize "grass-roots" support at the precinct level.

Only some of these examples are explicitly ethical, but the phenomenon is not limited to the choice of ethical rules or acts. The large-number dilemma pervades many areas of social interaction.

IV. Free Riders and Perfect Competition

The proposition that this paper extends to ethical theory has been widely recognized in economics, although even here the vital distinction between individual choice behavior in small-group and in large-group situations has not always been fully appreciated. Two separate applications will be summarized here. The first of these, commonly called "the free-rider problem," is a direct analogue to the ethical theory extension, and my work on this problem provided the specific stimulus for this paper. The second application is, in one sense, the inverse analogue. This is the whole notion of "perfect competition," a notion that has been basic to economic theory for almost a century.

---

part to the divergent "public consciousness" of these groups (see their "Public-Regardingness as a Value Premise in Voting Behavior," *American Political Science Review* 58 [December 1964]: 876–87).

The free-rider problem arises in the theory of public finance, or, more properly, in the theory of public-goods supply. This analysis attempts to derive an explanation for the supply of public goods, as contrasted with private goods, from the choice behavior of individuals. The question is: Why is political or governmental organization required at all? Why does the market or exchange process "fail," in some meaningful sense, when goods and services exist that must necessarily be shared in common by large numbers of persons? An examination of the conditions for equilibrium attained under private or independent trading adjustment reveals that the results are clearly non-optimal. If so, what is there to prevent further pressures designed to remove the remaining mutual gains from trade? The answer to these questions is found in the tendency of each person who is a potential beneficiary from the commonly shared public good to choose, rationally, to remain a "free rider." If the potential benefits are genuinely non-divisible among separate persons, each one will find it to his own private advantage to refrain from making voluntary contributions toward the costs of provision. This remains true despite the possibility that the total benefits to be derived from supplying the good, over all persons, may greatly exceed the total costs. And this may apply for each and every member of the group simultaneously without changing the results. Each person may consider that he would be better off in a situation where he, along with each of his fellow citizens, contributes a share in the common cost than he is in a situation where no one contributes anything. Yet each person may refuse, rationally, to contribute to this cost on an individualistic and voluntary basis. The equilibrium position is evidently non-optimal, and this may be recognized by all participants; but unless the rules are somehow changed, the large-number dilemma holds. This result emerges, of course, only when the size of the group is critically large. Only in such large groups will the individual consider his own action to exert substantially no effect on the actions of others.[7]

---

7. The first explicit recognition of the problem here is found in Knut Wicksell's classic work, *Finanztheoretische Untersuchungen* (Jena: Gustav Fischer, 1896). Relevant portions of this work are published in translation as "A New Principle of Just Taxation," in *Classics in the Theory of Public Finance*, ed. R. A. Musgrave and A. T. Peacock (London: Macmillan & Co., 1958), 72–118.

The classic modern treatments of the theory of public goods all recognize the existence of the free-rider problem. See Paul A. Samuelson, "The Pure Theory of Public Ex-

The very usage of the term "free rider," however, suggests that the significance of the large-group dilemma may not have been fully appreciated. This term suggests some deliberate effort on the part of the choosing individual to secure benefits at the expense of his fellows. In the only situation where the problem really emerges, however, the choosing individual enjoys no sensation of "riding free," of "letting George do it." There is no personal interaction present at all. The individual is simply reacting to an environment in which he finds himself, to "nature," so to speak, not in any way against his fellow citizens.

Once the large-number dilemma is understood, the failure of the market process to produce optimal results when public goods are present is explained. Further, as the argument has been developed, an explanation is provided for the tendency of individuals to turn to changes in the rules, specifically to the introduction of political-governmental processes as substitutes for market processes. Such changes in the institutions or rules can, of course, impose upon all members of the group common standards of conduct. From the analysis developed along these lines it becomes conceptually possible to demonstrate why, under certain circumstances, individuals will, on purely rational grounds, agree to allow themselves to be coerced.

The similarities between this analysis of individual choice behavior in contributing to the cost of public goods and that applied to the choice of an ethical rule are obvious. The second application of essentially the same proposition has an even longer history in economic theory, although its similarity is perhaps less evident due to its inverse relevance. This concerns the behavior of the individual or the firm under conditions of perfect competition. This state of affairs is, in fact, normally defined strictly by the presence of the

---

penditure," *Review of Economics and Statistics* 36 (November 1954): 387–89; and his "Diagrammatic Exposition of a Theory of Public Expenditure," ibid., 37 (November 1955): 350–56; and R. A. Musgrave, *The Theory of Public Finance* (New York: McGraw-Hill Book Co., 1959).

The discussion in this paper owes much to a still-unpublished paper by Otto A. Davis and Andrew Whinston: "Some Foundations of Public Expenditure Theory" (Carnegie Institute of Technology, mimeographed). Also many of the aspects of the problem, especially in relation to large organizations, have been discussed by Mancur Olson. In an early draft to which I have had access, Olson's work is entitled "The General Theory of Public Goods" (U.S. Air Force Academy, March 1963, mimeographed) (forthcoming under a slightly different title from Harvard University Press).

large-number dilemma. Perfect competition is said to exist when a single buyer or single seller exerts so small an influence on the total market demand or supply of a product that he acts as if his own behavior exerts no influence on the price that is established in the market. Each seller and each buyer is a price-taker.

Among the sellers of a single commodity, as a group, each single unit finds itself in a position precisely analogous to that of the "free rider." Each of the sellers would prefer to be in a position where all sellers restrict supply (with the net result being an increase in market price), but no single unit acting alone will find it profitable to restrict production. Given the situation, each must simply react to the external environment.

The large-number dilemma in this competitive context is different from that confronted in the ethical-choice or in the public-goods examples. Its applicability is the inverse of these other instances of the same proposition. Broadly speaking, the direction of desired change in the first examples is toward reducing group size, or at least modifying the rules so that something similar to small-group results emerges. In the organization of markets, however, explicit attempts are made to place buyers and sellers in the large-number dilemma. The economic system works efficiently only to the extent that the large-number dilemma prevails over wide areas, and institutional reforms are aimed directly at extending group size. Legal restrictions are imposed on attempts to consolidate, and enforcible rules over whole groups are forbidden. The essential difference between the ethical-choice–public-goods models and the perfect-competition models stems from the fact that in the first instances the groups are presumed inclusive of all members in the interacting social group. In market process, by contrast, only the particular sellers of one product, as a subgroup, find themselves in the large-number dilemma. And any change in the rules that will provide them with relief will automatically result in their exploitation of still other groups in the larger social system. Broader considerations involving the "social" constitution for the whole system may dictate that institutions of the economy be organized so as to foster deliberately the placing of single buyers and sellers in the large-number dilemma. This is simply another means of stating that the public at large may rationally choose to enforce the rules for perfect competition to the extent that this is possible.

Frank Knight often stresses that "in perfect competition there is no competition." This statement summarizes the essence of the large-number dilemma. The single seller in a perfectly competitive market, the single individual who considers his own voluntary contribution to a commonly shared public good, the single individual who tries to decide on an ethical rule in a large group: in each case rational choice dictates that he make the best of the environmental situation that he confronts. He can, by the nature of the conditions that he finds himself in, experience no sense of personal influence on the behavior of others directly or indirectly.

V. Implications

The large-number hypothesis in the theory of public goods supplies a possible logical explanation for the emergence of political-government institutions as replacements for market-exchange institutions in the provision of goods and services that exhibit the requisite "publicness." Before specific reforms can be suggested, however, additional questions must be answered. First, what value do individuals place on the voluntaristic elements of market processes, elements that must necessarily be sacrificed, at least to some degree, under political organization? What is the appropriate trading ratio between freedom of individual choice and economic efficiency? Even if this question were provisionally answered, another and equally difficult one would arise. How can the analyst, as an external observer, distinguish or classify those goods and services that exhibit "publicness"? Merely to raise these questions indicates that the pure theory of public goods remains in its infancy; the theorist remains a long way from that position which would allow him to provide normative advice to statesmen concerning the specifics of institutional reform.

This may seem a pessimistic estimate of the current state of theory, but modern developments have placed economists in the position where they now ask the proper questions. With this has surely come a more comprehensive understanding of political as well as economic processes. Such an understanding can yield suggestions for reforms that may not be initially apparent. Public finance theorists have, by and large, accepted the classification between "private goods," which may be efficiently supplied through market institutions, and "public goods," which cannot be so supplied, as being determined by forces not subject to social control. Closer examination reveals, however, that this important dividing line may itself be variable. To the extent that it is, under certain circumstances it may be possible to secure both the greater freedom of choice that market organization allows and the potential enhancement of efficiency that modified rules can introduce. Careful analysis of the structure of legal and property rights may reveal prospects for converting apparent cases of "free-rider" behavior into situations where individual behavior can produce substantially optimal results.

This paper is not the place to develop this particular line of argument; my purpose here is to contribute something to the analysis of ethical choice. The brief review of the implications of similar theorizing about the public-goods problem is specifically helpful only to the extent that the analogy with ethical choice is relevant. If the sweep of history is considered to make inevitable and irrevocable the interaction of larger and larger numbers of persons in an ethical context, the analysis must imply that a smaller and smaller proportion of individuals will come to base their own actions on some version of the generalization or universalization principle. The scope for an individualistic, voluntaristic ethics must, of necessity, be progressively narrowed through time. As individuals, increasingly, find themselves caught in the large-number dilemma with respect to ethical choices, a possible logical explanation is provided for resort to political-governmental processes which can, effectively, change the rules and impose standards of conduct common to all individuals. In this respect, the analysis yields helpful insights concerning the "legislation of morals" in terms of straightforward predictions if not of propriety. Common standards of conduct imposed and enforced by authority of the collectivity can, in the limiting case, result in "improvement" for all members of the community by their own standards. The limiting case is precisely that, however, and the overwhelming probability would be that collectively enforced standards of conduct would be those desired for "others" by "some." Here, as in the public-goods case, the question that must be asked is: What is the appropriate trading ratio between the greater freedom of choice allowed the individual under a voluntaristic ethics and the greater social "efficiency" that might possibly emerge under legislated and enforced common standards of behavior? The theorist can provide no answers here, and analysis suggests only that the price paid for freedom increases with the size of the relevant interacting group.

As in the public-goods case, avenues of reform other than collectivization should be explored. Must the effective size of interacting groups become ever larger, in the context of ethical choice? What are the possible means of factoring down complex social interaction systems into small-group patterns? Imaginative and exciting modifications in traditional property-right arrangements are currently emerging to "internalize the externalities" in private market processes for certain types of interactions.[8] Can an analogous change in institutions be predicted to emerge in the realm of ethics? Perhaps those whose professional competence and interest lies primarily in ethics should begin to re-examine the biblical admonition to "love thy neighbor," with the last word italicized. In the large-number group, who is my "neighbor"? The lawyer's question was evaded, not answered, in Jesus' parabolic response.

---

8. Cf. Spencer MacCallum, "The Social Nature of Ownership," *Modern Age* 9 (Winter 1964–65): 49–61.

The Samaritan's Dilemma

This paper is an essay in prescriptive diagnosis. It represents my attempt to show that many different "social problems" can be analyzed as separate symptoms of the same disease. The diagnosis, as such, may be accepted without agreeing that the disease amounts to much or that, indeed, it is disease at all. Prescription for improvement or cure is suggested only if the disease is acknowledged to be serious. Even if the diagnosis and prescription be accepted, however, prospects for "better social health" may not be bright because, as the analysis demonstrates, the source of difficulty may lie in modern man's own utility function. We may simply be too compassionate for our own well-being or for that of an orderly and productive free society.

I.

Consider a very simple two-by-two payoff matrix confronting two players, A and B. Player A chooses between rows; Player B chooses between columns. The payoffs are utility indicators, and these are arranged in ordinal sequence; there is no need to introduce cardinal utility at this point. As indicated in Figure 1, for Player A the second row dominates the first, in the strict game-theory sense. In a simple game setting, he will choose Row 2 regardless of what Player B does or is predicted to do. Furthermore, and this is important

From *Altruism, Morality and Economic Theory,* ed. E. S. Phelps (New York: Russell Sage Foundation, 1975), 71–85. Reprinted by permission of the publisher.

A preliminary version of this paper was presented in seminars at Harvard, Kentucky, UCLA, West Virginia, and Western Michigan Universities in the spring of 1971, and an early revised version was presented in the Seminar on the Mathematical Theory of Collective Decisions, Hilton Head, South Carolina, in August 1971. The final version was prepared for presentation at the Conference on Altruism and Economic Theory held at Russell Sage Foundation.

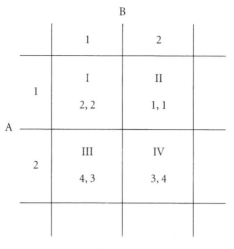

Figure 1

for the main points of this paper, Player A will select Row 2 even if he fails to recognize that he is in a game at all. Row 2 is simply his pragmatic or independent-behavior response to the choice situation that he confronts, whether or not A recognizes that B exists as a choice-making entity who opposes him in a game-like situation.

Note, however, that Player B does not find himself in a comparable position to A. The way that B chooses does depend on A's action, observed or predicted. If A should choose Row 1, B will choose Column 1. But if A chooses Row 2, Player B will always select Column 2. If B knows A's payoff matrix, he will predict that A will choose Row 2. Hence, the "solution" of this simple game would seem to be Cell IV of the matrix. If we look carefully at this outcome, however, we see that Player A is worse off than he would be in Cell III. His payoff is maximized in Cell III, but he cannot, in and of himself, accomplish a shift into Cell III. Nonetheless, since Player B's choices depend strictly on those of A, the latter should be in the driver's seat in one way or the other. Player A surely could, by some appropriate changes in behavior or strategy, insure an outcome in Cell III. To secure this, however, A must first recognize that he is in a game with B. That is to say, he must realize that his own choice behavior does, in fact, influence the choice behavior of B. Secondly, Player A must begin to behave "strategically"; that is, he must make his own choices on the basis of predictions about the effects of these on B's behavior. If A knows precisely what B's utility payoffs are, he can insure that an outcome in Cell III is realized. He can do so by playing the game in terms of the false payoffs that would be indicated by switching his own utility indicators as between Cells II and IV.

This strategy may be quite difficult for A, however, when we allow for the problems of communication and credibility between the players. Player A cannot simply announce to B what his strategy is and then expect Player B to believe him. We are interested here only in a sequential game, and A's strategy is revealed only through his behavior on particular plays of the game itself. In order to convince B that he is playing strategically, A must actually act as if the false payoffs are real. Only in this way can he establish credibility.

But this raises difficulties for A precisely because of the dominance features of his true payoff matrix. If strategic behavior dictates that he actually act as if the false rather than the true payoffs exist, Player A must suffer utility loss. He must, in order to make the strategy viable, choose Row 1 rather than Row 2 when Player B is observed or predicted to select Column 2. This will "hurt" A. Admittedly, the utility losses may be short-term only, and there may be offsetting long-term utility gains in a sequential game. But once the tradeoff between short-term utility and long-term utility is acknowledged to be present, we must also acknowledge that A's subjective discount rate will determine his behavior. If this rate is sufficiently high, A may choose to behave nonstrategically, even in the full recognition of the game situation that he confronts.

I shall return to this when I introduce examples, but, before this, let us consider a second game, which involves merely the transposition of the payoff numbers for Player A as between Cells I and III. This is illustrated in Figure 2. In this setting, dominance no longer characterizes A's choice; his behavior initially becomes dependent on that of B, either observed or predicted. Here we shall expect to secure either a Cell I or a Cell IV outcome, depending strictly on who gets there first, so to speak. For purposes that will, I hope, become clear later, let us assume that a continuing sequential solution in Cell I is in being. Player A faces no dilemma of the sort discussed earlier. He need not introduce strategic behavior.

Suppose, however, that Player B becomes cognizant of A's utility payoff matrix and that B begins to behave strategically. Suppose that B, independently, shifts to a Column 2 strategy, in the knowledge that A will quickly

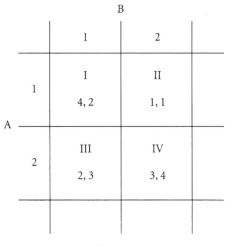

Figure 2

adopt a Row 2 course of action. B will, of course, suffer in the process, but let us suppose that he willingly takes the short-term utility losses that are required here. Clearly, A will have been placed in a position less desirable than the initial one by B's strategic behavior. Player A will be forced into the Cell IV outcome. In this event, B can be said to have exploited A successfully.

If we look at this situation from A's vantage point, the required strategic offsets to B's behavior are the same as those indicated for the first game discussed. To prevent being exploited by B, Player A must refuse to be influenced by B's shift to Column 2. Once again, A must act as if his utility payoffs as between Cells II and IV are reversed. Once again, however, A may find this difficult to carry out because he must suffer utility losses in the process. B's introduction of strategic behavior in this game places A in an acute position of suffering unless he acquiesces in a shift into Cell IV.

II.

I have quite deliberately presented these two very simple two-player interactions without identification or example, although the title of the paper may have already tipped my hand. I have left off labeling the players because I want to forestall, to the maximum extent that is possible, the instant emotional identification that my examples seem to arouse. But I cannot go beyond this point without examples, so I shall now attach specific labels. I shall call the first situation the *active samaritan's dilemma*, and the second situation the *passive samaritan's dilemma*. Let me emphasize, however, that I am attempting to develop a hypothesis that is generalizable to much of the behavior that we observe in the modern world. The samaritan example is used for descriptive clarity, in part because I could think of no better one. You may have suggestions here. The hypothesis does apply to certain aspects of the current policy discussion of welfare reform, but this is only one among many applications, and by no means the most important one.

Stated in the most general terms possible, the hypothesis is that modern man has become incapable of making the choices that are required to prevent his exploitation by predators of his own species, whether the predation be conscious or unconscious. The weakness here may be imbedded in man's utility function. The term "dilemma" seems appropriate because the problem may not be one that reflects irrational behavior on any of the standard interpretations. Origins of the dilemma are, in part, economic, and these are found in the increasing affluence of choice-makers. Analysis here lends substance to the cliché that modern man has "gone soft." His income-wealth position, along with his preference order, allows him to secure options that were previously unavailable. What we may call "strategic courage" may be a markedly inferior economic good, and what we may call "pragmatic compassion" may be markedly superior.

If my general hypothesis is accepted, the direction of reform and improvements lies first in an explicit recognition of the dilemma by those who are caught up in it. Before "play" can even begin, the players must recognize that a game exists. Once this sort of recognition is passed, the players involved must, individually and collectively, accept the possible necessity of acting *strategically* rather than pragmatically. The very meaning of a game implies that the behavior of one player can control, to some extent, the behavior of his opponent. Optimal behavior for one player is dependent on the predicted reciprocal or response behavior on the part of the others in the game. One objective of strategy is precisely that of influencing the behavior of others in such a way as to produce the preferred outcome or solution. The implied strategy may and normally will violate norms for simple utility maximization in an assumed nongame or state of nature setting.

In the first game discussed, which I have now called the active samaritan's dilemma, strategic behavior may be dictated for the samaritan even if the opposing player does not, himself, recognize the existence of the game, as such. That is to say, the player who is in the role of the potential samaritan may find it desirable to behave strategically even if his opponent, whom I have labeled the potential parasite, behaves pragmatically. In the second game, however, strategic behavior on the part of the potential samaritan may be dictated only when a specific gaming situation is forced upon him by his opponent.

In a very broad sense, the argument suggests the appropriateness of adopting rules for personal choice behavior as opposed to retaining individual flexibility of action. The ethic that is closely related to, if not exactly derivable from, the samaritan's dilemma is one of individual responsibility. Initially, the dilemma is discussed in an individualistic choice setting, but there are important social and group implications that emerge from widespread adherence to the behavioral norms. More significantly, the analysis lends itself readily to extension to situations where separate individual choices are clearly interdependent.

III.

To facilitate specific discussion, let me identify Player A as a "Potential Samaritan" and Player B as a "Potential Parasite." Furthermore, let us suppose that the potential samaritan faces two possible courses of action. He may do nothing vis-à-vis the potential parasite; that is, he may behave noncharitably (Row 1). Alternatively, the potential samaritan may behave charitably, and, for purposes of discussion here, let us suppose that this involves the transfer of $30 per month to the potential parasite (Row 2). To the other person in the interaction, there are also two courses of action open. He may work (Column 1), in which case we may assume he earns an income, say, one-fourth as large as that earned by the more capable samaritan (or more talented or more lucky). Or, the potential parasite may refuse work (Column 2).

As indicated earlier in the discussion of the nonidentified game, an outcome in Cell IV might be predicted to emerge as the continuing solution of the sequential game unless the samaritan recognizes the strategic prospects open to him and begins to behave accordingly. But this may be difficult for him. Vague threats or promises to cut off his charity in the absence of work on the part of the recipient parasite will remain empty unless there is demonstrated willingness to carry out such threats. But to carry these out, the samaritan will, in actuality, suffer disutility which may be severe. He may find himself seriously injured by the necessity of watching the parasite starve himself while refusing work. Furthermore, even if the parasite works, the samaritan suffers by his own inability to provide charity. The samaritan's task becomes more difficult to the extent that the parasite also recognizes the game situation and himself responds strategically. If the samaritan's strategic plan is to be at all effective, which requires first of all that credibility be established, he must accept the prospect of personal injury.

A family example may be helpful. A mother may find it too painful to spank a misbehaving child ("This hurts me more than it does you"). Yet spanking may be necessary to instill in the child the fear of punishment that will inhibit future misbehavior. If the temporal interdependence of choice is fully recognized, adjustments in behavior may, of course, be noted. A samaritan's payoff matrix that incorporates present values may not look like that shown in Figure 1. Unfortunately, however, the samaritan's dilemma cannot be resolved fully by appeal to a temporal extension of the rationality postulate. Failure of the samaritan's telescopic faculty may explain much of what we seem to observe, and a correction in this faculty may be important. But such a correction, in itself, cannot remove the dilemma in all cases. Even when she fully discounts the effects of her current action on future choice settings, the mother may still find it too painful to spank the misbehaving child. Behavior that will influence the potential parasite to act in preferred ways must involve short-term utility losses to the samaritan. And if his subjective discount rate is high, present-value payoffs may still indicate that the charitable or acquiescent course of action is the dominating one.

Is there any objective sense in which we may say that the samaritan's discount rate is "too high"? This rate is purely subjective, and it is derived solely from the person's intertemporal utility function. It seems improper to label any rate as "too high" without resort to some externally based "social welfare function."

We might, for example, say that a person's portfolio adjustment reflects irrationality if he is observed to be borrowing at, say, 10 percent, while simultaneously lending at 5 percent, transaction costs neglected. Rational behavior implies that marginal rates of return on all alternatives be equalized.

It is not clear, however, just how a discount rate appropriate for portfolio adjustment might be brought into equality with that which is implicit in a person's intertemporal behavioral tradeoffs, nor is it self-evident that a rationality postulate implies such equalization. Will the mother vary the severity of child discipline as the real rate of return of investment varies? If she does not, the hypothesis of equalization is refuted. This would, in turn, allow for the possibility that observed behavior of persons in samaritan-like settings reflects discount rates greatly in excess of those to which these same persons adjust their portfolios. Unfortunately, there seems to be no direct means to corroborate or to refute this proposition.

When the illusory nature of the short-term utility losses dictated by strategic behavior is fully recognized, the rationality of applying almost any positive discount rate may be questioned. For the samaritan, utility losses are directly related to the potential parasite's disbelief in his strategic plan. To the extent that the parasite believes that the samaritan has, in fact, adopted a strategic behavioral plan and that he will, in fact, abide by this plan once adopted, there need be *no* utility loss to the samaritan at all. The situation is one where the samaritan must convince the potential parasite of his willingness to suffer utility loss in order to insure that the expected value of this loss be effectively minimized.

An understanding of the dilemma confronted by those whom I have called "active samaritans" points directly toward means through which credibility can be increased and/or utility loss reduced. In the setting described, there should be genuine advantages to be gained by the samaritan from locking himself into a strategic behavior pattern in advance of any observed response on the part of his cohort. A Schelling-type advance commitment may be central to the more sophisticated rationality that is dictated here.[1] This may be accomplished in several ways. The samaritan can, in the first place, delegate the power of decision in particular choice situations to an agent, one who is instructed to act in accordance with the strategic norms that are selected in advance. The agency device serves two purposes simultaneously.

---

1. Cf. Thomas C. Schelling, *The Strategy of Conflict* (Cambridge: Harvard University Press, 1960). Also, see his later paper, "Game Theory and the Study of Ethical Systems," *Journal of Conflict Resolution* 12 (March 1968): 34–44. This paper raises somewhat indirectly the central issues discussed here. See in particular p. 40.

The potential parasite is more likely to believe that the agent will behave in accordance with instructions. Secondly, by delegating the action to the agent, the samaritan need not subject himself to the anguish of situational response which may account for a large share of the anticipated utility loss.

We may return to our family example. The mother may delegate child-spanking to the nanny, with definite and clear instructions for spanking upon specific instances of misbehavior. This delegation increases the child's awareness of the consequences of misbehavior. At the same time, it removes from the mother the actual suffering which personal infliction of punishment might involve. The nonspanking, misbehaving option (Cell IV) is effectively eliminated from the mother's choice set as well as the child's.

In general terms, the analysis points toward the choice of utility-maximizing rules for personal behavior as opposed to the retention of single-period or single-situation choice options. Having once adopted a rule, the samaritan *should not* be responsive to the particulars of situations that might arise. He should not act pragmatically and on a case-by-case basis. The argument specifically confutes the rationality of situational ethics in samaritan-like settings.

Practical examples are readily available. Standards for determining welfare eligibility, either for governmental or private programs, should not be left to the discretion of social workers who get personally involved with potential recipients. This institutional arrangement would force social workers into an acutely painful form of the dilemma discussed. University administrators should not enter into direct dialogues with "concerned" students and faculty members. By so doing, the administrators invite difficulties which might be avoided by detached adherence to preselected rules.

IV.

Much of the analysis can be extended directly to the problem confronted by "passive samaritans," the second game discussed. In the case with the active samaritan, pragmatic or nonstrategic behavior by both parties produces results that are not desired by the samaritan. He must first recognize the game that he plays and then behave strategically. In contrast with this, the passive samaritan finds himself in an optimally preferred position so long as *both* players continue to behave nonstrategically. In the illustrative matrix of Figure 2, the only change from Figure 1 is the transposition of the samaritan's utility payoff indicators between Cell I and Cell III.

So long as the potential parasite fails to recognize the game setting, he will view Column 1 as his only alternative. The outcome in Cell I will be stable over a sequence of choices. The dilemma of the passive samaritan emerges only when the potential parasite wakes up to his strategic prospects while the samaritan is left sleeping at the switch. If the parasite begins to adopt a Column 2 course of action, the samaritan who responds pragmatically will modify his own behavior to avoid the threatened utility loss of Cell II. As a result, the outcome will settle in Cell IV. Once in this situation, the passive samaritan's position becomes fully analogous to that confronting the active samaritan previously discussed. He must recognize that he is in the game, and he must consider behaving strategically rather than reactively. The analysis points similarly toward the advance selection of rules for behavior, rules that are chosen independently and in advance of particular choice situations.

Real world examples of this model are perhaps even more familiar than the first one, both in international relations and in domestic affairs. Ecuador and Peru seize tuna boats on the presumption that the United States will not itself respond strategically. North Korea captures the *Pueblo*. Terrorists kidnap diplomats in South American countries. Militant students throw Molotov cocktails and burn buildings. Prisoners go on hunger strikes.

V.

In a strict sense the analysis to this point has been limited to interactions between two players with an anticipated sequence of choices. However, as the several examples possibly suggest, the problem discussed has much wider applicability. To the extent that comparable choice settings are faced by different players and to the extent that behavior is interdependent, the implications can be readily extended.

Consider, first, a setting where a samaritan is confronted with only one choice vis-à-vis a single opponent. Simple utility maximization will be indicated only if a comparable choice with some other opponent is not anticipated, or, if such is anticipated, there are no behavioral interdependencies. On the other hand, if the samaritan expects to confront a whole set of possible parasites, one at a time, and if he predicts that his own choice behavior in confronting any one will influence the behavior of others, the motivation for considering the prospects for strategic behavior is as strong as or stronger than in the simpler sequential choices with a single opponent. Most instructors are familiar with instances in which modification of the grade of a single complaining student offers the short-run utility-maximizing course of action. Experienced instructors will recognize, however, that this behavior will increase the number of student complaints generally, and that long-run utility maximization may require rigid adherence to some sort of no-grade-change rule.

So long as the interdependence anticipated is that among the treatment of different cohorts of the single persons in a samaritan-like setting, we may remain within an individualistic decision model. More relevant implications emerge, however, when interdependencies among the behavior patterns of different samaritans are recognized as pervasive. Each samaritan may find himself confronted with the necessity of making a once-and-for-all choice concerning his treatment of a single potential parasite. The uniqueness of this choice insures that there are no direct future-period consequences; simple utility-maximizing behavior dictates that the samaritan take the soft option. If other persons are expected to confront similar choices with respect to other potential parasites, and if the treatment afforded in one setting modifies the expectations of payoff from similar ones, the dilemma becomes a "public" or "social" one rather than "private." In this case, self-interest on the part of an individual samaritan might never imply strategic behavior of the sort discussed. The rules describing such behavior become fully analogous to "public goods" in that the person producing them secures only a small portion (zero in the limit) of the benefits. His action confers external economies on remaining samaritans in the community, on all those who might anticipate being placed in comparable situations.

Airplane hijacking provides a single dramatic example. A single captain is unexpectedly confronted with a choice, and simple utility maximization dictates accession to the demands of the hijacker. Nonetheless, the benefits to the whole community of airline captains (and other members of the community) from a no-surrender course of action may far exceed the more concentrated possible losses. Strategic courage exercised by a single captain or crew member may generate spillover benefits to all others who might face hijacking threats. This will occur if the predictions of potential hijackers are modified and if their behavior is adjusted accordingly. This direction of effect can be denied only if all elements of rationality are assumed absent in potential hijackers' choices.

VI.

Avoidance of the samaritan's dilemma in its "public" form can be secured by voluntary adherence to individual rules of conduct or by explicit cooperative action to impose such rules. Voluntary acceptance of what we may call "responsible" standards requires that acting parties behave in ways different from those indicated by direct and apparent self-interest. Some pressure toward following such rules will exist if persons fully recognize the interdependence among behavior patterns, that is, if they acknowledge the generalized game setting in which they find themselves. An individual ethic of responsibility is akin to the Kantian generalization principle, although here it is necessarily limited to the group of potential samaritans in the community.

Individual adherence to such an ethic has in no way disappeared from the modern scene. Its widely observed appearance may, however, be explained as an anachronistic carryover from earlier periods rather than as a reflection of voluntarily chosen current commitment. At least two influences have been at work to undermine motivations for responsible behavior in the sense defined here. An individual's motivation for behaving so as to influence the behavior of others in the direction of generating preferred outcomes for the all-inclusive community varies inversely with the size of the group.[2] The expected influence of any one person's behavior on that of others diminishes sharply as numbers are increased. Beyond some critical size limit, the individual who finds himself in a samaritan-like setting must rationally treat the behavior of others, parasites and samaritans alike, as beyond his power of influence. When this point is reached, the pattern of behavior in others is accepted as a parameter for his own choice; others' actions become a part of the "state of nature" that the individual confronts. The game setting disap-

2. See James M. Buchanan, "Ethical Rules, Expected Values, and Large Numbers," *Ethics* 76 (October 1965): 1–13. See also Mancur Olson, *The Logic of Collective Action* (Cambridge: Harvard University Press, 1965).

pears in his subjective calculus, and there are no rationally derived reasons for behaving with the strategic courage that the community may require.

The effective size of community has become larger over time, and this size factor has been reinforced by a complementary influence. Western societies have been increasingly "democratized" in the sense that a larger and larger proportion of the potential membership has been effectively enfranchised in the formation of the social environment. The power of an "establishment," a possibly small and well-defined group of "leaders" to set patterns of behavior that might then serve as norms for others has been reduced, often dramatically. A familiar descriptive cliché classifies the modern age as one without heroes. Without heroes to emulate, each man "does his own thing."

VII.

The quasi-revolutionary shift in modern behavioral standards that widespread adherence to the responsibility ethic would represent does not seem likely to occur. Indeed all signs point in the opposing direction, and we shall probably witness a continuing erosion in strategic courage at all levels of decision.[3] There may be no escape from the generalized samaritan's dilemma, in its public form, except through the collective adoption and enforcement of rules that will govern individual situational responses. As they are applied, such rules must be coercive, and they must act to limit individual freedom of action. This need not, however, imply that individuals may not freely agree to their adoption at some prechoice, or constitutional stage of deliberation. Indeed, if the public form of the dilemma is a genuine one, it will be in the potential interest of most members of the community to adopt some such rules.[4] The implied limitations on individual freedom of response

3. Implicit in this whole analysis is my own attitude that "improvement" lies in reversing the direction of change, in escaping, wholly or partially, from the samaritan's dilemma. This value judgment may, of course, be rejected. Even if the analysis is fully accepted, and the vulnerability to exploitation acknowledged, the benefits from behavior that reflects increased "compassion" generally may be judged larger than the costs that would be involved in any attempt to encourage more discrimination in personal choices.

4. For a general discussion of the distinction between the constitutional stage and the operational stage of choice-making, see James M. Buchanan and Gordon Tullock, *The Calculus of Consent* (Ann Arbor: University of Michigan Press, 1962).

which such rules must embody are no different, conceptually, from those limitations that are embodied in the necessity to pay taxes for the financing of jointly consumed public goods and services.

If the collectivity acts to impose uniform behavioral rules on all potential samaritans, and if these rules are observed to be enforced, the response patterns of potential parasites will be modified. As a result, the whole community of potential samaritans enjoys the benefits. Examples may be found in university administration or in airplane hijacking. Separate university administrators in, say, a statewide or nationwide system may welcome the imposition of uniform rules for dealing with militant students, rules which effectively bind their own choice-making under pressure. Similarly, separate airline companies may welcome the imposition of governmental regulations regarding countermeasures against potential hijackers, despite the fact that no company would find it profitable to introduce such measures independently.

It should be evident both from the analysis and from the examples that the samaritan's dilemma as it appears often involves a mixture of its several forms. There may be an expected sequence of choices with the same potential parasite such that the samaritan is placed in a dilemma of the sort discussed in Section I. At the same time, however, the samaritan may expect to confront a series of decisions with respect to different potential parasites. Furthermore, he may also recognize that some effects of his own behavior will impose potential costs or benefits on other potential samaritans. Once again, the university provides a good example. Administrative officials, faced with a single disruptive group, know that they must make decisions over a sequence of events. To the extent that they expect to be confronted by the same group, they are, in the personal or private version of the dilemma, discussed in Section I. They may recognize, however, that their own behavior with respect to the single group will also affect the behavior of other groups which they may confront in subsequent periods. Finally, who can doubt but that the choice behavior of administrators on one campus exerts significant effects on disruptive activity on other campuses?

Because the dilemma appears mixed in several forms there are interdependencies in corrective adjustments. The adoption of individual rules for behavior aimed at removing the personal dilemma does much toward resolving the group or social dilemma that may exist simultaneously. Strategic utility maximization may reduce the necessity of reliance on an explicit ethic of responsibility. Conversely, general acceptance of this ethic makes personal calculations of optimal strategies less necessary, and resort to collective action less important. On the other hand, collective selection and enforcement of uniform codes of conduct reduces the pressure on the individual to select either an economically or an ethically optimal course of action. The dilemma is most pervasive in a situation where individuals do not maximize utility in the strategic sense, where they do not adhere to an ethic of responsibility, and where no collective action is taken toward laying down jointly preferred codes of conduct. Perhaps this describes modern society all too well.

VIII.

Increasing economic affluence is only one among many explanations for the pervasive importance of the phenomenon that I have called the samaritan's dilemma in twentieth-century Western society. As incomes have increased, and as the stock of wealth has grown, men have increasingly found themselves able to take the "soft options."[5] Mothers can afford candy to bribe misbehaving children. Welfare rolls can be increased dramatically without national bankruptcy.

The economic explanation may, however, be dwarfed in significance by other historical developments. The influence of organized religion in earlier periods was exerted in the direction of inhibiting personal behavior that was aimed solely at gratification of instant desires, whether these be charitable or selfish. There is content in the "Puritan ethic," and when this is interpreted

---

5. In earlier and impoverished epochs, survival may have depended on man's willingness and ability to make strategic choices, and evolutionary selectivity may have instilled behavioral characteristics in man that remain irrational in modern environments. As these characteristics disappear from observed behavior patterns, the necessity for conscious recognition of the dilemma increases.

Benjamin Klein has suggested that the sheer animal instinct for protecting property, which has been emphasized by Robert Ardrey and others, may serve an important "social" purpose in inhibiting courses of action that seem to be preferred in a short-term or nonstrategic context.

In more general terms, Schelling discusses at some length the role of instincts in imposing constraints on behavior. Cf. "Game Theory and the Study of Ethical Systems," in *The Strategy of Conflict*, 36–39.

favorably, it resembles the ethic of responsibility suggested above. As it was institutionally represented, Christian "love" was "love of God" which was effectively translated into a set of precepts for personal behavior.

It is difficult to be optimistic about the prospects for escaping the samaritan's dilemma. There are few if any signs of a return to the behavioral standards of a half-century past. If anything, short-term utility maximization seems on the ascendancy, and even for the individual, long-term utility maximization seems less characteristic of behavior now than in periods that are past.[6] Individuals who find themselves in positions comparable to that of the samaritans in the models of this paper seem unwilling to behave strategically or to adopt rules of conduct that will achieve the differing outcomes through time.

There is little to be observed in the behavior of collective units to counter the individualistic patterns of selecting the soft options. There might be grounds for guarded optimism if we should observe collectivities laying down rules for personal behavior in those situations where individual norms have not appeared. What we see is just the opposite. Collectivities, in their separate arms and instruments, are expanding the soft options. They seem everywhere to be loosening up on prescribed rules for behavior, and, in this way, they encourage similar reactions on the part of individuals. When the conventional wisdom of government is exemplified in the slogan "kindness for the criminals," we can hardly expect individuals to become enforcers. The correspondence between the individual and collective responses might be predicted. Governments do little more than reflect the desires of their citizens, and the taking of soft options on the part of individuals should be expected to be accompanied by an easing up on legal restrictions on individual behavior.

The phenomenon analyzed here takes on its most frightening aspects in its most general biological setting. A species that increasingly behaves, individually and collectively, so as to encourage more and more of its own members to live parasitically off and/or deliberately exploit its producers faces

6. Interestingly in this connection, it is precisely short-term utility maximization, as opposed to long-term utility maximization, that E. C. Banfield singles out to be characteristic of the lower classes. In this context, and if my predictions are correct, what we are witnessing is a transition into lower class habits on a massive and pervasive scale. Cf. E. C. Banfield, *The Unheavenly City* (Boston: Little Brown, 1970).

self-destruction at some point in time. Unless an equilibrium is established which imposes self-selected limits on samaritan-like behavior, the rush toward species destruction may accelerate rather than diminish. The limit that is defined by existing utility functions may lie beyond that which is required for maintaining viable social order. By some leap of biological faith, we may believe that behavior will be constrained to insure species survival. I can conceive of no such leap of faith which might allow us to predict that our innate behavior patterns must preserve a social-civil order that is at all similar to that which we have historically experienced.

I conclude with a paradox. If you find yourself in basic agreement with me, my hypothesis is at least partially falsified. Agreement would signal that you are fully aware of the dilemma that I have discussed, and your awareness could be taken as reflective of general awareness in the academic community.

On the other hand, and I suspect this is the case, if you find yourself in basic disagreement with me, my hypothesis is at least partially corroborated. Disagreement would signal your failure to recognize the dilemma, along with your implied willingness to submit to further exploitation than we yet have witnessed.

The Supply of Labour
and the Extent of the Market

The greatest improvement in the productive powers of labour, and the greater part of the skill, dexterity, and judgment with which it is anywhere directed, or applied, seems to have been the effects of the division of labour.

(I, i, 1)

As it is the power of exchanging that gives occasion to the division of labour, so the extent of this division must always be limited by the extent of that power, or, in other words, by the extent of the market.

(I, iii, 1)

Introduction

As these early, and familiar, statements in *The Wealth of Nations* make clear, Adam Smith sought to ground his argument for widening the exchange nexus on the increase in the production of economic value that extended specialization makes possible. Smith's primary targets were the restrictions on voluntary exchanges imposed by ill-advised mercantilist policies. The elimination of restrictions on trade effectively extends the market, thereby allowing for the exploitation of previously unrealized gains from specialization.

From *Adam Smith's Legacy: His Place in the Development of Modern Economics*, ed. Michael Fry (London: Routledge, 1992), 104–16. Reprinted by permission of the publisher.

Smith did not, to my knowledge, attend to the prospect for extending the market along the internal work-leisure margins of individualized choice.[1] If, however, gains are there to be secured by the mere opening up of markets, there must also be gains to be realized from a generalized increase in the quantities of input, specifically labour input, supplied to the exchange or market nexus. By supplying more inputs to the market in exchange for the increments in income that will, in turn, be expended on the goods and services generated in the market, individuals may, internally, extend the size of the network. An economy in which there are one million workers who supply, on average, forty hours of work per week, is twice the size of an economy, other things being equal, in which the same one million workers supply, on average, twenty hours of work per week.

In this paper, I shall concentrate on this internal means of extending the size of the market. I shall first defend the basic proposition that the size of the market can indeed be extended through such internal means. This defence will require a definition of the necessary conditions under which such extension in market size does generate the Smithian results. Under the existence of such conditions, independent individual choices between work effort supplied to the market and leisure need not generate Pareto optimal results, even when all of the standard requirements are met. Relevant external economies may remain in voluntaristic equilibrium. I shall argue that one means of internalizing these externalities is through the instillation and maintenance of a work ethic. By making work praiseworthy and leisure blameworthy, at least over some relevant ranges in labour supply, participants may effectively internalize the external economy that the Smithian theorem on the extent of the market implies.

Adam Smith would not quarrel with my argument here, nor indeed would most modern economists when they present the elementary principles of their discipline to general audiences in the very first chapters of their textbooks. On the other hand, and by contrast, many modern economists

---

1. Adam Smith did, of course, make the somewhat confused distinction between productive and unproductive labour, which may, in some stretch of imaginative generosity, be interpreted as a recognition of the relevance of the internal choice margin. For a fascinating treatment of the productive-unproductive distinction in the history of economics, see Helen Boss, *Theories of Surplus and Transfer: Parasites and Producers in Economic Thought* (Boston: Unwin and Hyman, 1990).

would find it difficult to reconcile these elementary Smithian principles with the centre notion of competitive equilibrium, a notion that occupies so much attention in later chapters of the self-same textbooks. The formal conditions required for competitive equilibrium must be adjusted, in some fashion, to accommodate the theorem that economic value increases with an extension of the market. The contradiction between two widely accepted principles necessarily comes into attention when internal rather than external increases in market size are examined at all closely.

"Production" for Own Consumption as a Non-tradeable Good

International trade theorists make a categorical distinction between goods (and services) that are tradeable across the boundaries of national economies and goods (and services) that are non-tradeable, with the latter being produced exclusively for domestic consumption or final end-use. To my knowledge the fully analogous distinction between tradeable and non-tradeable goods at the level of each individualized "economy" has not been emphasized, at least not sufficiently that its implications for the extent of the market, and, hence, for potential gains from the division of labour, have been widely recognized. The international trade theorist would not question the proposition that a shift from the production of non-tradeables to the production of tradeables would facilitate an extension of the trading network among nations and that such an extension would make possible increased international specialization, with consequent aggregate increases in economic value. Indeed, Adam Smith's central message might well be interpreted as a variant of this proposition. To the extent that artificially maintained political restrictions reduce the effective set of potentially tradeable goods, a removal of such restrictions will enhance the wealth of citizens.

The analogous proposition seems, however, to be much less acceptable, or at least analytically more challenging, when applied to the "economy" of each single owner of a potentially productive resource. The basic distinction between the utilization of a resource for trade, that is, for the production of goods or services entered into market exchange, and the utilization of a resource for own consumption, that is, for production of something that is internally used, may be made here. Owners of resources, or resource capacities, may (if they are free to choose) supply these resource units to the market, directly or indirectly, or they may withhold such units from the market, thereby "producing" for own or internal consumption.

The implications of the distinction here may assume important practical relevance only for labour, where non-market utilization, at least over some ranges of potential supply, is presumed to produce "goods" that are of positive value to the owner-supplier-chooser. The individual, as holder-owner of labour capacity, faces a choice between offering this capacity (or any part thereof) to the market, either by producing goods directly for sale to others, or by selling capacity, as such, to others (persons, firms) who combine such purchases of inputs to organize the production of goods finally offered for sale, and withholding this capacity, thereby "producing" something that is of value internally, whether this be leisure in the sense of inactivity or the active pursuit of other preferred end-uses of effort.

The simple point to be made here is that the choices made by individuals along the work-leisure margin determine the extent of the market or exchange nexus, and, through this, the degree of specialization to be potentially exploited. That part of resource capacity that is withheld from the market for own use is non-tradeable and, therefore, places a limit on the overall size of the tradeables sector. The point becomes obvious when placed in an extreme setting. If all persons in a community should choose to become fully self-sufficient and, hence, to withhold all resource capacity from exchange, there could be no specialization at all.

Work and Welfare

Note that, in the analytical construction suggested, leisure, inclusively defined as the non-supply of work to the market, remains a "good" as a positively valued argument in the individual's utility function. But the choice made by the individual between this "good" and other goods that are demanded indirectly through the supply of work effort to the market must exert an external effect on others through the impact on the extent of the market itself. Each supplier of work, at the margin, exerts an external economy on others in the economy. By supplying more hours, days, weeks, or years, to the market, the individual who so acts benefits others indirectly through the extension of the market that results from the expenditure of income incrementally earned on marketed goods and services, that is, on tradeables.

Further, the external economy may be Pareto relevant in that some generalized agreement among all input suppliers, and output demanders, may be worked out which will involve more input supply and which will generate results that benefit all parties. (I abstract here from all sectoral effects where differential relationships of complementarity and substitutability, that stem, in part, from non-homogeneity among inputs, may obscure the underlying effect that I want to emphasize. Ideally, appropriate compensations could always be worked out and implemented so as to insure that the beneficial effects from the extension in market size are enjoyed by every market participant.)

The claim here is that the market, even in competitive equilibrium, is not a "moral free zone," to use David Gauthier's terminology.[2] Choices made by individuals reciprocally exert an impact on each other. This result seems to contrast dramatically with that part of conventional competitive theory which concentrates on the demonstration of the Pareto optimality properties of the idealized competitive equilibrium, sustained by the voluntary choices of all participants. The optimality property stems, of course, from the idealized conditions imposed on the presumed interaction process, one of which must deny the applicability of the fundamental Smithian theorem concerning the effects of market extension. Among the idealized conditions for the optimality of competitive equilibrium, there is the requirement that all production takes place under constant returns.

Note that, under constant returns, a change in the size of the market, whether generated internally or externally, does not modify the price vector of inputs relative to outputs. There is no Pareto relevant external economy involved in a decision made by one person to supply more units of work input to the marketplace. In so doing, the person in question secures the *full* value of the increment of output that the action generates. There is no effect, positive or negative, on the economic position of anyone else in the exchange nexus. The market is, indeed, "moral free" in this setting, and no one need

2. David Gauthier, *Morals by Agreement* (Oxford: Oxford University Press, 1985).

express or feel concern as to the choices made by others along the work-leisure, or any other, margin.

The generation of this result, whether expressed in optimality-efficiency or in moral-free terms, must necessarily deny the existence of any overall increase in economic value associated with a generalized increase in the size of the market. The range of applicability for gains from the division of labour, from specialization, must be presumed to have been exhausted at some size of the economy smaller than that which operates to produce the idealized competitive equilibrium. But economists seem to have devoted little effort to any attempts to specify even some proximate sizes at which specialization ceases to generate gains, sizes that must, if indeed they should exist, depend critically on the state of technology and other socio-political variables.[3]

Generalized Increasing Returns

The minimal departure from the setting for competitive equilibrium that is required to accommodate the basic Smithian theorem on the extent of the market involves some allowance for increasing returns to the production of tradeable goods in the economy, but these increasing returns need not take the form that is most familiar to economists. And I should stipulate here that my interest lies exclusively in the minimally required departures from the conditions for idealized competitive equilibrium; the possible presence and extent of increasing returns of the garden-variety sort, as might be empirically observed, falls outside the area of interest of this paper.

We can approach the issues here initially by reference to Marshallian external economies in production, although, even here, the analogy is somewhat misleading. In the Marshallian setting, firms in an industry produce competitively without knowledge that their costs depend, inversely, on the size of industry output. Individual firms have, therefore, no incentive to ex-

---

3. In a curiously inconclusive paper, "The Division of Labor Is Limited by the Extent of the Market," *Journal of Political Economy* 59 (June 1951): 185–93, George Stigler fully appreciates the analytic dilemma here, but he seems to want to accept both the validity of Smith's theorem and the usefulness of the competitive equilibrium constructions. This stance is, perhaps, justified in part by Stigler's primary interest in the implications for the organization of industry.

pand particular output so as to capture industry-wide advantages of scale. The generalized increasing returns that will allow for the applicability of the Smithian theorem need not show up in any Marshallian sense, at least not *ex ante*. For the increase in the extent of the market, for all tradeable goods, to generate increases in economic value, properly measured, returns must be increasing (costs must decrease) *somewhere* in the economy, but the identification of the location of this source of gain may not be possible until *after* the expansion of demand that calls additional production (in such an industry and elsewhere) into being.

Consider the following scenario. Assume that, for any reason, there is a generalized increase in the supply of work effort; persons offer more hours of work at the going wages, and institutional barriers do not prevent their implementation of these choices. Persons in the economy, generally, are observed to work harder than before the change. But persons who have supplied the additional quantity of labour inputs to the market have presumably done so for the purpose of being able to purchase an increased quantity of output from the market. Suppliers are motivated by the prospect of becoming demanders. Say's law is surely valid at this juncture of the analysis. Supply emerges only because it enables its own demand to become possible.

The additional income secured from the sale of additional input returns to the market as additional demand for market-produced tradeable output. This extension in demand, which is matched by the initiating increase in supply that made it possible, will create the potential for the exploitation of further specialization, *in some production*, that remained just below the margin of economic variability in the pre-change equilibrium. The real cost of production in the affected industry falls (measured in minimally necessary quantities of inputs required to produce any given output). But the firms in the affected industry, or anywhere else in the economy, need not have been able to identify in advance which industry would experience the increasing returns. And, even if prior identification could have been made, the full exploitation of the scale advantages would not have been possible without the increase in demand in the economy generally.[4]

---

4. Identification of the increasing-returns industry (or industries) would, of course, make possible efficiency-enhancing *shifts* in demand patterns, within an overall fixity in

My emphasis here is on the *demand-side* source of possible opportunity to exploit gains from specialization, a source that stems initially from the proceeds of the sale of additional inputs to the market. In his seminal paper on increasing returns, Allyn Young stressed that "buying power" is what "constitutes a large market."[5] My emphasis is exclusively microeconomic, but there are also analytical affinities between the argument sketched out and that developed by Martin Weitzman, whose interests and emphases are exclusively macroeconomic.[6] His argument suggests that generalized increasing returns can offer plausible microeconomic foundations for understanding the emergence of quasi-competitive unemployment equilibria. In particular, Weitzman notes the contradiction between the Smithian emphasis on the division of labour and the constant returns condition in standard competitive theory. Earlier, N. Kaldor stressed the same point in the context of a generalized critique of equilibrium theory.[7]

Characteristics of the Work-Supply Externality

The particular characteristics of the work-supply externality analysed here warrant more detailed discussion. First, the externality need not be identified by any such attributes as location, occupation, or industry classification. The behavioural margin of relevance involves the supply of productive effort to the exchange nexus at any point and at any level of productivity, although, of course, the more productive the effort, the larger the external economies. It is worth stressing, in particular, that the operating features of the industry within which the work-leisure choice is made are totally irrelevant. The external economy emerges from all work-leisure choice margins, whether in increasing, constant, or decreasing returns to industries. The increase in

---

input utilization. But there would remain some remaining gains to be captured by expanded input supply.

5. Allyn Young, "Increasing Returns and Economic Progress," *Economic Journal* 38 (1928): 527–42.

6. Martin Weitzman, "Increasing Returns and the Foundations of Unemployment Theory," *Economic Journal* 92 (December 1982): 787–804.

7. N. Kaldor, "The Irrelevance of Equilibrium Economics," *Economic Journal* 82 (1972): 1237–55.

value to the overall nexus exerts its external effect only as and when the input supplier returns the added value to the market as a consumer-purchaser, generating thereby an increase in effective demand. If the extent of the market limits the potential for deriving the advantages of specialization, at least one industry in the totality that describes the production-exchange nexus must exhibit increasing returns of the sort indicated. And the direct or primary beneficiaries stemming from the increase in effective demand are those persons who include in their consumption portfolio the goods so produced.

The externality identified here differs from those that are more often treated in welfare economics in at least two basic characteristics. There need be no relation of contiguity, locational or otherwise, between the generator of the external effect and the recipients of the benefit (or harm). By comparison, consider a few familiar examples. The pollution of the river reduces the fishing and swimming opportunities for those who live downstream. The resident who maintains a fine flower garden increases the utility of the neighbours. Coasian cattle trample the crops of nearby wheatgrowers. Marshallian firms are in the same industry. On the other hand, the work-supply externality is potentially economy-wide. The individuals who supply additional work generate value to persons who may be "far away" in all dimensions.

A second difference between the work-supply externality and others that are more familiar lies in the way in which the benefits (or harms) enter the utility functions of those who are externally affected. If the good, X_i, exhibits increasing returns, then, consequent on an increased production of X_i, the externality affects all purchasers of X_i through a reduction in the price, P_i. There is no effect directly on the utility function analogous to that generated by the addition of floral splendour by the neighbouring gardener or the production of honey by the nearby bees. The consumer-purchaser of X_i finds the budget constraint shifted by the change in price. And this price effect is not, in this case, offset by a compensating price shift elsewhere in the economy, as faced by this or any other purchaser. The effect emerges as a pure price change, in real terms, made possible by the increase in aggregate supply of valued productive capacity to the economic nexus. Here the analyst must resist the temptation to disregard the externality because it enters the utility function through price. In the traditional terminology, the externality is "technological," and, hence, Pareto relevant, because it expands the choice set of some persons in the nexus, without fully offsetting restrictions in the choice sets of others.

Two emendations to the conventional externality logic can be helpful in facilitating an understanding of the work-supply effect. If we assume that consumption is generalized in the sense that all final goods are included in each participant's preferred consumption bundle, then everyone in the economic nexus, in the role of final user of the good produced under conditions of increasing returns, becomes a beneficiary of the increase in the supply of work effort on the part of any worker in the whole system. Or, if we introduce a model of household production, where Beckerian Z goods are "produced" with an appropriate set of X goods directly purchased from the market, then any reduction in the price of an X good modifies the production function for some Z good, making the externality appear analogous to those that are more familiar with the orthodox analysis.

Internalization through a Work Ethic

In a more extended treatment, I have discussed in some detail the alternative means through which the work-supply externality might be internalized.[8] In that discussion, I have suggested that none of three familiar institutional means of correction seem likely to prove effective, largely because of the economy-wide nature of the external effects. Coasian bargaining, politicized correction, and spontaneous institutional evolution—all of these avenues for possible internalization seem to be severely limited in application. We are left with a fourth choice, that which involves an internalization of the work-supply externality through the installation, maintenance and transmission of an ethical precept that will effectively modify the constraint set that describes individual choice between work and non-work.

It is difficult to introduce ethical or moral constraints into the analytical apparatus of the economic theory of choice.[9] The person who supplies work

8. James M. Buchanan, "Economic Interdependence and the Work Ethic" (Center for Study of Public Choice, George Mason University, 1989, duplicated).

9. David Levy, "Utility Enhancing Consumption Constraints," *Economics and Philosophy* 4 (1988): 69–88.

to the market appears simply to adjust quantities of supply to the parametric wage per time unit that is confronted. It is possible, however, to depict the effect of an ethical precept if we modify the constraint set appropriately as illustrated in Figure 1. The indifference contours represent the relative evaluation of the two arguments, leisure (non-work) and income (other goods purchasable from the market). The market wage to which the individual adjusts hours (days, weeks) of work supply is shown by the slope of the line *BY*. This line need not, however, represent the effective constraint set for the chooser if there exists an ethical norm which makes a sense of guilt emerge when work supply falls below certain minimal limits. The presence of a work ethic may modify the effective constraints for the person to produce the kinked frontier, *YMR*. Over the range, *MR*, the individual suffers an internalized psychic cost. In this setting, the individual attains his maximum utility at the corner solution, *M*. Given the ethical constraint that is presumed to be operative, the position *E*, which could seem to maximize utility, is simply unavailable.

If the individual could, in some fashion, escape from the binding constraint of the work ethic, and if this were possible *in isolation*, the preferred position at *E* might seem to be feasible. But note that, if *all* persons in the economy should similarly escape from the ethical constraint, *E* would no

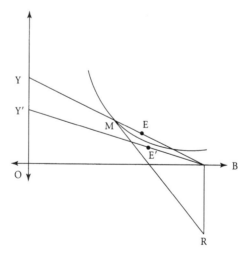

Figure 1. Effect of an ethical precept

longer be available. As all persons reduce the supply of work as might be dictated by their pure naked preferences, the extent of the market would shrink, and, by the Smithian theorem, the exploitable range of specialization would be reduced. Wage rates would fall to some position such as that shown by the line BY'; individual equilibrium would be reached at E', which, by construction, lies on a preference contour lower than that which passes through M. If generalized over all work suppliers in the economy, the existence of the ethical constraint allows for at least some internalization of the externality.

I have, of course, deliberately constructed the figure to demonstrate the projected result. Clearly, as further geometric manipulation could show, the constraint that is exercised by a generalized work ethic might be so strong as to produce results less preferable than those attainable in total absence of such constraint, even given the extent of the market influence on resource productivity. The construction does suggest, however, that, so long as the Smithian theorem applies, the noninternalized voluntaristic equilibrium must remain non-optimal. From this result it follows that, within limits, the presence of some constraining influence of a work ethic must be deemed to be efficiency-enhancing.

Work as Benevolent Self-Interest

Perhaps the single most familiar statement in *The Wealth of Nations* is that which tells us that "it is not from the benevolence of the butcher, the brewer, or the baker, that we expect our dinner, but from their regard to their own interest" (I, ii, 2). We understand Adam Smith's argument here, but if we take the conventional theory of distribution in the competitive economy seriously we immediately sense an apparent contradiction. If the butcher, and everyone else, takes from the economy precisely the equivalent of the value added to the economy by their efforts, how do we benefit from individuals' self-interested behaviour?

Suppose that the butcher decides to retire early and to go fishing, and that he does so out of strict self-interest. How will this change in his behaviour affect the rest of us? Not at all in the long-term sense if we accept the marginal productivity theory of distribution and assume that the economy is effectively competitive. The size of the market will become a mite smaller upon the butcher's retirement, but after other butchers expand their scales of operation, prices will return to the same levels that existed before the butcher ceased to butch.

I have argued that the conventional theory of competitive adjustment must surely be in error in this inference, and that we must look for ways to modify the conventional reasoning to allow for some accommodation of Smith's central theorem concerning the gains from trade that an extended division of labour facilitates. I have sought to show that, in order for the utilities of participants to be affected by a change in the size of the market, some relaxation of the constant returns condition for idealized competitive equilibrium must be effected. There must exist increasing returns in at least one industry in the all-inclusive exchange nexus.

Fortunately for my purposes, I am not required to enter directly into controversial areas of analysis involving the consistency between increasing returns and competitive equilibrium.[10] Nor is it necessary for me to specify, even conceptually, the relative share in total production that may emerge from increasing returns operation, or to identify those industries where increasing returns prevail.

I have suggested that the burden of internalization of the work-supply externality may rest with the embodiment of ethical norms in the work choice. To the extent that an ethic of work enters into the choice calculus of input suppliers, whether or not this be conscious, consumers somewhere in the economy secure spillover benefits. There is economic content in the ethic of work. And because there is economic content, there is some justification for both individualized and collective efforts to promulgate, maintain and transmit this ethic through the culture as well as intergenerationally.

The butcher's benevolent self-interest dictates that work does "good" for others and this is lost when he goes fishing. The anti-work ethic of the 1960s summarized in the admonition "take the time to smell the flowers" involves an explicit invitation to destroy economic value for others than the addressee. And, of course, the size of the external effects is directly related to the market value of the input potentially supplied. A radiologist who loafs

---

10. A general summary of the whole set of increasing-returns controversies, along with appropriate references to the literature, is found in the Palgrave entry of S. Vassilakis, "Increasing Returns to Scale," in *The New Palgrave Dictionary of Economics*, vol. 2, ed. J. Eatwell, M. Milgate, and P. Newman (London: Macmillan, 1987), 761–65.

around harms others more than the comparable behaviour of a McDonald's employee.

I have deliberately limited discussion in this paper to the work-leisure choice along the time unit dimension as the potential source of expansion or contraction in the size of the market. The analysis is obviously applicable to qualitative as well as quantitative dimensions, and to the choices of potential suppliers of resources other than work effort.

My suggestion that the work-supply externality is fully analogous to the "trade extension" externality would not, as noted earlier, be surprising to trade theorists.[11] But the analysis has implications for many other policy areas such as population control, immigration, women's entry into the labour force, work requirements for welfare, and retirement programmes, along with evident inferences for tax institutions. My concern does not, however, extend to the derivation of implications for these policy questions. I limit emphasis here to the work-supply externality, as such, motivated in large part by my initial query concerning the possible economic content in a work ethic. If my purpose must be generalized, it is to convince fellow economists that we remain ethically as well as economically interdependent, along the work-leisure choice margin as along so many others.

11. See W. J. Ethier, "National and International Returns to Scale in the Modern Theory of Institutional Trade," *American Economic Review* 72 (June 1982): 389–405, for useful analysis that also contains references to the international trade literature.

Markets, States,
and the Extent of Morals

Man acts within a set of institutional constraints that have developed historically: in part by sheer accident; in part by survival in a social evolutionary process; in part by technological necessity; in part by constructive design (correctly or incorrectly conceived). These constraints which define the setting within which human behavior must take place may, however, be inconsistent with man's capacities as a genuine "social animal." To the extent that moral-ethical capacities are "relatively absolute,"[1] there may be only one feasible means of reducing the impact of the inconsistency. Attempts must be made to modify the *institutions* (legal, political, social, economic) with the objective of matching these more closely with the empirical realities of man's moral limitations.

In a certain restricted sense, the observed behavior of the modern American is excessively "self-interested." Rather than hope for a "new morality," I shall focus on the potential for institutional reform that may indirectly modify man's behavior toward his fellows. Institutions may have been allowed to develop and to persevere that exacerbate rather than mitigate man's ever present temptation to act as if he is an island, with others treated as part of his natural environment. In a properly qualified sense, the latter pattern of behavior is the economist's "ideal," but the costs have not been adequately recognized.

From *American Economic Review* 68 (May 1978): 364–68. Reprinted by permission of the publisher.

I am indebted to Roger Congleton, Thomas Ireland, Janet Landa, Robert Tollison, and Richard Wagner for helpful suggestions.

1. Reinhold Niebuhr, *Moral Man and Immoral Society* (New York, 1932), 3, 267.

Let me proceed by simple illustration. Consider two traders, each of whom is initially endowed with a commodity bundle. Gains from trade exist and cooperation through trade is suggested, but there arises the complementary conflict over the sharing of net surplus. As we extend the model by introducing additional traders, however, the conflict element of the interaction is squeezed out, and, in the limit, each trader becomes a pure price-taker. "In perfect competition there is no competition," as Frank Knight was fond of emphasizing. (However, we must never lose sight of the elementary fact that this "economic ideal," including its most complex variants, presumes the existence of laws and institutions that secure private property and enforce contracts.)

Let me change the illustration and now assume that the same two persons find themselves in a genuine "publicness" interaction. (They are villagers alongside the swamp, to use David Hume's familiar example.) As before, there exist potential gains from trade, and these can be secured by agreement. Cooperation and conflict again enter to influence choice behavior, but here the introduction of more traders does nothing to squeeze down the range of conflict. Indeed, it does quite the opposite. Beyond some critical limit, each person will come to treat the behavior of others as part of the state of nature that he confronts as something wholly independent of his own actions.

Numbers work in opposing directions in the two cases. Under a set of laws and institutions that are restricted to the security of property and contract, the extension of the market in partitionable goods moves the efficiency frontier of the community outwards. But, under the same laws and institutions, if there exist nonpartitionable interdependencies (public goods), an increase in the size of the group may move the attainable efficiency frontier inwards.

I have introduced the familiar private goods–public goods comparison to illustrate my general argument to the effect that there are opposing behavioral implications involved in any extension in the membership of a community. The effects of group size on choice behavior, and, through this, on the normative evaluation of institutions, have not been sufficiently explored by economists, most of whom have remained content to concentrate on the formal efficiency properties of allocations. With relatively few exceptions they have worked with fixed-sized groups. And even in 1978, most economic policy discussion proceeds on the implicit presumption that "government" is benevolently despotic.[2]

What is the orthodox economists' response when pure public goods are postulated? It is relatively easy to define the formal conditions that are necessary for allocative efficiency, but it is not possible to define the governmental process that might generate these results.[3] Work in public choice theory has contributed to our understanding of how governmental processes actually operate, but this theory is, in a general sense, one of governmental failure rather than success.

Political scientists have objected to the imperialism of public-choice economists who extend utility-maximizing models of behavior to persons who act variously in collective-choice roles, as voters, as politicians, and as bureaucrats. These critics intuitively sense that a polity driven solely by utility maximizers (with empirical content in the maximand) cannot possibly generate an escape from the large number analogue to the prisoners' dilemma suggested in the simple example of a public goods interaction. These critics have not, however, understood the basic causes for the general dilemma that modern collectivist institutions impose on citizens, politicians, and bureaucrats. Even more than the economists, orthodox political scientists have tended to ignore the possible effects of group or community size on individual behavior patterns.

Any political act is, by definition, "public" in the classic Samuelsonian sense. An act of voting by a citizen potentially affects a result that, once determined, will be applied to *all* members of the community. Similarly, an act by a legislator in voting for one tax rule rather than another becomes an input in determining a result that will define the environment for all members of the polity. Comparable conclusions extend to each and every act of a civil servant and to each decision of a judge.[4] Under what conditions could we predict that such political acts will provide public good? For instruction here,

2. Economists have continued for eight decades to ignore the warnings of Knut Wicksell (*Finanztheoretische Untersuchungen* [Jena, 1896]).

3. A possible qualification to this statement is required with reference to the demand-revealing process, summarized by T. Nicolaus Tideman and Gordon Tullock ("A New and Superior Process for Making Social Choice," *Journal of Political Economy* 84 [December 1976]: 1145–60). Even its proponents recognize, however, that this process remains a conceptual ideal rather than an institution capable of practical implementation.

4. See G. Tullock, "Public Decisions as Public Goods," *Journal of Political Economy* 79 (July–August 1971): 913–18.

we can return directly to our elementary example. We should expect at least some such behavior to exhibit cooperative features in effectively small groups. We should not, and could not, expect persons who act politically to provide public good voluntarily in large number settings.

We can reach this conclusion by economic analysis that incorporates standard utility-maximizing behavior on the part of all actors. My principal hypothesis, however, involves the possible inconsistency between man's *moral* capacities and the institutions within which he acts. Is not man capable of surmounting the generalized public goods dilemma of modern politics by moral-ethical principles that will serve to constrain his proclivities toward aggrandizement of his narrowly defined self-interest? It is here that my secondary hypothesis applies. The force of moral-ethical principle in influencing behavior is directly dependent on the size of community within which action takes place. Other things equal, the smaller the number of persons with whom a person interacts, the higher the likelihood that he will seem to behave in accordance with something akin to the Kantian generalization principle: in our terminology, that he will provide public good in his choice behavior.

Even this secondary hypothesis can be discussed in a way as to bring it within a utility-maximizing framework. The extent that a person expects his own behavior to influence the behavior of those with whom he interacts will depend on the size of the group. Hence, utility maximization in a small number setting will not exhibit the observable properties of utility maximization in a large number setting.[5] I want, however, to go beyond this strictly small-group phenomenon of direct behavioral feedback. I want to introduce moral-ethical constraints in a genuine noneconomic context here. I propose to allow *Homo economicus* to exist only as one among many men that describe human action, and, in many settings to assume a tertiary motivation role.

The precise dimension of human behavior that I concentrate on here is the location of the effective mix between the two motivational forces of economic self-interest and what I shall term "community."[6] I do not want to,

5. See J. M. Buchanan, "Ethical Rules, Expected Values, and Large Numbers," *Ethics* 74 (October 1965): 1–13.
6. In a tautological sense, all behavior, including that which I label as moral-ethical, can be analyzed in a utility-maximizing model. In this paper, however, "utility maximization" and "self-interest" are defined operationally.

and I have no need to, identify with any particular variant of nonself-interest: fellowship, brotherhood, Christian love, empathy, Kantian imperative, sympathy, public interest, or anything else. I want only to recognize the existence of a general motive force that inhibits the play of narrowly defined self-interest when an individual recognizes himself to be a member of a group of others more or less like himself. Robinson Crusoe could be motivated by nothing other than self-interest until Friday arrives. Once he acknowledges the existence of Friday, a tension develops and Crusoe finds that his behavior is modified. This tension exists in all human action and observed behavior reflects the outcome of some resolution of the inner conflict. The institutional setting determines the size of community relevant for individual behavior. This influence of size is exerted both directly in the sense of limits to recognition, and indirectly in the relationship between a community's membership and its ability to command personal loyalties. Conceptually, the "structure of community" within which an individual finds himself can shift the location of behavior along a spectrum bounded on one extreme by pure self-interest and on the other by pure community interest within which the actor counts for no more than any other member.

The institutions (economic, geological, legal, political, social, technological), which define the sizes of community within which an individual finds himself, impose *external* bounds on possible behavior. Parallel to these external constraints there are also *internal* limits or bounds on what we may call an individual's moral-ethical community. There are, of course, no sharp categorical lines to be drawn between those other persons whom someone considers to be "members of the tribe" and those whom he treats as "outsiders." I make no such claim. I assert only that, for any given situation, there is a difference in an individual's behavior toward members and nonmembers, and that the membership lists are drawn up in his own psyche. This is not to say either that persons are uniform with respect to their criteria for tribal membership or that these criteria are invariant with respect to exogenous events. Clearly, neither of these inferences will hold. However, the fact of behavioral discrimination is empirical and subject to test. I am not arguing normatively to the effect that individuals should or should not discriminate among other members of the human species, or even as between humans and other animals.

My colleague Tullock enjoys asking egalitarians whether or not they would extend their precepts for social justice to the people of Bangladesh. He gets few satisfactory answers. Why should precepts for distributive justice mysteriously stop at the precise boundaries of the nation-state? If one responds that they need not do so, that national boundaries are arbitrary products of history, then one is led to ask whether or not effective precepts of justice might stop short of such inclusive community, whether or not the moral-ethical limit for most persons is reached short of the size of modern nations.[7] At provincial or regional boundaries? At the local community level? The extended family? The clan? The racial group? The ethnic heritage? The church membership? The functional group?

What can a person be predicted to do when the external institutions force upon him a role in a community that extends beyond his moral-ethical limits? The tension shifts toward the self-interest pole of behavior; moral-ethical principles are necessarily sublimated. The shift is exaggerated when a person realizes that others in the extended community of arbitrary and basically amoral size will find themselves in positions comparable to his own. How can a person act politically in other than his own narrowly defined self-interest in an arbitrarily sized nation of more than 200 millions? Should we be at all surprised when we observe the increasing usage of the arms and agencies of the national government for the securing of private personal gain?

The generalized public goods dilemma of politics can be kept within tolerance limits only if there is some proximate correspondence between the external institutional and the internal moral constraints on behavior.[8] This century may be described by developments that drive these two sets of constraints apart. An increase in population alone reduces the constraining influence of moral rules. Moreover population increase has been accompanied by increasing mobility over space, by the replacement of local by national

---

7. In an argument related to that in this paper, Dennis Mueller concentrates on the relationship between the size of community and the ability of a person to imagine himself behind a Rawlsian veil of ignorance ("Achieving the Just Polity," *American Economic Review Proceedings* 64 [May 1974]: 147–52).

8. Gerald Sirkin refers to the "Victorian compromise" which is, in several respects, similar to the correspondence noted here ("Resource X and the Theory of Retrodevelopment," in *The Economics of Resources*, ed. Robert D. Leiter and Stanley J. Friedlander [New York, 1976], 193–208).

markets, by the urbanization of society, by the shift of power from state-local to national government, and by the increased politicization of society generally. Add to this the observed erosion of the family, the church, and the law—all of which were stabilizing influences that tended to reinforce moral precepts—and we readily understand why *Homo economicus* has assumed such a dominant role in modern behavior patterns.[9]

Indirect evidence for the general shift from morally based resolution of conflict and morally based settlement of terms of cooperation to political-legal instruments is provided by the observed rapidly increasing resort to litigation. Modern man seeks not to live with his neighbor; he seeks instead to become an island, even when his natural setting dictates moral community. This movement, in its turn, prompts lawyers to turn to economic theory for new normative instruction.

Despite the flags and the tall ships of 1976, there is relatively little moral-ethical cement in the United States which might bring the internal moral-ethical limits more closely in accord with the external community defined inclusively by the national government. There is no "moral equivalent to war," and, since Viet Nam, we must question whether war itself can serve such a function. Nonetheless, experience suggests that war and the threat thereof may be the only moral force that might sustain the governmental leviathan. Viewed in this light, it is ominous that each president, soon after entering office, shifts his attention away from the divisive issues of domestic politics toward those of foreign affairs. We must beware the shades of Orwell's *1984*, when external enemies are created, real or imaginary, for the purpose of sustaining domestic moral support for the national government.

While I am not some agrarian utopian calling for a return to the scattered villages on the plains, I shall accept the label of a constitutional utopian who can still see visions of an American social order that would not discredit our Founding Fathers. To achieve such an order, drastic constitutional change is surely required. Effective federalism remains possible, within the technological constraints of the age, and "constitutional revolution" need not require

---

9. My diagnosis is restricted to the Western, specifically the American, setting. Perhaps the strongest empirical support for my argument is, however, provided in non-Western collectivized countries through the observed failures to create "new men" via institutional change.

the massive suffering, pestilence, and death associated with revolution on the left or right. Dramatic devolution might succeed in channelling some of the moral-ethical fervor in politics toward constructive rather than destructive purpose.

I become discouraged when I observe so little discussion, even among scholars, of the federal alternative to the enveloping leviathan. Where is the Québec of the United States? Where is the Scotland? Could a threat of secession now succeed? More importantly, could the emergence of such a threat itself force some devolution of central government power? Who will join me in offering to make a small contribution to the Texas Nationalist Party? Or to the Nantucket Separatists? From small beginnings. . . .

We should be clear about the alternative. The scenario to be played out in the absence of dramatic constitutional reform involves increasing resort to the power of the national government by those persons and groups who seek private profit and who are responding predictably to the profit opportunities that they observe to be widening. Individually, they cannot be expected to understand that the transfer game is negative sum, and, even with such understanding, they cannot be expected to refrain from investment in rent seeking. Furthermore, as persons and groups initially outside the game come to observe their own losses from political exploitation, they too will enter the lists. As the process moves forward through time, we can predict a continued erosion of trust in politics and politicians. But distrust will not turn things around. "Government failure" against standard efficiency norms may be demonstrated, analytically and empirically, but I see no basis for the faith that such demonstrations will magically produce institutional reform. I come back to constitutional revolution as the only attractive alternative to the scenario that we seem bent to act out. In the decade ahead, we shall approach the bicentenary of the Constitution itself. Can this occasion spark the dialogue that must precede action?

The Ethics of Constitutional Order

Early in my own career as a political economist, Robert Dahl and Charles Lindblom published a challenging book entitled *Politics, Economics, and Welfare* (1953). One of the central themes or arguments of the book was that we, as individual citizens, do not make choices among the grand organizational alternatives; we do not choose between "capitalism" and "socialism." We choose, instead, among the pragmatically defined and highly particularized policy alternatives as these are indirectly presented to us through the political process. And we make our choices on the basis of that combination of ignorance, ideology, and interest that best describes our psychological state.

I distinctly recall that I was somehow quite disturbed by this Dahl-Lindblom argument, but that I could not quite work out for myself a fully satisfactory response or counter-argument. Perhaps now, nearly four decades later, I can make such an effort.

First, let me translate the problem into terminology that is more familiar to me, and also more general. Let me refer to the whole constitutional order, that is, the structure of legal-political rules, within which we act both in our private and our public capacities. The Dahl-Lindblom thesis is that we do not consciously choose this structure. Empirically, they seem to be correct. We go about making our ordinary choices, which involve complex interactions with other persons and groups, within a framework or a structure of rules that we simply take as a part of our environment, a part of the state of nature, so to speak. This descriptive characterization applies equally to ordinary socio-economic and to political interaction.

If, however, we do not consciously choose, or even think about choosing,

From *Essays on the Political Economy* (Honolulu: University of Hawai'i Press, 1989), 25–31. Reprinted by permission.

among structures of rules, that is, among alternative constitutional orders, how can we be responsible for the regimes under which we live? And if we are not responsible for the ultimate choice among constitutional alternatives and could not, in fact, choose among them, is it not then meaningless to talk about constitutional change or constitutional reform?

The implication seems clear. We must, willy-nilly, acquiesce in the regime under which we live, and simply do our best to behave rationally as we confront the pragmatically generated choices that emerge. Something seems wrong with this argument. For most of the time, and for most practical purposes, it is perhaps best that we accept the existing constitutional order as a "relatively absolute absolute" (about which I have more to say in Chapter 5 ["On the Work Ethic"]). But such acceptance is not equivalent to a denial that change is possible, even for the single person who thinks about, analyzes, evaluates, and proposes alternative structures. I want to suggest here that each one of us, as a citizen, has an ethical obligation to enter directly and/or indirectly into an ongoing and continuing constitutional dialogue that is distinct from but parallel to the patterns of ordinary activity carried on within those rules that define the existing regime.

Let me illustrate the problem here by reference to a poker game example that will be familiar to those who have ever had any exposure to my own attempts to present the elements of constitutional political economy. In any observed and ongoing poker game, individuals, as players, abide by the rules that exist and that define the game itself. Players adopt this or that strategy in attempts to win within the existing rules. At the same time, however, the same persons may evaluate the rules themselves, and they may enter into side discussions about possible changes in the rules so as to make for a "better" game. If, as a result of such discussion, agreement is reached, then rules are changed and the regime shifts. A new constitution emerges.

This poker example helps me to make two elementary but highly important points. First, the example facilitates the distinction between the choice of strategies within the existing set of rules and the choice among alternative sets of rules, or, more generally, between in-constitutional and constitutional choice. Secondly, the examples allow us to see that an individual, as player, may behave responsibly and rationally in choosing and implementing strategies, within the rules that define the game, without necessarily concerning himself or herself about changes in the rules themselves. That is to say, the individual player may, but need not, enter into the dialogue and discussion about changes in the rules. To remain a player in the game, the choice among strategies of play is necessary, but participation in the potential choice among sets of rules is not necessary. The first of these two points has been elaborated at length in the modern analyses; the second point has not been fully examined, and it provides the focus of attention here.

Let me remain within the more familiar realm of discussion about the first point in order to summarize the now-standard argument. The distinction between the levels of choice—between post-constitutional, or within-rules, choice and choice among rules—has proved helpful in allowing a bridge to be constructed between rational choice behavior by the individual and the emergence of agreement on something that might be called the "general interest." If persons are unable to identify their own narrowly defined interests, due to the presence of some sufficiently thick veil of ignorance or uncertainty, they will choose among alternatives in accordance with some generalizable criteria such as fairness. In this setting of constitutional choice, therefore, no need for an explicit ethical norm seems to arise.

The poker-game, veil-of-uncertainty model has proved helpful in introducing the setting for constitutional choice, and it is a model that I have often used. But the model is highly misleading in respects relevant for my purposes here. If we are considering games with effectively large numbers of participants, there may exist little or no incentive for any single player to participate actively in any serious evaluation of the rules. Each player will, of course, have an incentive to maximize his or her own payoffs within whatever set of rules that exist, and each player may also have an interest in the presence of rules that satisfy generalizable criteria when that player does not know what his or her own position will be. But having the latter interest is not equivalent to having an interest-based incentive to act unless the individual expects that his own action will influence the outcome of the collective selection among alternatives. This point will be familiar to those who recognize the elementary public-choice logic, and especially in application to the theory of rational voter abstention and rational voter ignorance. In a large-number setting, the individual player may not consider himself or herself influential in controlling the ultimate selection among sets of rules; hence, the fully rational player may well refrain from participating in the choice among regimes.

The poker-game analogy is misleading in a second respect, and especially by extension to politics. A poker game is voluntary; hence, rules must, at least in some sense, be agreed to by all players because those who are dissatisfied may withdraw from play altogether. In this context, the large-number setting may not be so problematic as it seems, since each player retains a low-cost exit option. But there is no such exit possible in national political regimes. The political game is compulsory, and we all must play. Individually, therefore, we cannot exercise even residual influence over the rules through an effective exit option. The conclusion is clear: if the individual cannot ultimately influence the choice among regimes, it is not rational to participate actively in any discussion of constitutional change or to become informed about constitutional alternatives.

The argument suggests that becoming informed about, and participating in the discussion of, constitutional rules must reflect the presence of some ethical precept that transcends rational interest for the individual. The individual who acts on such a precept behaves "as if" his or her own influence on the ultimate selection among regimes is more than that which a rational-choice calculus would imply. Behavior in accordance with such a precept embodies an ethical responsibility for the choice among regimes.

Note that this ethic of constitutional citizenship is not directly comparable to ethical behavior in interaction with other persons within the constraints imposed by the rules of an existing regime. An individual may be fully responsible, in the standard ethical sense, and yet fail to meet the ethical requirement of constitutional citizenship. The individual may be truthful, honest, mutually respectful, and tolerant in all dealings with others; yet, at the same time, the same individual may not bother at all with the maintenance and improvement of constitutional structure.

On many occasions I have referred to what I have called a loss of constitutional wisdom, and especially as observed over the decades of this century. My argument here suggests that this loss of understanding and loss of interest in political structure may reflect the straightforward working out of rationally based individual self-interest, accompanied by an erosion of the ethical principle of constitutional responsibility. To the extent that we, as individuals, do not act "as if" we do, individually, choose among the grand alternatives, then the constitutional regime that we inherit must be vulnerable both to nonprincipled exploitation and to the natural erosion of historical change.

The result is precisely what we seem to have observed over recent decades.

The vision of constitutional order that informed the thinking of James Madison and his peers among the Founders was carried forward for more than a century of our national history. This vision embodies both an understanding of the principles of constitutional order and recognition that the individual, as citizen, must accept the ethical responsibility of full and informed participation in a continuing constitutional convention.

The Madisonion vision, with its embodied ethic of constitutional citizenship, is difficult to recapture once it is lost from the public consciousness. The simple, yet subtle, distinction between strategic choices within rules and constitutional choices among sets of rules, the distinction that was illustrated in the poker-game example introduced earlier, must inform all thinking about policy alternatives. The individual, as citizen, cannot restrict his or her attention to policy options within rules; the individual cannot simply reflect on the alternatives that emerge under the operation of a collective decision rule, say, majority voting in a legislature. Choice cannot be limited to a determination of that which is "best," either in terms of the individual's own interests or in terms of the individual's own version of some general interest. Constitutional citizenship requires that the individual also seek to determine the possible consistency between a preferred policy option and a preferred constitutional structure. (This point may be illustrated by a personal-choice example. An individual may prefer a dish of ice cream, but eating a dish of ice cream may not be consistent with the furtherance of the rules dictated by a self-imposed diet plan, an eating constitution.)

Much of what we have observed in modern politics is best described as action taken without understanding or even consideration of the rules that define the constitutional order. I have referred to this politics as "constitutional anarchy," by which I mean a politics that is almost exclusively dominated by and derivative from the strategic choices made by competing interests in disregard of the effects on political structure. This politics has come to its current position because we, as citizens, have failed to discharge our ethical obligations. We have behaved as if the very structure of our social order, our constitution defined in the broadest sense, will remain invariant or will, somehow, evolve satisfactorily over time without our active participation.

Simple observation of the behavior of our political and judicial agents should indicate that such a faith is totally without foundation. We may, of course, continue to default on the ethical obligation of constitutional citizenship. If we do so, however, we leave unchecked the emerging tyranny of the nonconstrained state, a tyranny that can be dislodged only with revolution. Neither such tyranny nor its consequent revolution is necessary if we, as individuals, can recover, even in part, the ethical principle upon which our constitutional order is established.

We must attend to the rules that constrain our rulers, and we must do so even if such attention may not seem to be a part of a rational-choice calculus. The amorality of acquiescence generates despair and longing; the morality of constitutional understanding embodies hope as a necessary complement.

PART SIX

The Reason of Rules

The Domain
of Constitutional Economics

Constitutional political economy is a research program that directs inquiry to the working properties of rules, and institutions within which individuals interact, and the processes through which these rules and institutions are chosen or come into being. The emphasis on the choice of constraints distinguishes this research program from conventional economics, while the emphasis on cooperative rather than conflictual interaction distinguishes the program from much of conventional political science. Methodological individualism and rational choice may be identified as elements in the hard core of the research program.

Introduction

Richard B. McKenzie introduced the term *constitutional economics* to define the central subject matter of a Heritage Foundation conference that he organized in Washington, D.C., in 1982.[1] In his fortuitous addition of the adjective *constitutional* to the familiar disciplinary base, McKenzie provided precisely the combination of meaning that was needed to identify and to isolate a research program that had emerged as an integral, but distinguishable, part of the subdiscipline of public choice over the three decades of the latter's existence. The term *constitutional politics* calls attention to the relevant sub-

From *Constitutional Political Economy* 1 (1990): 1–18. Reprinted by permission.

Paper prepared for Liberty Fund Symposium on "German Ordnungstheorie and American Constitutional Economics," Bonn, 3–6 June 1989.

1. R. McKenzie, ed., *Constitutional Economics* (Lexington, Mass.: Lexington Books, 1984).

ject phenomena but fails to convey the relevance and applicability of economics, as a disciplinary base, in the examination and evaluation of the foundational rules of social order. By borrowing McKenzie's term, I was then able to suggest, and later to write, an extended entry on *constitutional economics* for *The New Palgrave*.[2] With these beginnings, the ongoing research program (which is readily translatable into the more inclusive *constitutional political economy*) attained full semantic legitimacy in the 1980's. The journal *Constitutional Political Economy* becomes the institutionalized complement.

This paper describes the domain of the still-emerging research program, the boundaries of which must be considered to be sufficiently provisional to allow for analytical developments along any of several now-predictable dimensions. My first task is to clarify the separate parts of the name itself, and to distinguish the usage of the partial terms from other applications. *Constitutional* economics must be shown to be different from *non-constitutional, orthodox* or *standard* economics. At the same time, constitutional economics must be shown to be different from constitutional politics as the latter may be commonly understood. Sections I and II are designed to accomplish this task. My second task is to place or to locate constitutional political economy within a more inclusive intellectual tradition, and in particular in relation to classical political economy and contractarian political philosophy (Section III). My third self-assigned task, attempted in Section IV, is to expose for criticism and to defend the central philosophical presuppositions upon which the whole constitutional economics enterprise rests. Section V introduces some of the more controversial issues concerning the role that perception, vision, and belief must play in constitutional economics, as in other areas of social inquiry. And I should note that some of the arguments advanced in this section may be viewed as personally idiosyncratic, even by some of my fellow constitutional political economists. It is also here that nonsympathetic critics may suggest, appropriately, that in some ultimate sense the whole enterprise is normative. This normative grounding must not, however, be used to deny the relevance of the wholly positive analyses that consists of comparing alternative structures from within the perspective defined by the hard core of the research program. The whole inquiry involves the

---

2. J. Buchanan, "Constitutional Economics," *The New Palgrave* (London: Macmillan, 1987).

study of rules, how rules work and how rules might be chosen. But any such effort may be meaningless without some stipulation of the game that rules are to describe.

I. Constitutional and Non-constitutional Economics

There is a categorical distinction to be made between constitutional economics and non-constitutional, or ordinary, economics, a distinction in the ultimate behavioral object of analytical attention. In one sense, all of economics is about choice, and about the varying and complex institutional arrangements within which individuals make choices among alternatives. In ordinary or orthodox economics, no matter how simple or how complex, analysis is concentrated on choices made *within* constraints that are, themselves, imposed exogenously to the person or persons charged with making the choice. The constraints that restrict the set of feasible choice options may be imposed by nature, by history, by a sequence of past choices, by other persons, by laws and institutional arrangements, or even by custom and convention. In the elementary textbook formulation of demand theory, for example, the individual consumer-purchaser confronts a range of goods available at a set of prices, but is restricted by the size of the budget. This budget is not within the choice set of the consumer-purchaser during the period of choice under scrutiny. Indeed it would seem unnatural or bizarre, within the mind-set fostered by ordinary economics, to consider the prospect that an individual might deliberately choose to constrain or limit the set of available choice options. Within this mind-set, the utility of the chooser is always maximized by allowing for choices over the whole range allowed by the exogenously determined constraints.

It is precisely at this critical point that constitutional economics, in its most inclusive definition, departs from the conventional framework of analysis. Constitutional economics directs analytical attention to the *choice among constraints*. Once stated in this fashion, economists will recognize that there is relatively little in their established canon that will assist in analyzing choices of this sort. To orthodox economists, only the elementary reality of scarcity makes choice necessary; without scarcity there would be no need to choose. And it would appear to be both methodologically and descriptively absurd to introduce the artificial creation of scarcity as an object for behavioral analysis. Such bedrock conservatism presumably explains much of ordinary economists' inattention and disinterest in constitutional questions, at all levels.

If we move beyond the models of orthodox economics, however, even while remaining at the level of individual behavior, we observe that individuals do, in fact, choose their own constraints, at least to a degree and within some limits. Within recent decades, a few innovative thinkers from economics and other social sciences have commenced to study the choice processes that are involved here.[3] The *economics of self-control* has reached the status of a respectable, if minor, research program, which may be destined to become more important in this era of emphasis on diet, exercise, health, and the environment. We must surely be sufficiently catholic to allow analysis in this *individual constitutional economics* to qualify for inclusion in the domain.

As they carry on within their own guaranteed private spaces, however, individuals would presumably subject themselves to a relatively small set of prior constraints. Individuals basically *trust themselves* to choose rationally when confronted with the externally imposed constraints that are dictated in their historically emergent conditions. If the choice among constraints, in all its complexity, is limited to the economics of self-control, or stated conversely, to the economics of temptation, there might be little to be gained in delineating a constitutional economics enterprise.

It is essential to acknowledge, near the outset of discussion, that individuals choose to impose constraints or limits on their own behavior primarily, even if not exclusively, as a part of an *exchange* in which the restrictions on their own actions are sacrificed in return for the benefits that are anticipated from the reciprocally extended restrictions on the actions of others with whom they interact along the boundaries of private spaces and within the confines of acknowledged public spaces. That is to say, a domain of constitutional economics would exist even if individuals, in their private spaces, chose never to impose constraints on their own behavior. Note that by inter-

---

3. J. Elster, *Ulysses and the Sirens* (Cambridge: Cambridge University Press, 1979); Th. Schelling, "Egonomics, or the Art of Self Management," *American Economic Review* 68 (1978): 290–94; R. Thaler and H. M. Shefrin, "An Economic Theory of Self-Control," *Journal of Political Economy* 89 (1981): 392–406.

preting the individual's choice of a generalized constraint that restricts the actions both of others and himself (herself) as a part of a reciprocal exchange, we have moved toward the familiar domain of orthodox economics. So interpreted, the individual who joins in a collective decision to impose a generally applied constitutional rule is not, at base, acting differently from observed behavior in a setting that involves giving up one desired good, apples, for another desired good, oranges. In the latter example, we can, without violating the meaning of words, say that the individual chooses to constrain, or to limit, the potential consumption of apples in exchange for the expanded opportunity to consume oranges. Expressed in this way, all that is required is that we classify the restrictions on others' actions as *goods* in the individual's preference function along with the more natural classification or restrictions on his (her) own actions as *bads*.

In this simplistic and individualistic perspective, the choice of a reciprocally binding constraint by individuals who are related one to another in an anticipated set of interactions becomes fully analogous to trade in ordinary goods and services, and, so treated, becomes quite different from the choice of a self-imposed constraint in the much more difficult economics of self-control, briefly discussed above.

Why have the practitioners of orthodox economics seemed so reluctant to extend analysis to include the reciprocal exchanges of liberties that are central to the domain of constitutional economics?

I can advance several related reasons. Economists, along with their peers in the other social sciences as well as other academic disciplines, have had no difficulty, through the ages, in implicitly classifying restrictions on some of the activities of some persons in the body politic to be *good*. But the classification procedure has been quite different from the subjective evaluations presumed to be embodied in individuals' preference functions. The nonconstrained voluntary behavior is not classified to be *bad* because an individual simply disprefers such behavior in the ordinary way. Some such behavior is deeded to be bad, and hence its rectification to be good, on the basis of an externally derived criterion of *goodness* or *truth*. The attributes or qualities of goodness and/or badness applied to actions of persons are treated as if they are intrinsically public, in the Samuelsonian taxonomic sense. An action cannot, properly, be adjudged to be good by one person without an implied generalization of such judgment to other persons. In this conceptualization, persons must, ideally, be brought into agreement on some ultimate classification of actions through a process that resembles scientific discourse. Agreement does not emerge from a trading process where different interests are essentially compromised, with each party reckoning to enjoy some benefits while suffering some sacrifice of preferred position.

In some respects, it is surprising that economists have "jumped out" of their own analytical framework so readily when they consider the possible imposition of generalized constraints on behavior. They have expressed little curiosity in deriving justification for such constraints from a calculus of individual interests. Economists have, instead, been willing intellectual captives of idealistic political philosophers, and they have readily embraced variants of the Platonic and Hellenic mind-sets. Amartya Sen's usage of the term *meddlesome preferences*,[4] by sharp contrast with such terms as *merit goods* and *merit wants*, tends to focus analysis back toward a straightforward calculus of interest and away from nonindividualistic attributes of either goods or actions.

A second, and related, reason for economists' general failure to use the exchange setting when they consider the possible imposition of generalized constraints on individual behavior lies in the methodological dominance of the maximization paradigm. In the latter, *the economic problem* is defined as one of allocating scarce means (resources) among alternative ends. Choice is made necessary by the scarcity of means, and that which is desired (utility) is maximized when like units of resources yield equivalent returns in all uses to which they are put. In this elementary formulation, emphasis is almost exclusively placed on the choices that are made within the scarcity constraints that are, themselves, presumed to be beyond the scope for chooser selection. There is little or no attention paid to the identification of the choosing unit in this abstracted definition, and this feature allows for a relatively unnoticed transference of analysis from individual choice to *social* or *collective* choice on the basis of some implicit presumption that collectivities choose analogously to individuals.

This shift from individual to supraindividual choice was supported, and

4. A. K. Sen, "The Impossibility of a Paretian Liberal," *Journal of Political Economy* 78 (1970): 152–57.

indirectly justified, by the emergence of macroaggregation and macroeconomic theory and policy during the early decades of the post-Robbins half century. Target levels of macroaggregates (national product, rates of growth, levels of employment) were established to be objectively *good* and to serve as guideposts for choices to be made by collective entities (governments) subject only to the constraints imposed by natural scarcities and technological limits. By some implicit extension of the model for individual choice behavior, constrained only by external forces, governments came to be viewed romantically and were deemed capable of achieving the *good*, as defined for them by the economists and other social philosophers. Microeconomists had long been ready at hand to proffer policy advice to governments concerning ways and means to promote greater overall economy efficiency.

A third reason for economists' general failure to extend their analytical apparatus to the derivation of institutional-constitutional structure is to be found in their presumption that structural constraints are not, themselves, subject to deliberative choice, and, hence, to change. Economists have not neglected to recognize the relevance of institutional rules in affecting patterns of human behavior. Property-rights economics, in particular,[5] has opened up a research program that concentrates attention directly on the effects of alternative structures. For the most part, however, the emphasis here is on existing arrangements rather than on the comparative analysis involved in extension to structures that might be designed and implemented.

Constitutional economics differs from nonconstitutional or orthodox economics along each of the dimensions that may be inferred from the reasons for neglect detailed above. Analysis is consistently individualistic, in the several senses that are relevant. The derivation of institutional constraints is based on a calculus of individual interests, which, in turn, requires the introduction and use of an exchange paradigm as opposed to the idealists' search for the unique *good*. Furthermore, there is no extension of the choice calculus from the individual to collectivities, as such. Collective *choice* is factored down into the participatory behavior of individual members. Finally, emphasis is centered directly on the selection of rules, or institutions, that will, in turn, limit the behavior of the persons who operate within them. Institu-

---

5. A. Alchian, *Economic Forces at Work* (Indianapolis: Liberty Fund, 1977).

tions, defined broadly, are variables subject to deliberative evaluation and to explicit choice.[6]

As noted, at one extreme, constitutional analysis may be applied to the individual in total isolation, who may act solely in private space. At the other extreme, constitutional analysis is applied to the whole set of persons who make up the membership of the polity. This subcategory of research emphasis is the most familiar, since the very word *constitutional* tends to convey political connotations. The derivation of constraints on government does, indeed, occupy much of our attention. But the inclusive domain of constitutional economics also includes the derivation, analysis of, and justificatory argument for rules that constrain both individual and collective behavior in a wide array of membership groupings, larger than the one-unit limit but smaller than the all-inclusive limit of the whole polity. Clubs, trade unions, corporations, parties, universities, associations—these, and many more, exist and operate under constitutions that are amenable to scientific inquiry.

II. Constitutional *Economics* and Constitutional *Politics*

In Section I, I have attempted to distinguish between *constitutional* and *nonconstitutional* economics. I propose, in Section II, to distinguish between constitutional *economics* and constitutional *politics*, as the latter term may be generally and widely interpreted. As I have noted, most constitutional inquiry and analysis is concentrated at the level of the politically organized collectivity and is, in this sense, political. The distinction to be emphasized, however, is one of perspective rather than one that relates directly to either the form of organization or to the type of activity. If an exchange rather than a maximizing paradigm is taken to be descriptive of the inclusive research program for the discipline, then *economics* involves inquiry into *cooperative* arrangements for human interaction, extending from the simplest of two-person, two-good trading processes through the most complex quasi-constitutional arrangements for multi-national organizations. As noted in Section I, orthodox economics has rarely been extended to noncommercial

6. J. Buchanan and G. Tullock, *The Calculus of Consent* (Ann Arbor: University of Michigan Press, 1962).

or political activity, as such, but the exchange perspective readily allows this step to be taken.

The cooperative perspective, however, must be categorically distinguished from the contrasting *conflictual* perspective, which has been applied, almost automatically, to all political interactions, whether or not these are classified as constitutional. It will be useful here to examine the differences between the cooperative and the conflictual perspectives more carefully. The very term *politics* tend to conjure up a mental image of potential conflict among those persons who are members of the politically organized community. This conflict may be interpreted to be analogous to scientific disputes, in which separate participants or groups seek to convince one another of the *truth* of their advanced propositions. The age-old tradition of idealism in political philosophy conceives of all of politics in this light, and, as noted earlier, the dominance of this model of politics has tended to discourage economists from political extensions of the exchange or cooperative paradigm. But, even if the teleological interpretation is rejected, politics may seem, by its very nature, to involve conflict between and among individuals and groups within a polity.

From the institutionally determined characteristics of collective decisions, the characteristics that dictate mutual exclusivity among the alternatives for selection (only one candidate can be electorally chosen) imply some ultimate division of the membership into two subsets, *winners* and *losers*. This perspective almost directly suggests that politics is primarily if not exclusively a distributional game or enterprise, a process that involves transfers of value (utility) among and between separately identified coalitions of persons.

Note that the predominance of the distributional elements in the conflictual model of politics need not imply that the game be zero-sum, although this limiting case may be useful for some analytical purposes. Conflictual politics may be positive, zero, or negative-sum, as gains and losses are somehow aggregated over all participants (members). And this seems to be the natural model for analyzing politics so long as rules for reaching collective decisions require less than full agreement. If a majority, whether simple or qualified, is allowed to be decisive and impose its will on a minority, then the observed opposition of the minority to the alternative preferred by the majority can be taken to indicate that members of the minority expect to suffer utility losses, at least in a lost-opportunity sense. In this model of conflictual politics, which appears to be descriptive of ordinary political activity, there seems to be no direct way of introducing a cooperative interpretation. A necessary condition for cooperation in social interaction is the prospect for positive expected gains by all parties, or, in the gainer-loser terminology, the prospect that there be no net losers. At a first descriptive cut, this condition seems to be foreign to the whole political enterprise.

It is precisely at this point, however, that constitutional politics, or politics at the constitutional level of choices among alternative sets of basic rules or constraints, rescues the cooperative model, at least in some potential explanatory and normative sense. As it operates and as we observe it to operate, ordinary politics may remain conflictual, in the manner noted above, while participation in the inclusive political game that defines the rules for ordinary politics may embody positively valued prospects for all members of the polity. In other words, constitutional politics does lend itself to examination in a cooperative analytical framework, while ordinary politics continues to lend itself to analysis that employs conflict models of interaction.

Generalized agreement on constitutional rules that allow for the reaching of ordinary collective decisions by means that do not require general agreement is surely possible, as is empirically demonstrated in the context of almost all organizations. The analytical-scientific inquiry that involves comparisons of the working properties of alternative sets of rules along with the examination of processes through which agreement on rules may be attained defines the domain of primary concern. The usage of the terminology *constitutional economics* or *constitutional political economy* rather than the somewhat more accurate *constitutional politics* is prompted by the linkage in scientific heritage between *economics* and *cooperation*, by the inference of the appropriateness of the exchange as opposed to the conflict paradigm.

III. The Intellectual Traditions of Constitutional Political Economy

In Sections I and II, I have attempted to set the research program in constitutional political economy apart from ongoing programs within the interrelated and more inclusive disciplines of economics and political science. It would be totally misleading, however, to infer from my discussion that this research program has emerged full blown, as if divorced from any traditions of intellectual inquiry. As I have noted, constitutional economics, in its modern variant, did indeed blossom only in the second half of this century. But the program was not based either on a new scientific discovery, at least as usually defined, or on a new set of analytical tools. Constitutional political economy is best interpreted as a re-emphasis, a revival, a re-discovery, of basic elements of earlier intellectual traditions that have been set aside, neglected, and sometimes forgotten in the social sciences and social philosophy.

These traditions are those of classical political economy and contractarian political philosophy. It will be useful to discuss each of these traditions briefly.

Classical political economy, represented especially in the works of Adam Smith, was directed toward offering an explanation and understanding of how an economy (set of markets) would work without detailed political interventions and control. Smith's aim was to demonstrate that the *wealth* of the nation would be larger under a regime of minimal politicization than under the alternative closely controlled mercantilist regime.[7] And the whole thrust of the argument was to the effect that all groups in the economy and especially the laboring classes, could be expected to share in the benefits promised upon the shift in regimes. The emphasis was on the generalization of expected gains over all persons and classes. The suggested change in the structure, or basic rules, that depoliticization involves was, therefore, within the feasible limits of potential agreement by all parties. The normative focus, again especially in Adam Smith, was not explicitly distributional. Only with the Marxian extensions of Ricardo's abstract analysis did interclass conflict enter into classical attention.

It is also important to recognize that the Smithean emphasis was not allocational in the modern economists' meaning of this term. The analysis was not designed to show that economic resources would be more effectively allocated to higher valued uses under a market than under a politicized regime, as measured by some external and objective standard of value. The aim was, instead, to show that the market order would allocate resources such that the evaluations (preferences) of individuals would be more fully satisfied, *regardless of what these evaluations might be.* In terms of his familiar example of the butcher, Smith's lesson was to show that self-interest in the

7. A. Smith, *The Wealth of Nations* (Oxford: Clarendon Press, 1979).

marketplace works to supply meat for supper, provided that meat is what consumers want. There is no implication here that self-interest in the marketplace works to supply meat because meat is valuable in some nutritional sense as defined by experts.

So interpreted, therefore, Adam Smith's enterprise falls squarely within the domain of constitutional political economy. In a strictly positive sense, his analysis described both how the existing regime worked and how an alternative regime might work. And, since the alternative seemed to generate more wealth to all parties, as measured by their own standards, the normative extension of the positive analysis was quite straightforward. In this extension, the object upon which collective attention must be placed is the set of rules or constraints within which persons behave in their capacities as consumers-buyers and producers-sellers. The laws and institutions that define the economic-political order become the variables subject to possible adjustment and reform.

I have, in the immediately preceding paragraphs, selected elements from the tradition of classical political economy that seem to provide precursory foundations for the modern research program in constitutional political economy. My treatment would surely be accused of bias, however, if I failed to indicate the presence of considerable ambiguity and confusion in the philosophical underpinnings of the classical economics enterprise. An interpretation of that enterprise in terms of classical utilitarianism would be quite different from my own; this alternative interpretation would stress quite separate elements of the tradition. The interpersonal comparability and aggregate measurability of utility were not explicitly rejected by the classical economists and, in a selected reading, these may be attributed, as presumptions, to their analyses. In this case, the whole enterprise becomes precursory to the maximizing rather than to the exchange paradigm in economics, with both allocational and distributional implications, and with a wholly different avenue for moving from the individual to the collective levels of choice. The categorical distinction between choices among rules and choices within rules all but disappears in the utilitarian configuration.

The elements of Adam Smith's intellectual enterprise become directly precursory to the research program in constitutional economics only when these elements are imbedded within the tradition of contractarian political philosophy, the tradition that was developed prior to but became competitive with and quite different from classical utilitarianism. From the 17th century, from the works of Althusius, Hobbes, Spinoza, and Locke[8] in particular, attempts were made to ground justificatory argument for state coercion on agreement by those individuals who are subject to coercion. This intellectual tradition invented the autonomous individual by shucking off the communitarian cocoon. The assignment to the individual of a capacity for rational independent choice, as such, allowed a *science* of economics and politics to emerge, a *science* that embodied a legitimatizing explanation for the emergence of and existence of the state. In agreeing to be governed, explicitly or implicitly, the individual exchanges his own liberty with others who similarly give up liberties in exchange for the benefits offered by a regime characterized by behavioral limits.

The contractarian logic leaves open any specification of the range and scope for agreed-on coercive authority. The early contractarians and notably Hobbes, had no understanding of the efficacy of market order, as it might function under the umbrella of the protective or minimal state. This understanding was provided only in the 18th century, and was fully articulated only in the great work of Adam Smith. Classical political economy, as appended to the contractarian intellectual foundations, allowed the development of a scientifically based analysis aimed at comparing alternative structures of political-legal order, analysis that could introduce and use principles of rational choice behavior of individuals and without resort to supraindividualistic norms. Utilitarianism also rejected all supraindividual norms, as such, and grounded all norms in a calculus of pleasure and pain. Nonetheless, this Benthamite intrusion created ambiguity in the efforts to add up utilities over persons. In this way, the contractarian justification derived from conceptual agreement was obscured, and the way was opened for a nontranscendental utilitarian supercession of individualistic norms. The contractarian philosophical basis upon which classical political economy should have been exclusively developed was, at least partially, undermined and neglected for al-

---

8. J. Althusius, *Politica Methodica digesta*, ed. C. J. Friedrich (Cambridge: Harvard University Press, 1932); Th. Hobbes, *Leviathan* (London: Everymans Library, 1943); B. Spinoza, *A Treatise in Politics*, trans. William McCall (London: Holyoake, 1854); J. Locke, *Second Treatise of Civil Government* (Chicago: Gateway, 1955).

most two centuries, only to be rediscovered in the research program of constitutional economics.

IV. The Hard Core and Its Critics

Throughout this paper I have referred to constitutional economics or constitutional political economy as a *research program*, thereby deliberately using the Lakatosian classification. In this scheme, there exist elements in the hard core of the program that are rarely, if ever, challenged by those scholars who work inside the intellectual tradition defined by the program. These central elements are taken as presuppositions, as relatively absolute absolutes, and, as such, they become, themselves, the constraints (the constitution) within which the scientific discourse is conducted. External intellectual challenges to the whole enterprise tend to be directed at these elements in the core of the program. The ongoing research within the constraints can, of course, proceed without concern for these external criticisms, but practitioners need to be aware of the core-imposed limits on the persuasive potential of the internalized analytical exercise.

For constitutional economics, the foundational position is summarized in *methodological individualism.* Unless those who would be participants in the scientific dialogue are willing to locate the exercise in the choice calculus of individuals, *qua* individuals, there can be no departure from the starting gate. The autonomous individual is a *sine qua non* for any initiation of serious inquiry in the research program. Individual autonomy, as a defining quality, does not, however, imply that the individual chooses and acts as if he or she exists in isolation from and apart from the community or communities of other persons with whom he or she may be variously associated. Any form of community or association of individuals may reflect some sharing of values, and, further, any individual's formation of values may be influenced by the values of those with whom he or she is variously associated in communities. The communitarian challenge to methodological individualism must go beyond the claim that individuals influence one another reciprocally through presence in communities. The challenge must make the stronger claim that individuation, the separation of the individual from community, is not conceptually possible, that it becomes meaningless to think of potential divergence between and among individual interests in a community. Stated in this way, it is evident that methodological individualism, as a presupposition of inquiry, characterizes almost all research programs in economics and political science; constitutional economics does not depart from its more inclusive disciplinary bases in this respect.

The communitarian critique does not often appear in such blatant guise. For constitutional economics, in particular, the critique apparently leaves the individualistic postulates unchallenged, while either implicitly or explicitly asserting the existence of some supraindividualistic source of evaluation. Individual evaluations are superseded by those emergent from God, natural law, right reason, or the state. This more subtle stance rejects methodological individualism, not on the claim that individuation is impossible, or that individual evaluations may not differ within a community, but rather on the claim that it is normatively improper to derive collective action from individual evaluations. To the communitarian who posits the existence of some supraindividualistic value scale, the whole analysis that builds on a base of an individualistic calculus can only be useful as an input in schemes of control and manipulation designed to align individualized preferences with those orderings dictated by the overarching norms for the community.

Concomitant with methodological individualism as a component of the hard core is the postulate of rational choice, a postulate that is shared over all research programs in economics. The autonomous individual is also presumed to be capable of choosing among alternatives in a sufficiently orderly manner as to allow a quality of rationality to be attributed to observed behavior. For constitutional economics, the capacity for rational choice is extended to include a capacity to choose among constraints, both individually and collectively applied, within which subsequent choices may be made.

Rationality implies that choices may be analyzed as if an ordering of alternatives exists, arrayed in accordance with some scalar of *preferredness*. We may, but need not, use the term utility to designate that which the individual calls upon to make up the ordinal ranking. At the analytical level, there is no need that the ranking correspond with any array of the choice alternatives that may be objectively measurable by some outside observer. The test for individual rationality in choice does require, however, the minimal step of classifying alternatives into *goods* and *bads*. The central rationality precept states only that the individual choose more rather than less of goods, and less rather than more of bads. There is no requirement that rationality dictates choice in accordance with the individual's economic interest, as this might be measured by some outside observer of behavior.

The individualistic postulate allows the interests or preferences of individuals to differ, one from another. And the rationality postulate does not restrict these interests beyond the classificatory step noted. *Homo economicus*, the individual who populates the models of empirical economics may, but need not, describe the individual whose choice calculus is analyzed in constitutional political economy. When selecting among alternative constitutional constraints, however, the individual is required to make some predictions about the behavior of others than himself. And, in such a setting, there is a powerful argument that suggests the appropriateness of something akin to the *Homo economicus* postulate for behavior.[9]

I have briefly discussed the individualistic and the rationality presuppositions for the research program. These elements are not controversial, and they would be listed as components of the hard core both by practitioners and critics of constitutional economics. A less obvious element that is, however, equally fundamental involves the generalization of the individualistic and the rationality postulates to *all* persons in the political community. All individuals must be presumed capable to make rational choices among alternatives in accordance with individually autonomous value scales. And this generalization does not allow derivation of collective action, whether or not directed toward choices among constraints, from individual evaluations on anything other than an *equal weighting*. To introduce a weighting scheme through which the evaluation of some persons in the community are deemed more important than other persons would require resort to some supraindividualistic source, which is, of course, ruled out by adherence to the individualistic postulate. In this sense the whole of the constitutional economics research program rests squarely on a *democratic* foundation.

The identification of the elements in the hard core of the research program in constitutional economics allows for the simultaneous identification of its vulnerabilities. As noted, critics who call upon extraindividual sources of value cannot participate in the ongoing dialogue, nor can those skeptics who refuse to apply models of rational choice to the behavior of individuals

---

9. G. Brennan and J. Buchanan, *The Reason of Rules* (Cambridge: Cambridge University Press, 1985).

as autonomous actors. To this point in its development, the program is vulnerable also in its failure to address the issue of defining membership in the community of persons over whom the postulates are to be applied. Who is to count as an autonomous individual? How are children to be treated, and at what age or stage of development does childhood cease and is full membership in community granted? How are the mentally and emotionally incompetent to be handled, and who is to decide who is incompetent? Is the community considered to be open to potential entrants?

These and related issues are relevant for inquiries in constitutional economics, but the program, by its nature, cannot address them readily. The starting point for analysis is a set of autonomous individuals, either already organized or potentially organizable in a political unit. Once the set is initially defined, the program can be extended to include examination and analysis of how the defined community itself addresses such issues. But the initial definition lies beyond the boundaries of any analytical construction within the program, as such.

V. Perception, Vision and Faith

Nietzsche used the metaphor of viewing the world of reality through differing windows,[10] and Ortega y Gasset went so far as to define ultimate reality itself as a perspective.[11] In a sense, any research program involves a way of looking at, and thereby imposing an order on, that which is perceived. This characterization applies particularly to any program in social science, where the ultimate object of inquiry is behavior in a social interaction process. I have on several occasions referred to the *constitutional perspective*, which I have acknowledged to be different from other perspectives that might be used in examining and evaluating the interaction of individuals in social and/or political settings. This elementary fact that perspectives differ, or may differ, raises difficult issues in epistemology that cannot be ignored.

Consider, first, perception at its simplest level. Presumably, individuals are sufficiently alike, one to another, biologically that we see, hear, taste, smell, and feel physical phenomena similarly if not identically. We all see a wall as

10. W. Kaufman, *Nietzsche* (Princeton: Princeton University Press, 1950), 61.
11. J. Ortega y Gasset, *Meditations on Quixote* (New York: Norton, 1961), 45.

a barrier to movement, and no one of us makes an attempt to walk through walls. Someone who failed to perceive a wall as the others of us do would be classified to be abnormal in at least one of the basic perceptual senses. As phenomena come to be increasingly complex, however, individuals may come to differ in their perceptions, despite the fact that, biologically, they continue to possess the same perceptual apparatus. Elementary sense perception must be accompanied by imaginative constructions that require some mental processing before a basis for evaluation, and ultimately for action, can be established.

As phenomena increase in complexity, the imaginative elements in perception increase relative to those that emerge directly from the senses. In this progression from the simple to the complex, the similarity in perceptions among persons must decrease. What may be called the *natural* way of observing phenomena fades away at some point along the spectrum. Individuals may then be brought into agreement on that which they observe only by entry into some sort of association of shared values or norms, which members, either explicitly or implicitly, choose. This statement may seem contradictory when first made; it may seem to state that persons choose how they see reality. But the statement becomes less challenging to ordinary notions when we replace *see* with *think about*.

I have been accused of committing the naturalistic fallacy, in some of my own works, of failing to respect properly *the fact-value, positive-normative* distinction, and, hence, of deriving the *ought* from the *is*, at least implicitly. I submit, however, that my critics mount such charges only because of their own confusion about the nature of perception of complex phenomena. If there exists no *natural* way of observing reality, some evaluation and choosing process is a necessary complement to the imaginative step that allows apparent chaos to be converted into order. We select the *is* that defines the hard core of our research program, and this holds true whether or not we are professional scientists. Within this *is*, we can adhere strictly to the precepts laid down for positive analysis. But the normative implications that may be drawn are, indeed, derivative from the chosen perceptive framework, and could not, or would not, be otherwise available.

Constitutional economics is a domain of inquiry and discourse among scientists who choose to perceive social interaction as a set of complex relationships, both actual and potential, among autonomous persons, each of whom is capable of making rational choices. The domain, as such, cannot be extended to include inquiry by those who choose to perceive social interaction differently. There is simply no common basis for scientific argument, and ultimately agreement, with those who choose to perceive social interaction either in purely conflictual or purely idealistic visions. These visions are, indeed, alternative "windows" on the world. And the process through which individuals choose among such windows remains mysterious. How can empirical evidence be made convincing when such evidence must, itself, be perceived from only one vantage point at a time? The naivete of modern empirical economists in this respect verges on absurdity.

When all is said and done, *constitutional economics*, for me, must be acknowledged to rest upon a precommitment to, or a faith in if you will, man's cooperative potential. Persons are neither bees in hives, carnivorous beasts in a jungle, nor angels in God's heaven. They are independent units of consciousness, capable of assigning values to alternatives, and capable of choosing and acting in accordance with these values. It is both physically necessary and beneficial that they live together, in many and varying associations and communities. But to do so, they must live by rules that they can also choose.

Predictability
The Criterion of Monetary Constitutions

*(Illustrated with reference to the proposal
for a common-brick monetary standard)*

As I interpret the organization of these articles, the several authors are examining monetary policy in the broadest possible sense of this term. We are considering the alternatives for monetary policy independently of the many political-institutional-historical constraints that may serve, and have served, to inhibit discussion at many levels. We are, in other words, engaged in a discussion of constitutional law; we are analyzing the alternative monetary constitutions that may be appropriate to the functioning of a competitive or enterprise economy.

If we conceive our efforts, our separate contributions, in this manner, the question of criteria emerges at the outset of our discussion. What results do we desire to see accomplished? How may the comparative performances of the separate monetary frameworks be evaluated? If we can initially agree upon, and accept, a single criterion for judging the performance of a set of monetary institutions, we should already have made a major step toward securing the required consensus on the more specific elements of monetary reform.

I submit that we can reach agreement on such a criterion, agreement not only among ourselves but among scholars generally. In other words, I am stating that the issues in monetary policy can be resolved wholly into issues of means, not ends. Contrary to other areas of economic policy, there is, or should be, no basic value conflict on matters of monetary policy. Having said this, I am now obliged to define the criterion about which I speak. I suggest that the most meaningful criterion for monetary policy, regardless of the level of discussion, is *predictability* in the value of the monetary unit, or, reciprocally, in the absolute level of prices.

Predictability and Stability as Norms

It will be useful to compare and contrast *monetary predictability* with *monetary stability* as the criterion of policy. As we know, the latter has been more often advanced. Note that, with monetary stability, we encounter immediately the issue of definition. What is meant by stability, even in some "ideal" sense? Is stability to be defined in terms of a product or a factor price level? These questions could, no doubt, be answered satisfactorily, and significant agreement reached among large numbers of monetary theorists. But the necessity for such questions to arise at this level of discussion can be eliminated by the substitution of predictability for stability as the appropriate monetary norm. More importantly for our purposes, however, this substitution widens considerably the consensus on criteria that is required for genuine progress. Even those who have argued in favor of creeping inflation should agree on the predictability criterion. In fact, a major virtue of predictability as a criterion lies in the obvious difficulty which confronts the serious monetary scholar who proposes to refuse acceptance. As we shall discuss in the following section, predictability in the value of the monetary unit is required for maximum economic efficiency, as normally defined, and, of course, for economic growth, which has become the modern equivalent of the efficiency norm when considered in a dynamic context.

Perhaps the greatest advantage of the proposed substitution of *predictability* for *stability* lies in the fact that it allows us to isolate problems and issues relating to the monetary constitution from those which introduce problems and issues concerned with the efficacy of monetary policy in producing specific effects on the so-called macroeconomic variables. Monetary policy, either at the constitutional framework level or at the institutionally constrained level, may or may not produce the effects called for by some stabilization criteria. The quantity of money may or may not be the key control variable in an over-all macroeconomic policy model. The variation in this quantity may or may not satisfactorily explain historical experience as to fluctuations in economic magnitudes. The point is that issues such as these, regardless of individual views, *need not be raised* in the basic consideration of alternative monetary constitutions. And I think that the air would be cleared substantially if we should agree to leave aside these essentially subsidiary issues until the more basic ones are settled.

Predictability and Efficiency

It is difficult for me to understand how anyone could seriously reject predictability as an appropriate norm for monetary policy. And yet I think that the consensus on this norm represents much more than empty agreement on such other economic policy goals as "efficiency," "rapid growth," and the like. With the latter, the fundamental agreement on goals merely puts aside argument and dispute until problems of specifying and defining the agreed-on goals are faced. Monetary predictability is not a norm of this sort. The predictability of the value of money is quite precise as a conceptual notion. Problems of definition do, of course, arise, but these are problems that are subject to discussion and, presumably, to solution. In other words, reasonable men can readily agree on the meaning of monetary predictability.

The analogy which comes to mind is weather. Predictability in weather is a widely accepted criterion for meteorologists, and we all know what is meant by improved weather prediction. I have seen no claim or argument to the effect that improvement in weather forecasting, in predictability, will not also "improve" over-all efficiency in resource usage. The correspondence between improvements in predictability here and improvements in economic performance generally is, in fact, taken for granted and rarely mentioned explicitly at all. Improved weather forecasting is acknowledged to be one of the "desirable" results to be expected from greater investment in scientific research.

This accords strictly with common-sense notions. If man can further his skills in predicting the weather, economic resources will be more effectively employed; major mistakes will be avoided. Note particularly that this conclusion holds quite independently of the trend in the weather over time. The winters in the northern hemisphere may gradually be getting "worse" or "better" by certain commonly accepted standards of "worseness" or "betterness." But the direction of change in the weather, described in this way, is irrelevant to the conclusion that improved predictability can lead to greater economic efficiency.

Our analogy becomes even closer if we move forward in time and imagine ourselves in a situation where the weather can be deliberately controlled. It is relatively easy to see that, under such circumstances, serious disputes might arise concerning criteria for betterness. But the improvements in predictability should still be recognized as universally desirable, regardless of the particular criterion of betterness that is adopted.

The analogy, as modified, seems almost perfect, but, as with all analogies, it is treacherous unless it is carefully handled. The meteorologist can direct his efforts toward improving predictability in the current situation, quite independently of his efforts toward securing greater control over the elements. The monetary theorist can, of course, do likewise. He can accept the institutional complex as it exists and devote his energies to improving forecasting techniques. But this is clearly relatively unproductive if he can, at a lower cost, devise means of modifying the institutional structure itself in such a way as to ensure greater predictability as a result. The monetary theorist would probably have much more difficulty than the meteorologist of the future, however, in separating the predictability aspects of a proposed "constitutional" change from the "improvements in results" that he might be able to secure through the change. The situation here should, of course, be reversed when we consider the relative importance of predictability and improvements in results in the two cases. With the weather, significant "improvement" can be contemplated by most people, quite apart from improved forecasting. With a monetary framework or constitution, if predictability were to be ensured, there would seem to be relatively little difference among alternative patterns of performance. There should be relatively little difference in the social costs of organizing a monetary system that would, for example, produce stability in the product price level, one that would produce a gradual decline in the product price level, and a system that would produce a gradual increase, *provided that the predictability was equivalent in the several cases.*

This is not to suggest that the choice among alternative monetary systems, independent of predictability elements, is not an important one. I should emphasize only that this choice, when constrained to a system among those that are expected to produce substantially the same predictability, is considerably less important than the initial choice between systems expected to generate monetary predictability and those which are not.

Predictability and Perfect Foresight

I doubt that I have said anything up to this point with which issue could be taken. I should insist, however, that the emphasis on predictability is more important than it may at first appear. But objections may be raised on the grounds that predictability is a norm that can be useful for analytical purposes but which is unattainable and, therefore, not practicable in any policy sense. Is monetary predictability as a norm not similar to the requirement for perfect foresight when we discuss the efficiency with which the competitive economic system organizes resource use? We agree that the ideally operating competitive system requires perfect foresight on the part of all or at least a substantial number of participants, but rarely do we introduce such foresight as an organizational norm. We recognize that little can be done toward substantially increasing the "predictability" of the whole economic organization, considered over all. Such efficiency as the competitive order produces is ensured through its flexibility and adaptability to changes in tastes, in resource supply, and in technology: changes that are, almost by their nature, unpredictable. The structure of relative prices responds to such of these changes as happen to occur, and any attempt to "freeze" the future course of relative price relations in some misguided efforts to increase predictability, that is, to reduce uncertainty, would make little logical sense. The act of fixing the course of relative price movements in advance would do nothing toward reducing the uncertainties that are inherent in the movements of the wholly unpredictable exogenous variables of the free economy. Surplus disposal and rationing problems would surely arise from such an attempt to increase predictability, and, rather than accomplishing this result, the reductions in responsiveness of the system to unexpected changes would be measured in avoidable inefficiency.

The pre-fixing of the course of the absolute price level would, however, be completely different. If predictability in the level of absolute prices, that is, in the value of the monetary unit, could be introduced, net gains in efficiency would surely follow. Such predictability implies, of course, *continuous mon-*

etary equilibrium. And if this were accomplished, the actual course of change in the absolute price level would become largely irrelevant.

In comparing positions of full equilibrium, the classical dichotomy between relative prices and the absolute price level is valid. And by imposing the assumption of predictability at the outset, I am ensuring that an equilibrium state is continuously maintained. Changes in the absolute price level may, of course, require accompanying changes in the supply or quantity of money. Implicit in my argument to this point is the idea that this variable might be employed to accomplish the goal desired. The main point is that, as the neoclassical writers emphasized, the absolute price level is independent of the structure of relative prices. It follows from this that the movements in the absolute price level over time can be varied without affecting the relative price structure. And, contrary to the situation applicable to the latter, the actual course of movement is largely unimportant in relation to the predictability of this movement.

But I am not yet in the clear, since I have not really got over the possible objection that the assumption of predictability in the absolute price level is analogous to the assumption of perfect foresight in the competitive model and, as such, useful analytically but not helpful normatively. Predictability as an appropriate policy norm must still be shown to be practicably achievable or, at the least, approachable.

The unique difference between potential predictability in the absolute price level and the potential satisfaction of the perfect foresight condition lies in the Walrasian recognition that one commodity or service in an interrelated economy must be selected as a *numéraire* in order to prevent underdetermination in the solution of the system of equations describing the economy. Until and unless one such commodity or service is selected, relative price relations can be expressed only in ratios or relatives; no common denominator of value exists. The selection of such a *numéraire* does not reduce the flexibility or the adaptability of the system to changes in the exogenous variables. Quite the contrary; agreement on a *numéraire* becomes a necessary condition for organizational efficiency. It follows directly from this that the imposition of predictability in the value of this *numéraire*, when computed in terms of other commodities and services, does not substantially reduce the flexibility allowed the other variables in the system.

"Ideal" Aspects of Price-Level Predictability

If the predictability norm is accepted as appropriate for monetary policy, and if it is accepted that this represents a meaningful and conceptually attainable norm, the next question to be faced involves the choice of means to implement it. In one sense, everything I have said to this point is introductory to this latter question, which is the main part of my discussion. For it is on the means of attaining monetary predictability that the various students of constitutional monetary policy may, and do, differ sharply. Before discussing some of these differences, I should like to emphasize again that the attainment of predictability, under any monetary framework, is more important than the means through which the goal is accomplished. Despite the amount of discussion devoted to arguments for or against various means of introducing monetary predictability, the underlying and central importance of ensuring predictability, *by any means,* should never be overlooked.

The result we seek is not difficult to define. What we want a monetary framework to produce is predictability in the value of money. We desire a monetary system that will allow the individual decision-maker, whether he be consumer, entrepreneur, seller of productive services, or speculator, to remove from his calculus uncertainty about the future course of the absolute price level. He will face quite sufficient and necessary uncertainty in his efforts to predict the future course of relative prices, uncertainty which, quite properly, should enter directly into his calculus.

We define the result desired in terms of the value of money, or reciprocally, the absolute price level. These are conceptual abstractions, however, not physical units of measure. These magnitudes assume arithmetical meaning only after some averaging process is undertaken, a process that utilizes movements in the prices of real physical commodities and services. The predictability about which we speak is predictability in the movement of an average over time. This average can be expressed in terms of an index number, but this number can never be expected to serve for more than an arbitrary scale factor. As such, movement in the index number can provide a criterion to suggest the suitability of action being taken on *other* variables, real or physical variables. The index itself cannot be acted upon in any direct manner.

We may provide an illustration by an analogy with temperature. The thermometer measures temperature, but temperature as such can do nothing other than to provide us with a criterion for taking action directly on other variables. We cannot directly increase temperature; we must instead take action on other variables, such as the quantity of coal in the furnace, which will, in turn, influence the heat index, or temperature, that we are observing.

Fundamentally, there exist two ways in which predictability in the movement of a price index can be incorporated into a monetary constitution. First, we may utilize the price index as the *instrumental* criterion for policy changes, changes that must involve action taken on other variables of the system. Second, and alternatively, we may try to organize the institutions of private decision-making in such a way that the desired monetary predictability will emerge spontaneously from the ordinary operations of the system.[1]

It is easy to see that the first approach possesses somewhat greater appeal when the problem is conceived in its "ideal" sense. If, in fact, the "ideal" or "norm" can be defined with some precision, as we have said is the case with monetary predictability, it can always be achieved by "ideal" men operating under "ideal" conditions. Hence the tendency in this area, as in others, is for students to jump somewhat too quickly into support of the first approach suggested above. When, however, we recognize that in all matters of economic policy specific actions can only be taken by individual human beings, and that these human beings are fallible and subject to mistakes and error, we begin to sense the merit of the second, alternative, approach, that which aims at securing the desired results spontaneously rather than instrumentally.

Managed versus Automatic Systems

This represents the difference between what we call a "managed" monetary system and what we call an "automatic" monetary system. I am aware that these terms introduce still further questions; all monetary systems are, in a sense, managed; none can be wholly automatic. For our purposes, however,

---

1. An analogy with economic efficiency, defined in the orthodox way, will be useful. Insofar as such efficiency is a norm for competitive economic organization, it is achieved as a result that emerges from the operation of the economy and not as a result of instrumentally oriented attempts to achieve this goal in any direct manner.

we may think of a managed system as one that embodies the instrumental use of price-level predictability as a norm of policy, either loosely by discretionary authorities possessing wide latitude for independent decision-making powers, or closely in the form of specific rules constraining discretionary authority within narrow limits. On the other hand, we may think of an automatic system as one which does not, at any stage, involve the explicit use of the absolute price level, the price index, or any other macroeconomic variable,[2] in guiding monetary policy. In the automatic system, monetary policy as such consists solely of the designation of a single commodity or service as the basis for the monetary unit, as the standard, and the firm fixing of the future course of the price, in money units, of this commodity. Note that I do not, in this description of an automatic system, require that the money price of the commodity chosen as the standard be stabilized over time. All that is required is that this price be fixed at each particular moment in time and that its level be known in advance. The price of the standard commodity may, of course, be stabilized, which is the case usually analyzed, but my point is that the normative argument for such stability arises at a level of discussion different from that considered here. Predictability is the important normative element that must first be incorporated into either a managed or an automatic system.

The ultimate policy decision as between a managed monetary system and an automatic system should be made only after a careful analysis of the relative costs and benefits expected from the operation of each system. Comparisons must be made on the basis of the expected properties of the alternative systems in the real world, not on the basis of properties of ideally constructed models. But we do not get very far until and unless we specify quite carefully and precisely the nature of the alternative systems that we propose to compare. There are many institutions described by the term "managed system," and there are many different commodities and services that are possible standards. Too often generic evaluations will be made as a result of comparisons between a particular managed system and some poorly work-

2. A system characterized by the *exclusive* attention of stabilization authorities being given to other macroeconomic variables, such as an employment index, could hardly be called a monetary system at all. Nevertheless, insofar as it should become necessary to classify such a system, it would clearly fall within the managed set.

ing automatic system or between a particular automatic system and some poorly working managed system.

The "Ideal" Managed System

We may avoid this difficulty, to some extent, by commencing with a comparison between the best or "ideal" managed system and the best or "ideal" automatic or commodity-money system.

I do not propose here to argue the case for any particular managed system. I shall state my conviction that some such scheme as that proposed by Henry Simons and Lloyd Mints would come closest to introducing predictability in the absolute price level. That is to say, I should opt squarely in favor of some predetermined, quasi-constitutional "rule" that would define quite precisely the task of the monetary authority, the "managers." This authority would then be charged with the responsibility of following the rule or set of rules. This system would, ideally, produce divergencies between observed and predicted values for money only as a result of errors and miscalculations stemming from the attempts of the authorities to follow the predetermined rules. By contrast, under a discretionary managed system, divergencies between observed and predicted values would arise not only from this source but also from the additional one involving departures of the actually followed rules from predicted ones. But, as suggested, it is not my function to argue this point.

The "Ideal" Automatic System

Those monetary theorists who generally tend to favor managed systems of one sort or another have not, as a rule, specified the alternative automatic standard or system with which their mental comparisons are made. Too often, I suspect, they have dismissed automatic systems, generically, because they associate all such systems with one specific member of a very large set, a member that is known to have produced undesirable results when it was partially operative. I speak here, of course, of the gold standard. As we know, the historical gold standard was not even a good model of a monetary system based on the commodity gold. But this need not concern us here. My point is that we should always specify carefully the characteristics of the alternative monetary system under consideration, and until and unless we have examined the "best" practicable automatic system, we should not opt for managed systems out of hand.

I propose, therefore, that we think first in terms of the characteristics of an "ideal" commodity system of money. If it could be found, what commodity or service would "ideally" accomplish the goal of monetary predictability? Viewed in this light, it seems that we should seek some commodity that is perfectly representative of the production of goods and services over the whole economy. That is, we need to locate some commodity whose production embodies some appropriately weighted set of coefficients that are representative of production processes for all goods and services in the economy. The elasticity of supply of this ideal monetary commodity would be equivalent to that possessed by production as a whole. The production of this ideal monetary commodity would be in a real sense an image of the whole economy in operation. Or, to use a mathematical metaphor, the whole economy would be "mapped" into the single production process.

The weights that would be implicit in this ideal commodity must in some manner reflect the relative importance of the various goods and services produced. But this relative importance can only be judged in terms of values. We must introduce market prices as the only meaningful reflection of consumer evaluation. We are led in this way to the conclusion that the ideal commodity for a monetary constitution utilizing some automatic or indirect means of achieving monetary predictability must be some commodity whose price, in the absence of its designation as the standard commodity, would move *pari passu* with movements in the absolute level of prices, that is, with the price index.

If there should exist such a commodity, that is, one whose price varies in perfect correspondence with the absolute price level in the absence of its designation as the monetary standard or basis, the achievement of monetary predictability to the degree desired would require a relatively simple institutional change. The government could state simply that the monetary authority, in this case, the Mint, would stand ready and willing to buy and to sell for money units unlimited quantities of this ideal commodity at a schedule of prices fixed in advance (and not necessarily to be stabilized over time). The economy would, as a result, be operating on a basis of monetary predictability, since the decentralized and impersonal forces of the competitive mechanism could be depended upon to produce and to destroy "money" as the economy required. If the absolute price level fell below predicted values, production and sale of the ideal commodity would take place. The quantity of money units in circulation would increase, and this increase would continue until observed and predicted values for the absolute price level roughly coincided. Conversely, if the absolute price level rose above predicted values, purchase of the ideal monetary commodity from the Mint would be stimulated. This purchase would continue until observed and predicted values for some price index were roughly in equivalence. Note that predictability under this system would be achieved without the instrumental usage of any price index as a criterion of policy action. The primary virtue of any "automatic" or commodity standard of money lies in the fact that only in such a system would the forces of the competitive market be directly utilized to achieve monetary predictability. In one sense, there would be no explicit monetary policy involved in the operation of such a system.

The Price-Level Rule as a Simulated Ideal Commodity Standard

For purposes of comparative analysis, we may conceive the operation of the Simons-Mints rule for price-level predictability in terms of such an "ideal" commodity standard. In one sense, the system of managed money in accordance with this type of rule is designed to simulate the more automatic system. Under such a rule-oriented system, the government is essentially "selling" units of an ideal composite commodity at a schedule of predetermined prices and "buying" units of this commodity at the same schedule of prices. If the administrators of such a managed system make few errors, the results will be substantially equivalent to those produced under the operation of an actual ideal commodity standard. But there are no market checkreins on the behavior of the monetary authorities. This important control feature of an actual commodity standard is missing. Decisions must be centralized.

Some of the monetary theorists who support such a rule for monetary management will argue convincingly that, given some predictability in the future course of the absolute price level, the forces of the competitive market mechanism will become operative. The profit-seeking actions of speculators will tend to ensure that the predictability implicit in the rule-as-directive to the monetary authorities will, in fact, characterize the rule-as-result. The phenomena here have been referred to as self-reinforcing expectations. If people are sufficiently sure that a particular result is to be achieved, their own private actions will tend to guarantee that their prediction becomes true. I do not want to go further into the interesting philosophical issues raised by the question of rules as predictions.

There is, however, one important factor that prevents self-reinforcing speculation from being fully effective under the operation of a rule for monetary predictability. Even if we can discount the major problems involved in crossing the "belief threshold," that is, the problems of convincing speculators that the predetermined rule will in fact continue to be employed as the overriding criterion for policy, the force of competitive counterspeculation will be reduced because individuals are unable to buy or sell "an average," "a price level," or "a price index." The general expectation that the over-all price level will, for example, rise to some predicted value (as indicated in the rule-as-criterion) from some currently observed value will cause speculators to shift their asset holdings from money into real goods, but in such a shift, the absence of any ideal composite commodity necessitates taking on relative price uncertainties. Some choices must be made among the many possible real assets that may be purchased. On the other hand, if there exists a general expectation that the price level will decline to some predicted value from some currently observed value, speculators will shift from real goods into money, thereby shedding some relative price uncertainties. The actions of speculators will, on balance, seem to exert a slight downward bias on the price level that the monetary authorities would have to discount, assuming of course that individuals, on the average, prefer certainty to uncertainty. I do not want to explore here this interesting area of speculation in a system characterized by a set of rules for ensuring monetary predictability. I think that I have discussed self-reinforcing speculation sufficiently for it to be compared briefly with that which would take place under a regime of an ideal commodity standard.

Stabilizing Speculation under an "Ideal" Commodity Standard

Let us now examine again the monetary system that bases the value of the monetary unit on the "ideal" commodity discussed above. Leave aside for a bit longer the attempt to locate such an "ideal" commodity. Assume that one such commodity does exist. In effect, this system utilizes the forces of the free market to ensure predictability. The market price for the designated standard commodity cannot diverge significantly from the Mint price, which is predetermined. The absolute price level can, of course, move above or below a certain predictable trend value. But the phenomena of self-reinforcing expectations will be equivalent to those arising under a system of predetermined rules for monetary management. But these market forces, which should not be underestimated in either case, become *secondary* to the main competitive force in the automatic standard, this main force being represented by the direct shifts into and out of the designated standard commodity as its price in relation to other prices (costs) moves upward or downward. The speculative forces, secondary to this main force, increase predictability to the extent that speculators in the nonstandard commodities share a general faith in the strength of economic motives in the calculus of those individuals who are potential direct traders in the money commodity. In other words, the relevant comparison here is the one between the average or representative speculator's faith in the forces of the market as stabilizing devices and his faith in the monetary authority's success in following a predetermined rule.

Common Brick as the Standard Commodity

Having gone through ten sections of this paper, I come now to the place where I had intended to begin. I hope that by this time some of the groundwork has been laid for a more careful consideration of what must seem, at first glance, to be a proposal of a monetary extremist.

There exists no "ideal" commodity for purposes of achieving monetary predictability under an automatic system. There is no single real commodity or service that serves at all adequately to represent composite production over the whole economy, or that could appropriately be used as an image of the economy. Having recognized this, however, we should not dismiss all automatic or commodity money systems as unworkable and impracticable. There are still better and worse commodity standards, "better" and "worse" being measured in terms of the degree to which specific real commodities possess the characteristics required of the "ideal" commodity discussed above.

It is in this sense that the use of common brick as the standard commodity should be considered. Among existent real commodities, a good argument can be made out for common building brick as the best practicable commodity that could be employed as the basis for an automatic monetary system. The ingenious proposal that the value of money be based on common building brick was first advanced by Dr. C. O. Hardy, one of the seminal minds in monetary theory during the interwar and early postwar years. So far as I can discover, Dr. Hardy never published the proposal in a formal paper.[3] It has, however, come to be recognized as one of his many important contributions to monetary theory, and its substance has been passed along in an oral tradition by several scholars, among them Professor Lloyd Mints and a few of his former students, who have been impressed by the logical completeness and, confessedly, by the shock value of the common-brick proposal.

It will be useful to consider the advantages and disadvantages of common brick as the basis for an automatic monetary system. First let us specify briefly but carefully the structure of the system as it is expected to operate. The government sets a schedule of money prices for common building brick of specified quality. For simplicity in exposition, let us assume that this schedule of prices can be represented by a single price that is to be held constant over time. Again I should emphasize, however, that neither a single price nor constancy over time is significant to the proposal. At the same time that this price is announced, a public authority, which we shall call the Mint, announces its willingness to buy and sell units of common brick at the specified price in unlimited amounts. Money is issued from the Mint only in exchange for common brick, and money proceeds from the sale of common brick by the Mint are impounded in the Mint. Every individual has the assurance that he can, at any time, take a common brick, or any quantity of common brick (or a certificate of ownership of brick) to the Mint and receive in exchange a monetary unit, say, a paper dollar. He also knows that he can, at any time and in any desired amount, go to the Mint and purchase, for paper dollars, common brick of the specified quality. No additional mone-

3. In my search for some published version of the original proposal, I am indebted to Mrs. Myra M. Hardy of Washington, D.C., and to Dr. William H. Moore of the staff of the Joint Economic Committee.

tary or fiscal policy need take place. Having no powers to create or to destroy money other than those implicit in the rules governing the operations of the Mint, the government has to finance expenditures through taxation or through real borrowing. Commercial banks may be assumed to operate on the basis of 100 per cent reserves behind deposits, although this assumption is not essential to the analysis of the brick standard itself.[4]

This sort of monetary system could be predicted to work in a manner analogous to any other monetary system based upon a commodity standard. When the general level of prices rises above some presumed initial or "equilibrium" level, it becomes profitable for traders in common brick to *purchase* physical units of the standard commodity from the Mint. They can do so readily by exchanging paper money for brick or certificates of ownership of brick. As these traders turn in units of paper money to the Mint, the money supply outside the Mint is reduced, since the Mint is obligated to destroy or neutralize paper so received. As the supply of money in the system is reduced, the upward pressure on general prices is changed into downward pressure, and the price level begins to fall toward a predicted value. At the same time, of course, the brick-production industry becomes depressed in relation to other industries. The rate of brick production is reduced and resources tend to shift to other industries. This induced increase in the supply of nonstandard commodities and services does, of course, exert an effect that is substantially less significant than the demand effect resulting from the monetary contraction generated by the expansion of brick purchases from the Mint. Both the demand and the supply processes continue until they, along with supporting speculation in nonstandard commodities, are successful in bringing the absolute price level back into some accepted relation with a generally expected or predicted value. This result is accomplished, however, without any agency, authority, business firm, or single individual paying explicit attention to the absolute price level as such. Traders and potential traders in the standard commodity, brick, are guided by profit-maximization criteria, not by any private or public concern for monetary stability.

4. I should point out that the brick-standard proposal as outlined here, and the analysis of its operation that follows, represent my own version of the original proposal. I should like to give Dr. Hardy the full credit due him for originating the proposal without attributing to him any of the possible errors that might be present in this version.

The system is fully symmetrical in the case of a fall in the absolute price level below some predicted value. This fall generates offsetting equilibrating behavior. Firms find it profitable to sell brick to the Mint. As this takes place, additional money finds its way into the payments stream of the economy. This primary effect tends to increase aggregate demand for all nonstandard goods and services. It is supplemented by a supply-side effect generated by the shift of resources away from the production of nonstandard commodities, reducing the excess supplies forthcoming, and into the production of brick, the standard commodity. Again, the process continues until the absolute price level returns to some expected or predicted value or, to state the same thing in terms of the criteria directing private actions, until the relative profitability of production and sale of brick to the monetary authority disappears.

To this point, the same analysis might be applied to any physical commodity designated as the standard for an automatically operating monetary system. Indeed one of the points in discussing this analysis in terms of an everyday commodity like common building brick is the demonstration that a commodity standard need not be conceived in terms of precious metals. But we may go much further than this. There are many positive advantages of the brick-standard system in comparison with other possible commodity systems. In reviewing some of these advantages, it is useful to compare and contrast common brick with gold as the basis for an automatic monetary system.

First of all, common brick can be produced advantageously in almost every local area in the United States. The required adjustments in the industry producing the standard commodity would not, therefore, be localized in particular regions or areas. When general inflationary or deflationary pressures in the economy imposed depression or boom on this brick-producing industry, the dispersion of production over space would tend to prevent differential regional impact. Contrast this situation with one involving a standard commodity, such as gold or anthracite coal, which is produced only in highly localized areas. In periods of incipient depression or recession, the employment effects of the brick-standard system would be noteworthy. Opportunities for employment in local brickyards would tend to mitigate the necessity for the accelerated labor mobility that would be required in the shifting of resources into a regionally localized industry. This advantage is symmetrical with respect to the unemployment effects during periods of inflation.

A second major advantage lies in the fact that production processes for common brick do not seem to be overly complex, although I plead technical ignorance here. Efficient producing plants probably need not be of extremely large size, and entry into and egress from the industry should not be difficult. For these and other reasons, reactions to relative price and cost changes should take place rapidly and without serious dislocation of resources. A closely related third advantage is that production seems to require relatively few highly specialized resources. These three features combine to ensure that the elasticity of supply would be reasonably high.

A final advantage that should not be overlooked is that common building brick would probably not be suitable for adjusting international balances of payments. The system would, in this way, facilitate rather than hinder the separation of the domestic monetary system from the international payments mechanism, a separation whose impossibility would seriously restrict the use of gold as the standard commodity. The brick-standard system would be a suitable companion to a system of floating exchange rates.

On each of the four counts noted, a monetary standard of common building brick would seem superior to one of gold or any other precious metal.

There would, of course, be some offsetting disadvantages to the brick-standard system. Any commodity standard must involve some storage costs not present under managed systems: some proportion of the resources of the economy must of necessity be devoted to maintaining a stock of the commodity designated as the monetary standard, a stock over and above that which would be normal for nonmonetary uses. With brick, there would be little deterioration or depreciation involved in storage over time, but the sheer bulk of the commodity could make storage costs substantial. Economic resources would be tied up in maintaining unused a sizable stock of common brick. This stock need not go entirely unused, however. A substantial proportion could be devoted to the construction of government buildings. If in fact it could be predicted that the system would operate effectively on some fractional-reserve withdrawal, that is, if it could be predicted that the required responses to general upward or downward pressures would involve no more than, say, one fourth of the existing stock of "money brick," then three fourths of this stock, against which the Mint would at some time have issued dollars, could be employed in the construction of government buildings. In this way, the general taxpayer would secure some indirect benefit. As a recognized ultimate reserve or backing for the outstanding money issues, the brick used in such construction projects would have to be carefully distinguished from those government bricks acquired through ordinary market channels, and a potential withdrawal of this "money brick" would have to be acknowledged. Should a general wave of dishoarding on the part of the public generate serious inflationary pressure, thus making it highly profitable for private buildings to be constructed with brick purchased from the Mint, then offsetting destruction of some government buildings might have to take place. It is difficult to imagine that such major swings around a predicted norm would take place, however, once a monetary system of this nature came to be in full operation. For this reason there would seem to be little grounds for concern about the periodic possible destruction of private or public buildings.

One of the major disadvantages of any commodity standard, especially when viewed in the light of the predictability norm, lies in its vulnerability to unpredictable changes in the relative costs of producing standard and nonstandard commodities. A major technological improvement in production processes in the brick industry could, for example, be the source of serious inflation in the economy. We know that one of the disadvantages of the historical gold standard was its subjection of general economic conditions to the sometimes fortuitous discoveries of new gold fields. While brick would on this count clearly be superior to gold, the possible inflation that could result from a differential technological breakthrough should not be neglected in any thorough comparative evaluation. There would seem to be little chance of such a depletion of suitable raw materials as to make deflation from this source a serious possibility.

A second disadvantage of any commodity standard lies in its potential vulnerability to unpredictable shifts in the nonmonetary demand for the standard commodity. For example, an upsurge in the fashionableness of brick houses would, under the operation of a brick standard, impose deflationary pressure on the economy generally. To some extent, however, these unpredictable shifts in the private demand for the monetary commodity could be offset by variations in the government demand. In so far as such demand shifts occur and are not effectively offset, the commodity standard will not be able to produce monetary predictability. But broadly considered, such shifts are different in degree only from shifts in the desire to hold money, that is, hoarding and dishoarding, which seem to reduce the predictability of any monetary system.

A Labor Standard of Value?

It seems clear that common brick would be a more desirable monetary commodity than gold. But are there other commodities or services that might serve the desired purposes as well as, or perhaps better than, common brick? Before and after the time of Adam Smith, economists have been intrigued with and attracted by the idea that, of all existent commodities and services, common labor provides the best single measure of value in an economy. I should like to explore briefly the idea of utilizing common labor as the basis for an automatic monetary system.

In thinking about pedagogical devices for clarifying the logic of such a standard, I have toyed with an idea jokingly suggested by Professor Armen Alchian. He proposed that the general unemployment problem could be solved quite simply by installing money machines on each street corner. Each machine would be equipped with a crank or foot pedal, and upon turning the crank or pumping the pedal anyone could secure money at a fixed rate in exchange for effort measured solely by energy inputs. The energy generated by turning the crank or pumping the pedal could, perhaps, be turned into electricity by tying each machine into a power grid of some sort. This proposal represents one side of an automatic monetary system that bases the value of money on common-labor units. As a substitute for the Alchian machine, we could think of the Mint purchasing common labor at a fixed price in unlimited quantities. The labor so purchased could then be "sold" at auction to private entrepreneurs, or used to construct public works.

The other half of a common-labor-standard system is somewhat more difficult to conceive. Labor is not a storable commodity but a service. A fully automatic system would require that the Mint stand ready to sell as well as to buy units of the service. How could the Mint "sell" labor in unlimited quantities during times of threatened inflation? The idea is not wholly implausible. We could think of a scheme in which the government obligates itself to "sell" common labor to business firms without a stock of labor being maintained. For example, if the market price of common labor should rise above the "standard" price, the business firm could "purchase" labor services from the government. To meet this demand the government would have to purchase, at the market wage rate, sufficient labor services to meet business demands on it. This public outlay would have to be financed wholly from general tax revenues. The government would be obligated to neutralize the fixed money sum turned in by the business firm in "purchasing" each unit of labor service. I do not have the space to discuss further the interesting features of a scheme such as this, but I should emphasize the importance of considering all possible alternatives.[5]

Predictability and Constitutional Attitude

I am convinced that an automatic monetary system utilizing some basic commodity or service, such as common brick or common labor as the standard of value, would work. And by this I mean that such a system would embody a high degree of predictability about the course of movements in the absolute level of prices, in the value of money. I am also convinced that a managed system characterized by some specific rules for action would work; and I make no strong argument for one alternative over the other. Both alternatives will work, or both will fail, for the same reason.

I recall a statement once made by Professor F. A. Hayek to the effect that "nothing is inevitable but thinking makes it so." I should paraphrase this to apply here as "nothing is predictable, but thinking makes it so." The implementation of a monetary constitution that will produce predictability requires more than consensus among experts. Even if we could substantially agree on the most practicable monetary reform, and even if we were given the power to institute such reform, we would have no assurance that the continuing monetary problem would be solved. We should never lose sight of the fact that the average man knows little of economics and, worse than this, he does not know how little he does know. Man has, throughout modern

---

5. Dr. Francesco Forte has suggested to me that the proposal for a labor standard has been discussed at length by P. Jannaccone. I have not, however, been able to consult Jannaccone's work.

history, tended to blame the monetary system for many of his economic ills, and he has been quite right on many occasions. But by now he has learned through observation that his own actions, or the actions of men acting "for him," the government, can change, modify, and reform the monetary system. Thus, with respect to monetary matters, we find the average man able to raise objections, to criticize, without being able himself to provide rationally motivated alternatives to existing institutions. No longer is the average man willing to adopt a quasi-fatalistic attitude, to attribute the workings of the monetary system to the gods, to accept some mythology of money. To some small extent, such a mythology, such an attitude, was engendered by the operation of the historical gold standard. This system was to many people sacrosanct, and even today there is within all of us some of this mythology of gold as the appropriate monetary metal. It is this mythology that makes us look upon any such proposal as the one for a brick standard as amusing, and which causes us to dismiss such a proposal before we have seriously considered its working properties.

Careful observation should convince us, however, that even the mythology of the gold standard is substantially gone, and once gone, a mythology can never be reconstructed. If it could be, it would, by definition, not constitute a mythology. Nor can the wisest of monetary reforms create a monetary mythology surrounding a brick standard, a price-level rule, a Federal Reserve Board, or whatever.

Yet without something that serves the same purposes, *no* monetary reform can be expected to work, to ensure the predictability in the value of money that we all should accept as the appropriate norm. I suggest that what is required, what is essential here, is a "constitutional attitude"; that is to say, people must agree on the basic rules that define the operation of a monetary system and then agree to abide by these rules as adopted. The attitude of which I speak is one that prevents continual tampering with the rules as adopted. This constitutional attitude seems to me to be one of the most difficult of human behavioral characteristics to adopt, or even to explain and to understand. Since the Enlightenment men have refused to acknowledge the validity of any absolutes, either in terms of ethical principles or in terms of social institutions. Ideas, laws, social structures: all have been subjected to discussion and to question, and through these, to deliberately organized modification and change. Chaos is likely to result if change is made too quickly and not for rational reasons. Until and unless we know what changes are in fact "best," it is far better to accept certain "relatively absolute absolutes," both in ethics and in the rules defining the social order. And we cannot really know what fundamental or constitutional changes are needed until we are able to observe the working of a given set of institutions over time, through a long succession of events. The willingness to do this, to play a series of games by the same rules in order to evaluate properly the rules themselves, is the essential attitude that is required. The need for this attitude is not, of course, confined to the monetary problem. The monetary problem does serve, however, to point up sharply the general relevance of the attitude that is more generally required for the maintenance of orderly civilized life.

Specifically, with the emergence of a genuinely constitutional attitude, there are many possible monetary systems that would work well, that would ensure an adequate degree of monetary predictability. Without the emergence of this attitude, there is no monetary system that will work well, and continued monetary chaos, of sorts, can be expected to prevail.

Generality as a
Constitutional Constraint

I. Introduction

I appreciate the opportunity to visit Japan again and, especially, to speak to this meeting of the Asian Public Choice Society. It is nice to see so many of my Japanese friends again, many of whom have been visiting scholars at our Public Choice Center in Virginia, either in Blacksburg or in Fairfax (and, for some, both). For three decades now, I have been both pleased and surprised at the reception accorded to the public choice research program in Japan. My residual fear has always been, and this applies to all national communities outside the United States, that the research program in public choice has been too closely tied to the historical and institutional United States setting to have much international applicability, even if, on its own, the program has been developed in quite abstract formulations. The interest expressed by both Japanese and European scholars over the years has helped to mitigate this fear.

As many of you know, my own interest and research emphasis have always been on the constitutional part of the public choice program—on the choices among rules or constraints within which ordinary political decisions are made. This work involves, in its positive variant, analyses of the working properties of alternative sets of rules on patterns of political outcomes and, in its normative extension, discussion of optimal or efficient structures. Again, as many of you know, in recent years we have called this part of the

Originally presented at a meeting of the Japanese Public Choice Society in Tokyo, Japan, in August 1997. In *Trap of Democracy* (Tokyo: Editorial Board of Public Choice Studies).

inclusive public choice program "constitutional political economy," and we have tried to encourage particular research through establishment of the journal *Constitutional Political Economy*.

I do not propose here to try to summarize the comprehensive research programs in constitutional political economy. I want to limit this lecture to a summary treatment of my own program over the last four years—a program that has now culminated in a book written jointly with Roger Congleton and entitled *Politics by Principle, Not Interest*, which will be published by Cambridge University Press, presumably early in 1998.[1] This book develops, both analytically and in applicability, the generality principle, or norm, as a constraint that might be imposed constitutionally on the operation of majority rule politics.

II. Relation to Other Work

I can perhaps give you an introductory idea of this work by relating it to other writings, both my own and that of others. The most direct precursor is F. A. Hayek in his 1960 treatise, *The Constitution of Liberty*.[2] Those of you who know this book will recall that Hayek's main theme is the necessary place of the rule of law in any liberal order—with the rule of law defined in terms of the generality norm. Persons are to be equal before the law and are to be equally treated by the law. Everyone is to play by the same rules; there are no persons or groups who are to be either specially privileged or specially disadvantaged.

This principle or precept is a long and well-understood part of post-Enlightenment liberal thought, and it has informed legal philosophy for at least two centuries. The principle also finds embodiment in legal structures throughout the world—both as formally stated and as informally applied. Only very recently, and then only in fringe groups, have we found legal scholars who would overtly advocate departure from the generality norm in

1. James M. Buchanan and Roger D. Congleton, *Politics by Principle, Not Interest: Toward Nondiscriminatory Democracy* (Cambridge and New York: Cambridge University Press, forthcoming).

2. F. A. Hayek, *The Constitution of Liberty* (Chicago: University of Chicago Press, 1960).

the application of law itself. (I should add that I speak here only for United States legal scholarship.)

Our effort in the book may be described, in one sense, as an extension and elaboration of Hayek's theme. What we do, reduced to its essentials, is to suggest that the generality principle be extended to the realm of political action, that is, beyond the law as ordinarily interpreted. Indeed the subtitle of our book is *Toward Nondiscriminatory Democracy.* We suggest that, in part, the generality norm has not been explicitly extended to politics due to the heritage of idealism in political theory and that a rather direct implication of the public choice exorcism of romance from political action should be the recognition that some generality-like constraint is required.

I can also relate this current effort to earlier works of my own. In our book, *The Calculus of Consent*, Gordon Tullock and I analyzed the choice among constitutional rules for making collective decisions.[3] That work was motivated and informed by Knut Wicksell's seminal insight concerning the relationship between economic efficiency—defined in the standard manner—and unanimity as a collective decision rule. In a sense, our book might have been interpreted as a criticism of majority rule or majoritarianism with the subsidiary theme that, for many collective actions, a supermajority or qualified majority, short of unanimity but more inclusive than a simple majority, might be preferred.

I should not propose to modify in any way the analytical argument in *The Calculus of Consent.* However, in the three and one-half decades since that book was initially published, I have come increasingly to recognize, and acknowledge, that majority rule is equated in public attitudes with democracy, in some rather deep evaluative sense, and that proposals to impose constitutional requirements for qualified or supermajorities are likely to get little support. This recognition has prompted me to analyze alternative means through which collective action might be constrained. The present effort is, therefore, predicated on the maintenance of majoritarianism as the basic decision rule, while opening up the possibility of constraining the operation of this rule by restrictions on the set of feasible outcomes.

3. James M. Buchanan and Gordon Tullock, *The Calculus of Consent: Logical Foundations in Constitutional Democracy* (Ann Arbor: University of Michigan Press, 1962).

III. The Elementary Logic of Majority Rule

Public choice theory has been seriously flawed from its beginnings by the implicit presumption that the alternatives for choice—the members of the choice set—are exogenous to the constitutional rule through which choices are to be made. Early analysis in public choice concentrated on pairwise voting choices between alternatives (candidates, motions, positions) that were simply presented to the relevant electorate, as if by some external source. There was no recognition of the obvious fact that alternatives must, themselves, come from somewhere and that the rules might be influential in generating the choice set. In application to simple majority voting, an alternative that is majority-dominated or preferred for all members of any and all possible majority coalitions would never be presented for consideration. The criteria of domination and nondomination, familiar from Paretian welfare economics, can be directly extended to any collective choice rule.[4]

The elementary logic of a majority voting rule is straightforward. Majority voting means what it says—the majority rules the minority. Almost by definition, symmetry in result or outcome is ruled out; any symmetrical result will be dominated by a nonsymmetrical result, regardless of the makeup of the coalition that assumes control.

Consider the simple majority voting game in which a given value is to be divided among three persons. The symmetrical solution would assign one-third of this total value to each of the three members of the group. Note immediately, however, that this solution is dominated, for any majority, by a solution that assigns all of the value to the two members who happen to make up the majority coalition. The symmetrical solution, or distribution of value, would never, therefore, be presented for a vote by any potential majority coalition.

I have found it helpful to use the simple two-by-two matrix illustration to demonstrate the elementary logic here, despite the necessary collapse into two dimensions. Consider two persons, *A* and *B*, but think of these persons as coalitions that might rotate sequentially in positions of collective choice authority. Draw in payoffs in the four cells of the matrix, ordered precisely as such payoffs are found in standard versions of PD (prisoners' dilemma)

---

4. See my paper "Majoritarian Logic," forthcoming in *Public Choice.*

games. For our purposes here, however, the interaction in question is presumed to have been collectivized. A solution does not emerge from the separated and independent choices of the two persons. Instead a single outcome or solution is to be chosen by the person or coalition that assumes collective decision authority. The results are evident. If *A* is in a position of political power, the off-diagonal solution that differentially rewards *A* and penalizes *B* will be chosen. And similarly for *B*. If *B* is the decision maker, the off-diagonal solution that differentially rewards *B* and penalizes *A* will be selected. The symmetrical or on-diagonal solution in which both players or participants are benefited, by comparison with the no-action or status quo alternative, will never emerge from a "voting rule" that assigns decision-making authority to less than the full membership of the group. Note that replacement of majority (or in this case one-person rule) by unanimity will generate the symmetrical, and Pareto-superior, outcome.

IV. Eliminating the Off Diagonals

I am forced by space and time constraints here to summarize much analysis—some of it highly abstract—into a relatively short summary treatment, but I hope that the direction of the argument is clear. The elementary logic of majority rule must generate off-diagonal solutions; this logic dictates that members of majority coalitions are differentially advantaged relative to members of the polity outside these coalitions; majoritarian democracy is necessarily discriminatory in its operation, until and unless this feature is explicitly constrained.

It is at this point that the generality principle takes on its normatively desirable attributes. If we can think of generality in terms of symmetry in treatment, as if choices are among the cells of the diagonal whatever the dimensionality of the problem, we do not need to replace majority rule with some rule that requires more than majority agreement. For me, this point is the critical one. Majority rule can be forced, by the nature of the constraints on the choice set imposed by the generality norm, to operate much as if it were a unanimity rule. In the previous illustration of the simple two-person model, application of the generality constraint would, of course, make the operation of majority rule fully equivalent to the unanimity rule. In more extended, and more realistic, models in which both the number of options and number of members of the total electorate are expanded, majority rule constrained to choose only among locations or final positions along the diagonal would not produce results fully analogous to the unanimity rule. But as a generality norm constrains choice options to those along the diagonal, even if n-dimensional, the set of feasible options is dramatically reduced, and, importantly, overtly discriminatory treatment of minority members is effectively prohibited.

V. From Abstract Models to Applications

The elementary analysis, which I have done little more than sketch out earlier, is relatively straightforward, and, to me in any case, this analysis is both aesthetically and ethically appealing. In effect, this analysis translates the normative implications of elementary public choice theory into a politics that would embody the equivalent of the idealized rule of law. Through this analysis, we can perhaps begin to sense, abstractly, just what a genuinely nondiscriminatory majoritarian democracy would look like. As an ideal, it becomes quite exciting.

It is more difficult to translate the abstracted ideal into reality—even the reality that we deal with as academicians—than the analysis might itself indicate. To take this step, we must, and quite specifically, put precise labels on the rows and columns of our imagined n-dimensional matrices. What does it mean to say that solutions are either on or off the n-dimensional diagonal in the reality of modern politics?

In our book, we try to make several applications, with more or less success. Let me consider, first, the elementary fiscal setting, in which a commonly used public good is financed by taxes paid by separate members of the political community. David Hume's familiar example of the farmers who live alongside the common swamp or meadow that needs to be drained is called to mind here. To the extent that the benefits are equally available to all, once the investment is made, we can, plausibly I think, make the claim that the members of the group are treated symmetrically on this side of the fiscal account. But what is the tax side equivalent? Here it seems that symmetry in treatment would involve equal tax payments by each farmer. In this simple setting, with the outcomes constrained to those that embody equal taxes and equal availability of the public good, majority rule could be allowed full operation with no concern about undue or discriminatory exploitation of minority by majority. This remains true even if and when separate persons do not agree on their preferred results; the majoritarian solution is that which tends to meet the preferences of the median voter, as among the alternatives along the diagonal.

We move a step closer toward political reality when we drop the implicit assumption that the members of the political community are equal in their taxpaying capacity. What is the tax side equivalent of generality or symmetry in treatment when persons differ, perhaps very substantially, in their ability to pay taxes? What, if any, plausibly acceptable base for taxation, income or wealth, must commence from major differences among persons in their pre-tax positions?

It seems to me here that an argument can be made to the effect that a flat rate or proportional rate on an income base offers the closest approximation to meeting the generality norm. The elementary logic of the analysis suggests to me that Einaudi's scheme to the effect that each and every unit of value should be treated as equal for tax purposes carries considerable normative weight. In many respects, a flat tax, without exemptions, deductions, credits, or other special dispensation, meets the criterion of generality.

Differing members, and groups, in the electorate will, of course, differ as to the level of taxes to be imposed, and, residually, on the size of the overall budget. But the tax-rate structure cannot be used, deliberately, by a majority coalition as a means of exploiting members of a political minority, whether applied directly or indirectly. If constrained in this way, I, for one, would be quite willing to allow majoritarian decision processes to work their will.

If we shift outside the financing of public goods and consider direct transfers, it seems to me that the generality norm suggests that all direct transfers should take the form of equal-per-head payments—sometimes called demogrants—again without exemptions through means tests or otherwise. Note that the financing of demogrants through the levy of proportional or flat-rate taxes will, indeed, allow for some, perhaps considerable, redistribution through the fiscal process. Persons who are net taxpayers under this scheme will tend to prefer lower rates of tax, and transfers, than those persons who are net transferees. Even here, however, there is no overt discrimination involved, or so it seems to me.

I cannot, of course, go over the many other applications of the analysis here. Clearly, any particularized regulation or restriction on this or that market would violate the generality constraint. If government is to regulate or to protect one industry, profession, or product category, such a constraint would require that all comparable groups be treated similarly. This constraint would, almost immediately, remove all pressures toward market restrictions, since those who seek to secure differential benefits do so in the expectation that their group will be treated advantageously relative to other groups.

VI. Efficiency, Rent Seeking, and Generality

I previously suggested that the generality constraint was both aesthetically and ethically appealing. Let me now move into areas of discussion where economists are more at home—let me discuss the efficiency implications of a generality requirement.

First of all, let me acknowledge that, if we adopt the mind-set of the orthodox welfare economist and hold fast to the standard definitions of economic efficiency, there may seem to be little or no relationship between the two criteria: efficiency and generality. Would a flat-rate tax on incomes, without exemptions or deductions, with revenues devoted to the financing of a Samuelsonian public good, satisfy the necessary conditions for Pareto-Lindahl efficiency? Only under a specific combination of elasticities of demand and supply could this question be answered affirmatively.[5] If divorced completely from the politics of implementation, efficiency in financing public goods and services, or transfers, would dictate differential taxes on any given base, not general taxes of the sort imposed under any generality constraint.

We cannot, however, leave out the political structure through which we might expect both budgetary and taxing decisions to be made. That is to say, public choice cannot be ignored. And I should argue that, when political decision structures are analyzed, and particularly those of majority voting rules, a generality constraint will enhance rather than retard the approach to any efficiency standard. There is no more likelihood that political majorities

5. See my early treatment of this issue, "Fiscal Institutions and Efficiency in Collective Outlay," *American Economic Review* 54 (May 1964): 227–35.

would, indeed, implement the criteria for tax allocation dictated by the economists' efficiency calculus than that the two-person majority in the simple distribution game previously discussed would adopt the symmetry solution.

However, if constituents know, in advance, that is, constitutionally, that taxes for the financing of public goods are to be imposed *generally* on a designated base, there is no incentive for investment in efforts to secure differentially or discriminatorily favorable treatment, on the one hand, or to avoid differentially unfavorable treatment, on the other. The waste of resources in tax-related rent seeking would be very substantially reduced, if not totally eliminated. There would, of course, remain advantages to membership in majority coalitions, since constituency groups may differ over preferred budgetary size and composition, even under generality constraints on taxes, transfers, and on public goods. But clearly the difference between majority and minority status would be very substantially reduced under generality and, along with this, a reduction in fiscally motivated rent seeking. Resources that are spent on lobbying effort can, of course, be productively employed in alternative value-generating uses.

VII. Generality in Modern Democracy

One reaction to the inquiry that I have sketched out in this lecture might well be to the effect that the program is much ado about little or nothing. Critics may suggest that, indeed, generality is an important aspect of modern liberal societies, but, they might suggest that the principle does describe the basic working of structures in existence and departures may be relatively exceptional. Here, I must plead provincialism in my illiteracy about other fiscal-political structures than those of the United States. In the latter, there are well-understood constitutional limits on the degree, as well as the kind, of differential or discriminatory treatment of specially identified persons and groups. Attempts to differentiate against persons in terms of defined political affiliation would be ruled out of bounds constitutionally. So would attempts to discriminate on the basis of gender, race, ethnic background, and other like characteristics.

On the other hand, and by contrast, there is no constitutional restriction against discrimination on the basis of economic position or many other characteristics. Rates of tax may vary among different income or wealth categories; and, more importantly, rates of spending benefits can be targeted to specific locations, professions, industries, production or consumption categories, and age levels. Or, on the other side of the political account, particular groups may be subjected to discriminatorily unfavorable treatment.

It is possible to imagine an activist judiciary that might rediscover in the American constitutional documents a more robust generality constraint than modern courts are likely to enforce. The United States experience in the nineteenth century does suggest that the generality principle might not require a totally novel interpretation of constitutional law.

In one sense, therefore, at least in the American context, my argument in support of generality as a constraint on the operation of majoritarian democracy becomes a plea for rediscovery of what was once a wider understanding by politicians, by judges, by academicians, and by the public—an understanding that recognizes that overly discriminatory democracy cannot retain legitimacy. My own fear, at century's end, is that the extended commitments of modern welfare democracies may have created conditions where ruling coalitions will be tempted to resolve apparent fiscal crises by moving away from, rather than toward, generality. Quasi-general programs of income support, for old-age payments in particular, may be subjected increasingly to means testing. "Targeted," rather than general, tax adjustments may become increasingly important on the agenda of political coalitions in authority, in part motivated by residual *dirigiste* attitudes, but also driven by demands of fiscal expediency.

It is surely time that we read and understand what Hayek was telling us almost four decades past. "The Constitution of Liberty" must embody adherence to the principle of generality, whether emergent in the application of ordinary law or to the operation of majoritarian politics. All citizens must be made to play by the same rules, and all politics must be nondiscriminatory in its application.

Before Public Choice

A contract theory of the State is relatively easy to derive, and careful use of this theory can yield major explanatory results. To an extent at least, a "science" exists for the purpose of providing psychologically satisfying explanations of what men can commonly observe about them. Presumably, we "feel better" when we possess some explanatory framework or model that allows us to classify and interpret disparate sense perceptions. This imposition of order on the universe is a "good" in the strict economic sense of this term; men will invest money, time, and effort in acquiring it. The contract theory of the State, in all of its manifestations, can be defended on such grounds. It is important for sociopolitical order and tranquility that ordinary men explain to themselves the working of governmental process in models that conceptually take their bases in cooperative rather than in noncooperative behavior. Admittedly and unabashedly, the contract theory serves, in this sense, a rationalization purpose or objective. We need a "logic of law," a "calculus of consent," a "logic of collective action," to use the titles of three books that embody modern-day contract theory foundations.[1]

Can the contract theory of the State serve other objectives, whether these be normative or positive in character? Can institutions which find no conceivable logical derivation in contract among cooperating parties be condemned on other than strictly personal grounds? Can alleged improvements

From *Explorations in the Theory of Anarchy*, ed. Gordon Tullock (Blacksburg, Va.: Center for Study of Public Choice, 1972), 27–37. Reprinted by permission of the publisher.

1. See Gordon Tullock, *The Logic of Law* (New York: Basic Books, 1970); James M. Buchanan and Gordon Tullock, *The Calculus of Consent* (Ann Arbor: University of Michigan Press, 1962); Mancur Olson, *The Logic of Collective Action* (Cambridge: Harvard University Press, 1965).

in social arrangements be evaluated on anything other than contractarian precepts, or, to lapse into economists' jargon, on anything other than Paretian criteria? But, even here, are these criteria any more legitimate than any other?

In earlier works, I have tended to go past these fundamental questions. I have been content to work out, at varying levels of sophistication, the contractarian bases for governmental action, either that which we can commonly observe or that which might be suggested as reforms. To me, this effort seemed relevant and significant. "Political economy" or "public choice"— these seemed to be labels assignable to honorable work that required little or no methodological justification. It was only when I tried to outline a summary treatment of my whole approach to sociopolitical structure that I was stopped short. I came to realize that the very basis of the contractarian position must be examined more thoroughly.

We know that, factually and historically, the "social contract" is mythological, at least in many of its particulars. Individuals did not come together in some original position and mutually agree on the rules of social intercourse. And even had they done so at some time in history, their decisions could hardly be considered to be contractually binding on all of us who have come behind. We cannot start anew. We can either accept the political universe, or we can try to change it. The question reduces to one of determining the criteria for change.

When and if we fully recognize that the contract is a myth designed in part to rationalize existing institutional structures of society, can we simultaneously use the contractual derivations to develop criteria for evaluating changes or modifications in these structures? I have previously answered this question affirmatively, but without proper argument. The intellectual quality as well as the passionate conviction of those who answer the question negatively suggest that more careful consideration is required.

How can we derive a criterion for determining whether or not a change in law, or, if you will, a change in the assignment of rights, is or is not justified? To most social scientists, the only answer is solipsist. Change becomes desirable if "I like it," even though many prefer to dress this up in fanciful "social welfare function" or "public interest" semantics. To me, this seems to be pure escapism; it represents retreat into empty arguments about personal values which spells the end of rational discourse. Perhaps some of our colleagues do possess God-like qualities, or at least think that they do, but until and unless their godliness is accepted, we are left with no basis for discourse. My purpose is to see how far we can rationally discuss criteria for social change on the presumption that no man's values are better than any other man's.

Is *agreement* the only test? Is the Wicksellian-contractarian-Paretian answer the only legitimate one here? If so, are we willing to accept its corollaries? Its full implications? Are we willing to forestall all social change that does not command unanimous or quasi-unanimous consent?

Provisionally, let us say that we do so. We can move a step beyond, while at the same time rationalizing much of what we see, by resorting to "constitutionalism," the science of rules. We can say that particular proposals for social change need not command universal assent provided only that such assent holds for the legal structure within which particular proposals are enacted or chosen. This seems to advance the argument; we seem to be part of the way out of the dilemma. But note that this provides us with no means at all for evaluating particular proposals as "good" or "bad." We can generate many outcomes or results under nonunanimity rules. This explains my initial response to the Arrow impossibility theorem, and to the subsequent discussion. My response was, and is, one of nonsurprise at the alleged inconsistency in a social decision process that embodies in itself no criteria for consistency. This also explains my unwillingness to be trapped, save on rare and regretted occasions, into positions of commitment on particular measures of policy on the familiar efficiency grounds. We can offer no policy advice on particular legislative proposals. As political economists, we examine public choices; we can make institutional predictions. We can analyze alternative political-social-economic structures.

But what about constitutional change itself? Can we say nothing, or must we say that, at this level, the contractarian (Wicksellian, Paretian) norm must apply? Once again, observation hardly supports us here. Changes are made, changes that would be acknowledged to be genuinely "constitutional," without anything remotely approaching unanimous consent. Must we reject all such changes out of hand, or can we begin to adduce criteria on some other basis?

Resort to the choice of rules for ordinary parlor games may seem to offer assistance. Influenced greatly by the emphasis on such choices by Rutledge

Vining, I once considered this to be the key to genuinely innovative application of the contractarian criteria. If we could, somehow, think of individual participants in a setting of complete uncertainty about their own positions over subsequent rounds of play, we might think of their reaching
genuine agreement on a set of rules. The idea of a "fair game" does have real
meaning, and this idea can be transferred to sociopolitical institutions. But
how far can we go with this? We may, in this process, begin to rationalize
certain institutions that cannot readily be brought within the standard Wicksellian framework. But can we do more? Can we, as John Rawls seems to
want to do in his monumental *Theory of Justice*,[2] think ourselves into a position of original contract and then idealize our thought processes into
norms that "should" be imposed as criteria for institutional change? Note
that this is, to me, quite different from saying that we derive a possible rationalization. To rationalize, to explain, is not to propose, and Rawls seems
to miss this quite critical distinction. It is one thing to say that, conceptually,
men in some genuinely constitutional stage of deliberation, operating behind the veil of ignorance, might have agreed to rules something akin to
those that we actually observe, but it is quite another thing to say that men,
in the here and now, should be forced to abide by specific rules that we imagine by transporting ourselves into some mental-moral equivalent of an original contract setting where men are genuine "moral equals."

Unless we do so, however, we must always accept whatever structure of
rules that exists and seek constitutional changes only through agreement,
through consensus. It is this inability to say anything about rules changes,
this inability to play God, this inability to raise himself above the masses, that
the social philosopher cannot abide. He has an ingrained prejudice against
the status quo, however this may be defined, understandably so, since his
very role, as he interprets it, is one that finds itself only in social reform. (Perhaps this role conception reflects the moral inversion that Michael Polanyi
and Craig Roberts note; the shift of moral precepts away from personal behavior aimed at personal salvation and toward moral evaluation or social institutions.)

Just what are men saying when they propose nonagreed changes in the
basic structure of rights? Are they saying anything more than "this is what I

2. John Rawls, *Theory of Justice* (Cambridge: Harvard University Press, 1971).

want and since I think the State has the power to impose it, I support the State as the agency to enforce the change"? We may be able to get some handles on this very messy subject by going back to Hobbes. We need to examine the initial leap out of the Hobbesian jungle. How can agreement emerge? And what are the problems of enforcement?

We may represent the reaction equilibrium in the Hobbesian jungle at the origin in the diagrammatics of Figure 1. If we measure "B's law-abiding behavior" on the ordinate, and "A's law-abiding behavior" on the abscissa, it is evident that neither man secures advantage from "lawful" behavior individually and independently of the other man's behavior. (Think of "law-abiding" here as "not-stealing.") Note that the situation here is quite different from the usual public-goods model in which at least some of the "good" will tend to be produced by one or all of the common or joint consumers even under wholly independent adjustment. With law-abiding as the "good," however, the individual cannot, through his own behavior, produce so as to increase his own utility. He can do nothing other than provide a "pure" external economy; all benefits accrue to the other parties. Hence, the independent adjustment position involves a corner solution at the origin in our two-person diagram. But gains-from-trade clearly exist in this Hobbesian jungle, despite the absence of unilateral action.

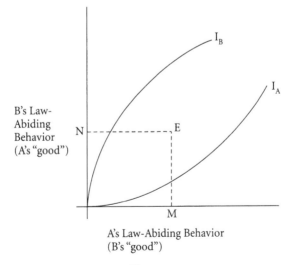

Figure 1

It is easy enough to depict the Pareto region that bounds potential positions of mutual gains by drawing the appropriate indifference contours through the origin as is done in Figure 1. These contours indicate the internal or subjective rates of tradeoff as between *own* and *other* law abiding. It seems plausible to suggest that the standard convexity properties would apply. The analysis remains largely empty, however, until we know something, or at least postulate something, about the descriptive characteristics of the initial position itself. And the important and relevant point in this respect is that individuals *are not equal*, or at least need not be equal, in such a setting, either in their relative abilities or in their final command over consumables.[3] To assume symmetry among persons here amounts to converting a desired normative state, that of equality among men, into a fallacious positive proposition. (This is, of course, a pervasive error, and one that is not only made by social philosophers. It has had significant and pernicious effects on judicial thinking in the twentieth century.) If we drop the equality or symmetry assumption, however, we can say something about the relative values or tradeoffs as between the relative "haves" and "have-nots" in the Hobbesian or natural adjustment equilibrium. For illustrative purposes here, think of the "natural distribution" in our two-person model as characterized by A's enjoyment of 10 units of "good," and B's enjoyment of only 2 units. Both persons expend effort, a "bad," in generating and in maintaining this natural distribution. It is this effort that can be reduced or eliminated through trade, through agreement on laws or rules of respect for property. In this way, both parties can secure more "goods." The posttrade equilibrium must reflect improvement for both parties over the natural distribution or pretrade outcome. There are prospects for Pareto-efficient or Pareto-superior moves from the initial no-rights position to any one of many possible posttrade or positive-rights distributions.

Let us suppose that agreement is reached; each person agrees to an assignment of property rights and, furthermore, each person agrees to respect such rights as are assigned. Let us suppose, for illustration, that the net distribution of "goods" under the assignment is 15 units for A and 7 units for B. Hence, there is a symmetrical sharing of the total gains-from-trade secured

---

3. The formal properties of the "natural distribution" that will emerge under anarchy have been described by Winston Bush in his paper "Income Distribution in Anarchy."

from the assignment of rights. Even under such symmetrical sharing, however, note that the relative position of B has improved more than the relative position of A. In our example, A's income increases by one-half; but B's income increases more than twofold. This suggests that the person who fares relatively worse in the natural distribution may well stand to gain relatively more from an initial assignment of rights than the person who fares relatively better in the pretrade state of the world.

Agreement is attained; both parties enjoy more utility than before. But again the prisoners' dilemma setting must be emphasized. Each of the two persons can anticipate gains by successful unilateral default on the agreement. In Figure 1, if E depicts the position of agreement, A can always gain by a shift to N if this can be accomplished; similarly, B can gain by a shift to M. There may, however, be an asymmetry present in prospective gains from unilateral default on the rights agreement. The prospective gains may well be higher for the person who remains relatively less favored in the natural distribution. In one sense, the "vein of ore" that he can mine by departing from the rules through criminal activity is richer than the similar vein would be for the other party. The productivity of criminal effort is likely to be higher for the man who can steal from his rich neighbor than for the man who has only poor neighbors.

This may be illustrated in the matrix of Figure 2, where the initial pretrade

		B		
		Abides by "Law"	Observes no "Law"	
	Abides by "Law"	I 15, 7	II 6, 12	
A				
	Observes no "Law"	III 17, 3	IV 10, 2	

Figure 2

or natural distribution is shown in Cell IV, and the posttrade or positive rights distribution is shown in Cell I. Note that, as depicted, the man who is relatively "poor" in the natural equilibrium, person B in the example, stands to gain relatively more by departing unilaterally from Cell I than person A. Person B could, by such a move, increase his quantity of "goods" from 7 to 12, whereas person A could only increase his from 15 to 17. This example suggests that the relatively "rich" person will necessarily be more interested in policing the activities of the "poor" man, as such, than vice versa. This is, of course, widely accepted. But the construction and analysis here can be employed for a more complex and difficult issue that has not been treated adequately.

Assume that agreement has been attained; both parties abide by the law; both enjoy the benefits. Time passes. The "rich" man becomes lazy and lethargic. The "poor" man increases his strength. This modifies the natural distribution. Let us say that the natural distribution changes to 6:6. The "rich" man now has an overwhelmingly more significant interest in the maintenance of the legal status quo than the "poor" man, who is no longer "poor" in natural ability terms. The initial symmetry in the sharing of gains as between the no-trade and the trade position no longer holds. With the new natural distribution, the "rich" man secures almost all of the net gains.

The example must be made more specific. Assume that the situation is analogous to the one examined by Winston Bush. The initial problem is how is manna which drops from Heaven to be divided among the two persons. The initial natural distribution is in the ratio 10:2 as noted. Recognizing this, along with their own abilities, A and B agree that by assigning rights, they can attain a 15:7 ratio, as noted. Time passes, and B increases in relative strength, but the "goods" are still shared in the 15:7 ratio. The initial set of property rights agreed to on the foundations of the initial natural distribution no longer reflects or mirrors the existing natural distribution. Under these changed conditions, a lapse back into the natural equilibrium will harm B relatively little whereas A will be severely damaged. The "poor" man now has relatively little interest in adherence to law. If this trend continues, and the natural distribution changes further in the direction indicated, the "poor" man may find himself able to secure even net advantages from a lapse back into the Hobbesian jungle.

The model may be described in something like the terms of modern game theory. If the initial natural distribution remains unaltered, the agreed-on assignment of rights possesses qualities like the core in an n-person game. It is to the advantage of no coalition to depart from this assignment or imputation if the remaining members of the group are willing to enforce or to block the imputation. No coalition can do better on its own, or in this model, in the natural distribution, than it does in the assignment. These core-like properties of the assigned distribution under law may, however, begin to lose dominance features as the potential natural distribution shifts around "underneath" the existing structure of rights, so to speak. The foundations of the existing rights structure may be said to have shifted in the process.

This analysis opens up interesting new implications for net redistribution of wealth and for changes in property rights over time. Observed changes in claims to wealth take place without apparent consent. These may be interpreted simply as the use of the enforcement power of the State by certain coalitions of persons to break the contract. They are overtly shifting from a Cell I into a Cell II or Cell III outcome in the diagram of Figure 2. It is not, of course, difficult to explain why these coalitions arise. It will always be in the interest of a person, or a group of persons, to depart from the agreed-on assignment of claims or rights, provided that he or they can do so unilaterally and without offsetting reactive behavior on the part of the remaining members of the social group. The quasi-equilibrium in Cell I is inherently unstable. The equilibrium does qualify as a position in the core of the game, but we must keep in mind that the core analytics presumes the immediate formation of blocking coalitions. In order fully to explain observed departures from status quo we must also explain the behavior of the absence of the potential blocking coalitions. Why do the remaining members of the community fail to enforce the initial assignment of rights?

The analysis here suggests that if there has been a sufficiently large shift in the underlying natural distribution, the powers of enforcing adherence on the prospective violators of contract may not exist, or, if they exist, these powers may be demonstrably weakened. In our numerical example, B fares almost as well under the new natural distribution as he does in the continuing assignment of legal rights. Hence, A has lost almost all of his blocking power; he can scarcely influence B by threats to plunge the community into Hobbesian anarchy, even if A himself should be willing to do so. And it should also be recognized that "willingness" to enforce the contract (the structure of legal rules, the existing set of claims to property) is as important as the objective ability to do so. Even if A should be physically able to force B to return to the *status quo ante* after some attempted departure, he may be unwilling to suffer the personal loss that might be required to make his threat of enforcement credible.[4] The law-abiding members of the community may find themselves in a genuine dilemma. They may simply be unable to block the unilateral violation of the social contract.

In this perspective, normative arguments based on "justice" in distribution may signal acquiescence in modifications in the existing structure of claims. Just as the idea of contract, itself, has been used to rationalize existing structure, the idea of "justice" may be used to rationalize coerced departures from contract. In the process those who advance such arguments and those who are convinced may "feel better" while their claims are whittled away. This does, I think, explain much attitudinal behavior toward redistribution policy by specific social groups. Gordon Tullock has, in part, explained the prevailing attitudes of many academicians and intellectuals.[5] The explanation developed here applies more directly to the redistributionist attitudes of the scions of the rich, e.g., the Rockefellers and Kennedys. Joseph Kennedy was less redistributive than his sons; John D. Rockefeller was less redistributive than his grandsons. We do not need to call on the psychologists since our model provides an explanation in the concept of a changing natural distribution. The scions of the wealthy are far less secure in their roles of custodians of wealth than were their forebears. They realize perhaps that their own natural talents simply do not match up, even remotely, to the share of national wealth that they now command. Their apparent passions for the poor may be nothing more than surface reflections of attempts to attain temporary security.

The analysis also suggests that there is a major behavioral difference fostered between the intergenerational transmission of nonhuman and human capital. Within limits, there is an important linkage between human capital and capacity to survive in a natural or Hobbesian environment. There seems

4. For a more extensive discussion of these points, see my paper "The Samaritan's Dilemma" (1971), to be published in *Economic Theory and Altruism*, edited by Edmund Phelps, Russell Sage Foundation (forthcoming).

5. See Gordon Tullock, "The Charity of the Uncharitable," *Western Economic Journal* 9 (December 1971): 379–91.

to be no such linkage between nonhuman capital and survival in the jungle. From this it follows that the man who possesses human capital is likely to be far less concerned about the "injustice" of his own position, less concerned about temporizing measures designed to shore up apparent leaks in the social system than his counterpart who possesses nonhuman capital. If we postulate that the actual income-asset distribution departs significantly from the proportionate distribution in the underlying and existing natural equilibrium, the system of claims must be acknowledged to be notoriously unstable. The idle rich, possessed of nonhuman capital, will tend to form coalitions with the poor that are designed primarily to ward off retreat toward the Hobbesian jungle. This coalition can take the form of the rich acquiescing in and providing defense for overt criminal activity on the part of the poor, or the more explicit form of political exploitation of the "silent majority," the Agnew constituency that possesses largely human rather than nonhuman capital.

This description has some empirical content in 1972. But what can the exploited groups do about it? Can the middle classes form a coalition with the rich, especially when the latter are themselves so insecure? Or can they form, instead, another coalition with the poor, accepting a promise of strict adherence to law in exchange for goodies provided by the explicit confiscation of the nonhuman capital of the rich? (Politically, this would take the form of confiscatory inheritance taxation.) The mythology of the American dream probably precludes this route from being taken. The self-made, the *nouveau riche*, seek to provide their children with fortunes that the latter will accept only with guilt.

All of this suggests that a law-abiding imputation becomes increasingly difficult to sustain as its structure departs from what participants conceive to be the natural or Bush-Hobbes imputation, defined in some proportionate sense. If the observed imputation, or set of bounded imputations that are possible under existing legal-constitutional rules, seems to bear no relationship at all to the natural imputation that men accept, breakdown in legal standards is predictable.

Where does this leave us in trying to discuss criteria for "improvement" in rules, in assignments of rights, the initial question that was posed in this paper? I have argued that the contractarian or Paretian norm is relevant on the simple principle that "we start from here." But "here," the status quo, is the existing set of legal institutions and rules. Hence, how can we possibly distinguish genuine contractual changes in "law" from those which take place under the motivations discussed above? Can we really say which changes are defensible "exchanges" from an existing status quo position? This is what I am trying to answer, without full success, in my paper in response to Warren J. Samuels discussion of the *Miller et al. v. Schoene* case.[6] There I tried to argue that, to the extent that property rights are specified in advance, genuine "trades" can emerge, with mutual gains to all parties. However, to the extent that existing rights are held to be subject to continuous redefinition by the State, no one has an incentive to organize and to initiate trades or agreements. This amounts to saying that once the body politic begins to get overly concerned about the distribution of the pie under existing property-rights assignments and legal rules, once we begin to think either about the personal gains from law-breaking, privately or publicly, or about the disparities between existing imputations and those estimated to be forthcoming under some idealized anarchy, we are necessarily precluding and forestalling the achievement of potential structural changes that might increase the size of the pie for *all*. Too much concern for "justice" acts to insure that "growth" will not take place, and for reasons much more basic than the familiar economic incentives arguments.

In this respect, 1972 seems a century, not a mere decade, away from 1962, when, if you recall, the rage was all for growth and the newfound concern about distribution had not yet been invented. At issue here, of course, is the whole conception of the State, or of collective action. I am far less sanguine than I was concerning the possible acceptance of the existing constitutional-legal framework. The basic structure of property rights is now threatened more seriously than at any period in the two-century history of the United States. In the paper, "The Samaritan's Dilemma," noted above, I advanced the hypothesis that we have witnessed a general loss of strategic courage, brought on in part by economic affluence. As I think more about all this, however, I realize that there is more to it. We may be witnessing the disintegration of our effective constitutional rights, regardless of the prattle about

6. See Warren J. Samuels, "Interrelations Between Legal and Economic Processes," *Journal of Law and Economics* 14, no. 2 (October 1971): 435–50, and my "Politics, Property and the Law," *Journal of Law and Economics* (forthcoming).

"the constitution" as seen by our judicial tyrants from their own visions of the entrails of their sacrificial beasts. I do not know what might be done about all this, even by those who recognize what is happening. We seem to be left with the question posed at the outset. How do rights re-emerge and come to command respect? How do "laws" emerge that carry with them general respect for their "legitimacy"?

The Relatively Absolute Absolutes

Introduction

When I was invited to give the lecture on which this essay is based, I indicated my provisional acceptance on the condition that I be allowed to talk on the topic "The Relatively Absolute Absolutes." I specified this topic for two reasons. First, I am tired of lecturing here, there, and elsewhere on the deficit, tax reform, welfare state, public choice—all topics of some interest to potential audiences and all relevant to some parts of my past work—because these topics do not challenge my deeper current interests. Secondly, I wanted, by announcing a title, to precommit myself and thereby impose a discipline that would force me to write out a lecture on a subject of major importance and one that I have put off for far too long. Further, I have long planned to write a small book on the "relatively absolute absolutes." I hoped that the lecture and this essay, in their preparation and presentation, would at least give me the required introductory shove toward completion.

These are my private, personal reasons for selecting a topic that might seem esoteric and meaningless. I can only hope that I can convey in the following discussion some of the importance and relevance of the relatively absolute absolutes, both in organizing and maintaining a coherent intellectual and moral stance in some highly personalized sense and in providing a practically useful foundation from which to advance persuasive normative judgments on socioeconomic-political alternatives.

I shall mention only three more points by way of preface. First, I hope I can disturb the complacency of practicing, working economists who never

From *Essays on the Political Economy* (Honolulu: University of Hawai'i Press, 1989), 32–46. Reprinted by permission.

stop to think seriously about either epistemological or normative foundations of their discipline. Secondly, the generalized adherence to the principle of the relatively absolute absolutes is a stance that embodies tolerance on the one hand and continuing tension on the other. It avoids the coziness of both the relativist and the absolutist at the cost of taking on attributes of Janus, attributes of a necessary duality in outlook. Finally, let me emphasize that the principle of the relatively absolute absolutes is not in any sense my own invention. It shows up in many disciplines and in the works of many scholars, often in precisely the same terminology. For my own part, the emphasis derives directly from Frank Knight, who restates the principle in almost every one of his philosophical essays, as well as from Henry Simons, Knight's colleague at the University of Chicago during my salad days at that institution.[1]

Plan for a Book

If and when I write my little book on the relatively absolute absolutes, I propose to develop the argument in a series of separate applications, several of which are familiar. I want to develop applications in economic theory, in psychology, in politics, in epistemology, in law, in sports, in war, in language, in morals, in political philosophy, and perhaps even other disciplines. Through the presentation of these applications, I want to suggest that most economists do, indeed, accept the principle of the relatively absolute absolutes, even if we do not explicitly realize just what the principle is; that is, even if we do not, in this sense, know what we are doing.

I shall allocate the limited space in this essay as follows: I shall first introduce an application of the relatively absolute absolutes that is familiar to all economists, although seldom recognized in this particular terminology. Following that, I shall move somewhat beyond orthodox economics into the borderlines with psychology. I shall then introduce an application from politics, one that is again familiar and one that I have long emphasized in my own work, but an application that, again, is not normally discussed under the relatively absolute absolutes rubric. The discussion of these economic,

---

1. See, in particular, the essays in Frank H. Knight, *Freedom and Reform* (Indianapolis: Liberty Fund, 1982). Also, see Henry Simons, *Economic Policy for a Free Society* (Chicago: University of Chicago Press, 1948).

psychological, and political applications can be considered introductory to the central part of the essay, which extends the analysis to moral-ethical discourse. In a sense, the main part of the essay can be interpreted, at least indirectly, as my own response to, or review of, Allan Bloom's best-selling book, *The Closing of the American Mind* (1987), that has been getting so much recent attention.

Marshallian Time: The Long View and the Short

One of Alfred Marshall's central contributions to basic economic theory was his introduction and use of time in analyzing the choices of economic agents, and particularly in the choices made by decision makers for business firms. By heroic and indeed arbitrary abstraction, Marshall imposed a temporal order on the complex environment within which firms act. The process of production involves the organization of costly inputs in the generation of outputs. For some purposes, it is useful to model this process as continuous and simultaneous, without reference to time. But, for Marshall, the timeless model offered little assistance toward an understanding of decision making. He recognized that inputs differ in their specificity, and that contractual obligations embody a time dimension. He proceeded to classify inputs into logically distinguishable and highly stylized categories defined by the time dimension of the choices faced by the firm's agent.

In its simplest formulation, and all that is relevant for my purposes, Marshall distinguished between those inputs that are variable within a short-run period of decision and those inputs that are fixed for decision prospects within such a period. The distinct time periods, the short run and the long run, are themselves defined with reference to input variability, rather than directly in terms of calendar time. The short-period planning decision involves a consideration of alternative rates of output achievable within the limits of variability of the first set of inputs constrained by the fixity of the second set. By contrast, the long-period planning decision involves consideration of alternative rates of output achievable by varying all of the input units as these are optimally adjusted one to another.

This summary sketch of a chapter in elementary price theory illustrates the principle of the relatively absolute absolutes, even if this terminology remains foreign to economic theorists. To demonstrate the meaning of the principle in this application, consider again the short-period planning decision that must be made by the agent for the producing firm. This decision involves the selection of some preferred rate of output, and, in consequence, rates of purchase, hire, or lease of all variable inputs, with the characteristics of the fixed inputs taken as constraints beyond the range of short-period choice. Compare this decision with that which emerges from long-period planning. In the latter, the agent considers alternative levels of fixed-input utilization.

For the short-period planning problem, the agent takes the fixed input (the size of physical plant) as an absolute, as a given, a parameter that is not subject to choice within the limits of the relevant planning horizon. At a different level of consciousness, however, the same agent fully recognizes that the fixed inputs are also variable; these inputs shift from the constraint set to the set of objects from which choice becomes possible. It is in this sense that it seems appropriate, and useful, to refer to the fixed inputs as "relatively absolute absolutes" for short-period choice, subject only to variation at a level of consciousness or decision that is conceptually separate from that which defines short-period planning.

Note that the differentiation here is not itself made along a time dimension. The short-period and the long-period planning processes may occur simultaneously. The differentiation lies, instead, in the number of variables that are allowed within the relevant choice set relative to the number of variables that are relegated to the set of constraints.

Individual Choice within Constraints

In the familiar Marshallian setting, there is some initial starting point when all of the relevant variables are within the choice set. The principle of the relatively absolute absolutes emerges only in choice settings that occur after the initial one. If we extend the analysis to the individual, there is nothing analogous to the creation, *ab initio*, of an institution, as such. An individual does not create himself from nothing. There is no identifiable moment when a person confronts *tabula rasa*, a situation when all of the potential constraints are variables subject to choice. A person's life is an unfolding narrative in which choices are continuously confronted, choices that may determine both subsequent constraints and subsequent preferences. At any moment, an individual finds himself or herself in a setting fully analogous to the agent for the Marshallian firm. The individual must reckon on the temporal adaptability of the potential choice variables, and norms for rational choice require that some variables be treated analogously to fixed inputs in the Marshallian model, that is, as relatively absolute absolutes for the purpose of making short-period choices.

In any choice environment, an individual confronts genuine absolutes, relatively absolute absolutes, and alternatives from which choice may be made. Constraints summarized as genuine absolutes are those described by natural limits, temporal and physical; these are not my concern here. These aside, however, there are relatively absolute absolutes that serve as constraints or boundaries on short-period planning options.

Let us say for the moment that we are professional economists. It remains within the realm of the possible that we could change our profession, and with years of training become physicians or physicists. For most of us, however, it would be rational to take our profession as a given, as a relatively absolute absolute, as a constraint within which relevant choices as to career, work effort, and life-style are made. Within limits, the same argument may, of course, be extended to other characteristics of any person's choice setting. A professional relocation to another employing institution is within the possible, but, for many of us, it may be rational to accept the employment status quo as a constraint, as a relatively absolute absolute, while, at a different level of conscious consideration, we review alternative opportunities. It seems clear that we can extend the same argument to any durable good or service that enters into any consumption or production stream. Durability becomes a reasonably good surrogate for the classification of characteristics into variables and constraints.

Preferences as Constraints

In the two choice settings disclosed, the implicit presumption has been that individual preferences over the relevant choice alternatives are not themselves among the objects for choice. The individual, whether as agent for the firm or for himself, confronts a set of alternatives that is exogenous. If we remain within these standard choice settings, the relatively absolute absolute, as a notion, would be little more than a fancy label for familiar aspects of the general choice problem.

The relatively absolute absolute becomes important as well as useful, however, if we move beyond the choice settings of standard economics, and particularly as we recognize that persons do not approach all choices with a fixed preference ordering over all alternatives. Once we recognize that preferences change and, further, that preferences can be changed by deliberate choice; the temporal differentiation originating from the physical characteristics of the choice options must be replaced by differentiation that is deliberately produced by choice itself.

We may think of a person who chooses to impose upon his or her own choices an artificial preference function, who explicitly adopts rules or norms for choosing among options that exclude some otherwise available options from the choice set, who chooses among options in such fashion as to insure that there will be directional bias in choice patterns actually implemented. Personal examples abound. A person really prefers the calorie-laden dessert, but also wants to maintain or achieve a desirable weight. The "higher" preference, losing weight, constrains the preference for sweets.

The example suggests that an individual may exercise a rational choice among a set of choice alternatives that is, at least in part, determined by his or her own choice exercised at a different level of consciousness. The rule against eating dessert is self-imposed, and is recognized as such. But, for making the cafeteria selections, this precommitment is taken as a relatively absolute absolute. The revealed preference against sweets may reflect a prior preference for preferences, about which the chooser remains fully aware.

It is useful to introduce the term "constitutional" in its most inclusive and general sense here to refer to deliberately chosen constraints on choice alternatives. In the example here, the individual chooses within a set of previously and separately selected precommitments, or rules, which describe a personal constitution for that individual's choice behavior. The point to be emphasized is that the two levels of choice are distinct and that constitutional choice is necessarily more comprehensive than in-constitutional choice.

The Political Constitution

We can move beyond economics while remaining in familiar territory if we shift attention from the personal to the political constitution. In constitutional democracy, and in the United States in particular, it is recognized that ordinary politics takes place within the constraints defined by the set of rules defined as the constitution. The very purpose of these rules is to constrain ordinary political choices. And these ordinary choices take existing constitutional rules as relatively absolute absolutes. As they participate variously in ordinary politics—as voters, aspiring politicians, elected politicians, and bureaucrats—individuals operate within the existing rules of the political game. At the same time, however, individuals recognize that these rules, themselves, at some differing and more comprehensive level of choice, are subject to evaluation, modification, and change. The constitutional rules are not absolutes to be put beyond the pale of rational consideration. But neither are these rules comparable with ordinary politics, which are dominated by current and possibly fleeting dictates of expediency.

Political dialogue and discussion proceed simultaneously at two levels, the in-constitutional and the constitutional. Precisely because constitutional rules are not absolute, they, too, are subject for evaluation and debate. At the same time, and conversely, precisely because they are not subject to change within the decision-making structure of ordinary politics, they can, and do, act to constrain this politics within limits determined by the rules that exist.

We are, as United States citizens, fortunate in that our political structure embodies a much more evident conceptual distinction between the set of constraining rules and the choice-making of politics within that set of rules. Parliamentary democracies, which do not embody such clarity in this distinction, generate confusion, for citizen and scholar alike. Discussion proceeds as if parliamentary majorities operate totally nonconstrained by constitutional rules, while at the same time, some prior commitment to rules for continuing open franchises, along with periodic elections, seems to be presumed in existence. That is to say, politics in parliamentary democracies also proceeds within a set of relatively absolute absolutes, even if these are not explicitly recognized in any formal sense.

Rules for Games

In shifting discussion from personal to political constitutions, we have effected a categorical transformation from private to public choice. The applications from economics suggest the usefulness of modeling strictly private choices in such a manner that decisions made at one level constrain choices at other levels. As we focus on individual choice behavior in interaction with other persons, in a political or social "game," there emerges a new, and conceptually distinct, basis for constitutional precommitment. The individual participant need not, in such a setting, consider it to be useful to impose constraining rules on *his or her own choice behavior.* At the same time, however, since the individual is only one participant in the collective choosing process, and since his own choice need not correspond with that which the collective decision–rule will generate, rational considerations may dictate support for constitutional constraints or limits on the range and scope of collective decisions. In this sense, the individual chooses not to precommit his own choice behavior but rather to constrain the choice behavior of *others than himself,* who might prove dominant in the decision process.

In terms of game theory here, the individual rationally agrees to play by the rules, and to accept these rules as relatively absolute absolutes, not necessarily to constrain his own actions but rather to limit the actions of others than himself. There are two rather than one possible sets of constraining rules once we move into social interaction, once we consider games between and among separate decision-making units. The first set of rules is that which defines the game itself, those rules that constrain the actions of individual players and which are applicable to all players. These are, in a sense, public rules. There may be, but need not be, a different set of constraining rules, through which a single player may, independently of other players, constrain his own choices as he plays the game in accordance with the public rules. This second set of possible constraints may be called private rules; these need not constrain all players, and such rules need not be comparable over all players.

The second set of rules, private rules, are those of the personal constitution discussed earlier. But, in social interaction, we often refer to these rules as individualized strategies, rules that dictate to a player how choices will be made over a whole sequence of plays of a game. In sports, reference is often made to a team's or a player's game plan, which is to be distinguished both from the rules of the game itself and from the tactics of play within these rules. But the game plan, as such, also constrains the choices within the tactical setting. And, as the player attempts to follow the game plan, he is behaving as if this plan is relatively absolute absolute.

The same logical structure is often applied to discussion of wars or conflict between opposing parties or groups. The common distinction is between strategy and tactics. And, especially in earlier centuries, even wars were conducted within implicit rules for the game itself. This aside, however, military strategy for a campaign describes a set of constraining rules within which tactical choices are to be made. The strategy is treated as being relatively absolute absolute when tactical decisions are made, while at the same time, the commander considers shifting the strategy itself.

Epistemology

What I have covered to this point will have seemed repetitious and redundant to those who are at all acquainted with my published writings of recent vintage. I have deliberately gone over familiar ground in preparation for the important applications of the principle of the relatively absolute absolutes, at least from my own perspective. Let me first consider epistemology, a branch of inquiry that occupies so many of the good minds of this and other times. How do we know anything once we recognize that all knowledge must, somehow, be filtered through our minds, which, in turn, translate perceptions into ideas? I have never been attracted to go deeply into epistemology; at the same time, I have never felt at a loss before the highly complex set of issues discussed by my learned colleagues. My own ability to withstand temptation in this respect has, I think, its foundations in the relatively absolute absolute.

I am able, armed with this principle, to proceed as if we do indeed possess knowledge, even if at another level of inquiry I can realize that we may not. I can keep in lockstep with the positivist, who accepts the genuine reality of the world to be discovered and literally believes that this reality exists, while at the same time I can express agreement with those antipositivist critics, provided only that the argument be carried on at a separate and distinct level of discourse. The real world exists, as a relatively absolute absolute, and we can get on with our work.

I can take much the same stance toward the whole Popperian enterprise, with its emphasis on the falsifiability of hypotheses and on the provisionality of all truth. Ordinary or everyday science proceeds as if its hard core Lakatosian program embodies a set of relatively absolute absolutes. Scientists can work within this methodological framework without being frustrated by the deeper epistemological issues around the edges. We may, on occasion, walk on ice as if it were solid ground, even if we recognize that to do so requires that certain conditions of temperature, time, and place be met.

Value Relativism

I now turn to the alleged relativism of all values. For well over a century, or with philosophers indeed since David Hume, we have lived with the collapse of certitude previously offered by the dogmas of religion and reason. Blueprints outlining either the precepts of behavior for the "good man" or the principles of the "good society" are not to be found on tablets left on mountaintops or in communion with the spirits of ancient Greeks. Modern human beings seem to be trapped in the dilemma imposed by the disappearances of moral-ethical absolutes. Where does the individual turn when he or she is unable to counter Dostoyevsky's "all is permitted" or Cole Porter's "anything goes"? If we are, ourselves, the ultimate source of evaluation, how can disparate value norms be ordered, either within the psyche of an individual or as advanced by separate persons?

It is precisely when such questions as these are posed that resort to the principle of the relatively absolute absolutes is most useful. This principle combines the desired ordering properties of moral-ethical absolutism with the equally esteemed properties of intellectual integrity. It offers us a philosophical standing place between the two equally unacceptable extremes, between the pretension and arrogance of the moral absolutist on the one hand, and the total abnegation of judgmental capacity on the other.

The evocation and utilization of the principle of the relatively absolute absolutes depends critically on our ability and willingness both to choose among constraints and to act within the constraints that are chosen. In the absence of self-imposed constraints, we are simple human animals. And a measure of our advance from this animal state is provided by the distance that separates us from the internally anarchistic psychological benchmark defined by the total absence of self-imposed rules.

As Frank Knight emphasized, a human being is a rule-following animal. We live in accordance with a set of moral-ethical rules or norms for behavior, a set that we take, consciously or unconsciously, to be relatively absolute absolutes. We do not, and should not, treat these norms for our behavior as having been revealed to us by god or by reason. Nor should we treat these norms as sacrosanct merely because they exist as a product of a cultural evolutionary process that we may not fully understand. These personal norms are appropriate objects for critical inquiry and discussion, which may proceed at one level of our consciousness while we continue to choose and to act by the very dictates of these norms in our behavior as ordinary persons. We can, upon reflection, evaluate, criticize, and ultimately change the rules that describe "the constitution of our values." But it is vitally important to recognize the categorical distinction between this change in the moral constitution of ourselves and ordinary changes in such matters as diet, dress, recreational activity, and sexual partners.

Political Philosophy

My suggestion that the principle of the relatively absolute absolutes offers a philosophical standing place between the extremes of moral relativism and moral absolutism may be readily accepted in application to the realm of personal values that determine private rules. But I have not, to this point, demonstrated the applicability of the principle to public rules, to the commonality of values among persons, or, in more general terms, to political philosophy.

First of all, it is necessary to define the origin from which any discussion is to proceed. It is worth emphasizing that this origin is the individual who is identified in physical and temporal dimensions. The individual finds himself or herself located in time and place, with a genetic and cultural history, which includes participation in interactions with other persons, who are recognized to be reciprocally capable of choosing among constraints and acting within the constraints so chosen, both in their private and public choosing-acting roles.

To the extent that social interaction exhibits predictable patterns of order, there must exist rules or norms for individual behavior that are common over many participants. These shared public rules must, however, be operative in a setting that allows separate individuals to hold widely divergent constitutions of personal, private values in the sense discussed above. A central task of political philosophy is to derive principles of social order that will reconcile divergent private value structures and the minimally required public rules without which productive interaction among persons is impossible.[2] These public rules may be formal, as embodied in law and legal institutions, or they may be informal, as reflected in prevailing conventions. To the individual, these public rules exist; they define an aspect of the environment within which the individual chooses and acts. These rules exist as a precondition for participation in the "game" of social order. And the individual, any individual, must accept these public rules as relatively absolute absolutes. The fact that the individual may not have participated, actually and effectively, in the choice process that generated the set of public rules, if indeed such a process did take place, is irrelevant to his or her acceptance. In this respect, public rules are functional absolutes in ongoing social order. But they remain open to evaluation and change; these rules are relative rather than absolute absolutes.

At the appropriate level of inquiry, the individual may participate in an examination of the desirability of the existing set of public rules, an examination that must include comparison with alternative sets. But the process of evaluation here can only take place separately and apart from the continued interaction of all participants within the existing status quo set of rules. Individuals who privately abrogate public rules by violating those in existence, thereby imposing their own preferred rules on others, become, quite literally, outlaws, and deserve treatment as such.

My argument that the status quo set of public rules must be treated as a set of relatively absolute absolutes is not equivalent to assigning this set of rules some superior moral attribute in the relevant long-run or constitutional sense. In a setting where persons' basic values differ, we should expect that the set of public rules observed to be in existence will be nonoptimal to *everyone*, when evaluated against a given individual's ideal principles for social interaction. At the same time, however, the set of public rules may be optimal in the Pareto sense familiar to welfare economists, there may be no change that could be agreed to by *all* members of the community. Peaceful coexistence requires that we treat as relatively absolute absolutes those institutions or rules of social interaction within which relationships are orderly

2. See John Gray, "Contractarian Method, Private Property, and the Market Economy" (Jesus College, Oxford, December 1986, mimeographed).

rather than conflictual. These rules remain only relatively absolute, however, and they are always subject to inquiry, evaluative comparison, and reform, upon agreement among all affected persons and groups.

The central point to be emphasized is that the process of living rationally and efficiently within the public rules that exist must be understood to remain categorically distinct from potential discussion and rationally derived changes in these rules. To revert to the initial Marshallian analogy; the firm may be in long-run disequilibrium with the wrong size of its plant, but it remains rational for it to operate that plant which exists optimally.

I consider it to be the task of economists, as economic scientists, to make rudimentary predictions about the behavior of persons within existing and potential constraints, whether these be imposed physically or artifactually. I have considered it to be the task of economists, as moral and social philosophers, to evaluate alternative sets of constraints, and to seek consensus on changes in the direction of those that most nearly meet the discipline's ultimate normative criteria, which are themselves determined by agreement. I have found, personally, that the principle of the relatively absolute absolutes has been very helpful in sorting my way through the complex intellectual mazes that confront all economists. I hope that, in this very preliminary sketch of what I hope will be a more comprehensive effort, I have been able to suggest to others the productivity of a single simple idea.

The Constitution
of Economic Policy

December 8, 1986

I. Introduction

> The science of public finance should always keep ... political
> conditions clearly in mind. Instead of expecting guidance from a
> doctrine of taxation that is based on the political philosophy of
> by-gone ages, it should instead endeavor to unlock the mysteries
> of the spirit of progress and development. (Wicksell, p. 87.)[1]

On this of all occasions I should be remiss if I failed to acknowledge the influence of that great Swede, Knut Wicksell, on my own work, an influence without which I should not be at this podium. Many of my contributions, and especially those in political economy and fiscal theory, might be described as varied reiterations, elaborations, and extensions of Wicksellian themes; this lecture is no exception.

One of the most exciting intellectual moments of my career was my 1948 discovery of Knut Wicksell's unknown and untranslated dissertation, *Fi-*

From *Les Prix Nobel* (Stockholm: Almquist and Wicksell International, 1986), 334–43. Reprinted by permission.

I am indebted to Robert Tollison, Viktor Vanberg, and Richard Wagner for helpful comments.

1. This and subsequent citations are from Knut Wicksell, "A New Principle of Just Taxation," included in *Classics in the Theory of Public Finance*, ed. R. A. Musgrave and A. T. Peacock (London: Macmillan, 1958), 72–118. The more inclusive work from which this translated essay is taken is Knut Wicksell, *Finanztheoretische Untersuchungen* (Jena: Gustav Fischer, 1896).

nanztheoretische Untersuchungen, buried in the dusty stacks of Chicago's old Harper Library. Only the immediate post-dissertation leisure of an academic novice allowed for the browsing that produced my own dramatic example of learning by serendipity. Wicksell's new principle of justice in taxation gave me a tremendous surge of self-confidence. Wicksell, who was an established figure in the history of economic ideas, challenged the orthodoxy of public finance theory along lines that were congenial with my own developing stream of critical consciousness. From that moment in Chicago, I took on the determination to make Wicksell's contribution known to a wider audience, and I commenced immediately a translation effort that took some time, and considerable help from Elizabeth Henderson, before final publication.

Stripped to its essentials, Wicksell's message was clear, elementary, and self-evident. Economists should cease proffering policy advice as if they were employed by a benevolent despot, and they should look to the structure within which political decisions are made. Armed with Wicksell, I, too, could dare to challenge the still-dominant orthodoxy in public finance and welfare economics. In a preliminary paper, I called upon my fellow economists to postulate some model of the state, of politics, before proceeding to analyze the effects of alternative policy measures. I urged economists to look at the "constitution of economic policy," to examine the rules, the constraints within which political agents act. Like Wicksell, my purpose was ultimately normative rather than antiseptically scientific. I sought to make economic sense out of the relationship between the individual and the state before proceeding to advance policy nostrums.

Wicksell deserves the designation as the most important precursor of modern public choice theory because we find, in his 1896 dissertation, all three of the constitutive elements that provide the foundations of this theory: methodological individualism, *Homo economicus*, and politics-as-exchange. I shall discuss these elements of analytical structure in the sections that follow. In Section V, I integrate these elements in a theory of economic policy. This theory is consistent with, builds upon, and systematically extends the traditionally accepted principles of Western liberal societies. The implied approach to institutional-constitutional reform continues, however, to be stubbornly resisted almost a century after Wicksell's seminal efforts. The individual's relation to the state is, of course, the central subject matter of political philosophy. Any effort by economists to shed light on this relationship must be placed within this more comprehensive realm of discourse.

II. Methodological Individualism

> If utility is zero for each individual member of the community, the total utility for the community cannot be other than zero. (Wicksell, p. 77.)

The economist rarely examines the presuppositions of the models with which he works. The economist simply commences with individuals as evaluating, choosing, and acting units. This starting point for analysis necessarily draws attention to the choice or decision environment for the individuals who must make selections from among the alternatives. Regardless of the possible complexity of the processes or institutional structures from which outcomes emerge, the economist focuses on individual choices. In application to market or private-sector interactions, this procedure is seldom challenged. Individuals, as buyers and sellers of ordinary (legally tradable) goods and services are presumed able to choose in accordance with their own preferences, whatever these may be, and the economist does not feel himself obliged to inquire deeply into the content of these preferences (the arguments in individuals' utility functions). Individuals themselves are the sources of evaluation, and the economist's task is to offer an explanation-understanding of the process through which these unexamined preferences are ultimately translated into a complex outcome pattern.

The eighteenth-century discovery that, in an institutional framework that facilitates voluntary exchanges among individuals, this process generates results that might be evaluated positively, produced "economics," as an independent academic discipline or science. The relationship between the positively valued results of market processes and the institutional characteristics of these processes themselves emerged as a source of ambiguity when "the market" came to be interpreted functionally, as if something called "the economy" existed for the purpose of value maximization. Efficiency in the allocation of resources came to be defined independently of the processes through which individual choices are exercised.

Given this subtle shift toward a teleological interpretation of the economic process, it is not surprising that politics, or governmental process, was similarly interpreted. Furthermore, a teleological interpretation of politics had been, for centuries, the dominating thrust of political theory and political philosophy. The interpretations of "the economy" and "the polity" seemed, therefore, to be mutually compatible in the absence of inquiry into the fundamental difference in the point of evaluation. There was a failure to recognize that individuals who choose and act in the market generate outcomes that, under the specified constraints, can be judged to be value-maximizing for participating individuals, *without* the necessity of introducing an external evaluative criterion. The nature of the process itself insures that individual values are maximized. This "value maximization" perspective cannot be extended from the market to politics since the latter does not directly embody the incentive compatible structure of the former. There is no political counterpart to Adam Smith's invisible hand. It is not, therefore, surprising that the attempts by Wicksell and other continental European scholars to extend economic theory to the operation of the public sector remained undeveloped for so many years.

An economic theory that remains essentially individualistic need not have become trapped in such a methodological straight jacket. If the maximization exercise is restricted to explanation-understanding of the individual who makes choices, and without extension to the economy as an aggregation, there is no difficulty at all in analyzing individual choice behavior under differing institutional settings and in predicting how these varying settings will influence the outcomes of the interaction processes. The individual who chooses between apples and oranges remains the same person who chooses between the levers marked "Candidate A" and "Candidate B" in the polling booth. Clearly, the differing institutional structures may, themselves, affect choice behavior. Much of modern public choice theory explains these relationships. But my point here is the more basic one to the effect that the choice behavior of the individual is equally subject to the application of analysis in all choice environments. Comparative analysis should allow for predictions of possible differences in the characteristics of the results that emerge from market and political structures of interaction. These predictions, as well as the analysis from which they are generated, are totally devoid of normative content.

III. *Homo economicus*

> ... neither the executive nor the legislative body, and even less the deciding majority in the latter, are in reality ... what the ruling theory tells us they should be. They are not pure organs of the community with no thought other than to promote the common weal.

> ... members of the representative body are, in the overwhelming majority of cases, precisely as interested in the general welfare as are their constituents, neither more nor less. (Wicksell, pp. 86, 87.)

This analysis can yield a limited set of potentially falsifiable hypotheses without prior specification of the arguments in individual utility functions. If, however, predictions are sought concerning the effects of shifts in constraints on choice behavior, some identification and signing of these arguments must be made. With this step, more extensive falsifiable propositions may be advanced. For example, if both apples and oranges are positively valued "goods," then, if the price of apples falls relative to that of oranges, more apples will be purchased relative to oranges; if income is a positively valued "good," and, then, if the marginal rate of tax on income source A increases relative to that on income source B, more effort at earning income will be shifted to source B; if charitable giving is a positively valued "good," then, if charitable gifts are made tax deductible, more giving will be predicted to occur; if pecuniary rents are positively valued, then, if a political agent's discretionary power to distribute rents increases, individuals hoping to secure these rents will invest more resources in attempts to influence the agent's decisions. Note that the identification and signing of the arguments in the utility functions takes us a considerable way toward operationalization without prior specification of the relative weights of the separate arguments. There is no need to assign net wealth or net income a dominating motivational influence on behavior in order to produce a fully operational economic theory of choice behavior, in market or political interaction.

In any extension of the model of individual rational behavior to politics, this difference between the identification and signing of arguments on the one hand and the weighting of these arguments on the other deserves further attention. Many critics of the "economic theory of politics" base their criticisms on the presumption that such theory necessarily embodies the hypothesis of net wealth maximization, an hypothesis that they observe to be falsified in many situations. Overly zealous users of this theory may have sometimes offered grounds for such misinterpretation on the part of critics. The minimal critical assumption for the explanatory power of the economic theory of politics is only that identifiable economic self-interest (e.g., net wealth, income, social position) is a positively valued "good" to the individual chooser. This assumption does not place economic interest in a dominating position, and it surely does not imply imputing evil or malicious motives to political actors; in this respect the theory remains on all fours with the motivational structure of the standard economic theory of market behavior. The differences in the predicted results stemming from market and political interaction stem from differences in the structures of these two institutional settings rather than from any switch in the motives of persons as they move between institutional roles.

IV. Politics as Exchange

> It would seem to be a blatant injustice if someone should be forced to contribute toward the costs of some activity which does not further his interests or may even be diametrically opposed to them. (Wicksell, p. 89.)

Individuals choose, and as they do so, identifiable economic interest is one of the "goods" that they value positively, whether behavior takes place in markets or in politics. But markets are institutions of *exchange;* persons enter markets to exchange one thing for another. They do not enter markets to further some supra-exchange or supra-individualistic result. Markets are not motivationally functional; there is no conscious sense on the part of individual choosers that some preferred aggregate outcome, some overall "allocation" or "distribution" will emerge from the process.

The extension of this exchange conceptualization to politics counters the classical prejudice that persons participate in politics through some common search for the good, the true, and the beautiful, with these ideals being defined independently of the values of the participants as these might or might not be expressed by behavior. Politics, in this vision of political philosophy, is instrumental to the furtherance of these larger goals.

Wicksell, who is followed in this respect by modern public choice theorists, would have none of this. The relevant difference between markets and politics does not lie in the kinds of values/interests that persons pursue, but in the conditions under which they pursue their various interests. Politics is a structure of complex exchange among individuals, a structure within which persons seek to secure collectively their own privately defined objectives that cannot be efficiently secured through simple market exchanges. In the absence of individual interest, there is no interest. In the market, individuals exchange apples for oranges; in politics, individuals exchange agreed-on shares in contributions toward the costs of that which is commonly desired, from the services of the local fire station to that of the judge.

This ultimately voluntary basis for political agreement also counters the emphasis on politics as power that characterizes much modern analysis. The observed presence of coercive elements in the activity of the state seems difficult to reconcile with the model of voluntary exchange among individuals. We may, however, ask: Coercion to what purpose? Why must individuals subject themselves to the coercion inherent in collective action? The answer is evident. Individuals acquiesce in the coercion of the state, of politics, only if the ultimate constitutional "exchange" furthers their interests. Without some model of exchange, no coercion of the individual by the state is consistent with the individualistic value norm upon which a liberal social order is grounded.

V. The Constitution of Economic Policy

> ... whether the benefits of the proposed activity to the individual
> citizens would be greater than its cost to them, no one can judge
> this better than the individuals themselves. (Wicksell, p. 79.)

The exchange conceptualization of politics is important in the derivation of a normative theory of economic policy. Improvement in the workings of politics is measured in terms of the satisfaction of that which is desired by individuals, whatever this may be, rather than in terms of moving closer to some externally defined, supra-individualistic ideal. That which is desired by individuals may, of course, be common for many persons, and, indeed, the difference between market exchange and political exchange lies in the sharing of objectives in the latter. The idealized agreement on the objectives of politics does not, however, allow for any supersession of individual evaluation. Agreement itself emerges, again conceptually, from the revealed choice behavior of individuals. Commonly shared agreement must be carefully distinguished from any externally defined definition or description of that "good" upon which persons "should agree."

The restrictive implications for a normative theory of economic policy are severe. There is no criterion through which policy may be directly evaluated. An indirect evaluation may be based on some measure of the degree to which the political process facilitates the translation of expressed individual preferences into observed political outcomes. The focus of evaluative attention becomes the process itself, as contrasted with end-state or outcome patterns. "Improvement" must, therefore, be sought in reforms in process, in institutional change that will allow the operation of politics to mirror more accurately that set of results that are preferred by those who participate. One way of stating the difference between the Wicksellian approach and that which is still orthodoxy in normative economics is to say that the *constitution* of policy rather than policy itself becomes the relevant object for reform. A simple game analogy illustrates the difference here. The Wicksellian approach concentrates on reform in the rules, which may be in the potential interest of *all* players, as opposed to improvement in strategies of play for particular players within defined or existing rules.

In the standard theory of choice in markets, there is little or no concern with the constitution of the choice environment. We simply presume that the individual is able to implement his preferences; if he wants to purchase an orange, we presume that he can do so. There is no institutional barrier between the revealed expression of preference and direct satisfaction. Breakdown of failure in the market emerges, not in the translation of individual preferences into outcomes, but in the possible presentation of some choosers with alternatives that do not correspond to those faced by others in the exchange nexus. "Efficiency" in market interaction is insured if the participants are faced with the same choice options.

In political exchange, there is no decentralized process that allows "efficiency" to be evaluated deontologically, akin to the evaluation of a market.

Individuals cannot, by the nature of the goods that are collectively "purchased" in politics, adjust their own behavior to common terms of trade. The political analogue to decentralized trading among individuals must be that feature common over all exchanges, which is *agreement* among the individuals who participate. The unanimity rule for collective choice is the political analogue to freedom of exchange of partitionable goods in markets.

It is possible, therefore, to evaluate politics independently of results only by ascertaining the degree of correspondence between the rules of reaching decisions and the unique rule that would guarantee "efficiency," that of unanimity or agreement among all participants. If, then, "efficiency" is acknowledged to be the desired criterion, again as interpreted here, normative improvement in process is measured by movement toward the unanimity requirement. It is perhaps useful to note, at this point, that Wicksell's own characterization of his proposals in terms of "justice" rather than "efficiency" suggests the precise correspondence of these two norms in the context of voluntary exchange.

Politics as observed remains, of course, far from the idealized collective-cooperative exchange that the unanimity rule would implement. The political equivalent to transactions cost makes the pursuit of idealized "efficiency" seem even more out of the bounds of reason than the analogous pursuit in markets. But barriers to realization of the ideal do not imply rejection of the benchmark definition of the ideal itself. Instead, such barriers are themselves incorporated into a generalized "calculus of consent."

Wicksell himself did not go beyond advocacy of reform in legislative decision structures. He proposed a required linking of spending and financing decisions, and he proposed that a quasi-unanimity rule be introduced for noncommitted outlays. Wicksell did not consciously extend his analysis to constitutional choice, to the choice of the rules within which ordinary politics is to be allowed to operate. His suggested reforms were, of course, constitutional, since they were aimed to improve the process of decision making. But his evaluative criterion was restricted to the matching of individual preferences with political outcomes in particularized decisions, rather than over any sequence.

It is perhaps worth noting that Wicksell himself did not look upon his suggested procedural reforms as restrictive. By introducing greater flexibility into the tax-share structure, Wicksell predicted the potential approval of spending programs that would continue to be rejected under rigid taxing arrangements. Critics have, however, interpreted the Wicksellian unanimity constraint to be restrictive, and especially as compared to the extended activity observed in ordinary politics. This restrictive interpretation was perhaps partially responsible for the continued failure of political economists to recognize his seminal extension of the efficiency norm to the political sector. Such restrictiveness is very substantially reduced, and, in the limit, may be altogether eliminated, when the unanimity criterion is shifted one stage upward, to the level of potential agreement on constitutional rules within which ordinary politics is to be allowed to operate. In this framework, an individual may rationally prefer a rule that will, on particular occasions, operate to produce results that are opposed to his own interests. The individual will do so if he predicts that, on balance over the whole sequence of "plays," his own interests will be more effectively served than by the more restrictive application of the Wicksellian requirement in-period. The in-period Wicksellian criterion remains valid as a measure of the particularized efficiency of the single decision examined. But the in-period violation of the criterion does not imply the inefficiency of the rule so long as the latter is itself selected by a constitutional rule of unanimity.[2]

As noted, the shift of the Wicksellian criterion to the constitutional stage of choice among rules also serves to facilitate agreement, and, in the limiting case, may remove altogether potential conflicts among separate individual and group interests. To the extent that the individual reckons that a constitutional rule will remain applicable over a long sequence of periods, with many in-period choices to be made, he is necessarily placed behind a partial "veil of uncertainty" concerning the effects of any rule on his own predicted interests. Choice among rules will, therefore, tend to be based on generalizable criteria of fairness, making agreement more likely to occur than when separable interests are more easily identifiable.

The political economist who operates from within the Wicksellian research program, as modified, and who seeks to offer normative advice must,

---

2. In my own retrospective interpretation, the shift of the Wicksellian construction to the constitutional stage of choice was the most important contribution in *The Calculus of Consent,* written jointly with Gordon Tullock (Ann Arbor: University of Michigan Press, 1962).

of necessity, concentrate on the process or structure within which political decisions are observed to be made. Existing constitutions, or structures or rules, are the subject of critical scrutiny. The conjectural question becomes: Could these rules have emerged from agreement by participants in an authentic constitutional convention? Even here, the normative advice that is possible must be severely circumscribed. There is no external set of norms that provides a basis for criticism. But the political economist may, cautiously, suggest changes in procedures, in rules, that may come to command general assent. Any suggested change must be offered only in the provisional sense, and, importantly, it must be accompanied by a responsible recognition of political reality. Those rules and rules changes worthy of consideration are those that are predicted to be workable within the politics inhabited by ordinary men and women, and not those that are appropriate only for idealized, omniscient, and benevolent beings. Policy options must remain within the realm of the feasible, and the interests of political agents must be recognized as constraints on the possible.

VI. Constitutionalism and Contractarianism

> The ultimate goal . . . is equality before the law, greatest possible liberty, and the economic well-being and peaceful cooperation of all people. (Wicksell, p. 88.)

As the basic Wicksellian construction is shifted to the choice among rules or constitutions and as a veil of uncertainty is utilized to facilitate the potential bridging of the difference between identifiable and general interest, the research program in political economy merges into that of contractarian political philosophy, both in its classical and modern variations. In particular, my own approach has affinities with the familiar construction of John Rawls, who utilizes the veil of ignorance along with the fairness criterion to derive principles of justice that emerge from a conceptual contractual agreement at a stage prior to the selection of a political constitution.[3]

Because of his failure to shift his own analytical construction to the level of constitutional choice, Wicksell was confined to evaluation of the political

---

3. John Rawls, *A Theory of Justice* (Cambridge: Harvard University Press, 1971).

process in generating current allocative decisions. He was unable, as he quite explicitly acknowledged, to evaluate political action involving either prior commitments of the state, for example, the financing of interest on public debt, or fiscally implemented transfers of incomes and wealth among persons and groups. Distributional questions remain outside the Wicksellian evaluative exercise, and because they do so, we locate another source of the long-continued and curious neglect of the fundamental analytical contribution. With the shift to the constitutional stage of politics, however, this constraint is at least partially removed. Behind a sufficiently thick veil of uncertainty and/or ignorance, contractual agreement on rules that allow for some in-period fiscal transfers seems clearly to be possible. The precise features of a constitutionally approved transfer structure cannot, of course, be derived independently because of the restriction of evaluative judgment to the process of constitutional agreement. In this respect, the application is fully analogous to Wicksell's unwillingness to lay down specific norms for tax sharing independently of the process of agreement. *Any* distribution of tax shares generating revenues sufficient to finance the relevant spending project passes Wicksell's test, provided only that it meets with general agreement. Analogously, *any* set of arrangements for implementing fiscal transfers, in-period, meets the constitutional stage Wicksellian test, provided only that it commands general agreement.

This basic indeterminacy is disturbing to political economists or philosophers who seek to be able to offer substantive advice, over and beyond the procedural limits suggested. The constructivist urge to assume a role as social engineer, to suggest policy reforms that "should" or "should not" be made, independently of any revelation of individuals' preferences through the political process, has simply proved too strong for many to resist. The scientific integrity dictated by consistent reliance on individualistic values has not been a mark of modern political economy.

The difficulty of maintaining such integrity is accentuated by the failure to distinguish explanatory and justificatory argument, a failure that has described the position of almost all critics of social contract theories of political order. We do not, of course, observe the process of reaching agreement on constitutional rules, and the origins of the rules that are in existence at any particular time and in any particular polity cannot satisfactorily be explained by the contractarian model. The purpose of the contractarian exercise is not explanatory in this sense. It is, by contrast, justificatory in that it offers a basis for normative evaluation. Could the observed rules that constrain the activity of ordinary politics have emerged from agreement in constitutional contract? To the extent that this question can be affirmatively answered we have established a legitimating linkage between the individual and the state. To the extent that the question prompts a negative response, we have a basis for normative criticism of the existing order, and a criterion for advancing proposals for constitutional reform.[4]

It is at this point, and this point only, that the political economist who seeks to remain within the normative constraints imposed by the individualistic canon may enter the ongoing dialogue on constitutional policy. The deficit-financing regimes in modern Western democratic polities offer the most dramatic example. It is almost impossible to construct a contractual calculus in which representatives of separate generations would agree to allow majorities in a single generation to finance currently enjoyed public consumption through the issue of public debt that insures the imposition of utility losses on later generations of taxpayers. The same conclusion applies to the implicit debt obligations that are reflected in many of the intergenerational transfer programs characteristic of the modern welfare state.

The whole contractarian exercise remains empty if the critical dependence of politically generated results upon the rules that constrain political action is denied. If end states are invariant over shifts in constitutional structure, there is no role for constitutional political economy. On the other hand, if institutions do, indeed, matter, the role is well defined. Positively, this role involves analysis of the working properties of alternative sets of constraining rules. In a game theoretic analogy, this analysis is the search for solutions of games, as the latter are defined by sets of rules. Normatively, the task for the constitutional political economist is to assist individuals, as citizens who ultimately control their own social order, in their continuing search for those rules of the political game that will best serve their purposes, whatever these might be.

In 1987, the United States celebrates the bicentennial anniversary of the

---

4. A generalized argument for adopting the constitutionalist-contractarian perspective, in both positive and normative analysis, is developed in *The Reason of Rules*, written jointly with Geoffrey Brennan (Cambridge: Cambridge University Press, 1985).

constitutional convention that provided the basic rules for the American political order. This convention was one of the very few historical examples in which political rules were deliberately chosen. The vision of politics that informed the thinking of James Madison was not dissimilar, in its essentials, from that which informed Knut Wicksell's less comprehensive, but more focused, analysis of taxation and spending. Both rejected any organic conception of the state as superior in wisdom, to the individuals who are its members. Both sought to bring all available scientific analysis to bear in helping to resolve the continuing question of social order: How can we live together in peace, prosperity, and harmony, while retaining our liberties as autonomous individuals who can, and must, create our own values?

Appendixes

Appendix A
James M. Buchanan Biographical Data

Born
October 3, 1919, Murfreesboro, Tennessee

Education

University of Chicago	Ph.D.	1948
University of Tennessee	M.A.	1941
Middle Tennessee State College	B.S.	1940

Honors and Awards

Alfred Nobel Memorial Prize in Economic Sciences	1986
Honorary Doctorate (Dr. h. c. in Law), University of Valladolid, Valladolid, Spain	1996
Honorary Professorship, Universidad del Pacifico, Lima, Peru	1996
Honorary Doctorate (Dr. h. c.), University of Porta, Porta, Portugal	1995
Honorary Doctorate (Dr. h. c.), University of Bucharest, Bucharest, Romania	1994
Honorary Doctorate (Dr. h. c.), Academy for Economic Studies, Bucharest, Romania	1994
Honorary Doctorate (Dr. h. c.), University of Catania, Catania, Italy	1994

Honorary Doctorate (Dr. h.c.), Libera Università Internazionale degli Studi Sociali, Rome, Italy	1993
International "Uberto Bonino" Award for Science, Arts, and Letters, Messina, Italy	1993
President, Advisory Council for ESEADE Buenos Aires, Argentina	1992
Legion de la Libertad, Instituto Cultural Ludwig von Mises, Mexico City, Mexico	1992
Academia Nazionale dei Lincei, Honorary Foreign Member, Rome, Italy	1991
Adam Smith Award, Association for Private Enterprise Education, Chattanooga, Tennessee	1991
Distinguished Alumnus Award, American Association of State Colleges and Universities, San Francisco, California	1989
Special Festschrift Conference, sponsored by Liberty Fund on occasion of 70th birthday, Roanoke, Virginia	1989
George Washington Honor Medal, Freedoms Foundation at Valley Forge, Valley Forge, Pennsylvania	1988
Honoree, "James Buchanan Day," Rutherford County, Tennessee, Middle Tennessee State University, City of Murfreesboro, Tennessee	1988
Honorary Doctorate (Dr. h.c.), Ball State University, Muncie, Indiana	1988
Honorary Doctorate (Dr. h.c.), City University of London, London, England	1988

Lord Foundation Award for Leadership in Wealth Creation, Cambridge, Massachusetts	1988
Honorary Doctorate of Laws (Dr. h.c.), George Mason University, Fairfax, Virginia	1987
Honorary Doctorate (Dr. h.c.), New University of Lisbon, Lisbon, Portugal	1987
Honorary Doctorate (Dr. h.c.), University of Valencia, Valencia, Spain	1987
Alexis de Tocqueville Memorial Award, The Independent Institute, San Francisco, California	1987
Outstanding Faculty Award, Virginia State Council on Higher Education, Richmond, Virginia	1987
Distinguished Senior Fellow, Cato Institute	1987
Frank E. Seidman Distinguished Award in Political Economy	1984
Honorary Doctorate (Dr. h.c.), University of Zurich, Zurich, Switzerland	1984
Distinguished Fellow, American Economic Association	1983
Honorary Doctorate (Dr. h.c.), University of Giessen, Giessen, Germany	1982
Certificate of Honor, Freedom Foundation	1982
Distinguished Service Award, Virginia Social Science Association	1982
Prize in Law and Economics by the Law and Economics Center, for the book *The Limits of Liberty*, University of Miami Law School, Miami, Florida	1976

Adjunct Scholar,   1976–92
American Enterprise Institute

Fellow,   1976–
American Academy of Arts and Sciences

Outstanding Alumnus,   1971
Middle Tennessee State University

Career Data
Advisory General Director,   1988–
Center for Study of Public Choice,
George Mason University,
Fairfax, Virginia

General Director,   1983–88
Center for Study of Public Choice,
George Mason University,
Fairfax, Virginia

Holbert L. Harris University Professor,   1983–
George Mason University,
Fairfax, Virginia

General Director,   1969–83
Center for Study of Public Choice,
Virginia Polytechnic Institute &
State University, Blacksburg, Virginia

University Distinguished Professor,   1969–83
Virginia Polytechnic Institute &
State University, Blacksburg, Virginia

Professor of Economics,   1968–69
University of California,
Los Angeles, California

Director,   1958–69
Thomas Jefferson Center
for Political Economy,
University of Virginia,
Charlottesville, Virginia

Paul G. McIntire Professor of Economics,   1962–68
University of Virginia,
Charlottesville, Virginia

Chairman,   1956–61
James Wilson Department of Economics,
University of Virginia,
Charlottesville, Virginia

Professor,   1956–62
James Wilson Department of Economics,
University of Virginia,
Charlottesville, Virginia

Chairman,   1954–56
Department of Economics,
Florida State University,
Tallahassee, Florida

Professor,   1951–56
Department of Economics,
Florida State University,
Tallahassee, Florida

Professor,   1950–51
University of Tennessee,
Knoxville, Tennessee

Associate Professor,   1948–50
University of Tennessee,
Knoxville, Tennessee

Visiting Professorships
Visiting Professor,   February 1976
University of Miami Law School,
Miami, Florida

J. Fish Smith Professor of Economics,   Winter 1974
Brigham Young University
Provo, Utah

Visiting Professor,   Spring 1967
London School of Economics,
London, England

Fulbright Visiting Professor,   1961–62
Cambridge University,
Cambridge, England

Ford Faculty Fellow   1959–60

Fulbright Research Scholar in Italy   1955–56

Military Service
USNR   1941–46
Currently, LCDR, Retired Reserve

Awarded Bronze Star Medal   1945

Professional Appointments
Mt. Pelerin Society   1976–86
President (1984–86);
Vice President (1982–84);
Executive Committee,
Member of the Board (1976–82)

Western Economic Association   1981–84
President (1983–84);
President-Elect (1982–83);
Vice President (1981–82)

American Economic Association   1966–69, 1971
Executive Committee (1966–69);
Vice President (1971)

Southern Economic Association   1963
President

Member
American Economic Association
Mt. Pelerin Society
Public Choice Society (cofounder, 1963)
Royal Economic Society
Southern Economic Association

Appendix B
Contents of the Collected Works
of James M. Buchanan

Volume 1   *The Logical Foundations of Constitutional Liberty*

Volume 2   *Public Principles of Public Debt: A Defense and Restatement*

Volume 3   *The Calculus of Consent: Logical Foundations of Constitutional Democracy* (with Gordon Tullock)

Volume 4   *Public Finance in Democratic Process: Fiscal Institutions and Individual Choice*

Volume 5   *The Demand and Supply of Public Goods*

Volume 6   *Cost and Choice: An Inquiry in Economic Theory*

Volume 7   *The Limits of Liberty: Between Anarchy and Leviathan*

Volume 8   *Democracy in Deficit: The Political Legacy of Lord Keynes* (with Richard E. Wagner)

Volume 9   *The Power to Tax: Analytical Foundations of a Fiscal Constitution* (with Geoffrey Brennan)

Volume 10   *The Reason of Rules: Constitutional Political Economy* (with Geoffrey Brennan)

Volume 11   *Politics by Principle, Not Interest: Toward Nondiscriminatory Democracy* (with Roger D. Congleton)

Volume 12   *Economic Inquiry and its Logic*

PART 1. The Practice and Method of Economic Theory

"Is Economics a Science of Choice?" in *Roads to Freedom-Essays in Honour of Friedrich. A. von Hayek,* ed. Erich Streissler (London: Routledge & Kegan Paul, 1969), 47–64.

["What Should Economists Do?" *Southern Economic Journal* 30 (January 1964): 213–22.]*

"General Implications of Subjectivism in Economics," in *What Should Economists Do?* (Indianapolis: Liberty Fund, 1979), 81–91.

["Order Defined in the Process of Its Emergence," *Literature of Liberty* 5 (Winter 1982): 5.]

"There *Is* a Science of Economics," in *Post-Socialist Political Economy: Selected Essays* (Cheltenham, U.K.: Edward Elgar, 1997), 9–19.

"Economics as a Public Science," in *Foundations of Research in Economics: How Do Economists Do Economics?* ed. Steven G. Medema and Warren J. Samuels (Cheltenham, U.K.: Edward Elgar, 1996), 30–36.

"*Ceteris Paribus:* Some Notes on Methodology," *Southern Economic Journal* 24 (January 1958): 259–70.

["The Relevance of Pareto Optimality," *Journal of Conflict Resolution* 6 (December 1962): 341–54.]

James M. Buchanan and Charles Plott, "Marshall's Mathematical Note XIX," *Economic Journal* 75 (September 1965): 618–20.

Geoffrey Brennan and James Buchanan, "The Normative Purpose of Economic 'Science': Rediscovery of an Eighteenth Century Method," *International Review of Law and Economics* 1 (December 1981): 155–66.

Geoffrey Brennan and James Buchanan, "Predictive Power and the Choice Among Regimes," *Economic Journal* 93 (March 1983): 89–105.

---

*The items in brackets appear in volume 1 of the series. Had they not been selected for inclusion in this overview volume, they would have been placed as indicated in the following list.

["Natural and Artifactual Man," in *What Should Economists Do?* (Indianapolis: Liberty Fund, 1979), 93–112.]

"The Economizing Element in Knight's Ethical Critique of Capitalist Order," *Ethics* 98 (October 1987): 61–75.

["Politics and Science: Reflections on Knight's Critique of Polanyi," *Ethics* 77 (July 1967): 303–10.]

"Professor Alchian on Economic Method," in *What Should Economists Do?* (Indianapolis: Liberty Fund, 1979), 65–79.

PART 2. Competition and Entrepreneurship

James M. Buchanan and Alberto di Pierro, "Cognition, Choice, and Entrepreneurship," *Southern Economic Journal* 46 (January 1980): 693–701.

"Resource Allocation and Entrepreneurship," The Arne Ryde Symposium on the Economic Theory of Institutions, *Statsvetenskaplig Tidskrift* (The Swedish Journal of Political Science) 5 (1980): 285–92.

James M. Buchanan and Roger Faith, "Entrepreneurship and the Internalization of Externalities," *Journal of Law and Economics* (April 1981): 95–111.

PART 3. The Theory of Monopoly

"The Theory of Monopolistic Quantity Discounts," *Review of Economic Studies* 20 (June 1953): 199–208.

James M. Buchanan and Gordon Tullock, "The 'Dead Hand' of Monopoly," *Antitrust Law and Economics Review* 1 (Summer 1968): 85–96.

Geoffrey Brennan, James Buchanan, and Dwight Lee, "On Monopoly Price," *Kyklos* 36, fasc. 4 (1983): 531–47.

James M. Buchanan and John E. Moes, "A Regional Countermeasure to National Wage Standardization," *American Economic Review* 50 (June 1960): 434–38.

PART 4. Input Prices

"Saving and the Rate of Interest: A Comment," *Journal of Political Economy* 67 (February 1959): 79–82.

"The Simple Economics of the Menial Servant," in *Ethics and Economic Progress* (Norman: University of Oklahoma Press, 1994), 129–45.

James M. Buchanan and Yong J. Yoon, "Constitutional Implications of Alternative Models of Increasing Returns," *Constitutional Political Economy* 6 (Summer 1995): 191–96.

"Who Cares Whether the Commons Are Privatised?" in *Post-Socialist Political Economy: Selected Essays* (Cheltenham, U.K.: Edward Elgar, 1997), 160–67.

PART 7. Economic Theory in a Postsocialist World

"Asymmetrical Reciprocity in Market Exchange: Implications for Economies in Transition," *Social Philosophy & Policy* 10 (Summer 1993): 51–64.

"Economic Science and Cultural Diversity," *Kyklos* 48, fasc. 2 (1995): 193–200.

"Structure-Induced Behaviour in Markets and in Politics," in *Post-Socialist Political Economy: Selected Essays* (Cheltenham, U.K.: Edward Elgar, 1997), 136–50.

"We Should Save More in Our Own Economic Interest," in *Justice Across Generations: What Does It Mean?* ed. Lee M. Cohen (Washington, D.C.: AARP, 1993), 269–82.

"Economic Theory in the Postrevolutionary Moment of the 1990s," in *The Role of Economic Theory*, ed. Philip A. Klein (Boston/Dordrecht/London: Kluwer Academic Publishers, 1994), 47–60.

Volume 13   *Politics as Public Choice*

PART 1. General Approach

["Positive Economics, Welfare Economics, and Political Economy," *Journal of Law and Economics* 2 (October 1959): 124–38.]

["Politics without Romance: A Sketch of Positive Public Choice Theory and Its Normative Implications," Inaugural Lecture, Institute for Advanced Studies, Vienna, Austria, *IHS-Journal, Zeitschrift des Instituts für Höhere Studien, Wien* 3 (1979): B1–B11.]

["Politics, Policy, and the Pigovian Margins," *Economica* 29 (February 1962): 17–28.]

["Social Choice, Democracy, and Free Markets," *Journal of Political Economy* 62 (April 1954): 114–23.]

"An Economist's Approach to 'Scientific Politics'," in *Perspectives in the Study of Politics*, ed. Malcolm B. Parsons (Chicago: Rand McNally, 1968), 77–88.

"The Public Choice Perspective," *Economia delle scelte pubbliche* 1 (January–April 1983): 7–15.

"Toward Analysis of Closed Behavioral Systems," in *Theory of Public Choice: Political Applications of Economics*, ed. James M. Buchanan and Robert D. Tollison (Ann Arbor: University of Michigan Press, 1972), 11–23.

"From Private Preferences to Public Philosophy: The Development of Public Choice," in *The Economics of Politics* (London: Institute of Economic Affairs, 1978), 1–20.

"Notes on the History and Direction of Public Choice," in *What Should Economists Do?* (Indianapolis: Liberty Fund, 1979), 175–82.

Foreword to *The Politics of Bureaucracy*, by Gordon Tullock (Washington, D.C.: Public Affairs Press, 1965), 1–9.

"Notes on Politics as Process," in *Liberty, Market and State: Political Economy in the 1980s* (Brighton, England: Wheatsheaf Books, 1986), 87–91.

PART 2. Public Choice and Its Critics

Geoffrey Brennan and James M. Buchanan, "Is Public Choice Immoral? The Case for the 'Nobel' Lie," *Virginia Law Review* 74 (March 1988): 179–89.

"Foundational Concerns: A Criticism of Public Choice Theory," in *Current Issues in Public Choice*, ed. José Casas Pardo and Friedrich Schneider (Cheltenham, U.K.: Edward Elgar, 1995), 3–20.

"The Achievement and the Limits of Public Choice in Diagnosing Government Failure and in Offering Bases for Constructive Reform," in *Anatomy of Government Deficiencies*, ed. Horst Hanusch (Berlin: Springer-Verlag, 1983), 15–25.

PART 3. Voters

["Individual Choice in Voting and the Market," *Journal of Political Economy* 62 (August 1954): 334–43.]

"The Political Economy of Franchise in the Welfare State," in *Capitalism and Freedom: Problems and Prospects,* ed. Richard T. Selden (Charlottesville: University Press of Virginia, 1975), 52–77.

Geoffrey Brennan and James Buchanan, "Voter Choice: Evaluating Political Alternatives," *American Behavioral Scientist* 28 (November–December 1984): 185–201.

"Hegel on the Calculus of Voting," *Public Choice* 17 (Spring 1974): 99–101.

"Public Choice and Ideology," in *What Should Economists Do?* (Indianapolis: Liberty Fund, 1979), 271–76.

PART 4. Voting Models

"What If There Is No Majority Motion?" in *Towards a Science of Politics: Essays in Honor of Duncan Black,* ed. Gordon Tullock (Blacksburg, Va.: Center for Study of Public Choice, 1981), 79–90.

Roger L. Faith and James M. Buchanan, "Towards a Theory of Yes-No Voting," *Public Choice* 37 (1981): 231–45.

James M. Buchanan and Dwight R. Lee, "Vote Buying in a Stylized Setting," *Public Choice* 49 (1986): 3–16.

"Democracy and Duopoly: A Comparison of Analytical Models," *American Economic Review* 58 (May 1968): 322–31.

"Majoritarian Logic," *Public Choice* 97 (October 1998): 13–21.

PART 5. Rent Seeking

["Rent Seeking and Profit Seeking," in *Toward a Theory of the Rent-Seeking Society,* ed. James M. Buchanan, Robert D. Tollison, and Gordon Tullock (College Station: Texas A&M University Press, 1980), 3–15.]

"Rent Seeking under External Diseconomies," in *Toward a Theory of the Rent-Seeking Society,* ed. James M. Buchanan, Robert D. Tollison, and Gordon Tullock (College Station: Texas A&M University Press, 1980), 183–94.

"Rent Seeking, Noncompensated Transfers, and Laws of Succession," *Journal of Law and Economics* 26 (April 1983): 71–85.

James M. Buchanan and Roger D. Congleton, "The Incumbency Dilemma and Rent Extraction by Legislators," *Public Choice* 79 (April 1994): 47–60.

"The Coase Theorem and the Theory of the State," *Natural Resources Journal* 13 (October 1973): 579–94.

"Consumerism and Public Utility Regulation," in *Telecommunications, Regulation, and Public Choice,* ed. Charles F. Phillips, Jr. (Lexington, Va.: Washington and Lee University Press, 1975), 1–22.

"In Defense of Advertising Cartels," Pubblicita e Televizione (Rome: RAI, 1969), 84–93.

"Reform in the Rent-Seeking Society," *Toward a Theory of the Rent-Seeking Society,* ed. James M. Buchanan, Robert D. Tollison, and Gordon Tullock (College Station: Texas A&M University Press, 1980), 359–67.

PART 6. Regulation

James M. Buchanan and Viktor J. Vanberg, "The Politicization of Market Failure," *Public Choice* 57 (May 1988): 101–13.

"A Public Choice Approach to Public Utility Pricing," *Public Choice* 5 (Fall 1968): 1–17.

James M. Buchanan and Dwight R. Lee, "Cartels, Coalitions, and Constitutional Politics," *Constitutional Political Economy* 2 (1991): 139–61.

"Politics and Meddlesome Preferences," in *Smoking and Society: Toward a More Balanced Assessment,* ed. Robert D. Tollison (Lexington, Mass.: D. C. Heath, 1986), 335–42.

James M. Buchanan and Gordon Tullock, "Polluters' Profits and Political Response: Direct Controls versus Taxes," *American Economic Review* 65 (March 1975): 139–47.

PART 7. Public Choice and Public Expenditures

"Easy Budgets and Tight Money," *Lloyds Bank Review* 64 (April 1962): 17–30.

"Notes for an Economic Theory of Socialism," *Public Choice* 8 (Spring 1970): 29–43.

James M. Buchanan and Dwight R. Lee, "Tax Rates and Tax Revenues in Political Equilibrium: Some Simple Analytics," *Economic Inquiry* 20 (July 1982): 344–54.

Volume 14   *Debt and Taxes*

PART 1. Taxation, Politics, and Public Choice

["The Pure Theory of Government Finance: A Suggested Approach," *Journal of Political Economy* 57 (December 1949): 496–505.]

"Public Finance and Public Choice," *National Tax Journal* 28 (December 1975): 383–94.

"Public Choice and Public Finance," in *What Should Economists Do?* (Indianapolis: Liberty Fund, 1979), 183–97.

"Democratic Values in Taxation," in *Freedom in Constitutional Contract: Perspectives of a Political Economist* (College Station and London: Texas A&M University Press, 1977), 243–53.

"Tax Reform as Political Choice," *Journal of Economic Perspectives* 1 (Summer 1987): 29–35.

"The Theory of Public Finance," *Southern Economic Journal* 26 (January 1960): 234–38.

["Taxation in Fiscal Exchange," *Journal of Public Economics* 6 (1976): 17–29.]

"Richard Musgrave, Public Finance, and Public Choice," *Public Choice* 61 (June 1989): 289–91.

["Socialism Is Dead but Leviathan Lives On," the John Bonython Lecture, CIS Occasional Paper 30 (Sydney: Centre for Independent Studies, 1990), 1–9.]

PART 2. Earmarking and Incidence in Democratic Process

"The Economics of Earmarked Taxes," *Journal of Political Economy* 71 (October 1963): 457–69.

"The Constitutional Economics of Earmarking," in *Charging for Government: User Charges and Earmarked Taxes in Principle and Practice,* ed. Richard E. Wagner (London and New York: Routledge, 1991), 152–62.

James M. Buchanan and Francesco Forte, "Fiscal Choice Through Time: A Case for Indirect Taxation?" *National Tax Journal* 17 (June 1964): 144–57.

"Externality in Tax Response," *Southern Economic Journal* 33 (July 1966): 35–42.

James M. Buchanan and Mark V. Pauly, "On the Incidence of Tax Deductibility," *National Tax Journal* 23 (June 1970): 157–67.

PART 3. Analytical and Ethical Foundations of Tax Limits

Geoffrey Brennan and James M. Buchanan, "Towards a Tax Constitution for Leviathan," *Journal of Public Economics* 8 (December 1977): 255–73.

Geoffrey Brennan and James Buchanan, "The Logic of Tax Limits: Alternative Constitutional Constraints on the Power to Tax," *National Tax Journal* 32 (June 1979): 11–22.

James M. Buchanan and Roger Congleton, "Proportional and Progressive Income Taxation with Utility-Maximizing Governments," *Public Choice* 34 (1979): 217–30.

"The Ethical Limits of Taxation," *Scandinavian Journal of Economics* 86 (April 1984): 102–14.

"Coercive Taxation in Constitutional Contract," in *Explorations into Constitutional Economics,* comp. Robert D. Tollison and Viktor J. Vanberg (College Station: Texas A&M University Press, 1989), 309–28.

"Constitutional Constraints on Governmental Taxing Power," *ORDO* Band 30 (Stuttgart: Gustav Fischer Verlag, 1979): 349–59.

PART 4. The Fiscal Constitution

Geoffrey Brennan and James Buchanan, "The Tax System as Social Overhead Capital: A Constitutional Perspective on Fiscal Norms," in *Public Finance and Economic Growth, Proceedings of the 37th Congress of the International Institute of Public Finance,* Tokyo, 1981, ed. Dieter Biehl, Karl W. Roskamp, and Wolfgang F. Stolper (Detroit: Wayne State University Press, 1983), 41–54.

James Buchanan and Geoffrey Brennan, "Tax Reform without Tears," in *The Economics of Taxation,* ed. Henry J. Aaron and Michael J. Boskin (Washington, D.C.: Brookings Institution, 1980), 33–53.

"The Political Efficiency of General Taxation," *National Tax Journal* 46 (December 1993): 401–10.

James M. Buchanan and Yong J. Yoon, "Rational Majoritarian Taxation of the Rich: With Increasing Returns and Capital Accumulation," *Southern Economic Journal* 61 (April 1995): 923–35.

PART 5. Confessions of a Burden Monger

"Debt, Public," in *International Encyclopedia of the Social Sciences*, vol. 4 (London and New York: Macmillan, 1968), 28–34.

["Public Debt, Cost Theory, and the Fiscal Illusion, in *Public Debt and Future Generations*, ed. J. M. Ferguson (Chapel Hill: University of North Carolina Press, 1964), 150–63.]

"Confessions of a Burden Monger," *Journal of Political Economy* 72 (October 1964): 486–88.

"The Icons of Public Debt," *Journal of Finance* 21 (September 1966): 544–46.

"Public Debt and Capital Formation," in *Taxation and the Deficit Economy: Fiscal Policy and Capital Formation in the United States*, ed. Dwight Lee (San Francisco: Pacific Research Institute for Public Policy, 1986), 177–94.

PART 6. Ricardian Equivalence

"Barro on the Ricardian Equivalence Theorem," *Journal of Political Economy* 84 (April 1976): 337–42.

Geoffrey Brennan and James M. Buchanan, "The Logic of the Ricardian Equivalence Theorem," *Finanzarchiv* 38, no. 1 (1980): 4–16.

James M. Buchanan and Jennifer Roback, "The Incidence and Effects of Public Debt in the Absence of Fiscal Illusion," *Public Finance Quarterly* 15 (January 1987): 5–25.

PART 7. The Constitution of a Debt-Free Polity

Viktor Vanberg and James M. Buchanan, "Organization Theory and Fiscal Economics: Society, State, and Public Debt," *Journal of Law, Economics, and Organization* 2 (Fall 1986): 215–27.

"The Economic Consequences of the Deficit," *Economia delle scelte pubbliche* 3 (1986): 149–56.

["Keynesian Follies," in *The Legacy of Keynes*, Nobel Conference XII, ed. David A. Reese (San Francisco: Harper & Row, 1987), 130–45.]

"Budgetary Bias in Post-Keynesian Politics: The Erosion and Potential Replacement of Fiscal Norms," in *Deficits*, ed. James M. Buchanan, Charles Rowley, Robert D. Tollison (New York: Blackwell, 1987), 180–98.

James M. Buchanan and Richard E. Wagner, "Dialogues Concerning Fiscal Religion," *Journal of Monetary Economics* 4 (August 1978): 627–36.

"The Moral Dimension of Debt Financing," *Economic Inquiry* 23 (January 1985): 1–6.

"The Balanced Budget Amendment: Clarifying the Arguments," *Public Choice* 90 (1997): 117–38.

"The Ethics of Debt Default," in *Deficits*, ed. James M. Buchanan, Charles Rowley, Robert D. Tollison (New York: Blackwell, 1987), 361–73.

Volume 15   *Externalities and Public Expenditure*

PART 1. Public Services and Collective Action

The Bases for Collective Action (New Jersey: General Learning Press, 1971), 1–18.

Francesco Forte and James M. Buchanan, "The Evaluation of Public Services," *Journal of Political Economy* 69 (April 1961): 107–21.

"'La scienza delle finanze': The Italian Tradition in Fiscal Theory," in *Fiscal Theory & Political Economy: Selected Essays* (Chapel Hill: University of North Carolina Press, 1960), 24–74.

PART 2. Externalities

James M. Buchanan and Wm. Craig Stubblebine, "Externality," *Economica* 29 (November 1962): 371–84.

James M. Buchanan and Gordon Tullock, "Public and Private Interaction under Reciprocal Externality," in *The Public Economy of Urban Communities*, ed. Julius Margolis (Washington, D.C.: Resources for the Future, 1965), 52–73.

Charles J. Goetz and James M. Buchanan, "External Diseconomies in Competitive Supply," *American Economic Review* 61 (December 1971): 883–90.

"External Diseconomies, Corrective Taxes, and Market Structure," *American Economic Review* 59 (March 1969): 174–77.

"The Institutional Structure of Externality," *Public Choice* 14 (Spring 1973): 69–82.

PART 3. Clubs and Joint Supply

"An Economic Theory of Clubs," *Economica* 32 (February 1965): 1–14.

"Joint Supply, Externality, and Optimality," *Economica* 33 (November 1966): 405–15.

PART 4. Public Goods Theory

"Cooperation and Conflict in Public-Goods Interaction," *Western Economic Journal* 5 (March 1967): 109–21.

James M. Buchanan and Milton Z. Kafoglis, "A Note on Public Goods Supply," *American Economic Review* 53 (June 1963): 403–14.

"Public Goods in Theory and Practice: A Note on the Minasian-Samuelson Discussion," *Journal of Law and Economics* 10 (1967): 193–97.

"Breton and Weldon on Public Goods," *Canadian Journal of Economics and Political Science* 33 (February 1967): 111–15.

James M. Buchanan and António S. Pinto Barbosa, "Convexity Constraints in Public Goods Theory," *Kyklos* 33, fasc. 1 (1980): 63–75.

"Public Goods and Natural Liberty," in *The Market and the State: Essays in Honour of Adam Smith,* ed. Thomas Wilson and Andrew S. Skinner (Oxford: Clarendon Press, 1976), 271–86.

PART 5. Applications—City, Health, and Social Security

"Public Goods and Public Bads," in *Financing the Metropolis: Public Policy in Urban Economies,* vol. 4, ed. John P. Crecine (Beverly Hills: Sage Publications, 1970), 51–71.

"Principles of Urban-Fiscal Strategy," *Public Choice* 11 (Fall 1971): 1–16.

The Inconsistencies of the National Health Service, Occasional Paper no. 7 (London: Institute of Economic Affairs, 1965).

Technological Determinism Despite the Reality of Scarcity: A Neglected Element in the Theory of Spending on Medical and Health Care (Little Rock: University of Arkansas Medical School, 1990), 3–17.

"The Budgetary Politics of Social Security," in *Social Security's Looming Surpluses: Prospects and Implications,* ed. Carolyn L. Weaver (Washington, D.C.: AEI Press, 1990), 45–56.

"A Contractarian Perspective on Anarchy," in *Freedom in Constitutional Contract: Perspectives of a Political Economist* (College Station: Texas A&M University Press, 1977), 11–24.

"The Contractarian Logic of Classical Liberalism," in *Liberty, Property, and the Future of Constitutional Development,* ed. Ellen Frankel Paul and Howard Dickman (Albany: State University of New York Press, 1990), 9–21.

Constitutional Restrictions on the Power of Government, the Frank M. Engle Lecture, 1981 (Bryn Mawr, Pa.: American College, 1981), 1–16.

"Contractarian Political Economy and Constitutional Interpretation," *AEA Papers and Proceedings* 78 (May 1988): 135–39.

"Justification of the Compound Republic: The *Calculus* in Retrospect," *Cato Journal* 7 (Fall 1987): 305–12.

PART 2. The Method of Constitutional Economics

"A Contractarian Paradigm for Applying Economic Theory," *American Economic Review* 65 (May 1975): 225–30.

"Boundaries on Social Contract," *Reason Papers* 2 (Fall 1975): 15–28.

"Constitutional Design and Construction: An Economic Approach," *Economia* 3 (May 1979): 293–314.

"The Use and Abuse of Contract," in *Freedom in Constitutional Contract: Perspectives of a Political Economist* (College Station: Texas A&M University Press, 1977), 135–47.

PART 3. Incentives and Constitutional Choice

Viktor J. Vanberg and James M. Buchanan, "Constitutional Choice, Rational Ignorance, and the Limits of Reason," *Jahrbuch für Neue Politische Ökonomie* 10 Band (1991): 61–78.

"How Can Constitutions Be Designed So That Politicians Who Seek to Serve 'Public Interest' Can Survive and Prosper?" *Constitutional Political Economy* 4 (Winter 1993): 1–6.

Viktor Vanberg and James M. Buchanan, "Interests and Theories in Constitutional Choice," *Journal of Theoretical Politics* 1 (January 1989): 49–62.

"Student Revolts, Academic Liberalism, and Constitutional Attitude," *Social Research* 35 (Winter 1968): 666–80.

James M. Buchanan and Viktor Vanberg, "A Theory of Leadership and Deference in Constitutional Construction," *Public Choice* 61 (April 1989): 15–27.

"Individual Rights, Emergent Social States, and Behavioral Feasibility," *Rationality and Society* 7 (April 1995): 141–50.

PART 4. Constitutional Order

"Contractarianism and Democracy," in *Liberty, Market and State: Political Economy in the 1980s* (Brighton, England: Wheatsheaf Books, 1986), 240–47.

"Democracy within Constitutional Limits," in *Post-Socialist Political Economy: Selected Essays* (Cheltenham, U.K.: Edward Elgar, 1997), 182–89.

PART 5. Market Order

Untitled, in *The State of Economic Science: Views of Six Nobel Laureates,* ed. Werner Sichel (Kalamazoo: W. E. Upjohn Institute for Economic Research, 1989), 79–95.

"The Minimal Politics of Market Order," special issue, *From Plan to Market: The Post-Soviet Challenge,* parts 1 and 2, *Cato Journal* 11 (Fall 1991): 215–26.

PART 6. Distributional Issues

"Distributional Politics and Constitutional Design," in *Economics and Political Institutions in Economic Policy,* ed. V. A. Muscatelli (Manchester, U.K.: Manchester University Press, 1996), 70–78.

James M. Buchanan and Winston C. Bush, "Political Constraints on Contractual Redistribution," *American Economic Review* 64 (May 1974): 153–57.

James M. Buchanan and Roger L. Faith, "Subjective Elements in Rawlsian Agreement on Distributional Rules," *Economic Inquiry* 18 (January 1980): 23–38.

PART 7. Fiscal and Monetary Constitutions

["Predictability: The Criterion of Monetary Constitutions," in *In Search of a Monetary Constitution*, ed. Leland B. Yeager (Cambridge: Harvard University Press, 1962), 155–83.]

"Procedural and Quantitative Constitutional Constraints on Fiscal Authority," in *The Constitution and the Budget: Are Constitutional Limits on Tax, Spending, and Budget Powers Desirable at the Federal Level?* ed. W. S. Moore and Rudolf G. Penner (Washington, D.C.: American Enterprise Institute, 1980), 80–84.

"Tax Reform in 'Constitutional' Perspective," *Invited Essay* (September 1977): 1–5.

"The Relevance of Constitutional Strategy," *Cato Journal* 6 (Fall 1986): 513–17.

PART 8. Reform

"The Economic Constitution and the New Deal: Lessons for Late Learners," in *Regulatory Change in an Atmosphere of Crisis: Current Implications of the Roosevelt Years*, ed. Gary Walton (New York: Academic Press, 1979), 13–26.

"Sources of Opposition to Constitutional Reform," in *Constitutional Economics: Containing the Economic Powers of Government*, ed. Richard B. McKenzie (Lexington, Mass.: D. C. Heath, 1984), 21–34.

"Achieving Economic Reform," in *The Economics and the Ethics of Constitutional Order* (Ann Arbor: University of Michigan Press, 1991), 99–108.

James M. Buchanan and Alberto di Pierro, "Pragmatic Reform and Constitutional Revolution," *Ethics* 79 (January 1969): 95–104.

"Lagged Implementation as an Element in Constitutional Strategy," *European Journal of Political Economy* 10 (1994): 11–26.

"Prolegomena for a Strategy of Constitutional Revolution," in *The Economics and the Ethics of Constitutional Order* (Ann Arbor: University of Michigan Press, 1991), 89–97.

"The Structure of Progress: National Constitutionalism in a Technologically Opened World Economy," in *Doctorado "Honoris Causa" del excmo. sr. d. James M. Buchanan* (Valladolid, Spain: University of Valladolid, 1996), 19–29.

"Notes on the Liberal Constitution," *Cato Journal* 14 (Spring/Summer 1994): 1–9.

"Dismantling the Welfare State," in *Liberty, Market and State: Political Economy in the 1980s* (Brighton, England: Wheatsheaf Books, 1986), 178–85.

["Generality as a Constitutional Constraint," in *Trap of Democracy* (Tokyo: Editorial Board of Public Choice Studies).]

Volume 17   *Moral Science and Moral Order*

PART 1. Methods and Models

["The Foundations for Normative Individualism," in *The Economics and the Ethics of Constitutional Order* (Ann Arbor: University of Michigan Press, 1991), 221–29.]

"Economics and Its Scientific Neighbors," in *The Structure of Economic Science: Essays on Methodology*, ed. Sherman Roy Krupp (Englewood Cliffs: Prentice-Hall, 1966), 166–83.

"The Domain of Subjective Economics: Between Predictive Science and Moral Philosophy," in *Method, Process, and Austrian Economics: Essays in Honor of Ludwig von Mises*, ed. Israel M. Kirzner (Lexington, Mass.: D. C. Heath, 1982), 7–20.

"The Related but Distinct 'Sciences' of Economics and of Political Economy," special issue, *Social Psychology and Economics*, ed. Wolfgang Stroebe and Willi Meyer, *British Journal of Social Psychology*, vol. 21, pt. 2 (June 1982): 175–83.

"Rational Choice Models in the Social Sciences," in *Explorations into Constitutional Economics*, comp. Robert D. Tollison and Viktor J. Vanberg (College Station: Texas A&M University Press, 1989), 37–50.

"An Ambiguity in Sen's Alleged Proof of the Impossibility of a Pareto Libertarian," *Analyse & Kritik* 18 (September 1996): 118–25.

"Choosing What to Choose," *Journal of Institutional and Theoretical Economics* 150 (March 1994): 123–44.

"Law and the Invisible Hand," in *The Interaction of Economics and the Law*, ed. Bernard H. Siegan (Lexington, Mass.: D. C. Heath, 1977), 127–38.

James M. Buchanan and Warren J. Samuels, "On Some Fundamental Issues in Political Economy: An Exchange of Correspondence," *Journal of Economic Issues* 9 (March 1975): 15–38.

James M. Buchanan and Gordon Tullock, "Economic Analogues to the Generalization Argument," *Ethics* 74 (July 1964): 300–301.

"Monetary Research, Monetary Rules, and Monetary Regimes," *Cato Journal* 3 (Spring 1983): 143–46.

PART 2. Belief and Consequence

"The Potential for Tyranny in Politics as Science," in *Liberty, Market and State: Political Economy in the 1980s* (Brighton, England: Wheatsheaf Books, 1986), 40–54.

"Belief, Choice and Consequences: Reflections on Economics, Science and Religion," in *Wege der Vernunft: Festschrift zum siebzigsten Geburtstag von Hans Albert,* ed. Alfred Bohnen and Alan Musgrave (Tübingen: J. C. B. Mohr [Paul Siebeck], 1991), 151–63.

PART 3. Moral Community and Moral Order

["Ethical Rules, Expected Values, and Large Numbers," *Ethics* 76 (October 1965): 1–13.]

["The Samaritan's Dilemma," in *Altruism, Morality and Economic Theory,* ed. E. S. Phelps (New York: Russell Sage Foundation, 1975): 71–85.]

Moral Community, Moral Order, or Moral Anarchy, The Abbott Memorial Lecture no. 17 (Colorado Springs: Colorado College, 1981), 1–15.

"Moral Community and Moral Order: The Intensive and Extensive Limits of Interaction," in *Ethics and Animals,* ed. Harlan B. Miller and William H. Williams (Clifton, N.J.: Humana Press, 1983), 95–102.

"A Two-Country Parable," in *Justice in Immigration,* ed. Warren F. Schwartz, Cambridge Studies in Philosophy and Law (New York: Cambridge University Press, 1995), 63–66.

"Economic Origins of Ethical Constraints," in *The Economics and the Ethics of Constitutional Order* (Ann Arbor: University of Michigan Press, 1991), 179–93.

["Markets, States, and the Extent of Morals," *American Economic Review* 68 (May 1978): 364–68.]

PART 4. Moral Science, Equality, and Justice

"Political Economy and Social Philosophy," in *Economics and Philosophy,* ed. Peter Koslowski (Tübingen: J. C. B. Mohr [Paul Siebeck], 1985), 19–36.

Volume 18   *Federalism, Liberty, and the Law*

PART 1. The Analytics of Federalism

"Federalism and Fiscal Equity," *American Economic Review* 40 (September 1950): 583–99.

James M. Buchanan and Richard E. Wagner, "An Efficiency Basis for Federal Fiscal Equalization," in *The Analysis of Public Output*, ed. Julius Margolis (New York: National Bureau of Economic Research, 1970), 139–58.

James M. Buchanan and Charles J. Goetz, "Efficiency Limits of Fiscal Mobility: An Assessment of the Tiebout Model," *Journal of Public Economics* 1 (1972): 25–43.

PART 2. Federalism and Freedom

"Federalism as an Ideal Political Order and an Objective for Constitutional Reform," *Publius* 25 (Spring 1995): 19–27.

"Federalism and Individual Sovereignty," *Cato Journal* 15 (Fall/Winter 1995–96): 259–68.

"Economic Freedom and Federalism: Prospects for the New Century," special contribution to the inaugural issue, *Asian Journal of Business & Information Systems* 1 (Summer 1996): 5–10.

"Europe's Constitutional Opportunity," in *Europe's Constitutional Future* (London: Institute of Economic Affairs, 1990), 1–20.

"National Politics and Competitive Federalism: Italy and the Constitution of Europe," in *Post-Socialist Political Economy: Selected Essays* (Cheltenham, U.K.: Edward Elgar, 1997), 243–53.

James M. Buchanan and Dwight R. Lee, "On a Fiscal Constitution for the European Union," *Journal des Economistes et des Etudes Humaines* 5, no. 2/3 (June/September 1994): 219–32.

James M. Buchanan and Roger L. Faith, "Secession and the Limits of Taxation: Toward a Theory of Internal Exit," *American Economic Review* 77 (December 1987): 1023–31.

PART 3. Liberty, Man, and the State

"Man and the State," in *Socialism: Institutional, Philosophical and Economic Issues*, vol. 14 of *International Studies in Economics and Econometrics*, ed. Svetozar

Pejovich (Dordrecht, Boston, Lancaster: Kluwer Academic Publishing, 1987), 3–9.

"Criteria for a Free Society: Definition, Diagnosis, and Prescription," in *Freedom in Constitutional Contract: Perspectives of a Political Economist* (College Station: Texas A&M University Press, 1977), 287–99.

"The Individual as Participant in Political Exchange," in *Social Theory and Social Policy: Essays in Honor of James S. Coleman,* ed. Aage B. Sørensen and Seymour Spilerman (Westport, Conn.: Praeger, 1993), 11–21.

"Towards the Simple Economics of Natural Liberty: An Exploratory Analysis," *Kyklos* 40, fasc. 1 (January 1987): 3–20.

["The Justice of Natural Liberty," *Journal of Legal Studies* 5 (January 1976): 1–16.]

"Property as a Guarantor of Liberty," *The Shaftesbury Papers,* vol. 1 (Hants, England: Edward Elgar, 1993), 1–64.

PART 4. The Constitution of Markets

"On the Structure of an Economy: A Re-emphasis of Some Classical Foundations," *Business Economics* 24 (January 1989): 6–12.

"Market Failure and Political Failure," in *Individual Liberty and Democratic Decision-Making: The Ethics, Economics, and Politics of Democracy,* ed. Peter Koslowski (Tübingen: J. C. B. Mohr [Paul Siebeck], 1987), 41–52.

James M. Buchanan and Viktor J. Vanberg, "The Market as a Creative Process," *Economics and Philosophy* 7 (October 1991): 167–86.

"Cultural Evolution and Institutional Reform," in *Liberty, Market and State: Political Economy in the 1980s* (Brighton, England: Wheatsheaf Books, 1986), 75–86.

PART 5. Economists, Efficiency, and the Law

"Good Economics—Bad Law," *Virginia Law Review* 60 (Spring 1974): 483–92.

"Comment," *Journal of Law and Economics* 18 (December 1975): 903–5.

"Politics, Property, and the Law: An Alternative Interpretation of Miller et al. v. Schoene," *Journal of Law and Economics* 15 (October 1972): 439–52.

"In Defense of *Caveat Emptor*," *University of Chicago Law Review* 38 (Fall 1970): 64–73.

"Notes on Irrelevant Externalities, Enforcement Costs and the Atrophy of Property Rights," in *Explorations in the Theory of Anarchy*, ed. Gordon Tullock (Blacksburg, Va.: Center for Study of Public Choice, 1972), 77–86.

PART 6. Law, Money, and Crime

James M. Buchanan and T. Nicolaus Tideman, "Gold, Money, and the Law: The Limits of Governmental Monetary Authority," in *Gold, Money and the Law*, ed. Henry G. Manne and Roger LeRoy Miller (Chicago: Aldine, 1975), 9–70.

"A Defense of Organized Crime?" in *The Economics of Crime and Punishment*, ed. Simon Rottenberg (Washington, D.C.: American Enterprise Institute, 1973), 119–32.

Volume 19   *Ideas, Persons, and Events*

PART 1. Autobiographical and Personal Reflections

["Better than Plowing," *Banca Nazionale del Lavoro Quarterly Review* 159 (December 1986): 359–75.]

"Born-Again Economist," in *Lives of the Laureates: Ten Nobel Economists*, ed. William Breit and Roger W. Spencer (Cambridge: MIT Press, 1990), 163–80.

"From the Inside Looking Out," in *Eminent Economists: Their Life Philosophies*, ed. Michael Szenberg (Cambridge: Cambridge University Press, 1992), 98–106.

"Italian Retrospective," in *Better than Plowing: And Other Personal Essays* (Chicago: University of Chicago Press, 1992), 82–92.

"Political Economy: 1957–82," in *Liberty, Market and State: Political Economy in the 1980s* (Brighton, England: Wheatsheaf Books, 1986), 8–18.

"Virginia Political Economy: Some Personal Reflections," in *Better than Plowing: And Other Personal Essays* (Chicago: University of Chicago Press, 1992), 93–107.

James M. Buchanan and Robert D. Tollison, "A Theory of Truth in Autobiography," *Kyklos* 39, fasc. 4 (1986): 507–17.

["The Relatively Absolute Absolutes," in *Essays on the Political Economy* (Honolulu: University of Hawai'i Press, 1989), 32–46.]

PART 2. Reflections on Fellow Political Economists

"Frank H. Knight, 1885–1972" in *Remembering the University of Chicago: Teachers, Scientists, and Scholars,* ed. Edward Shils (Chicago: University of Chicago Press, 1991), 244–52.

"Knight, Frank H.," in *International Encyclopedia of the Social Sciences,* vol. 17, ed. David L. Sills (New York: Macmillan and Free Press, 1968), 424–28.

"The Qualities of a Natural Economist," in *Democracy and Public Choice: Essays in Honor of Gordon Tullock,* ed. Charles Rowley (Oxford: Basil Blackwell, 1987), 9–19.

Preface to *Essays on Unorthodox Economic Strategies: A Memorial Volume in Honor of Winston C. Bush,* ed. Arthur T. Denzau and Robert J. Mackay (Blacksburg, Va.: Center for Study of Public Choice, 1976), vi.

"Jack Wiseman: A Personal Appreciation," *Constitutional Political Economy* 2 (1991): 1–6.

"I Did Not Call Him 'Fritz': Personal Recollections of Professor F. A. v. Hayek," *Constitutional Political Economy* 3 (Spring–Summer 1992): 129–35.

"Methods and Morals in Economics: The Ayres-Knight Discussion," in *Science and Ceremony: The Institutional Economics of C. E. Ayres,* ed. William Breit and William Patton Culbertson, Jr. (Austin and London: University of Texas Press, 1976), 163–74.

"Economists and the Gains from Trade," special issue, *Managerial and Decision Economics* (Winter 1988): 5–12.

"Shackle and a Lecture in Pittsburgh," *Market Process* 7 (Spring 1989): 2–4.

Review of *Imagination and the Nature of Choice,* by G. L. S. Shackle, *Austrian Economics Newsletter* 3 (Summer 1980): 2–3.

Review of *Politics and Markets: The World's Political Economic Systems,* by Charles E. Lindblom, "Three Reviews of Charles E. Lindblom—*Politics and Markets: The World's Political Economic Systems,*" *Journal of Economic Issues* 13 (March 1979): 215–17.

"Liberty, Market and State," in *Liberty, Market and State: Political Economy in the 1980s* (Brighton, England: Wheatsheaf Books, 1986), 3–7.

PART 3. Political Economy in the Post-Socialist Century

"America's Third Century in Perspective," *Atlantic Economic Journal* 1 (November 1973): 3–12.

Analysis, Ideology and the Events of 1989 (Zürich: Bank Hofmann AG, 1991), 7–23.

"Politicized Economies in Limbo: America, Europe and the World, 1994," in *Nobelpreisträger James M. Buchanan in Jena, München und Bayreuth, 7–15 Juni 1994* (Munich: Herbert Quandt Stiftung, 1994), 18–23.

"The Epistemological Feasibility of Free Markets," in *Post-Socialist Political Economy: Selected Essays* (Cheltenham, U.K.: Edward Elgar, 1997), 151–59.

Consumption without Production: The Impossible Idyll of Socialism (Freiburg, Germany: Haufe, 1993), 49–75.

"Economics in the Post-Socialist Century," *Economic Journal* 101, no. 404 (January 1991): 15–21.

"Post-Socialist Political Economy," in *Post-Socialist Political Economy: Selected Essays* (Cheltenham, U.K.: Edward Elgar, 1997), 36–47.

"The Triumph of Economic Science: Is Fukuyama Wrong and, If So, Why?" *Government Auditing Review* 3, no. 7 (1993): 5–14.

"Public Choice after Socialism," *Public Choice* 77, no. 1 (1993): 67–74.

PART 4. Reform without Romance

"Adam Smith as Inspiration," in *The Academic World of James M. Buchanan*, ed. Byeong-Ho Gong (Seoul, Korea: Korea Economic Research Institute, 1996).

"The Potential for Politics after Socialism," in *Geschichte und Gesetz, Europäisches Forum Alpbach 1989*, ed. Otto Molden (Vienna: Österreichisches College, 1990), 240–56.

"Ideas, Institutions, and Political Economy: A Plea for Disestablishment," in *Real Business Cycles, Real Exchange Rates and Actual Policies, Carnegie-Rochester Conference Series on Public Policy 25*, ed. Karl Brunner and Alan Meltzer (Amsterdam: North Holland, 1986), 245–58.

"Can Policy Activism Succeed? A Public Choice Perspective," in *The Monetary versus Fiscal Policy Debate: Lessons from Two Decades*, ed. R. W. Hafer (Totowa, N.J.: Rowman and Allanheld, 1986), 139–50.

"Society and Democracy," in *The David Hume Institute—The First Decade,* ed. Nick Kuenssberg and Gillian Lomas (Edinburgh: David Hume Institute, 1996), 25–33.

"Reform without Romance: First Principles in Political Economy," in *Post-Socialist Political Economy: Selected Essays* (Cheltenham, U.K.: Edward Elgar, 1997), 233–39.

Name Index

James M. Buchanan is referred to as "JMB" in subentries.

Subject Index

James M. Buchanan is referred to as "JMB" in subentries.

This book is set in Minion, a typeface designed by Robert Slimbach specifically for digital typesetting. Released by Adobe in 1989, it is a versatile neohumanist face that shows the influence of Slimbach's own calligraphy.

This book is printed on paper that is acid-free and meets the requirements of the American National Standard for Permanence of Paper for Printed Library Materials, z39.48-1992. ♾

Book design by Louise OFarrell, Gainesville, Fla.
Typography by Impressions Book and Journal Services, Inc., Madison, Wisc.
Printed and bound by Worzalla Publishing Company, Stevens Point, Wisc.